# Roots of H

On the eve of the Holocaust, antipathy toward Europe's Jews reached epidemic proportions. Jews fleeing Nazi Germany's increasingly anti-Semitic measures encountered closed doors everywhere they turned. Why had enmity toward European Jewry reached such extreme heights? How did the levels of anti-Semitism in the 1930s compare to those of earlier decades? Did anti-Semitism vary in content and intensity across societies? For example, were Germans more anti-Semitic than their European neighbors, and, if so, why? How does anti-Semitism differ from other forms of religious, racial, and ethnic prejudice?

In pursuit of answers to these questions, William I. Brustein offers the first truly systematic comparative and empirical examination of anti-Semitism in Europe before the Holocaust. Brustein proposes that European anti-Semitism flowed from religious, racial, economic, and political roots, which became enflamed by economic distress, rising Jewish immigration, and socialist success. To support his arguments, Brustein draws upon a careful and extensive examination of the annual volumes of the *American Jewish Year Book* and more than forty years of newspaper reportage from Europe's major dailies. The findings of this informative book offer a fresh perspective on the roots of society's longest hatred.

William I. Brustein is Professor of Sociology, Political Science, and History and the director of the University Center for International Studies at the University of Pittsburgh. His previous books include *The Logic of Evil* (1996) and *The Social Origins of Political Regionalism* (1988).

# ROOTS OF HATE

ANTI-SEMITISM IN EUROPE
BEFORE THE HOLOCAUST

WILLIAM I. BRUSTEIN
*University of Pittsburgh*

CAMBRIDGE
UNIVERSITY PRESS

CAMBRIDGE UNIVERSITY PRESS
Cambridge, New York, Melbourne, Madrid, Cape Town, Singapore,
São Paulo, Delhi, Dubai, Tokyo, Mexico City

Cambridge University Press
32 Avenue of the Americas, New York, NY 10013-2473, USA

www.cambridge.org
Information on this title: www.cambridge.org/9780521774789

First published 2003
Reprinted 2010

A catalog record for this publication is available from the British Library.

Library of Congress Cataloging in Publication Data

Brustein, William.
Roots of hate : anti-semitism in Europe before the Holocaust /William I. Brustein.
p.  cm.
Includes bibliographical references and index.
ISBN 0-521-77308-3 – ISBN 0-521-77478-0 (pb.)
1. Antisemitism – Europe – History – 19th century.  2. Antisemitism – Europe –
History – 20th century.  I. Title.
DS146.E8B78    2003
305.892´404´09 – dc21        2003043478

ISBN  978-0-521-77308-9 Hardback
ISBN  978-0-521-77478-9 Paperback

To the memory of and with inspiration from
David Cooperman, Herbert Goldfrank,
and George L. Mosse.

# Contents

# Figures and Tables

## FIGURES

### TABLES

# PREFACE

The genesis of this work had several sources. As an American Jew and a scholar of political extremism, I could never quite fathom how people of the Jewish faith had remained the objects of such intense scorn in Western societies for close to two thousand years. It seemed equally perplexing that in many of the same societies in which the progressive thinking of the Enlightenment had found fertile soil, the level of anti-Semitism had reached epidemic proportions. Rather than receding as time passed, anti-Semitism, according to the historical record, increased during the last quarter of the nineteenth and the first half of the twentieth century. On the eve of the Holocaust, one could make a strong case that antipathy toward Jews had reached unprecedented levels. I wanted to understand the bases of anti-Semitism.

Other factors drove my quest. My previous research endeavors had not focused specifically on the phenomenon of anti-Semitism. In my earlier research on the social origins of the Nazi Party, I had posited that Nazi supporters were no different from citizens anywhere who select a political party or candidate they believe will promote their economic interests. I suggested that anti-Semitism, while certainly present in Nazi propaganda between 1925 and 1933, could not satisfactorily explain why so many million Germans adhered to the Nazi Party. I intimated that we err if we attribute the Nazi Party's success to its professed anti-Semitism. Prior to 1933, the Nazi Party's anti-Semitism lacked originality and shared strong similarities with that of many other Weimar political parties and of numerous ultranationalistic political movements and parties throughout interwar Europe. However, nowhere in my book *The Logic of Evil: The Social Origins of the Nazi Party, 1925–1933*, did I systematically test the importance of anti-Semitism as a motivation for joining the

Nazi Party, nor did I methodically compare German anti-Semitism to anti-Semitism elsewhere.

In the same year that my book on Nazi Party membership was published, a book by Daniel Jonah Goldhagen, *Hitler's Willing Executioners: Ordinary Germans and the Holocaust*, appeared. Among other things, Goldhagen implied that German anti-Semitism, by virtue of its eliminationist character, differed from antipathy to Jews found elsewhere in Western societies. But Goldhagen's account failed to compare systematically German and non-German anti-Semitism. In fact, as I was soon to discover, while much has been written on the subject of anti-Semitism, there has never been, with the notable exception of Helen Fein's superb 1979 book, *Accounting for Genocide: National Responses and Jewish Victimization during the Holocaust*, a comprehensive empirical study of societal variation in anti-Semitism in Western societies.[1]

The present book represents an initial effort to examine anti-Semitism systematically and empirically across space and time. This book does not focus directly on the Holocaust; rather, it seeks to explore the roots of Jewish hatred that, in many ways, prepared the ground for the Holocaust. Among the many questions to be confronted are: how and why had antipathy toward European Jews reached such heights on the eve of the Holocaust; how did the levels of anti-Semitism on the eve of the Holocaust compare to those of earlier decades; did anti-Semitism vary in content and in intensity across societies; how does anti-Semitism differ from other forms of religious, racial, and ethnic prejudice; and, how likely is it that worldwide anti-Semitism could once again reach epidemic levels?

My argument is that anti-Semitism is a multifaceted form of prejudice. Anti-Semitism contains religious, racial, economic, and political manifestations. These manifestations, which had become embedded in Western culture generally over the course of centuries, would periodically erupt at moments of large-scale Jewish immigration, severe economic crisis, or revolutionary challenge to the existing political and social order. At times and in places where a popular consciousness marked by the four forms of anti-Semitism to be explored here converged with

---

[1] Fein focused on national variation in Jewish victimization rates during the Holocaust. She found that the variable strength of pre–World War II anti-Semitic movements played a significant role in explaining differing levels of Jewish victimization. Fein's study did not attempt to explain the rise of and variations among European pre–World War II anti-Semitic movements. These objectives are central to the present study.

an increase in Jewish immigration, severe economic malaise, and/or revolutionary upheaval, anti-Semitism should have been most intense, I will argue. The countries that will constitute the cases for this study are France, Germany, Great Britain, Italy, and Romania. These countries were selected for important theoretical and methodological reasons. The primary time period examined covers the years from 1879 to 1939.

The organization of the book is straightforward. In Chapter 1, I explore several of the better-known explanations of the rise of and societal variation in European anti-Semitism, along with my own theory, and I present empirical evidence supporting the contention that anti-Semitism as measured by acts and attitudes varied across time and space before the Holocaust. Chapter 2 examines the religious root of anti-Semitism, and Chapters 3 through 5 investigate its racial, economic, and political roots, respectively. In the book's concluding chapter, I present, among other things, some brief reflections on the generalizability of my findings and on the uniqueness of anti-Semitism as a form of prejudice, a comparison of anti-Semitism and hatred of Gypsies, and some conjectures about anti-Semitism's future.

Over several years, I have accumulated many debts in the writing of this book. The research would not have been possible without the efforts of a superlative group of research assistants, largely comprised of American, German, Italian, French, and Romanian students and scholars. Within this wonderful group of assistants, Ryan King, whose help was immeasurable, holds a singular place. During the past five years, my many assistants worked tirelessly examining the volumes of the *American Jewish Year Book*; reading and coding the major daily newspapers from France, Great Britain, Germany, Italy, and Romania; and analyzing the data from these various sources. In particular, I deeply appreciate the contributions of Rita Bashaw, Marit Berntson, Denis Cart-Lamy, Dan Cazanacli, Haim Culer, Katharine Dow, Nicoletta Ferrario, Ariane Fiesser, Lisa France, Michael Kirschner, Paula Kramer, Kelly A. McDermott, Tina Newcomb, Sarah Noble, Aileen Crowe Oden, Julie Paisnel, Amy Ronnkvist, Jennifer Sartorius, Lorna Sopcak, and Marion Thurmes. I owe an additional special thanks to Marit Berntson, Ryan King, and Amy Ronnkvist, who assisted me in the organization and analysis of the large data collection. I give special thanks to Alex Grigescu, Claire Piana, Nicola I. Duehlmeyer, and Maria D'Anniballe for checking and correcting my French, German, Romanian, and Italian spelling, and to Janet Helfand for her helpful editorial suggestions.

A number of colleagues offered indispensable advice during my research and the writing of this book. For their helpful suggestions or comments, I am deeply grateful to Risto Alapuro, Helmut Anheier, Kathleen Blee, Seymour Drescher, Simcha Epstein, Helen Fein, William Gamson, David Good, Michael Hechter, Radu Ioanid, Ellen J. Kennedy, David I. Kertzer, Irina Livezeanu, Michael Mann, John Markoff, Nonna Mayer, Don McTavish, Tony Oberschall, Ido Oren, Rainer Praetorius, Ilya Prizel, Joachim Savelsberg, Edward Tiryakian, Christopher Uggen, Leon Volovici, and Susan Zuccotti. It goes without saying that I assume sole responsibility for any inaccuracies contained in this study.

Without the invaluable assistance of J. Mark Sweeney of the Library of Congress and, especially, Melissa Eighmy of the University of Minnesota's Interlibrary Loan Department, who oversaw the ordering of the multitude of newspaper microfilm reels over a three-year period, the research for this book would have been impossible. Hilda Mork Daniels was a godsend for her unmatched skill at managing the budgets of the numerous grants that funded this research.

I have benefited greatly from the material assistance of several foundations and institutions. At different stages, my research was funded by grants from the Dr. Sol & Mitzi Center Fund, the Philip and Florence Dworsky Endowment, the Edelstein Family Foundation, the University of Minnesota Graduate School, the Life Course Center of the Department of Sociology of the University of Minnesota, both the College of Liberal Arts and the Graduate School of the University of Minnesota, the University Center for International Studies at the University of Pittsburgh, and the National Science Foundation (#SES-9905000). I am indebted to the University of Minnesota College of Liberal Arts for providing me with paid leave during the 1999–2000 academic year to devote myself full-time to this project and the London School of Economics and Political Science for awarding me the position of Academic Visitor during the spring and summer of 1999, enabling me to work at the British Library-Newspaper Library and the Institute of Contemporary History and Wiener Library Limited.

I also want to thank the staffs of the Ullstein Verlag in Berlin, the Staatsbibliothek zu Berlin, the Library of Congress, the University of Minnesota's Interlibrary Loan Department, the Center for Research Libraries, the British Library-Newspaper Library, the Institute of Contemporary History and Wiener Library Limited, the U.S. Holocaust Memorial Museum Library, the Bibliotheque Nationale, the Biblioteca Nazionale Centrale, the Fondazione Centro di Documentazione Ebraica

Contemporanea, the Bibliotheque de l'Alliance Israelite Universelle, the Centre de Documentation Juive Contemporaine, the Biblioteca Academiei României, the University of Minnesota's Wilson Library, and the Yad Vashem Library. They have been most gracious in facilitating me and my research assistants in this research endeavor.

I have benefited greatly from the comments of many faculty colleagues and students who attended my guest lectures at the College of William and Mary, Duke University, Emory University, the Jagellonian University, Northwestern University, Pennsylvania State University, Stanford University, the University of Helsinki, the University of Minnesota, the University of Pittsburgh, the University of Toronto, the University of Trento, the University of Washington, and the University of Wisconsin at Madison.

Most important, I wish to thank my wife, Yvonne, and my two children, Arielle and Maximilian, for their patience, love, and encouragement during the many years it took to make this book happen.

# CHAPTER ONE

# INTRODUCTION:

# ANTI-SEMITISM IN EUROPE

# BEFORE THE HOLOCAUST

In the months following Nazi Germany's annexation of Austria in March 1938, Nazi persecution of Jews in Austria climbed dramatically. Jewish property was destroyed, persecution and violence against individual Jews became commonplace, and hundreds of Jews were marched off to prisons and concentration camps. These crimes against Jews drew worldwide attention. During the spring and summer of 1938, tens of thousands of Austrian Jews swelled the ranks of Jews seeking to flee pre-*Anschluss* Germany. In the early summer of 1938, Nazi Germany offered its Jews to the world. At the same time, neighboring Hungary and Yugoslavia closed their borders with Austria, while fascist Italy, which had recently permitted German and Austrian refugees to enter the country, halted Jewish immigration. Belgium, the Netherlands, and Switzerland allowed small numbers of these Jewish refugees to enter; Great Britain instituted a special new visa requirement sorting out Third Reich Jews from other refugees.[1]

President Franklin D. Roosevelt, responding to pro-refugee sentiments in the United States, called an international conference on refugees. Delegates from thirty-two countries assembled in the French resort town of Evian-les-Bains between July 6 and July 14, 1938, to discuss ways to help Jewish refugees fleeing the Nazi Third Reich. Many delegates attending the Evian Conference publicly professed their sympathies for the Jewish refugees, and the conference chairman, Myron C. Taylor, a former head of U.S. Steel, invoked a plea to those assembled that governments act and act promptly to address the refugee problem.

---

[1] Michael Marrus, *The Unwanted: European Refugees in the Twentieth Century* (New York and Oxford, 1985), 167–69.

However, most countries, including Australia, Great Britain, and the United States, offered excuses as to why they could not accept more refugees. The Australian delegate, explaining his country's refusal to increase its quota of refugee Jews, stated that the entry of more Jews would disturb his country's racial balance. Frederick Blair, representing Canada, proposed that the Evian delegates do nothing to alleviate the Jewish refugee crisis in order to force Nazi Germany to solve its Jewish Question internally. The official delegates from Hungary, Poland, and Romania used the opportunity to propose that they too be relieved of their Jews. Several Western delegates, seeking to justify their countries' reluctance to accept more Jews, emphasized the fear that a change in existing quotas would prompt some Eastern European governments to expel tens of thousands of their unwanted Jews. In the end, only the representatives of the Dominican Republic and later Costa Rica agreed to increase their quotas. That the world seemed to turn its back on the German and Austrian Jewish refugees, not surprisingly, provided the Nazi regime's anti-Semitic campaign a propaganda bonanza.[2]

The failure of the delegates at the Evian Conference to aid European Jewry was not exceptional as an example of worldwide indifference to the fate of European Jews on the eve of the Holocaust, for in the aftermath of the Evian Conference, indifference to the fate of Europe's Jews reached epidemic levels. Both Hungary and Czechoslovakia refused to give refuge to the expelled Sudetenland Jews. The American government failed to fulfill its immigration quotas for Austria and Germany; the Wagner-Rogers Child Refugee Bill, which would have admitted to the United States 20,000 Jewish refugee children from Europe, failed, after acrimonious debate, to reach the floor of Congress; and U.S. authorities refused to admit the 936 German-Jewish refugees aboard the ill-fated ship the *St. Louis*. Shifting from its earlier policy, the British government decided in the spring of 1939 to close off Palestine to Jewish immigration, while offering no alternative haven for Jewish immigration. The French government of Prime Minister Daladier declined to offer even a symbolic objection to Nazi Germany's barbaric *Kristallnacht* pogrom, and the governments of Argentina and Brazil reneged on pledges made to papal

---

[2] Arthur D. Morse, *While Six Million Died: A Chronicle of American Apathy* (New York, 1968), 214; John Weiss, *Ideology of Death: Why the Holocaust Happened in Germany* (Chicago, 1996), 331; Saul Friedlaender, *Nazi Germany and the Jews*, vol. 1, *The Years of Persecution, 1933–1939* (New York, 1997), 248–50; Marrus, *Unwanted*, 170–72; A. J. Sherman, *Island Refuge: Britain and Refugees from the Third Reich 1933–1939* (London, 1973), 101.

authorities to accept baptized Jews into their countries. Even as late as April 1943 at the Bermuda Conference, American and British representatives in possession of knowledge of Nazi atrocities against Europe's Jews, gathered by British and American intelligence services, continued to display little interest in altering existing policies on Jewish refugees. Across the globe, as the magnitude of anti-Semitic incidents grew exponentially during the 1930s, few public protests against the mistreatment of European Jewry occurred.[3]

On the eve of the Holocaust, apathy toward their rapidly deteriorating plight was not the only injustice experienced by millions of Europe's Jews. The introduction of official anti-Semitic policies and bans and the incidence of violence against Jewish persons and property climbed to levels unprecedented in the modern age. Violence against Jews took place not only in the German Third Reich and Eastern Europe. Marrus and Paxton[4] have observed that demonstrations against Jews, including physical attacks, occurred in September 1938 in Paris, Dijon, Saint Etienne, Nancy, and in several locations in Alsace and Lorraine. These anti-Semitic manifestations in France led the grand rabbi of Paris to caution his co-religionists during the High Holy Days of the autumn of 1938 to refrain from gathering in large numbers outside of synagogues.[5] By 1938, Germany and Austria did not stand alone in Europe in terms of the enactment of anti-Semitic laws. Anti-Semitic laws found a home in Bulgaria, Hungary, Poland, Romania, and Slovakia. Finzi[6] notes that in Poland, which contained one of Europe's largest Jewish communities, the 1930s ushered in a systematic economic boycott of many Jewish producers and a series of prohibitions excluding Polish Jews from several

[3] Friedlaender, *Nazi Germany*, 265–66, 299–300; George Mosse, *Toward the Final Solution: A History of European Racism* (Madison, 1985), 231; Marrus, *Unwanted*, 285–89; Peter Novick, *The Holocaust in American Life* (Boston and New York, 1999), 51–52; Sherman, *Island*, 265; Geoffrey Field, "Anti-Semitism with the Boots Off." In H. A. Strauss, ed., *Hostages of Modernization: Studies on Modern Antisemitism 1870–1933/39 Germany–Great Britain–France*, vol. 3/1 (Berlin and New York, 1993), 325; Paul Bookbinder, "Italy in the Overall Context of the Holocaust." In I. Herzer, ed., *The Italian Refuge: Rescue of Jews During the Holocaust* (Washington, DC, 1989), 106–07; Louis Golding, *The Jewish Problem* (London and Aylesbury, 1938), 117.

[4] Michael Marrus and Robert Paxton, *Vichy France and the Jews* (Stanford, 1981), 40.

[5] Ibid., 40.

[6] Roberto Finzi, *Anti-Semitism: From Its European Roots to the Holocaust* (New York, 1999), 108.

occupations and educational opportunities. In Romania, the formation of the Goga-Cuzist government following the December 1937 national elections produced Europe's second anti-Semitic regime.

These examples of insensitivity to the fate of persecuted European Jews and of anti-Jewish acts on the eve of the Holocaust point to an extraordinary depth and breadth of European anti-Semitism before the Holocaust and thus raise a number of important questions regarding anti-Semitism.[7] How and why had antipathy toward European Jewry reached such extreme heights? How did the levels of anti-Semitism in the 1930s compare to those of earlier decades? There appears to be a scholarly consensus that, beginning in the 1870s, European anti-Semitism entered a dramatically new phase. If this is indeed true, what brought about the post-1870s rise in anti-Semitism? Did anti-Semitism vary in content and in intensity across societies? In order words, did ordinary Germans embrace anti-Semitism in a way that ordinary American, British, French, Italian, Polish, or Romanian citizens did not, as has been suggested in a number of relatively recent works on German anti-Semitism?[8]

We have accounts of how thousands of ordinary non-Jewish citizens and, in some cases, high ranking government officials in a few European countries under Nazi occupation or allied with Nazi Germany during World War II risked their lives to help the persecuted Jews. Here are three well-known examples: King Boris of Nazi-allied Bulgaria and his country's Orthodox Church refused to hand over to the Nazis the country's fifty thousand Jews. Officers of the fascist Italian military during World War II resisted efforts by Croatian anti-Semitic paramilitary groups and

---

[7] I do acknowledge that insensitivity is not necessarily a precursor to anti-Semitic hatred.

[8] Daniel J. Goldhagen, *Hitler's Willing Executioners* (New York, 1996); Weiss, *Ideology*. In a provocative study of the role of ordinary Germans in the Holocaust, Goldhagen claims that German anti-Semitism was indeed qualitatively different by virtue of its eliminationist character and the extent of its embeddedness in German culture and society before 1945. Goldhagen's work suggests that pre–World War II popular anti-Semitism was both qualitatively and quantitatively different outside of Germany. Some might dismiss the value of the comparison, given that the Holocaust was perpetrated by Germans and not by other Europeans. However, the fact that Germans organized the Holocaust does not by itself demonstrate that German popular anti-Semitism was sui generis. For is it not unreasonable to argue that if a political movement like the German Nazi Party with its agenda of eliminating Europe's Jewish population had come to power in another country, a genocidal campaign against the Jews might have been undertaken?

Vichy French forces to arrest and deport thousands of Jews. And the Danish police, unlike their counterparts elsewhere in Europe, actively participated in the successful efforts to rescue almost all of Denmark's estimated 7,200 Jews during the Nazi occupation. Do these instances of remarkable benign treatment of Jews by Bulgarians, Italians, and Danes, which occurred at a time when ordinary citizens of so many other nations displayed apathy toward the plight of European Jewry or willingly participated in the slaughter of millions of Jews, indicate societal variations in anti-Semitism?

Finally, how does anti-Semitism differ from other forms of religious, racial, and ethnic prejudice? More specifically, is Jewish hatred similar to the antipathy manifested against the Arabs in Israel, the blacks in the United States, the Chinese in Indonesia, the Gypsies or Roma throughout Europe, or the Irish in Great Britain? If not, why? These are some of the key questions I will explore in this work.

The proposed study of anti-Semitism will focus on what I call "popular anti-Semitism." By "popular anti-Semitism," I mean hostility (as expressed in sentiments, attitudes, or actions) to Jews as a collectivity rooted in the general population. Stated in another fashion, this study of anti-Semitism seeks to understand the anti-Semitic beliefs and behaviors of average citizens, rather than simply those of the elites. Jewish hatred has a long and infamous lineage in the Christian West. This study endeavors to cover a small but significant slice of this anti-Semitic heritage.

Though some attention will be given to earlier centuries, the bulk of this study concerns itself with European anti-Semitism during a span stretching from the 1870s through the 1930s. Why this period? These seventy years, culminating in the Holocaust, marked a high point in popular anti-Semitism in Europe. This period signals a reversal in Jewish-Gentile relations within Europe that had begun with the European Enlightenment of the late eighteenth century. Between 1791 and 1870, European Jews experienced rising toleration and emancipation. Throughout Europe, ghetto walls came down; obstacles to professional advancement disappeared; and Jews became members of the highest echelons of the economic, social, cultural, and political elites. This is not to suggest the complete eradication of Western anti-Semitism. Indeed, there were some notable anti-Jewish incidents momentarily souring Jewish-Gentile relations between 1791 and 1870, such as the "hep hep" riots of 1819 in western regions of Germany, the Damascus Affair in 1840, and the Mortara Affair of 1858. These anti-Semitic events,

however, galvanized significant public outrage in Europe and led many
to characterize them as unfortunate vestiges of an unenlightened medieval past. Overall, the first three-quarters of the nineteenth century
witnessed a high-water mark in the movement toward Jewish civil and
political equality in Europe.

Thus, the sudden emergence after 1870 of anti-Semitic social and political movements, the widespread popularity of anti-Semitic pamphlets
and books, and the growth in anti-Semitic violence stunned many Jewish
and Christian observers, who, on the eve of 1870, had been predicting
a further blossoming of enlightenment and emancipation.[9] Among the
more prominent anti-Semitic occurrences of the 1870s were the public
declarations of Gyozo Istoczy, a Liberal Party Hungarian parliamentarian, who mentioned the possibility of a "mass extermination" of the
Jews in the mid-1870s; the establishment of the anti-Semitic Christian
Socialist Workers Party in 1878 by Adolf Stoecker, a German Lutheran
pastor and the Kaiser's court chaplain; and the 1879 publication of
Wilhelm Marr's *The Victory of Judaism over Germanism*, in which the
term "anti-Semitism" first appears. What began in the 1870s lost no
steam in the 1880s and 1890s. During these two decades, anti-Semitic
pogroms erupted in czarist Russia, culminating in the westward movement of millions of Eastern European Jews; a new wave of the "blood
libel" accusation against Jews unfolded in Central Europe; anti-Semitic
parties in Austria, France, Germany, and Hungary experienced stunning electoral successes; *La France juive*, Edouard Drumont's scathing
anti-Semitic tirade, appeared; and the infamous Dreyfus trial grabbed
worldwide attention.[10] The new wave of European anti-Semitism would
wane briefly between 1898 and 1914. But with the successful Bolshevik

---

[9] David N. Smith, "Judeophobia, Myth, and Critique." In S. D. Breslauer, ed.,
*The Seductiveness of Jewish Myth: Challenge or Response* (Albany, 1997), 125–26;
Herbert A. Strauss, "Introduction: Possibilities and Limits of Comparison." In
Strauss, ed., *Hostages of Modernization*, vol. 3/1 (Berlin and New York, 1993), 6.

[10] Jacob Katz, *From Prejudice to Destruction: Anti-Semitism, 1700–1933* (Cambridge,
MA, 1980), 9, 257–78; Richard J. Bernstein, *Hannah Arendt and the Jewish Ques-
tion* (Cambridge, MA, 1996), 49, 62; Robert F. Byrnes, *Antisemitism in Modern
France*, vol. 1 (New Brunswick, 1950), 81–82; Albert S. Lindemann, *The Jew
Accused: Three Anti-Semitic Affairs (Dreyfus, Beilis, Frank) 1894–1915* (Cam-
bridge, 1991), 92; Claire Hirshfield, "The British Left and the 'Jewish Conspir-
acy': A Case Study of Modern Antisemitism," *Jewish Social Studies*, vol. 28, no. 2,
Spring 1981, 95; Max I. Dimont, *Jews, God, and History* (New York, 1962), 313;
Meyer Weinberg, *Because They Were Jews* (New York and Westport, London,
1986), 93.

Revolution in Russia, the post–War World I collapse of empires, and the toppling of the world economy, anti-Semitism surged to unprecedented levels between 1933 and the Holocaust. The year 1939 will serve as the end point of this study, for that eventful year witnessed the outbreak of World War II and a qualitatively new phase in anti-Semitism leading to the near-annihilation of European Jewry.

In pursuit of an explanation for the rise of modern anti-Semitism and societal variations in anti-Semitism before the Holocaust, the present study endeavors to carry out a comparative and empirical examination of anti-Semitism before the Holocaust. A comparative study of popular anti-Semitism in Europe before the Holocaust could easily include any number of European countries. For compelling reasons, I have chosen to examine popular anti-Semitism in France, Germany, Great Britain, Italy, and Romania. The inclusion of these five countries appeals for a number of important reasons. Each of these countries was politically autonomous during the years between 1879 and 1939, and each permitted contested elections for much of the period (Italy's last free election occurred in 1921, and Germany's last free election occurred in 1933).[11] By including Italy, we have the added advantage of examining a society much like Germany, in that it too accomplished its unification relatively late, and it too came under fascist rule during the interwar period.[12] Moreover, the countries included offer what many scholars assume to be a wide range of anti-Semitism: Germany and Romania are ranked as high; France is ranked as intermediate; and Italy and Great Britain are ranked as low. This sample also includes significant variations in levels of economic development (Great Britain and Germany were quite advanced, and Italy and Romania were less developed) and religion (Great Britain and Germany were substantially Protestant; France

---

[11] There are a large number of other European countries, including Austria, Hungary, Poland, and Russia, that would have been ideal candidates for a comparative study of anti-Semitism in Europe before the Holocaust. Unfortunately, these countries were not included in my study because they were not politically autonomous for the entire period of the study, did not possess a relatively open and competitive press, or reappeared after World War I as a significantly different political or national entity.

[12] Late unification has been cited as a possible contributor to acute nationalism and racism by Martin Woodroffe, "Racial Theories of History and Politics: The Example of Houston Stewart Chamberlain." In Paul Kennedy and Anthony Nicholls, eds., *Nationalist and Racialist Movements in Britain and Germany before 1914* (London, 1981), 152–53.

and Italy were predominantly Roman Catholic; and Romania was largely Orthodox).

Did European anti-Semitism vary temporally and spatially before the Holocaust? Is there empirical proof of societal variations in pre–World War II anti-Semitism? More specifically, how are we to empirically ascertain if popular anti-Semitism was more widespread in Germany than in Italy, or if it was more intense in France between 1930 and 1934 than between 1924 and 1928? Over the course of several years, my international research team has coded and analyzed data on anti-Semitic acts and attitudes within France, Germany, Great Britain, Italy, and Romania, between 1899 and 1939. In order to compare popular anti-Semitism as expressed through acts and attitudes within Europe across space and time, this study systematically examines two rich sources of data. One of the most invaluable historical sources of information on Jewish issues and Jews is the *American Jewish Year Book* (AJYB). The *American Jewish Year Book* has been published annually since 1899 and contains a section dedicated to summarizing leading news events of the previous year (a year follows the Jewish calendar – autumn to autumn) from around the world.[13] This section usually focuses on events involving Jews. Included among the types of events covered are promotions of prominent Jews, accomplishments of Jews, special religious events, changes in laws pertaining to Jews, and accounts of violence against Jews. With rare exceptions, the news events are categorized by country, and, with a few exceptions, the events are identified by the day, month, and year in which they occurred. Because, among other things, the *American Jewish Year Book* served as a digest of anti-Semitic acts, it is an excellent source of historical information on anti-Semitic events. However, as is the case with much historical data, we must proceed with caution, given the limitations of these data. While we have no means to ascertain thoroughly the accuracy of the reported events, we should assume that the reported events are only representative of all anti-Semitic events, for the editors of the *American Jewish Year Book* probably selected to include events that they found of significance. Moreover, the reports of events from around the world were sent to the editors by local and national Jewish organizations, and the accuracy of the reports may have

---

[13] While the volumes of the *American Jewish Year Book* correspond to the Jewish year (autumn to autumn), years from the Christian calendar are noted in the volumes. Thus, coding the data according to the Christian calendar was not problematic.

some reliability problems. Nevertheless, given the absence of alternative sources of information on popular anti-Semitism, the information contained in the *American Jewish Year Book* can serve as a useful tool to examine variations in popular anti-Semitic acts across space and time.

The present study has extracted information on anti-Semitic acts from the yearbooks and sorted the acts by country, year, and type of anti-Semitic act. My typology of acts consists of thirteen categories, ranging from false accusations against Jews to murderous riots. Occasionally, I encountered an act that could realistically fit into more than one category. In such cases, I generally went with the more serious category or further examined the context of the act. For example, a serious assault within a riot could be tallied as a violent act, but since the assault was in the context of a riot, I recorded the act as a "riot resulting in physical injury to Jews." Additionally, my typology of anti-Semitic acts does not fully capture variations among acts in terms of their magnitude. The *American Jewish Year Book*, for instance, reports the *Kristallnacht* pogrom of November 1938 in Germany as four acts. One of the four acts mentions the destruction of 600 synagogues. Rather than count this act as 600 individual acts, I decided to collapse the multiple acts into one act. Fortunately, as it pertains to my examination, *Kristallnacht* was the exception and not the rule. The completed data file on anti-Semitic acts consists of (1,295) anti-Semitic acts spanning the forty-one-year period (1899–1939). These data from the *AJYB* provide us with a preliminary estimation of the spatial and temporal variation in anti-Semitic acts in France, Germany, Great Britain, Italy, and Romania for the period 1899 to 1939.[14]

My investigation of the *AJYB* revealed significant variations across the five countries of interest. Figure 1.1 compares the average number of anti-Semitic acts per million people for the forty-one-year period across the five countries, and it suggests that Great Britain, France, and Italy had relatively few anti-Semitic acts, recording less than .05 acts per million people. Yet the number of anti-Semitic acts in Germany was

---

[14] To account for population variance in the five countries, I have standardized anti-Semitic acts. In most analyses, I measure anti-Semitism as the number of acts per million people in the respective countries. This standardized variable allows a more fruitful comparison over time and between countries and allows us to pool our data for multivariate analyses.

TABLE 1.1. *Types of anti-Semitic Acts in Great Britain, France, Germany, Italy, and Romania, 1899–1939*

| Type of Anti-Semitic Act | Country | | | | | |
|---|---|---|---|---|---|---|
| | Great Britain | France | Germany | Italy | Romania | Total |
| Riots and demonstrations (no violence or vandalism reported) | 7 (10%) | 10 (20%) | 27 (4%) | 0 (0%) | 46 (11%) | 90 (7%) |
| Vandalism or destruction of property | 7 (10%) | 1 (2%) | 20 (3%) | 0 (0%) | 13 (3%) | 41 (3%) |
| Formation of anti-Semitic groups, protest speeches, leafleting | 7 (10%) | 4 (8%) | 54 (8%) | 3 (8%) | 36 (8%) | 104 (8%) |
| Boycotts or strikes | 2 (3%) | 1 (2%) | 21 (3%) | 0 (0%) | 10 (2%) | 34 (3%) |
| Laws/acts against Jewish practices | 5 (7%) | 4 (8%) | 35 (5%) | 1 (3%) | 20 (5%) | 65 (5%) |
| Laws/acts against Jewish immigration or naturalization; expulsions, citizenship reversals, or deportations | 2 (3%) | 7 (14%) | 56 (8%) | 0 (0%) | 36 (8%) | 101 (8%) |
| Laws/acts of discrimination | 8 (11%) | 1 (2%) | 195 (28%) | 11 (28%) | 75 (17%) | 290 (22%) |
| Media attacks | 19 (26%) | 11 (22%) | 39 (6%) | 12 (31%) | 6 (1%) | 87 (7%) |
| Violent acts against people; murder | 0 (0%) | 1 (2%) | 22 (3%) | 0 (0%) | 41 (10%) | 64 (5%) |
| Raids, confiscations, or shutdowns; dissolved organizations | 2 (3%) | 2 (4%) | 29 (4%) | 2 (5%) | 8 (2%) | 43 (3%) |
| False accusations, arrest, or imprisonment | 2 (3%) | 3 (6%) | 21 (3%) | 4 (10%) | 5 (1%) | 35 (3%) |
| Riots with vandalism, destruction of property, physical assault, and/or murder | 4 (6%) | 1 (2%) | 20 (3%) | 0 (0%) | 91 (21%) | 116 (9%) |
| Laws/acts forcing Jews to leave posts or appointments or to lose businesses | 8 (11%) | 3 (6%) | 164 (23%) | 6 (15%) | 44 (10%) | 225 (17%) |
| Total | 73 (100%) | 49 (100%) | 703 (100%) | 39 (100%) | 431 (100%) | 1295 (100%) |

*Note:* Column percentages in parentheses.
*Source: American Jewish Year Book.*

10

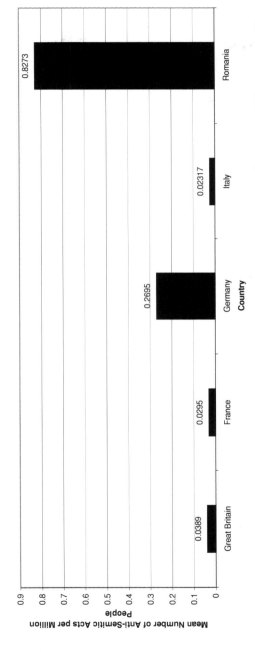

Figure 1.1. Mean number of anti-Semitic acts per million people by country, 1899–1939. *Note:* There were 1,295 acts recorded for the five countries. The distribution breaks down as follows: Great Britain = 73; France = 49; Germany = 703; Italy = 39; Romania = 431. *Source: American Jewish Year Book.*

over five times that of France, Great Britain, and Italy, and the number of anti-Semitic acts in Romania was three times that of Germany.[15]

The analysis also revealed variations in the nature of anti-Semitic acts across countries. Figure 1.2 suggests that anti-Semitic acts in France and Italy were exceptionally nonviolent, with a mean number of violent anti-Semitic acts of .002 and .000, respectively.[16] The mean number of violent acts was slightly higher in Germany (.024) as well as in Great Britain (.006). Romanian anti-Semitism appeared to be the most violent, with a mean number of .254. In Romania, 35 percent of all anti-Semitic acts reported were violent in nature.

In sum, we find that anti-Semitic acts were relatively infrequent in France, Great Britain, and Italy, yet significantly more frequent in Germany and particularly in Romania. It should be noted, however, that 401 of the 703 anti-Semitic acts reported for Germany occurred between 1933 and 1939. Moreover, our investigation of the volumes of the *American Jewish Year Book* revealed significant variation in the nature of anti-Semitic acts. For instance, we find that Romanian anti-Semitism was rather violent (over a third of all acts were violent). In contrast, German (and later Italian) anti-Semitism often involved dismissals and requests that Jews leave posts, appointments, or occupational positions, as well as discriminatory laws. Anti-Semitic acts in France, Great Britain, and Italy, meanwhile, were largely composed of media attacks (between 25 percent and 31 percent) and nonviolent acts. Taken together, we may conclude that the number and nature of European anti-Semitic acts before the Holocaust varied significantly across societies.

[15] When standardizing anti-Semitic acts by Jewish population, the distribution of acts is largely consistent with what I found in other figures depicting anti-Semitic acts per million people across countries. The mean proportion of anti-Semitic acts per 10,000 Jews per year is .05 for Italy (1899–1935), .07 for Great Britain, .09 for France, .16 for Germany (1899–1932), and .19 for Romania. If you add Germany (1933–39) and Italy (1936–39), the proportions change dramatically for these two countries, which points to the dramatic difference made by Hitler's seizure of power in 1933 and Mussolini's anti-Semitic turn in 1936. Analysis of variance (one-way ANOVA) tests suggest the variation in means across countries is statistically significant ($p < .001$). Also, although anti-Semitic acts were significantly more prevalent in Romania than in Germany over the forty-one-year period, we found no significant difference between Romania and Germany after 1933.

[16] Acts were coded as violent if they fell into one of the following categories: (1) vandalism or destruction of property; (2) riots with vandalism, destruction of property, and/or physical assault or murder; (3) violent acts on people, including murder.

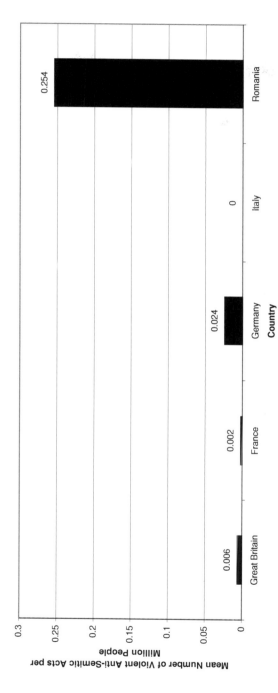

Figure 1.2. Mean number of violent anti-Semitic acts per million people by country, 1899–1939. *Note:* There were 1,295 acts recorded for the five countries. The distribution breaks down as follows: Great Britain = 73; France = 49; Germany = 703; Italy = 39; Romania = 431. *Source: American Jewish Year Book.*

To supplement this societal variation in anti-Semitism, we next examine temporal variation in European anti-Semitism before the Holocaust. Figure 1.3 combines all anti-Semitic acts per million people in the five countries of interest. Except for notable increases between 1909 and 1910, 1912 and 1914, and 1919 and 1921, the number of anti-Semitic acts remained relatively low prior to 1933. However, after Hitler's ascension to power in 1933, we witness a rather dramatic increase in anti-Semitic acts. The number of anti-Semitic acts per million people increased over seven times from 1932 to 1933. While much of this is due to anti-Semitic activity within the German borders, we also found increases in France, Great Britain, and Romania (Italy did not show an increase until after 1936). While the number of acts did subside over the following years, we still find a significantly greater number of acts during this period than over the previous thirty-three years.

Figure 1.4 illustrates yearly changes in anti-Semitic acts per million people in France, Germany, Great Britain, Italy, and Romania between 1899 and 1939. Figure 1.4 reveals four patterns. First, prior to 1933 (Hitler's ascension to power in Germany) the number of anti-Semitic acts in Romania is consistently greater than the number occurring in the other countries. However, after Hitler's ascension, the number of acts in Germany approximates the number in Romania. Second, the pattern of Romanian anti-Semitism is much more erratic than the pattern in the other four countries. We find rather dramatic increases in Romanian anti-Semitic acts in 1909, 1913, 1924, and again in 1937. Again, the other four countries do not display such dynamic trends. Third, we see relatively uniform increases in all countries except Italy in 1920 and 1933. These years mark the immediate aftermath of World War I and the Russian Revolution and the beginning of the Hitler era, respectively. Finally, and perhaps as one would suspect, we find significant increases in German and Italian anti-Semitism after 1933. In both cases, these acts largely involve laws and acts of discrimination or orders for Jews to leave posts, appointments, or occupational positions.

The *American Jewish Year Book* is a valuable source of information on anti-Semitic acts before the Holocaust. But an examination of anti-Jewish acts alone provides us a rather limited understanding of anti-Semitism. People may harbor negative feelings toward individuals or groups yet never engage in an explicit action against them. A more thorough investigation of the rise of and societal variations in anti-Semitism requires an empirical assessment of popular attitudes toward Jews. Despite some limitations as a source of historical information, the newsprint medium is a most valuable source of information on popular

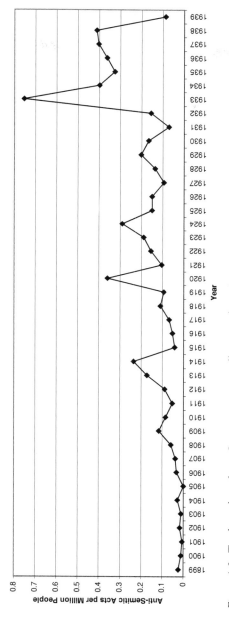

Figure 1.3. Total number of anti-Semitic acts per million people in Great Britain, France, Germany, Italy, and Romania (combined) by year, 1899–1939. *Source: American Jewish Year Book* (N = 1,295).

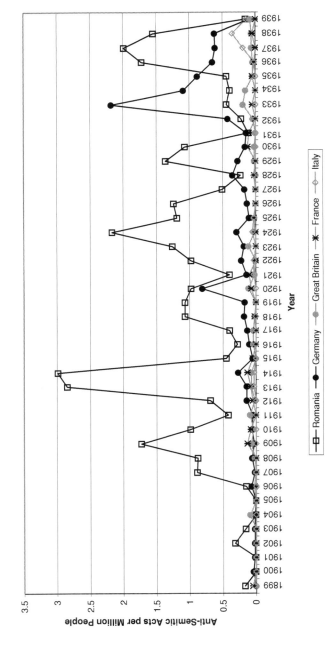

Figure 1.4. Anti-Semitic acts per million people in Romania, Germany, Great Britain, France, and Italy by year, 1899–1939. *Source: American Jewish Year Book* (N = 1,295).

anti-Semitic attitudes before the Holocaust.[17] Today we rely largely on survey research to assess people's racial, religious, gender, and ethnic attitudes, but this information-gathering tool was nonexistent before the 1940s. An examination of newspapers provides us with a comparable tool to assess what people were reading about Jews and Jewish issues in our five countries and how the coverage may have differed from country to country and year to year. The years from 1899 to 1939 fall within "the golden age of journalism." Gannon reminds us that before the advent of television, for the vast majority of people the newspaper press was the sole purveyor of information about the outside world. Newspapers served as a principal means by which average citizens became informed and by which popular attitudes on numerous issues took shape.[18] Kauders notes that newspapers "also reflect what was read, believed, and called for at the time more closely than many other printed records we have at our disposal."[19] According to Gamson, newspapers serve as an important tool or resource that enables people to make sense of issues in the news.[20] Thus, for these reasons, newspapers with large circulations should have played an important role in creating and shaping popular attitudes towards Jews. For each of the five countries, I examined the daily newspaper with the largest national circulation between 1899 and 1939.[21] The newspapers are *Le Petit Parisien* (France), the *Berliner*

---

[17] Roberto Franzosi, "The Press as a Source of Socio-Historical Data: Issues in the Methodology of Data Collection from Newspapers," *Historical Methods*, vol. 20, no. 1, 1987, 6–7; John D. McCarthy, C. McPhail, and J. Smith, "Images of Protest: Estimating Selection Bias in Media Coverage of Washington Demonstrations, 1982 and 1991," *American Sociological Review*, vol. 61, 1996, 478–99; David Snyder and W. R. Kelly, "Conflict Intensity, Media Sensitivity and the Validity of Newspaper Data." *American Sociological Review*, vol. 42, 1977, 105–23. See Franzosi ("Press") for a detailed assessment of the strengths and weaknesses of newspapers as a data source for historical research. According to Fanzosi ("Press," 6–9), newspapers (like yearbooks) do not provide exhaustive accounts of the occurrences of particular kinds of events, but they often constitute the only available source of information. McCarthy, McPhail, and Smith ("Images") posit that the selection biases exhibited by newspapers appear to be similar across newspapers and across nations.

[18] Franklin Reid Gannon, *The British Press and Germany 1936–1939* (Oxford, 1971), 1.

[19] Kauders, *German*, 5.

[20] William Gamson, *Talking Politics* (Cambridge, 1992), 180.

[21] Information on newspaper circulation comes from published volumes of *Editor and Publisher International Yearbook*, which is the most authoritative industry reference guide. I also referred to the volumes of *The Newspaper Press Directory* for

*Morgenpost* (Germany), the *Daily Mail* (Great Britain), the *Corriere della Sera* (Italy), and *Universul* (Romania).[22] In terms of daily circulation for much of the interwar period, the *Petit Parisien* and the *Daily Mail* averaged between 1.5 and 2.0 million readers, while the *Berliner Morgenpost* and the *Corriere della Sera* each had roughly one-half million readers. The circulation of *Universul* ranged between 150,000 and 300,000.[23]

Though I am confident that an examination of the widest-circulating newspaper in each country provides the best possible measure of popular attitudes on Jews, I also include a selective examination of a second widely circulating newspaper in each of the five countries. By incorporating a study of a second newspaper, I am able to compare intranational reportage on Jews and Jewish issues for possible political and/or regional variation. The newspapers selected for this examination are *La Dépêche de Toulouse* (France), the *Muenchner Neueste Nachrichten* (Germany), the *Daily Herald* (Great Britain), *Il Messaggero* (Italy), and *Lumea* (Romania). These principal secondary newspapers generally catered to a different audience than the primary newspapers used in this study.[24]

---

information on the newspapers' circulation, political identification, ownership, and origins.

[22] Each of these papers maintained uninterrupted publication throughout the 1899–1939 period and was available for examination either as hardbound or microfilm copies. My decision to select the newspaper with the largest daily circulation came after considerable deliberation and consultation. The key objective of the newspaper study is to gather information on what the average citizen of each of these countries was reading about Jews on a daily basis. One reasonable way to assess what people were reading is to examine the newspaper with the widest circulation within each country, regardless of political tendency. Not surprisingly, the newspapers with the widest circulation were typically politically independent or centrist and oriented toward the middle classes. But is it reasonable to ask if the major paper was either leftist or rightist, lest this fact contaminate my research objective? The simple answer is no. Again, the essential point of the newspaper study is to find out what most people were reading about Jews and Jewish issues, and if they received their news from a rightist or leftist paper, then that is what they were reading.

[23] Gannon, *British*, 32; Schor, *L'Opinion*, 14; *Editor and Publisher*, vols. 61–63, nos. 36–37.

[24] The daily circulation of these secondary papers varied considerably. The *Daily Herald* possessed a readership of between 1.5 and 2.0 million, the *Il Messaggero* and *La Dépêche de Toulouse* averaged between 200,000 and 300,000 readers, the *Muenchner Neueste Nachrichten* had between 100,000 and 200,000 subscribers, and *Lumea* had a circulation of between 15,000 and 25,000. Though the circulation of *Lumea* was relatively low by Western European standards, it was

Because of my limited resources and the restricted availability to some of these newspapers, I utilized a selective sampling of certain years of the reportage for these secondary newspapers. The years covered are 1921, 1933, 1935, and 1939.[25]

My examination of the various newspapers covers the period from 1899 to 1939, to match the years for which we have collected data on anti-Semitic acts from the *American Jewish Year Book*.[26] For this period, microfilm copies as well as hardbound copies of these newspapers are available through interlibrary loan. Rather than examine each edition of each of these daily newspapers, I have conducted both a random and purposive sample of each newspaper. The random sample includes newspaper editions for the fifteenth of each month from January 15, 1899 to December 15, 1939.[27] Every article of each edition for the fifteenth of the month was examined. The purposive sample focuses on newspaper coverage during critical discourse moments involving Jews or Jewish issues. By "critical discourse moments," I mean key events that directed public attention to a specific issue and that were covered widely and in-depth by the media. This study examines two supranational critical discourse moments. They are the Evian Conference of July 1938 and the *Kristallnacht* pogrom against Jews and Jewish property in Germany in November 1938. Both events received extensive coverage throughout

the leading daily paper of the Moldavian city of Iasi (Jassy). This newspaper was sold in major cities throughout Romania. In the hope of controlling for possible regional and political variation, I have included it as the secondary Romanian paper.

[25] In the case of *Lumea*, the newspaper was banned in 1937 and thus ceased publication in that year. Therefore, we have no articles for 1939.

[26] The examination of the various newspapers required a multiyear effort and was conducted by an international research team under my supervision. Where microfilm copies were available through interlibrary loan, copies of the newspapers were read at the University of Minnesota. To gain access to some of the newspapers, however, we were obliged to work in foreign libraries and archives. All editions of both Romanian newspapers, *Universul* and *Lumea*, were examined at the Biblioteca Academiei României in Bucharest, Romania. Editions of the Italian newspaper *Il Messaggero* were examined in Rome at the *Biblioteca Nazionale Centrale*. Copies of the two British newspapers, the *Daily Mail* and the *Daily Herald*, were examined at the Colindale branch of the British Library in London, and editions of the *Berliner Morgenpost* for the years 1899 to 1906 were examined at the private library of the *Ullstein-Verlag* and the Deutsche Staatsbibliothek in Berlin, Germany.

[27] If, in the rare case, the edition for the fifteenth of the month was unavailable, the next available edition was selected.

Europe. A principal benefit of an examination of critical discourse moments is that they offer us an in-depth comparison of the reportage of both national newspapers as well as a comparison of single events across five different national presses. For each of the two critical discourse moments, all editions of each newspaper (both the primary and secondary ones) were examined for a one-week period beginning with the initial report of the event.[28]

A coding instrument has been developed, consisting of a questionnaire containing thirty-four questions. The questionnaire has been completed for every extracted article from both the random and purposive samples. A copy of the questionnaire can be found in the Appendix.[29] Information from the questionnaire is used to compare popular anti-Semitic attitudes across countries and across years. I am particularly interested in how popular attitudes toward Jews differed across the five countries between 1899 and 1939. Did, for example, press reporting of negative attitudes toward Jews rise considerably in all five countries after 1919? Were the number of negative articles on Jews higher in France than in Great Britain between 1899 and 1939?[30]

My examination of the five principal European dailies for articles on Jews or Jewish issues for the fifteenth day of the month from January 15,

[28] Since *Lumea*, my secondary Romanian newspaper, ceased to publish in 1937, we cannot include it in the examination of these two critical discourse moments.

[29] The principal readers on the project were all native speakers. Each reader read the entire newspaper. Any article mentioning Jews or Jewish issues was photocopied using the readily available combination photocopy machines/microfilm readers. Possessing a hard copy of the article permitted the readers to check their coding of the newspaper's contents. After the initial coding of each article, a printout of the entered data was checked against the newspaper microfilm photocopies for accuracy. Readers had a set of coding guidelines with which to work. My two project leaders, Ryan King and Dr. Marit Berntson, held group sessions for readers and were available to answer questions about coding decisions. In those instances where the two project leaders did not agree, they came to me for a final decision. King and Berntson also randomly checked readers' coding for accuracy and consistency. In a random within-country reliability check (two separate German readers reading and coding the same newspapers), we found 18 errors for 868 possible opportunities for error. That is, the research assistants coded 18 questions differently. This indicates an error percentage of about 2 percent for this selection of coded articles.

[30] With the ascension to power of Mussolini in Italy and Hitler in Germany, respectively, major dailies in both countries became less reliable as a gauge or mirror of popular attitudes. Nevertheless, newspaper reportage probably continued to play a critical role in shaping popular attitudes.

TABLE 1.2. *Number of articles discussing Jews or Jewish issues by country, 1899–1939*

| | Country | | | | |
|---|---|---|---|---|---|
| | Great Britain | France | Germany | Italy | Romania |
| Number of Articles | 299 | 199 | 269 | 101 | 136 |

*Note:* Articles were taken from the fifteenth day of the month for every month between 1899 and 1939. Articles were taken from the *Daily Mail* in Great Britain, *Le Petit Parisien* in France, *Berliner Morgenpost* in Germany, *Corriere della Sera* in Italy, and *Universul* in Romania.

1899 to December 15, 1939, yielded a total of 1,004 articles.[31] Table 1.2 lists the number of articles for each of the five countries. The number of articles ranges from a high of 299 for Great Britain to a low of 101 in Italy. Figure 1.5 depicts temporal variation in the number of articles discussing Jews or Jewish issues for all five countries combined between 1899 and 1939. The data suggests some interesting findings regarding temporal variation. Among these findings are the exceptionally large number of articles for the year 1899, the low levels of reportage occurring between 1914 and 1921, and the appearance of a steadily rising coverage of Jews and Jewish issues from 1935 through 1938. Temporal variation in newspaper coverage on Jews and Jewish issues by country for the 1899 to 1939 period is presented in Figure 1.6. As demonstrated in the figure, among the five countries, Great Britain appears to have had the largest number of articles between 1899 and 1908, while Germany maintained relatively high reportage between 1908 and 1914, 1922 and 1925, and 1935 and 1938. French newspaper reportage spikes in 1899 and again from 1934 through 1936. Among the five countries, Italy stands out as the one in which the coverage of Jews and Jewish issues remains consistently low throughout the period. Only in 1938 do we witness a significant rise in Italian reportage.

In the next set of figures, we examine whether the reportage on Jews and Jewish issues was favorable, unfavorable, or neutral. Coders assigned an unfavorable orientation to an article if the author's tone was clearly

---

[31] For the five principal European dailies, my research team read 2,460 newspapers (editions). Of this number, 1,678 newspapers did not include any articles discussing Jews, while 782 did, with many of these 782 newspapers having multiple articles.

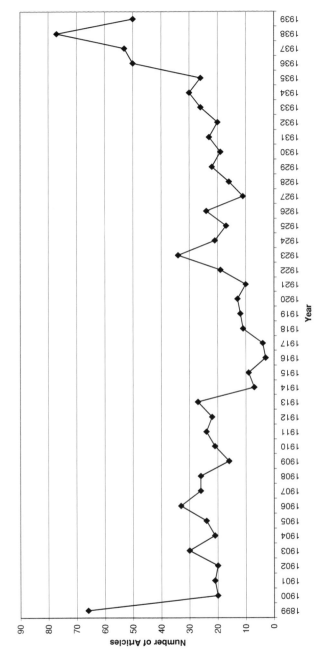

Figure 1.5. Total number of newspaper articles discussing Jews and/or Jewish issues in Great Britain, France, Germany, Italy, and Romania (combined) by year 1899–1939. *Note:* Articles are taken from the fifteenth day of the month for every month between 1899 and 1939. Articles were taken from the *Daily Mail* in Great Britain (N = 269), *Le Petit Parisien* in France (N = 199), *Berliner Morgenpost* in Germany (N = 269), *Corriere della Sera* in Italy (N = 101), and *Universul* in Romania (N = 136). The total number of articles from all five countries is 1,004.

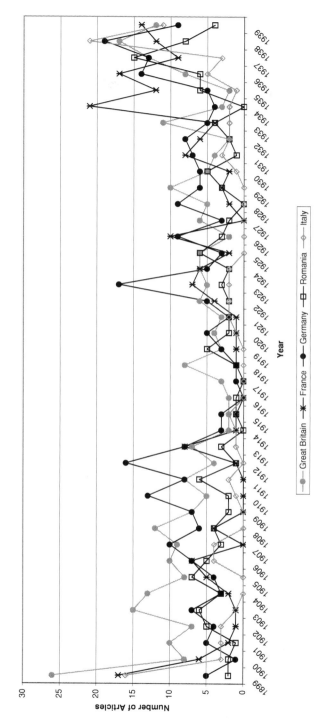

Figure 1.6. Newspaper articles discussing Jews and/or Jewish issues by country and year, 1899–1939. *Note:* Articles are taken from the fifteenth day of the month for every month between 1899 and 1939. Articles were taken from the *Daily Mail* in Great Britain, *Le Petit Parisien* in France, *Berliner Morgenpost* in Germany, *Corriere della Sera* in Italy, and *Universul* in Romania.

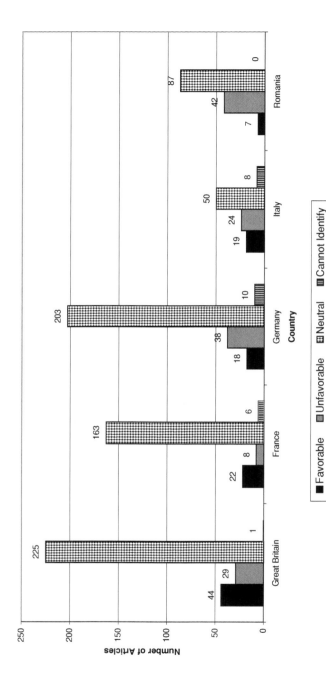

Figure 1.7. Newspapers' orientation toward Jews by country, 1899–1939. *Note:* Articles are taken from the fifteenth day of the month for every month between 1899 and 1939. Articles were taken from the *Daily Mail* in Great Britain (N = 299), *Le Petit Parisien* in France (N = 199), *Berliner Morgenpost* in Germany (N = 269), *Corriere della Sera* in Italy (N = 101), and *Universul* in Romania (N = 136). The total number of articles from all five countries is 1,004. Articles were coded "unfavorable" if the article reflected negatively on Jews, if the authors tone expressed disdain for Jews, or if the article supported actions that adversely affected Jews.

anti-Semitic. Conversely, if the author of the article spoke in defense of Jews, then the article was coded as favorable. If the article simply reported on an event without taking a side, the article was assigned a neutral tone. Figure 1.7 provides a breakdown for each country for the entire forty-one-year period in terms of the newspaper's orientation towards Jews (see Appendix, question 6). In all five countries, the content of the majority of articles about Jews was neutral. This was particularly true in the cases of Great Britain, France, and Germany. Great Britain, France, Germany, and Italy had higher levels of favorable articles than Romania. In Romania, for every favorable article concerning Jews, there were six unfavorable articles.

Figures 1.8a through 1.8d offer glimpses of temporal variation in newspapers' orientations toward Jews for each of the five countries for different time periods between 1899 and 1939. The most striking finding among these four figures is the phenomenal change in orientation after 1932. More specifically, we see a sharp increase in unfavorable articles in Germany, Italy, and Romania after 1932. Interestingly, Germany's reportage goes from disproportionately favorable in the first three time periods (1899–1913, 1914–23, and 1924–32) to overwhelmingly unfavorable between 1933 and 1939. Also, for Italy we find that of the twenty-four unfavorable articles published between 1899 and 1939, nineteen appeared during the seven years following 1933.

Did the orientations of the secondary newspapers in each of the five countries replicate those observed in the principal newspapers? Figure 1.9 provides a comparison of the principal and secondary newspapers for all five countries for the years 1921, 1933, 1935, and 1939. For these selected years, with the notable exception that the tone of the majority of articles for Great Britain, France, and Germany was neutral toward Jews, we find considerable divergence among the pairs of newspapers. The *Daily Herald* had a higher volume of articles than the *Daily Mail*, and its orientation appeared more favorable. *La Dépêche de Toulouse* also carried more articles on Jews and Jewish issues, and its reportage seemed only slightly more favorable. For Germany, the *Muenchner Neueste Nachrichten* published a considerably larger number of articles about Jews for the selected years than the *Berliner Morgenpost*. However, in both papers, the ratio of unfavorable to favorable articles ran largely unfavorable. The quantity of articles about Jews in the two Italian and two Romanian papers was far lower than in the other three countries. *Il Messaggero* matched the *Corriere della Sera* in terms of unfavorable articles, while the orientation of *Universul* was decidedly

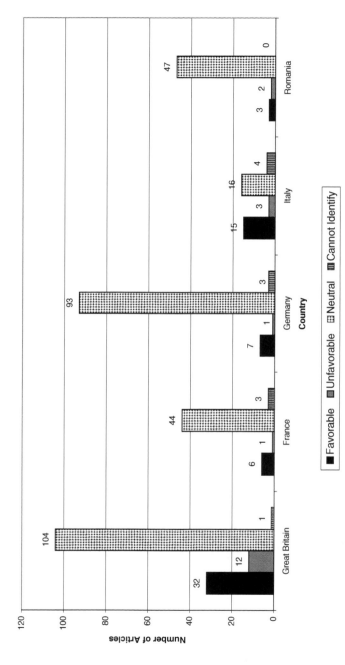

Figure 1.8a. Newspapers' orientation toward Jews by country, 1899–1913. *Note:* Articles are taken from the fifteenth day of the month for every month between 1899 and 1939. Articles were taken from the *Daily Mail* in Great Britain, *Le Petit Parisien* in France, *Berliner Morgenpost* in Germany, *Corriere della Sera* in Italy, and *Universul* in Romania. Articles were coded "unfavorable" if the article reflected negatively on Jews, if the author's tone expressed disdain for Jews, or if the article supported actions that adversely affected Jews.

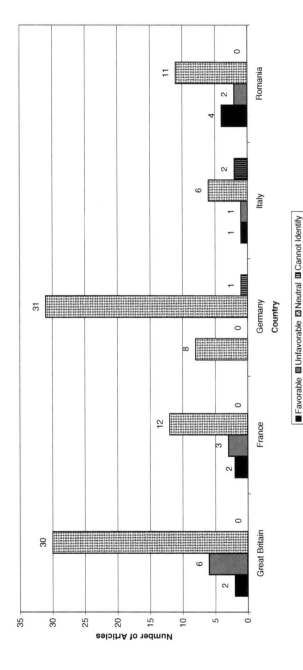

Figure 1.8b. Newspapers' orientation toward Jews by country, 1914–23. *Note:* Articles are taken from the fifteenth day of the month for every month between 1914 and 1923. Articles were taken from the *Daily Mail* in Great Britain, *Le Petit Parisien* in France, *Berliner Morgenpost* in Germany, *Corriere della Sera* in Italy, and *Universul* in Romania. Articles were coded "unfavorable" if the article reflected negatively on Jews, if the author's tone expressed disdain for Jews, or if the article supported actions that adversely affected Jews.

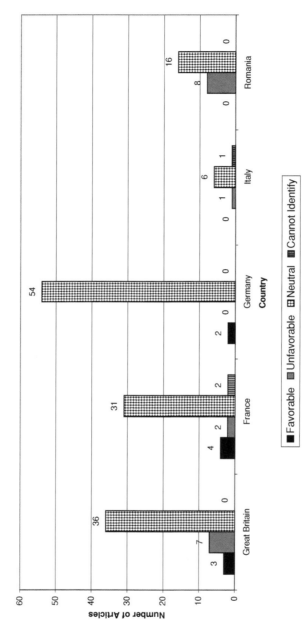

Figure 1.8c. Newspapers' orientation toward Jews by country, 1924–32. *Note:* Articles are taken from the fifteenth day of the month for every month between 1924 and 1932. Articles were taken from the *Daily Mail* in Great Britain, *Le Petit Parisien* in France, *Berliner Morgenpost* in Germany, *Corriere della Sera* in Italy, and *Universul* in Romania. Articles were coded "unfavorable" if the article reflected negatively on Jews, if the author's tone expressed disdain for Jews, or if the article supported actions that adversely affected Jews.

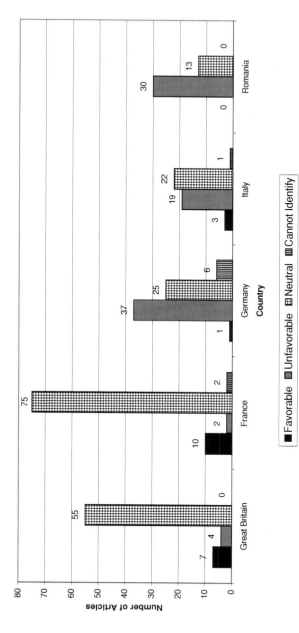

Figure 1.8d. Newspapers' orientation toward Jews by country, 1933–39. *Note*: Articles are taken from the fifteenth day of the month for every month between 1933 and 1939. Articles were taken from the *Daily Mail* in Great Britain, *Le Petit Parisien* in France, *Berliner Morgenpost* in Germany, *Corriere della Sera* in Italy, and *Universul* in Romania. Articles were coded "unfavorable" if the article reflected negatively on Jews, if the author's tone expressed disdain for Jews, or if the article supported actions that adversely affected Jews.

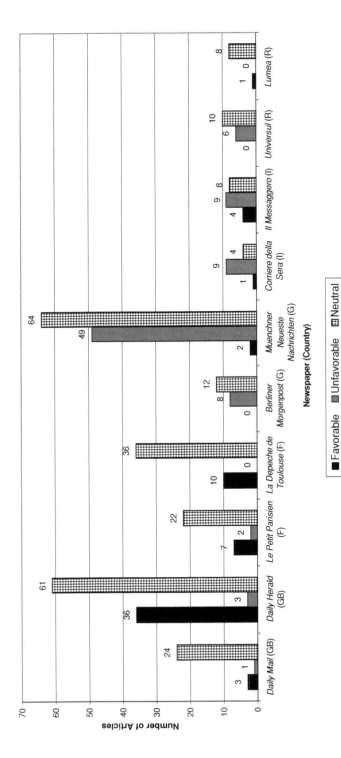

Figure 1.9. Newspapers' orientation toward Jews by newspaper for selected years. *Note:* All articles are taken from the fifteenth day of the month for every month in the years 1921, 1933, 1935, and 1939. The only exception is Romania, where *Lumea* was no longer in print in 1939; hence, for the Romanian newspapers I compare the years 1921, 1933, and 1935 only. Articles were coded "unfavorable" if the article reflected negatively on Jews, if the author's tone expressed disdain for Jews, or if the article supported actions that adversely affected Jews.

more unfavorable toward Jews than that of *Lumea*. What the findings
in Figure 1.9 suggest for the selected years is that for France, Great
Britain, and Germany, intranational reportage varied greatly vis-à-vis
the volume of articles about Jews, but the relationship among favorable, unfavorable, and neutral orientation within each country's press
remained roughly proportional. In the case of Italy, we find a greater
congruence between the two newspapers with respect to both volume
of articles and orientation. For Romania, the two newspapers diverged
in terms of both volume of articles and orientation.

The two critical discourse moments selected for an examination
of newspaper reportage are the July 1938 Evian Conference and the
November 1938 *Kristallnacht* pogrom. Between July 6 and July 14,
1938, delegates representing thirty-two nations met in the quaint resort town of Evian-les-Bains to address the Central European Jewish
refugee problem. The conference lasted for more than a week and received substantial international newspaper coverage. The *Kristallnacht*
pogrom occurred in Nazi Germany in the aftermath of the assassination
of Ernst vom Rath, first secretary of the German Embassy in Paris, by
Herschel Grynszpan, a seventeen-year-old German-born Polish Jew, on
November 7, 1938. Herschel Grynszpan assassinated the German diplo-
mat supposedly in an angry response to the forced expulsion from
Germany of his parents. His parents were among the thousands of
Polish Jews residing in Germany who were transported to the Polish
border town of Zbaszyn by German authorities during the last days
of October 1938. Within forty-eight hours of the assassination, Nazi
thugs rampaged Jewish quarters throughout the German Reich. During
two days of rioting, 267 synagogues were destroyed, more than 7,000
Jewish businesses were damaged, and 91 Jews were murdered. Not until
some days had passed did the German government intervene to halt
the anti-Jewish violence. Again, as it had for the Evian Conference,
the world press gave considerable coverage to the events surrounding
*Kristallnacht*. Figures 1.10 and 1.11 show the results of my cross-national
and intranational examination of the newspapers for the two critical discourse moments. For each critical discourse moment, newspapers were
read for seven consecutive days beginning with the first mention of the
critical discourse moment. The reportage on *Kristallnacht* exceeded the
reportage on Evian by a ratio of more than 2 to 1. The British, French,
and German newspapers provided the most extensive coverage of both
events.

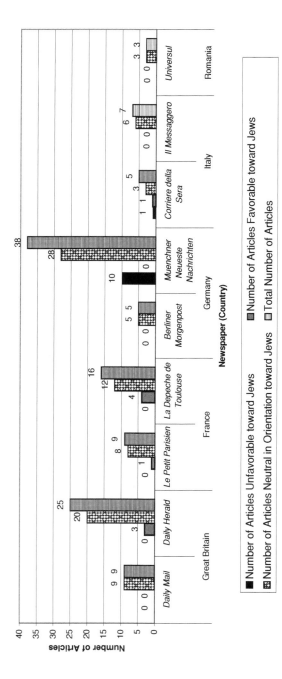

Figure 1.10. Newspapers' orientation toward Jews for the first seven days covering the Evian Conference (July 1938). *Note:* The totals represent articles pertaining to Jews or Jewish issues for a seven-day period covering the Evian Conference. Beginning with the first day of coverage, articles were coded for each newspaper edition for the following seven days. Most newspapers began their coverage on July 6, 1938, with the exception of *Le Petit Parisien* (July 7), *Corriere della Sera* (July 7), *Il Messaggero* (July 8), *Corriere della Sera* (July 7), *Il Messaggero* (July 7), and *Universul* (July 10). *Lumea* in Romania had been discontinued and thus was not included in this analysis. Articles were coded "unfavorable" if the article reflected negatively on Jews, if the author's tone expressed disdain for Jews, or if the article supported actions that adversely affected Jews.

The total for the *Daily Herald* includes two articles that could not be identified as favorable, unfavorable, or neutral.

The total for the *Il Messaggero* includes one article that could not be identified as favorable, unfavorable, or neutral.

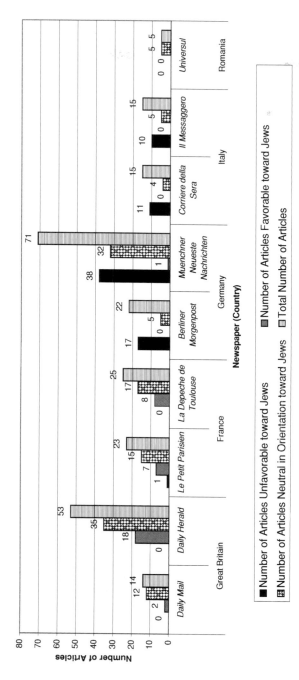

Figure 1.11. Newspapers' orientation toward Jews for the first seven days covering *Kristallnacht* (November 1938). *Note:* The totals represent articles pertaining to Jews or Jewish issues for a seven-day period covering the *Kristallnacht* pogrom. Beginning with the first day of coverage, articles were coded for each newspaper edition for the following seven days. Most newspapers began their coverage on November 8, 1938, with the exception of *Daily Mail* (November 9), *Corriere della Sera* (November 9), and *Universul* (November 11). *Lumea* in Romania had been discontinued and thus was not included in this analysis. Articles were coded "unfavorable" if the article reflected negatively on Jews, if the author's tone expressed disdain for Jews, or if the article supported actions that adversely affected Jews.

33

With few exceptions, the tone of the newspaper reportage on Evian was decidedly neutral. Only the *Muenchner Neueste Nachrichten*, with ten articles unfavorable toward Jews, ran counter to the overall neutral tone. The French press appeared to be the most sympathetic to the Jewish refugee problem, with four articles in *La Dépêche de Toulouse* and one article in *Le Petit Parisien*. Though both British newspapers were overwhelmingly neutral in their reportage, the *Daily Herald* did publish three articles favorable toward Jews during the event. The most pronounced intranational variation in reportage surrounded the volume of articles, notably in Britain, France, and Germany.

Newspaper reportage of *Kristallnacht* evoked a greater sympathetic tone towards Jews than did the Evian Conference. Nevertheless, the lion's share of articles published during the week's coverage was neutral. The *Daily Herald* and the *Muenchner Neueste Nachrichten* provided the largest volume of articles. The *Daily Herald*, *Le Petit Parisien*, and *La Dépêche de Toulouse* published nearly all the articles favorable toward Jews among the nine newspapers examined during the events of *Kristallnacht*. The Italian press, which had given trifling coverage to the Evian Conference, gave substantially more coverage to *Kristallnacht* – albeit unfavorable to Jews. The French and Italian presses exhibited negligible intranational variation in reportage on *Kristallnacht*. Within Great Britain, the *Daily Herald* was decidedly more favorable in its orientation toward Jews than the *Daily Mail*, and the German *Muenchner Neueste Nachrichten* contained nearly as many articles neutral in their orientation toward Jews as it did unfavorable articles.

In sum, while the volume of articles on Jews varied significantly for the two critical discourse moments, the tone of the newspaper reportage differed slightly: *Kristallnacht* produced a more sympathetic reportage on Jews than Evian, with the French newspaper coverage exhibiting the most favorable response. Compared to its coverage of the Evian Conference, Italian newspaper reportage of *Kristallnacht* was of a higher volume and more unfavorable toward Jews. *Kristallnacht* reportage also produced a greater degree of intranational divergence, particularly within the British and German national presses.

The evidence from this cursory examination of the *American Jewish Year Book* and the sample of European daily newspapers from 1899 to 1939 clearly shows that European anti-Semitism varied both temporally and spatially before the Holocaust. What explanations have scholars advanced to explain both the dramatic rise and the societal variations in popular anti-Semitism between 1870 and the Holocaust? Before I lay out the competing explanations of anti-Semitism, allow me to justify my alternating between reference points of 1870 and 1899. The year 1870 is a useful starting point for my study from a conceptual standpoint, for 1870 marks the beginning of a dramatic rise in European anti-Semitism. In a more perfect world, I might have been able to locate systematic empirical data beginning with the year 1870. However, in the absence of reliable data, my quantitative analysis allows a test only beginning with 1899.

Many of the popular explanations for the rise of anti-Semitism have analogs in the literature on ethnic prejudice (e.g., relative deprivation, ethnic competition, and frustration/aggression). Here, I choose to summarize several of the leading theories of anti-Semitism.[32] My examination will cover modernization, scapegoat, reaction against the strong state, and political culture theories of anti-Semitism.

Much of the scholarly literature emphasizes the role of modernization in explaining the rise of anti-Semitism in Europe. Modernization explanations of anti-Semitism typically assign causality to either the effects of rising economic competition or to growing anomic stresses resulting from the process of modernization. The process of modernization embodied the emergence of liberalism and capitalism, which, among other things, led to the political, social, and economic emancipation of Jews. Jewish social mobility and Jewish competition elicited fears among many Gentiles, reinforcing anti-Semitic attitudes. An underlying argument within this version of the modernization thesis is that modernization wrought a zero sum process that enhanced Jewish upward mobility at the cost of downward mobility for non-Jews. The losers in the process of modernization (either social groups or nations) tended to harbor the strongest anti-Semitic beliefs. The emphasis in these arguments is generally on the emergence of social tensions based on a competitive relationship

---

[32] For heuristic purposes, the following summary of the literature pertaining to theories of modern anti-Semitism reduces complex arguments to their most simplistic form and is by no means totally comprehensive of the vast literature on anti-Semitism. Furthermore, my brief review of the theoretical literature will not examine psychological theories, which emphasize psychological elements of personality acquired by individuals (see Werner Bergmann, "Psychological and Sociological Theories of Antisemitism," *Patterns of Prejudice*, vol. 26, nos. 1–2, 1992, 37–47), or theories that seek to differentiate among the various levels of Jewish hatred or concentric rings of antipathy within groups or within a particular society (see Michael Marrus, "The Theory and Practice of Anti-Semitism," *Commentary*, vol. 74, no. 2, August 1982, 38–42).

between Jews and non-Jews.[33] For instance, both Lindemann[34] and Hagen[35] derive an explanation of the late nineteenth-century explosion of anti-Semitism in Eastern and Central Europe from increasing economic competition. For the two authors, anti-Semitism erupted not in regions marked by economic backwardness, where the classes of Jewish middlemen and Christian peasants coexisted in relative peace, but in the rapidly transforming small towns and cities, where entrepreneurial Christian and Jewish middle-class groups eager to reap the benefits from capitalist modernization engaged in fierce competition.[36]

---

[33] Lindemann, *Accused*; Albert Lindemann, *Esau's Tears: Modern Anti-Semitism and the Rise of the Jews* (Cambridge and New York, 1997); Helen Fein, "Explanations of the Origin and Evolution of Antisemitism." In Helen Fein, ed., *The Persisting Question: Sociological Perspectives and Social Contexts of Modern Antisemitism*, vol. 1 (Berlin and New York, 1987), 17; Shmuel Almog, *Nationalism and Antisemitism in Modern Europe 1815–1945* (Oxford, 1990); Shmuel Ettinger, "Jew-Hatred in Its Historical Content." In Shmuel Almog, ed., *Antisemtism through the Ages*, trans. Nathan H. Reisner (Oxford, 1988); Ettinger, Jew-Hatred," p. 7; Herbert A. Strauss, "Hostages of 'World Jewry': On the Origin of the Idea of Genocide in German History." In Strauss, ed., *Hostages of Modernization*, vol. 3/1 (Berlin and New York, 1993).

[34] Lindemann, *Accused*, 229.

[35] William W. Hagen, "Before the 'Final Solution': Toward a Comparative Analysis of Political Anti-Semitism in Interwar Germany and Poland," *The Journal of Modern History*, vol. 68, no. 2, 1996, 361, 380.

[36] The Lindemann and Hagen explanations appear closely linked to Olzak's (see Susan Olzak, *The Dynamics of Ethnic Competition and Conflict*, Stanford, 1992) economic competition theory. Olzak proposed the economic competition theory as an alternative to Hechter's (see Michael Hechter, "Group Formation and the Cultural Division of Labor," *American Journal of Sociology*, vol. 84, 1978, 293–318) well-known ethnic segregation theory. The ethnic segregation theory argues that modernization promotes ethnic segregation, inequality, and grievances, which ultimately produce ethnic intolerance and conflict. According to Hechter, modernization leads to the introduction of a hierarchical cultural division of labor in which ethnic groups are assigned to particular occupational or social roles. Ethnic tensions are likely to erupt as ethnic groups become aware of the existence of inequality along ethnic lines. Olzak, on the other hand, holds that modernization fosters competition along ethnic lines. For Olzak, increasing ethnic competition results from decreasing occupational and residential segregation and increased ethnic group contact. All told, competition along ethnic lines for scarce goods increases ethnic intolerance. Again, ethnic tensions are likely to erupt as ethnic groups become aware of the existence of inequality along ethnic lines. Thus, we would expect from Olzak that levels of anti-Semitism should be higher in societies where Jews and non-Jews are highly integrated and competing for scarce resources; whereas from Hechter, we would expect that levels of anti-Semitism

Canepa advances an argument that appears to support Lindemann and Hagen.[37] Seeking to explain the relatively low levels of anti-Semitism in Italy before World War II, Canepa points to Italy's late industrialization as important in reducing the likelihood of economic competition between Italian Jews and non-Jews, in contrast to the earlier industrialization of France and Germany.

Modernization also figures in the rise of anti-Semitism by way of increasing anomic stresses. In contrast to the first set of modernization explanations, which emphasize economic competition between Jews and non-Jews, anti-Semitism in these accounts did not require actual encounters or conflicts between Jews and non-Jews. To this end, Hagen has aptly remarked that anti-Semitism emerged "from deflections onto the Jews of social antagonisms deriving from other sources."[38] This strand of the modernization argument draws on the Durkheimian notion that modernization has intensified the anomic character of society by cutting the masses loose from their traditional and communal moorings. In the absence of sufficient social integration and regulation, people are likely to exhibit deviant or irrational behaviors. Sternhell's research on French anti-Semitism provides one example of this tendency within the modernization camp.[39] Sternhell has illuminated the connection between anti-Semitism and the revolt against the intellectual heritage of the nineteenth century, which included the contributions of materialism, liberalism, and Marxism. In Sternhell's account, many anti-Semites attributed national decadence to this intellectual heritage and tied this heritage to Jews.

Arendt provides an interesting variant to the modernization thesis of anti-Semitism. Modernization for Arendt included the transformation of the role of Jews in European societies.[40] By the end of the nineteenth century, European states had become less dependent on wealthy Jewish financiers, and Jews experienced a new status – they had lost real power,

---

should be greater in societies where Jews and non-Jews are highly segregated both residentially and occupationally.

[37] Andrew Canepa, "Christian-Jewish Relations in Italy from Unification to Fascism." In I. Herzer, ed., *The Italian Refuge: Rescue of Jews during the Holocaust* (Washington, DC, 1989), 23.

[38] Hagen, "Before the Final Solution," 363.

[39] Zeev Sternhell, "The Roots of Popular Anti-Semitism in the Third Republic." In Frances Malino and Bernard Wasserstein, eds., *The Jews in Modern France* (Hanover and London, 1985), 129–32.

[40] Hannah Arendt, *The Origins of Totalitarianism* (San Diego, 1975), 4–5.

yet were still holders of major wealth. For Arendt, the inconsistency between insignificant power and phenomenal wealth created within the general public the image of Jews as a despised parasitical social group. Arendt cites as evidence that the greatest periods of modern anti-Semitism coincided with declines in Jewish influence.[41]

While the modernization thesis seemingly provides a plausible explanation for the rise of anti-Semitism in Europe after 1870, it fails to offer a convincing argument for temporal and spatial variations in anti-Semitism. For instance, the modernization thesis cannot explain why popular anti-Semitism in Europe climbed significantly during the 1880s and 1890s but fell dramatically in Europe between 1900 and 1914, to rise again to new heights during the early 1920s and the mid to late 1930s. Nor does the theory explain why levels of popular anti-Semitism tended to be higher in Germany and Romania than in Great Britain and Italy.

An alternative explanation for the rise of anti-Semitism is the scapegoat model. Like the anomic stress variant of the modernization thesis, the scapegoat theory highlights people's irrational socio-psychological impulses. The scapegoat theory of anti-Semitism emanates from a larger scholarly literature on minorities and ethnic prejudice. Blalock observes that highly visible or foreign minority groups, with high economic status and low political clout, filling a middleman role between the dominant elites and the impoverished masses, particularly in times of intense stress, are likely to become scapegoats.[42] Proponents of the scapegoat theory as it pertains to the Jews see the Jews as prototypical of a foreign middlemen minority. That European Jews constituted a minority group, dispersed among many countries, and traditionally engaged as traders and artisans relying on non-Jewish customers, made them convenient targets for the majority's frustrations in times of national crises. Jews became a group upon whom the majority population instinctively assigned blame for their misfortunes.[43] European societies had certainly experienced

---

[41] Ibid.

[42] Hubert Blalock, Jr., *Toward a Theory of Minority Group Relations* (New York, 1967).

[43] Marrus, "Theory"; Arthur Ruppin, *The Jews in the Modern World* (London, 1934), 239; Walter P. Zenner, "Middleman Minority Theories: A Critical Review." In Helen Fein, ed., *The Persisting Question: Sociological Perspectives and Social Contexts of Modern Antisemitism*, vol. 1 (Berlin and New York, 1987), 256–57; Strauss, "Introduction," 7; Katz, *Prejudice*, 247; Ettinger, "Jew-Hatred," 4–7; Helen Fein, *Accounting for Genocide: National Responses and Jewish Victimization during the Holocaust* (New York, 1979), 84–98.

significant trauma after 1870, including major wars and a series of economic and social upheavals, and for many groups, Jews became the
objects of their frustration and aggression. But the scapegoat thesis fails
to tell us why Jews rather than other minorities became scapegoats for
national distress, or why, in certain societies where Jews were present,
other groups served as scapegoats. For instance, in interwar Romania,
persecution of Jews far exceeded the harassment that fell upon other
Romanian minorities, including Bulgarians, Germans, Greeks, and
Hungarians. Yet in Italy, Jews did not become the scapegoats in times of
major national trauma, such as Italy's stunning military defeat in 1896
at the battle of Adowa, or in the failure of the Italian government to
procure territories in the post–World War I settlement.

The Pierre Birnbaum offers a very different theory of the rise of anti-
Semitism and of anti-Semitic variation among societies. Birnbaum attributes the rise of modern anti-Semitism to popular reaction against the
strong state.[44] Birnbaum proposes that where a strong state is perceived as
having imposed on society the emancipation of the Jews, anti-Semitism
tends to be strong (e.g., France and Germany). On the other hand,
where the state is relatively weak and Jews have obtained equal rights
through society rather than the state, anti-Semitism tends to be muted
(e.g., Great Britain and the United States).[45] But how would Birnbaum's
theory explain temporal variation in popular anti-Semitism? For instance, most scholars distinguish between the periods of high popular
anti-Semitism in France (the 1890s and 1930s) and the periods of low
popular anti-Semitism (1904–30). It makes little sense to argue that the
French state was significantly weaker between 1904 and 1930 than it
was during the 1890s. Or how would Birnbaum's thesis make sense of
the extraordinary high levels of popular anti-Semitism in Romania – a
country in which the state refused to grant the Jews civil rights until
after World War I, and then only after considerable pressure from the
victorious nations at Versailles?

The theories so far, with the exception of Birnbaum's, have focused
largely on the rise of modern anti-Semitism. Few general theories provide explanations for temporal and spatial variations in anti-Semitism.
One theory that has been applied to the study of societal variation in
anti-Semitism is the theory of political culture. The principal argument

[44] Pierre Birnbaum, *Anti-Semitism in France: A Political History from Leon Blum to
the Present*, trans. Miriam Kochan (Oxford, 1992).
[45] Birnbaum, *Anti-Semitism*, 6–10, 227–28.

of the theory is that distinct political cultures are responsible for national variations in anti-Semitism. Adherents of the political culture theory who argue that Germans possessed greater antipathy for Jews than did the English, for example, derive their belief from the differing constellations of internalized norms and beliefs about Jews in each of these countries. In Germany, the political culture supposedly nurtured intense dislike of Jews, whereas in other countries with lower levels of anti-Semitism, the political culture failed to nourish a similar degree of animosity. In light of twentieth-century history, it is understandable that the political culture argument has frequently been employed to explain German anti-Semitism; thus, few scholars have systematically employed the model to examine the political cultures of countries manifesting relatively low levels of anti-Semitism. Since the political culture model of anti-Semitism has focused largely on German anti-Semitism, we will briefly summarize and examine a few key arguments from this literature.

In their attempts to come to terms with the Holocaust, proponents of the political culture theory allege that the Holocaust is more the inevitable outcome of German history and culture than the consequence of Hitler's rise to power. These same proponents of the political culture theory have found evidence of the supposedly unique German anti-Semitic political culture as far back as the times of Martin Luther or the Napoleonic era.

Political culture as an explanation for national variations in anti-Semitism is implicit in three recent books on Germans and the Holocaust. Weiss, in accounting for the magnitude and breadth of modern German anti-Semitism, points to a "powerful culture of racism" existing in Germany.[46] He adds that during the Wilhelmine era, anti-Semitism became "essential to the definition of a patriotic German nationalist."[47] Weiss claims, moverover, that Nazi ideological anti-Semitism was hardly the creation "of a near psychotic and a few henchmen. It was an extreme version of ideas long familiar to millions. The tragedy is not that an obsessed fanatic somehow gained power, but that his bellicose racial hatreds were shared by legions of his fellow Germans and Austrians."[48] Weiss claims that millions of Germans no doubt knew what the Nazis had in mind for the Jews. The Nazi chant of "Death to the Jews" was widely known. For Weiss, that Germans were hardly ignorant of the

---

[46] Weiss, *Ideology*, viii.
[47] Ibid., 126.
[48] Ibid., 205

Nazi plan to destroy the Jews and did little to obstruct the plan makes it plainly clear that Jew hatred had embedded itself solidly within German political culture.[49] In terms of the relationship among anti-Semitism, Hitler, and the Holocaust, Weiss opines: "Anti-Semitism was an explosion waiting to happen; the Nazis would be the beneficiaries, the Holocaust the consequence."[50] And again with regard to the Holocaust and German political culture, Weiss remarks: "It is time to stop believing that 'without Hitler, no Holocaust.'"[51]

Goldhagen sees German anti-Semitism as a unique force throughout much of the nineteenth and twentieth centuries. For Goldhagen, anti-Semitism was an axiom of German culture that provided Germans "a model of cultural coherence."[52] In Germany, anti-Semitism embodied an "eliminationist" ideology, interpreting Jewish influence as naturally destructive and advocating the irrevocable elimination of Jewish influence from society.[53] Gonen, like Weiss and Goldhagen, contends that the widespread acceptance within Germany of an anti-Semitic ideology contributed prominently to Germany's leading role in the Holocaust. Gonen suggests, moreover, that "German myth and history" nurtured "shared group fantasies" of Jewish deceitfulness.[54]

Though many scholars object to Goldhagen's assertions that German political culture embodied "eliminationist" anti-Semitism and that Germany's unique culture of anti-Semitism enabled ordinary Germans to willfully participate in the murder of millions of Jews, they occasionally highlight the importance of a German culture of anti-Semitism. Several scholars have offered a more nuanced view of the anti-Semitic character of German political culture than those of Weiss, Goldhagen, and Gonen. For example, Kershaw, Bankier, Niewyk, and Friedlaender have argued that German public opinion at various times between 1933 and 1939 reacted negatively to Nazi party efforts to promote economic boycotts against Jewish businesses and to propagate violence against Jewish persons and property.[55] According to these scholars, such popular

[49] Ibid., 286.
[50] Ibid., 154–55.
[51] Ibid., 287.
[52] Goldhagen, *Hitler's*, 32, 54.
[53] Ibid., 48.
[54] Jay Y. Gonen, *The Roots of Nazi Psychology: Hitler's Utopian Barbarism* (Lexington, 2000).
[55] Ian Kershaw, *Popular Opinion and Political Dissent in the Third Reich: Bavaria 1933–1945* (Oxford, 1983), 233–69; David Bankier, *The Germans and the Final Solution:*

opposition was not rooted in some firmly held moral conviction or in
love for the Jews, but rather in pure economic self-interest.[56] On the
other hand, these same scholars imply a role for political culture when
they stress that German popular opinion did not seem to mind the imposition of other kinds of decrees or curbs on Jews, such as the "Law for
the Protection of German Blood and Honor."

As an explanation of temporal and spatial variations in anti-Semitism
as well as an interpretation of the German case, the political cultural arguments of Weiss, Goldhagen, and Gonen possess a number
of deficiencies. None of the proponents systematically examines non-
German political cultures and non-German anti-Semitism. How do they
know that the beliefs and norms about Jews contained within Polish,
Romanian, or Russian cultures diverged significantly from those in
the German culture? Would an observer canvassing popular prejudices
against Jews in 1905 in the wake of the Dreyfus Affair in France,
Karl Lueger's electoral victory in Vienna, or the Kishenev pogrom in
Czarist Russia have realistically concluded that German "Judeophobia"
had no rival? What is missing here is a thorough comparative study
of various European political cultures. Moreover, as numerous critics
have demonstrated, the political culture model, as depicted by Weiss,
Goldhagen, and Gonen, fails to account for the ebb and flow of
German anti-Semitism between 1814 and 1945. Several scholars of
German anti-Semitism have argued convincingly that the curve of anti-
Semitism fluctuated noticeably between 1870 and 1940. Levy and
Wistrich point to a major decline in the popularity of anti-Semitic po-
litical parties in Germany between 1896 and 1914.[57] Lindemann notes

*Public Opinion under Nazism* (Oxford, 1992), 69–73; Donald L. Niewyk, "The Jews
in Weimar Germany: The Impact of Anti-Semitism on Universities, Political
Parties and Government Services." In Strauss, ed., *Hostages of Modernization*,
vol. 3/1 (Berlin and New York, 1993), 225–26; Friedlaender, *Nazi Germany*, 162–
64, 324.

[56] Friedlaender (*Nazi Germany*, 324) describes the general attitude of the majority
of Germans during the Third Reich as one in which there was "tacit acquiescence
or varying degrees of compliance" but not one condoning widespread violence
against Jews. He notes furthermore (*Nazi Germany*, 4), in contrast to Goldhagen,
that after the 1941 invasion of the Soviet Union, the actions of ordinary German
participants in the murder of Jews on the eastern front differed little from the
actions of ordinary Austrians, Balts, Rumanians, and Ukrainians.

[57] Richard S. Levy, *The Downfall of the Anti-Semitic Political Parties in Imperial
Germany* (New Haven, 1975), 225; Robert S. Wistrich, *Antisemitism: The Longest
Hatred* (New York, 1991), 60–61.

that the anti-Semitic bills presented by anti-Semitic deputies in the German Reichstag from the 1880s to 1914 went overwhelmingly down to defeat.[58] Lohalm suggests that Weimar anti-Semitism was both qualitatively and quantitatively different from pre–World War I German anti-Semitism.[59] The political culture theory of anti-Semitism assumes a consistency in levels of anti-Semitism that runs counter to the preponderant evidence of temporal variations in German anti-Semitism. Pulzer has adroitly captured the inherent problem with the thesis that characterizes German history and culture as completely awash in anti-Semitism. Pulzer notes: "There is a danger in reading German history backwards, especially the history of anti-Jewish sentiments and activities in Germany so that events and developments point to a culmination in the Third Reich."[60]

Spatial and temporal variations in anti-Semitism bring into question the causal role of political culture. If it is true that nations, such as Germany, have experienced a waxing and waning of anti-Semitism, what does that say about the causal role of political culture? A theory that assumes *invariability* in political culture cannot explain *variation* in anti-Semitism. What I propose is that rather than being a cause of anti-Semitism, political culture may be a manifestation of anti-Semitic attitudes and actions, and, like anti-Semitism, be produced by antecedent and independent factors. Political culture, like anti-Semitism, requires an explanation of its origins. In particular, what needs to be explained is how a political culture characterized by heightened levels of anti-Semitism came into existence, or what conditions are responsible for the emergence of an anti-Semitic political culture. One chief objective of this study is to locate those factors that produced an anti-Semitic political culture.

All told, though the diverse explanations have substantially improved our theoretical understanding of the rise of modern anti-Semitism, they have typically lacked empirical verification and have rarely addressed spatial and temporal variations in anti-Semitism. With one notable exception, scholars have given minimal attention to a systematic and empirically based national comparison of popular anti-Semitism before

---

[58] Lindemann, *Accused*, 24.

[59] Uwe Lohalm, "Völkisch Origins of Early Nazism: Anti-Semitism in Culture and Politics." In Strauss, ed., *Hostages of Modernization*, vol. 3/1 (Berlin and New York, 1993),194–95.

[60] Peter Pulzer, *Jews and the German State: The Political History of a Minority, 1848–1933* (Oxford, 1992), 14.

1945.[61] The scholarly literature on anti-Semitism typically involves an examination of anti-Semitism within a particular nation or a nonempirical analysis of anti-Semitism across several countries.[62]

From the perspective of this study, what made anti-Semitism different from other forms of xenophobia or dislike of minorities is that Jew hatred is more multifaceted than other kinds of prejudice. White prejudice against blacks typically embraced a racial form of dislike; persecution of Armenians and Greeks in the former Asia Minor usually revolved around economic fears; and antipathy toward Irish-Catholics or Italian-Catholics in the nineteenth-century United States largely took a form of religious hatred. Popular anti-Semitism, by contrast, incorporated religious, racial, economic, and political prejudice. Consequently, we will see that Jews were disliked and *feared* for their religious beliefs and attitudes, their alleged racial characteristics, their perceived economic behavior and economic power, and their assumed leadership or support of subversive political and social movements. That anti-Semitism embodied numerous manifestations may help to explain why Jews rather

---

[61] Fein, *Accounting*.

[62] For a sample of the case studies, see Steven E. Ascheim, *Strange Encounters: The East European Jew in German and German Jewish Consciousness 1800–1923* (Madison, 1981); Birnbaum, *Anti-Semitism in France*; I. C. Butnaru, *The Silent Holocaust: Romania and Its Jews* (New York, 1992); Robert F. Byrnes, *Anti-Semitism in Modern France* (New Brunswick, 1950); Canepa, "Christian-Jewish"; Leonard Dinnerstein, *Antisemitism in America* (New York and Oxford, 1994)' Stephen Fischer-Galati, "Fascism, Communism, and the Jewish Question in Romania." In Bela Vago and George L. Mosse, eds., *Jews and Non-Jews in Eastern Europe 1918–1945* (New York, 1974), 157–76; Nancy Fitch, "Mass Culture, Mass Parliamentary Politics, and Modern Anti-Semitism: The Dreyfus Affair in Rural France," *American Historical Review*, vol. 97, no. 1 1992, 55–95; Friedlaender, *Nazi Germany*; Goldhagen, *Hitler's*; John Higham, *Strangers in the Land: Patterns of American Nativism 1860–1925* (New Brunswick and London, 1988); Colin Holmes, *Anti-Semitism in British Society 1876–1939* (New York, 1979); Carol Iancu, *Les Juifs en Roumanie (1866–1919): De L'Exclusion à L'Emancipation* (Aix-en-Provence, 1978); Radu Ioanid, *The Holocaust in Romania: The Destruction of Jews and Gypsies under the Antonescu Regime, 1940–1944* (Chicago, 2000); Kershaw, *Popular Opinion*; Gisela Lebzelter, *Political Anti-Semitism in England 1918–1939* (New York, 1978); W. F. Mandle, *Anti-Semitism and the British Union of Fascists* (London, 1968); Michael R. Marrus, *The Politics of Assimilation: A Study of the French Jewish Community at the Time of the Dreyfus Affair* (Oxford, 1971); Michael R. Marrus and Robert O. Paxton, *Vichy France and the Jews* (Stanford, 1981); Paul W. Massing, *Rehearsal for Destruction: A Study of Political Anti-Semitism in Imperial Germany* (New York, 1949); Meir Michaelis, *Mussolini and the Jews: German-Italian Relations and the Jewish Question in Italy 1922–1945*

than other minorities were frequently sought out as scapegoats or useful targets during periods of both worldwide and national difficulties. The multifaceted nature of anti-Semitism may also help to explain why other traditional "middlemen groups" – such as the Greeks in the Balkans, the Syro-Lebanese in West Africa and Latin America, the Parsis in India, and the Scots in South Africa and many parts of Canada – rarely experienced the magnitude of persecution encountered by Jews.[63] Yet we should not conclude that where Jewish minorities exist, they must always be singled out for persecution during times of crisis, for during the tumultuous years preceding the fascist takeover in Italy, Jews were rarely targeted for Italy's ills.

In order to account for the rise of popular anti-Semitism between 1870 and 1939, I contend that it is in this period that we witness the evolution and popularization of the four manifestations or strains of anti-Semitism. The four strains – religious, racial, economic and political – contain within themselves four distinct anti-Semitic narratives. Each of the anti-Semitic narratives entailed its own set of themes depicting Jewish malfeasance. We shall see that anti-Semitism in the years prior to 1870 was largely characterized by a dislike based primarily on religious differences and perceived Jewish economic practices. After 1870,

---

Oxford, 1978); George L. Mosse, *Germans and Jews: The Right, The Left, and the Search for a "Third Force" in Pre-Nazi Germany* (New York, 1970); Donald L. Niewyk, *The Jews in Weimar Germany* (Baton Rouge, 1980); William Oldson, *A Providential Anti-Semitism: Nationalism and Polity in Nineteenth Century Romania* (Philadelphia, 1991); Bruce F. Pauley, *From Prejudice to Persecution: A History of Austrian Anti-Semitism* (Chapel Hill, 1992); Pulzer, *Jews and the German State*; Sternhell, "The Roots"; Raphael Vago, "The Traditions of Antisemitism in Romania," *Patterns of Prejudice*, vol. 27, 1993, 107–19; Leon Volovici, *Nationalist Ideology and Antisemitism: The Case of Romanian Intellectuals in the 1930s* (Oxford, 1991); Weiss, *Ideology*: Stephen Wilson, *Ideology and Experience: Anti-Semitism in France at the Time of the Dreyfus Affair* (Rutherford, 1982); Susan Zuccotti, *The Italians and the Holocaust: Persecution, Rescue, and Survival* (New York, 1987). For examples of nonempirical analysis of anti-Semitism across several countries, see Almog, *Nationalism*; Bergmann, "Psychological"; Ettinger, "Jew-Hatred"; Paul E. Grosser and Edwin G. Halperin, *Anti-Semitism, Causes and Effects: An Analysis and Chronology of 1900 Years of Anti-Semitic Attitudes and Practices* (New York, 1978); Katz, *Prejudice*; Gavin I. Langmuir, *History, Religion, and Antisemitism* (Berkeley, 1990); Lindemann, *Esau's*; Marrus "Theory"; George L. Mosse, *Toward the Final Solution: A History of European Racism* (Madison, 1985); Meyer Weinberg, *Because They Were Jews* (New York, 1986); Wistrich, *Antisemitism*.

[63] Zenner, "Middleman," 256–57.

religious and economic anti-Semitism continued – albeit with new themes – and were joined by the rising racial and political strains.[64]

Understanding the evolution and popularization of the four strains of anti-Semitism should certainly help to explain the presence of a climate of popular anti-Semitism within Western Christian societies during the late nineteenth and early twentieth centuries. However, the presence of religious, economic, racial, and political anti-Semitic narratives cannot sufficiently explain the dramatic explosion of anti-Semitism after 1870 or the variations in anti-Semitism across space and time. European societies varied in terms of their popular anti-Semitism. In societies and in periods where Jews were perceived as a greater religious, economic, racial, and political threat or challenge to non-Jews, popular anti-Semitism should have attained higher levels. What factors may account for changes in the perception of Jews as a threat to non-Jews? I propose that, within the context of the four strains of anti-Semitism, temporal and spatial variations across the five nations resulted chiefly from the effects of four critical factors. The factors are the deterioration in a nation's economic well-being, the impact of increased Jewish immigration, the growth of popular support for the political left, and the extent to which leadership of the political left was identified with Jews. To state it somewhat differently: the four strains of anti-Semitism provided the fuel for hatred of Jews, while a decline in economic well-being, a rise in Jewish immigration, and the strength of the revolutionary left constituted the critical match for the post-1870 firestorm.

A decline in a nation's economic well-being, particularly in an environment in which Jews are seen as controlling or owning major economic resources, should produce higher levels of anti-Jewish feelings. On the other hand, we should not expect to find high rates of anti-Semitic sentiments in times of economic stability or growth or in situations where Jews are not perceived to be in positions of dominance within a nation's economy.

Increased levels of Jewish immigration (typically from Eastern and Central Europe) should affect popular anti-Semitism in several ways.

---

[64] Although there is considerable overlap among the four forms of anti-Semitism, for analytical purposes, I will present each type as a distinct form. Furthermore, my typology of anti-Semitism as comprised of the religious, racial, economic, and political strains is not meant to be exhaustive. Anti-Semitism embodied other forms. For example, anti-Semitism, at times, took the form of a belief that Jews dominated the arts and, thereby, exerted undo control over the production of intellectual capital.

Since many of the new Jewish immigrants from Eastern Europe possessed few resources and little formal education, they typically competed with many in the host population for low-paying jobs. Competition often bred animosity, resulting in heightened levels of anti-Semitism. The Yiddish-speaking new arrivals from Eastern Europe's Jewish ghettos, with their strange customs and religious practices, frequently struck Western European Gentiles as a very different sort of Jews from the more assimilated Sephardic or Ashkenazic Jews who had lived in the West for centuries. The influx of Eastern European Jews should have fueled the negative racial stereotypes existing within Western European culture and, thereby, contributed to growing anti-Semitism. Particularly in the aftermath of the 1917 Bolshevik Revolution, many European Gentiles associated recent Eastern European Jewish immigrants with Bolshevism. Given that many of these Jewish immigrants appeared to be impoverished, had fled persecution, and came from the former Russian empire, they were perceived to favor parties of the political left. Thus, increased Jewish immigration should have heightened religious, racial, economic, and political antipathies toward Jews, and we should expect that increasing Jewish immigration fueled increasing anti-Semitism.

The dramatic rise of a revolutionary left at the end of the nineteenth century led to the fear of a violent overturn of the existing social, economic, political, and religious order in Europe. In the popular consciousness, Jews were often linked to the revolutionary left. Making matters worse for Jews were the numerous press reports after 1917 insinuating that Jews were overrepresented within the leadership of the Bolshevik and Communist Parties. Anti-Bolshevik tendencies fed anti-Semitic attitudes. Anti-Semites had often accused Jews of seeking retribution against Christians by plotting to seize power. Many anti-Semites cited Jews as the founders of revolutionary socialism and anarchism and saw the hand of Jews in periodic labor unrest. Thus, we should expect to see increased anti-Semitism in societies where the political left exhibited growing strength and where prominent leftist leaders were identified as Jews. However, where support for the political left was weak or declining or where Jews were not seen as playing important roles in the left, we should expect lower levels of anti-Semitism.

The data clearly indicate the existence of temporal and spatial variations in anti-Semitic acts and attitudes before the Holocaust. To understand the rise of modern anti-Semitism in the West, we now turn to an investigation of the four roots of anti-Semitism within our five countries – France, Germany, Great Britain, Italy, and Romania. We will see that the intensity and breadth of the four roots varied both spatially (among societies) and temporally (year to year). I shall argue that declining economic conditions, rising Eastern and Central European Jewish immigration, and the growing popularity of the revolutionary left linked to the perception of a Jewish overrepresentation on the left would ignite the four strains, leading to explosive waves of popular anti-Semitism between 1870 and the Holocaust. These same factors would additionally account for much of the societal divergence in Jewish antipathy after 1870.

# CHAPTER TWO

# THE RELIGIOUS ROOT

*continuity*

Of the four roots of anti-Semitism, religious anti-Semitism has the longest history in Western Christian societies. Religious anti-Semitism encompasses hostility that stems from the Jewish people's refusal to abandon their religious beliefs and practices and, specifically within Christian societies, from the accusation of Jewish collective responsibility for the death of Jesus Christ. By the eighteenth century, the religious root would expand to include the French Enlightenment critique that Judaism was responsible for the antiprogressive and exclusionist characters of its followers. *reason*

Official Christian antipathy toward Judaism began to gather steam within one hundred years of the death of Christ. Christian bitterness may have stemmed largely from the new religion's competition with Judaism for a following. The competition between the two religions was unlike that between quite *dissimilar* religions – such as Buddhism and Christianity, or Hinduism and Christianity – for Jesus Christ had been a Jew, and Christianity saw itself replacing Judaism as the inheritor of God's covenant with Abraham. Because only the Jewish people can claim that the Christian Savior was one of its own, the relationship between Judaism and Christianity is special. The strong desire for Christian self-affirmation and Christian disconfirmation of Judaism, especially during the church's formative years, may help to explain its unique anti-Judaism. As both Rubenstein and Langmuir cogently remark, the greatest threat to the Christian belief system was the denial of Jesus by the Jews.[1] Given the historical familiarity of the Jews with

---

[1] Richard L. Rubenstein, *After Auschwitz: History, Theology, and Contemporary Judaism*, 2nd ed. (Baltimore and London, 1992), 35–36, 94; Gavin I. Langmuir, *History, Religion, and Antisemitism* (Berkeley, 1990), 284.

*deeply rooted natted] felt threatened*

Jesus of Nazareth, no other religion's rejection of Christian beliefs carried such weight in the eyes of the Christian Church. That Jesus' Jewish contemporaries refused to believe in him opened the door to Christian self-doubt about their own commitment to Jesus and the church. The competition, as perceived first by Christ's apostle Paul of Tarsus, envisioned the new Christian faith as the true successor faith to Judaism rather than as an entirely different religion.

In constructing the case for Christianity as the true successor faith to Judaism, early Christian fathers increasingly portrayed Judaism in a negative light.[2] The writings of Augustine of Hippo at the end of the fourth century captured the evolution of early Christian fathers' thinking that portrayed the Jews of the Old Testament as good Hebrews and bad Jews. By this interpretation, the followers of Christ descended from the good Hebrews. The Jews, demonstrating spiritual shortsightedness in rejecting Christ as the Messiah promised to Israel and as Lord, have become disqualified from receiving God's favor. In their stead, the Christians, constituting New Israel, assume the mantel of the legitimate successors of the now-disgraced Jews. Only when the Jews recognize the authenticity of Christ will they be able to enter the community of saints. In the meantime, according to Augustine of Hippo, Jews would exist to serve Christian purposes.[3]

Throughout the Middle Ages, the Christian Church would portray the Jewish faith in a light quite distinct from its characterizations of other faiths, for the Christian Church's holy books included the Jewish Old Testament, and Jesus, the Christian Savior, had been born Jewish. Judaism alone as a non-Christian and dissenting faith was to remain

---

[2] For examples of the errant ways of the Jews according to Paul, see Paul's writings in Galatians 5:2–7, Romans 1:16–18, Romans 10:1–5, and Romans 11:13–14. In one often-cited passage, Paul has Jesus chastising the Jews as the offspring of Satan (James Carroll, *Constantine's Sword: The Church and the Jews*, Boston and New York, 2001, 92–93). Interestingly, Carroll (*Constantine's Sword*, 143) portrays John more as an unfortunate victim than as a principal culprit in the early Jewish-Christian struggle.

[3] Rubenstein, *After Auschwitz*, 11–12, 31; Langmuir, *History*, 286–87, 293–94; Charles Y. Glock and Rodney Stark, *Christian Beliefs and Anti-Semitism* (New York and London, 1966), 45; Rosemary R. Ruether, "The Theological Roots of Anti-Semitism." In Helen Fein, ed., *The Persisting Question: Sociological Perspectives and Social Contexts of Modern Antisemitism*, vol. 1 (Berlin and New York, 1987), 30.

legal and tolerated (within strict limits) as a pariah faith in Christian-dominated medieval Europe.[4]

Further reinforcing the split between the two religions during the first two hundred years after Christ's death were the military defeats suffered by the Jews at the hands of the Romans in two wars fought between 66 and 70 C.E. and between 131 and 135 C.E. For Christians, such as Justin Martyr (100–165 C.E.), these Jewish defeats represented God's displeasure with the Jews for their refusal to accept Christ as the Messiah and their responsibility for the crucifixion of Jesus.[5]

Since the birth of the Christian faith, numerous accusations of malfeasance have been leveled against the Jews.[6] For centuries, Jews were held responsible for the crucifixion of Christ; chastised for not accepting Christ as the Messiah; accused of a series of acts and practices, including the ritual killing of Christian children in order to use their blood to make matzoth during the Jewish holiday of Passover; causing the Black Plague of the Middle Ages by poisoning the wells of Europe; desecrating the Host (stealing and destroying communion wafers after the Eucharist ceremony); serving as agents of the Antichrist; and, at various times, being usurers, sorcerers, and vampires.

Early Christian Church fathers were quite explicit in condemning the Jews, collectively, for the murder of Christ and were instrumental in the diabolization of Jews.[7] The Christian conception that holds Jews responsible for the death of Christ as the Son of God has embittered relations between the two religious faiths for nearly 2,000 years. The

---

[4] Ruether, "Theological," 34–35; David I. Kertzer, *The Kidnapping of Edgardo Mortara* (New York, 1998), 19. In the aftermath of the Roman emperor Constantine's acceptance of Christianity as the dominant religion of the empire during the first quarter of the fourth century, we find the case for the pariah status of Judaism emerging in the writings of Augustine. Augustine proposed that the Jews should be allowed to survive, but not thrive (Carroll, *Constantine's Sword*, 201–02, 217–18).

[5] Rubenstein, *After Auschwitz*, 31–32; Kertzer, *Kidnapping*, 19; Langmuir, *History*, 286.

[6] Interestingly, the dramatic increase in Christian popular hostility toward Jews, allegations of Jewish crimes, and legal restrictions on Jewish activities occurred largely after the beginning of the second millenium. The twelfth and thirteenth centuries mark a pronounced rise in Christian anti-Semitism in northern Europe.

[7] G. L. Jones, *Hard Sayings: Difficult New Testament Texts for Jewish-Christian Dialogue* (London, 1993); Lindemann, *Esau's*, 34–36; Carroll, *Constantine's Sword*, 90.

principal source of this "deicide" accusation is from Matthew 27:17–25. According to Matthew, the chief priests and elders of Judea persuaded Pontius Pilate, the Roman procurator of Judea, to arrest Jesus for claiming he was king of the Jews, a crime against both Roman and Jewish law. Pilate, following a long-standing Jewish custom that allowed for pardoning a condemned prisoner at feast time, offered the crowd a choice to save Jesus or Barabbas. Barabbas had been found guilty of murder and sedition. By Matthew's account, with the inspiration of the chief priests and elders, the crowd roared for the release of Barrabas and the crucifixion of Christ. Pilate, claiming to be innocent of the killing of Christ, is said to have reluctantly acceded to the wish of the Jewish assemblage. The Jewish multitude, on the contrary, is said to have accepted responsibility for Christ's death: "His blood be on us, and on our children." Thus begins the Christian conception of the collective responsibility of Jews for the death of Jesus – a conception that would gain momentum in the sermons and writings of the late fourth century Christian father John Chrysostom, bishop of Antioch. John held the Jews responsible for Christ's murder and added that they continued to rejoice in the death of the Christian Savior. Not until the Second Vatican Council in the mid-1960s did the Roman Catholic Church finally absolve the Jewish people of the deicide charge by declaring that the Jews as a people were not responsible for the death of Jesus Christ.[8]

Christian anti-Semitism, rooted in the beliefs that Jews were collectively responsible for the death of Jesus and that Jews failed to accept Christ as the Messiah, held center stage within the Christian anti-Jewish mental world until the twelfth century. Beginning in the twelfth century, religious anti-Semitism would undergo a major transformation in terms of its intensity and its incorporation of new anti-Jewish themes. One catalyst for the dramatic rise in anti-Semitism – an anti-Semitism that brought with it renewed popular hostility, allegations of new Jewish crimes, and a host of new legal restrictions on Jewish practices – put forward by Langmuir, was the realization by ecclesiastical authorities (including the Pope) during the middle of the thirteenth century that

---

[8] Glock and Stock, Christian, 50–51; Harold E. Quinley and Charles Y. Glock, "Christian Sources of Anti-Semitism." In Helen Fein, ed., The Persisting Question: Sociological Perspectives and Social Contexts of Modern Antisemitism, vol. 1 (Berlin and New York, 1987), 197; Rubenstein, After Auschwitz; Lindemann, Esau's, 34–36; Carroll, Constantine's Sword, 213. From the New Testament, see Matthew, Chapter 27, and John, Chapter 19.

Jews were relying on the Talmud rather than the Bible for their fundamental divine revelation.[9] In this new phase of religious anti-Semitism,
myths about Jews would expand to include accusations that they were
purveyors of the Black Plague, ritual murders, desecrators of the Host
wafer, agents of the Antichrist and the Devil, usurers, sorcerers, and
vampires.[10] One of the most bizarre accusations against the Jews con-
cerned their purported role in the Black Plague, which is believed to
have wiped out more than a third of Europe's population. More specifically, during the fourteenth century, Jews (along with lepers) were held
responsible for unleashing the Black Plague by poisoning the wells of
Europe in order to stamp out Christianity. According to the contemporary myth, Jews allegedly carried out their misdeed by administer-
ing a concoction of spiders, frogs, lizards, excrement, menstrual blood,
Christian hearts, and consecrated Hosts through secret tunnels that
flowed into the wells of Christian Europe. The resulting anti-Jewish violence led to the destruction of hundreds of Jewish communities throughout Europe.[11]

It would be difficult to date the origins of the ritual murder or "blood
libel" charge against the Jews, although Langmuir credits Thomas of
Monmouth, an English monk, as the originator.[12] Thomas of Monmouth
allegedly conspired with a Jewish convert to Christianity and the family
of a murdered youth in the vicinity of Norwich in 1144 during Easter-
tide. According to Thomas of Monmouth and his co-conspirators, the
Jews had crucified the boy as part of an annual Jewish ritual to convey
their hatred for Jesus, whom they could no longer directly assault. By
the late Middle Ages, the "blood libel" myth had gained widespread
ascendancy.[13] The ritual murder charge came to represent the Christian

---

[9] Langmuir, *History*, 296–97.

[10] Langmuir, *History*, 304–05; Glock and Stark, *Christian*, 148–49; Robert S.
Wistrich, *Antisemitism: The Longest Hatred* (New York, 1991), xix; David I.
Kertzer, *The Popes against the Jews: The Vatican's Role in the Rise of Modern Anti-
Semitism* (New York, 2001), p. 130.

[11] Ruether, "Theological," 40–41; Golding, *Jewish Problem*, 67; Pauley, *Prejudice*,
13; Lindemann, *Accused*, 34. According to Carroll (*Constantine's Sword*, 277),
from the time of the First Crusade in the last decade of the eleventh century to
the initial outbreak of the Black Plague in 1348, Jews had been alleged to have
poisoned wells in several cities of central Europe. Thus, Jewish responsibility for
the Black Plague is seen as a logical consequence of the earlier allegations.

[12] Langmuir, *History*, 298.

[13] Levine (Hillel Levine, *Economic Origins of Antisemitism: Poland and Its Jews in
the Early Modern Period*, New Haven and London, 1991, 138) observes that the

view that Jews were collectively and hereditarily responsible for the crucifixion of Christ. Additionally, religious sacrifice of a human victim to guarantee the community's prosperity and well-being was not totally unknown, and the "blood libel" allegation against the Jews may have represented the belief that Jews symbolically repeated the crime of murdering Christ by killing Christian children at Passover time, which coincided with Easter. Some religious anti-Semites during the medieval period took out of context the talmudic enjoinder that "the best among the Gentiles should be slain" in order to add credence to the "blood libel" charge. Jews supposedly killed their Christian victims in order to use their blood for their rituals, such as mixing the Christian blood into Passover matzoth.[14]

Sometime during the thirteenth century, the crime of "desecrating the Host" became affixed to the list of Jewish crimes against Christians. In many respects, this allegation closely paralleled the "blood libel" charge. Jews were accused of stealing communion wafers after the Eucharist ceremony, and it was further noted that, in their efforts to express their undying hatred for Christians, Jews spat on and urinated upon the communion wafers. Through this act, Jews supposedly were trying to torture and kill Christ, since the communion wafers symbolically stood for the mystically transformed body of Christ.[15]

Other harmful myths taking shape during the Middle Ages concerning Jews included the association of the Jews with the Devil and the Antichrist. Jewish persistence in refusing to accept Christ was attributed to the supernatural hold of their satanic master. Further, explicit in the fourth Gospel (John 8:42–45) is the identification of the Jew with the Devil. In another popular mythology, before the return of Christ, a final battle between the Antichrist and the forces of Christ would unfold. Because Christ was the son of God and born of a Jewish virgin, the

---

popularization of the "blood libel" accusation in medieval England probably benefited greatly from its sanctioning by Geoffrey Chaucer in his well-known *Canterbury Tales*. Following quickly on the Norwich ritual murder case, similar charges against Jews were made in Wuerzburg, Gloucester, Blois, and Saragossa (Carroll, *Constantine's Sword*, 272–73). In 1235, the "blood libel" charge was called on by Conrad of Marburg to accuse the Jews of Fulda in the murder of five boys. Conrad of Marburg alleged that the Jews killed the boys in order to obtain their blood for their rituals. The accused Jews were murdered (Langmuir, *History*, 299–300).

[14] Rubenstein, *After Auschwitz*, 40; Pauley, *Prejudice*, 3; Weinberg, *Because*, 86; Lindemann, *Accused*, 34; Lindemann, *Esau's*, 34–36.

[15] Lindemann, *Accused*, 34; Lindemann, *Esau's*, 34–36; Langmuir, *History*, 300.

Antichrist would be begot from the union of the Devil and a Jewish whore.[16] At the age of thirty, this Antichrist would announce himself to the Jews as the Messiah and raise up an army to do battle against the forces of righteousness. Later, anti-Semites would conveniently employ a variant of the myth of the Antichrist in alleging a Jewish world conspiracy aimed at destroying Christian Europe.[17]

In addition to the numerous allegations leveled against Jews in Christian medieval Europe, European Jews were subjected to a series of restrictions. By the fourth century, Christianity had become the state religion of the Roman Empire. In the following centuries, the Christian Church in Europe would progressively curtail the activities of the Jewish people. By the sixth century, Jews were forbidden from employing Christian servants and not allowed to show themselves in the streets during Passion Week. In the seventh century, the Synod of Clermont disfranchised Jews from holding public office. Between the seventh and thirteenth centuries, in the writings of many Church Fathers, in sermons of the clergy, and in the arts (e.g., passion plays and ballads), Jews were portrayed quite negatively. By the thirteenth century, Jews were no longer permitted to discuss religion with Christians, and the Jewish Talmud and other religious books were burned publicly in France. From the thirteenth to the sixteenth centuries, Jews were officially expelled from several European states. The list of expulsions includes England in 1291, France in 1394, and Spain in 1492. In 1555, a papal decree (*Cumnimis absurdum*) presented by Pope Paul IV called for the confinement of the Jews to a particular street or quarter within a town or city. Although Jewish ghettoes had a prior existence in Europe, they had never before received a Pope's public stamp of approval. Thereafter, Jewish ghettos sprang up throughout Europe. Segregation of the Jews was seen as a means to curb social contact with Christians and to punish Jews for rejecting Christ and for their stubborn resistance to baptism. Efforts to segregate Jews from Christians preceded the institutionalization of ghettos. At the Fourth Lateran Council in 1215, Church

---

[16] See Carroll, *Constantine's Sword*, 92–93, for the identification of Jews with Satan in the early Christian Gospels. Centuries later, Martin Luther asserted that the Jews must be "the devil's children" since they were no longer God's people (Jones, *Hard Sayings*, 9). Luther would also write in his pamphlet *Against the Jews and Their Lies* that aside from the Devil, Christ had no greater enemy than the true Jew who seeks to be a Jew (Weinberg, *Because*, 86).

[17] Rubenstein, *After Auschwitz*, 38–39.

authorities passed regulations barring Jews from serving in government and the military and enacted laws enforcing the wearing of a conical hat and the "Jew badge" by Jews. The "Jew badge" was typically a yellow circle, symbolizing Judas Iscariot's betrayal of Christ for gold. (Interestingly, the Gospels actually state that Judas betrayed Jesus for thirty pieces of silver.) The particular Jewish dress was universally enforced after the Council of Basel in 1434.[18]

By the end of the Middle Ages, in the minds of many Christians the imagery of the Jew incorporated three rather unsavory stereotypes. First, Jews were identified with Judas Iscariot, who allegedly betrayed Christ for thirty pieces of silver. In the Gospels, Judas supposedly conspired with the chief (Jewish) priests of the temple to have Jesus arrested for blasphemy. The Judas tale (with Judas portrayed with a vulgarly exaggerated Semitic appearance and as having an inordinate love of money) had become a centerpiece of the Passion drama performed during Christian Holy Week that retold the story of Christ's crucifixion.[19] This image of Jews as untrustworthy and as traitors would raise its ugly head several times in more recent centuries, as evidenced by the trial of Captain Alfred Dreyfus in France and by the Nazi "stab in the back" theory after World War I.[20] A second image of the Jew was personified by Shakespeare's avaricious Venetian Jew, Shylock, in *The Merchant of Venice*. The despised moneylender Shylock, lacking compassion, ruthlessly indentured Christians economically. The association of Jews with the figure of Shylock would accompany the Jews into the modern era. Ahasuerus, the wicked or wandering Jew, represented a third image of the Jew. Ahasuerus, is supposedly, the Jew who, without compassion, sped Jesus along to his crucifixion. For his deed, Ahasuerus is condemned to rove aimlessly and eternally, country to country. He can neither live nor

---

[18] Wistrich, *Antisemitism*, 37; Pauley, *Prejudice*, 13–16; Ruether, "Theological," 39; Rubenstein, *After Auschwitz*, 51; Paul Lendvai, *L'antisémitisme sans juifs* (Paris, 1971), 43; Mosse, *Final Solution*, xii; Kertzer, *The Popes*, 28; Carroll, *Constantine's Sword*, 376–77.

[19] It appears that in early Christian writings, particularly in the epistles crafted by the Apostle Paul during the first century after the death of Christ, there is no mention of the role of Judas in Jesus' crucifixion. During the next few centuries, Judas as the betrayer and a symbol of Jewish treachery emerged in the writings of Christian theologians, such as the highly influential St. Augustine (Larry B. Stammer, *Minneapolis Star Tribune*, April 29, 2000, reprinted from the *Los Angeles Times*).

[20] Rubenstein, *After Auschwitz*, 22, 50- 51; Friedlaender, *Nazi Germany*, 197.

die.[21] In more modern times, Ahasuerus came to represent the rootless and disinherited international Jew, who is devoid of a homeland.[22]

With the emergence of the French Enlightenment (circa 1700s), religious anti-Semitism based on a mythology of Jews as, among other things, the "deicide people" and desecrators of the Host increasingly receded into the background. That is not to say that the Christian Church abandoned its position that Judaism had erred and that the Jewish people must pay for their rejection of Christ, or to deny that many Europeans of the Christian faith continued to harbor antipathy toward Jewish religious beliefs and practices. Until very recently, regular Christian events and practices – such as the well-known *Oberammergau* Passion Play in Germany that portrayed Jewish priests as devil-like evildoers wearing horned hats, the Good Friday liturgy of the Roman Catholic Church that contained prayers "for the perfidious Jews," and unfavorable references to Jews in performances of the *Saint John Passion* and Bach's *Easter Oratorio* – have kept alive Christian hostility toward Jews. Accusations of ritual murder and Jewish conspiratorial designs to destroy Christianity persisted throughout the nineteenth and into the twentieth century. In fact, between 1887 and 1914, Europe witnessed an upsurge in ritual murder charges, with twenty-two separate ritual murder accusations reported in the Catholic Church press between 1887 and 1891 and at least twelve trials of Jews for ritual murder between 1890 and 1914. In 1930, a ritual murder charge against a Jew was initiated in the Rutho-Carpathian mountains of Czechoslovakia by a government prosecutor, and as late as 1946–47, participants in bloody anti-Jewish riots at Topolcany in Slovakia, Kunmadaras in Hungary, and Kielce in Poland cited the ritual murder allegation as a cause for their participation.[23] The Nazis would resurrect the myth of Ahasuerus, the

---

[21] As with several other anti-Jewish themes, the origins of the myth of Ahasuerus are hard to pinpoint. Pope Innocent III in 1208 linked Jewish eternal wandering to the Jewish crimes of deicide and blasphemy (Langmuir, *History*, 294–95).

[22] Rubenstein, *After Auschwitz*, 22, 50-51; Friedlaender, *Nazi Germany*, 197; Mosse, *Final Solution*, 114–15; Birnbaum, *Anti-Semitism*, 99.

[23] Kertzer, *The Popes*, 14, 156; Mosse, *Final Solution*, 114; Lendvai, *L'antisémitisme*, 42. According to Kertzer (*The Popes*, 234–36), the *Civiltà cattolica* – the Catholic Church's Jesuit journal – championed the campaign of ritual murder charges against the Jews at the end of the nineteenth and the beginning of the twentieth century. Kertzer points to two well-known articles by Father Paolo Silva, published at the time of the infamous Beilis ritual murder case in Kiev. In Father Silva's articles, sent in advance to the papal secretary of state, it was alleged that for Jews, drinking blood is like drinking milk for others.

wandering Jew, but they were not alone. In the aftermath of World War I, anti-Semites throughout Europe evoked the wandering Jew as the carrier of revolutionary Bolshevism that aimed to overthrow Western Christian civilization.

Here, I trace the evolution of modern religious anti-Semitism in France, Germany, Great Britain, Romania, and Italy. What should be obvious to my reader is that I have made the explicit choice in this study to concentrate exclusively on anti-Semitic rather than philosemitic or pro-Semitic contributions. I would be negligent if I failed to point out that throughout the 2,000-year history of Jewish-Christian relations, Christians of all backgrounds have spoken out in defense of and acted on behalf of Jews. Examples abound and would include the call for harmonious relations between Christians and Jews of Abelard and Nicolaus of Cusa, two great Catholic theologians of the Middle Ages; Pope Clement VI's denunciation of anti-Jewish violence during the Black Plague; and the decidedly positive portrayal of Jews in the writings of George Eliot.[24]

### FRANCE

Traditional religious anti-Semitism in France continued to flourish in many quarters during and after the *ancien régime*. The list of prominent French thinkers employing virulent anti-Semitism to blame the misfortunes of Christian France on Jews included theologians as well as novelists such as Pascal, Bossuet, de Bonald, Gougenot des Mousseaux, Léon Bloy, and Bernanos. Pascal and Bossuet justified Jewish dispersion and misery in terms of punishment for the Jewish role in the crucifixion of Christ and the Jews' continued rejection of Christ; both Pascal and Bossuet saw the fate of the Jews as theologically ordained. For French anti-Semites such as Edouard Drumont, the Jews were responsible for a host of French major misfortunes, including the French Revolution,[25]

---

[24] Carroll, *Constantine's Sword*, 339, 350. Also, I am indebted to Michael Hechter and Ilya Prizel, who reminded me of a pro-Semitic literary current as evidenced in Eliot's *Daniel Deronda*.

[25] Several French writers linking the evils of the French Revolution to the Jews have focused on the role of Marat, the famous Jacobin. Taine, Drumont, Daudet, Céline, and Bernardini have alleged that Marat was Jewish and that his Jewishness contributed to his role in the "Terror." In his 1944 book, *Le Juif Marat*, Bernardini invokes the image of Ahasuerus in portraying Marat as the grand inquisitioner of the "Terror" (Pierre Birnbaum, *La France aux Français: Histoire des haines nationalistes*, Paris, 1993, 54–57).

the defeat in the Franco-Prussian War of 1870–71, the Paris Commune, the establishment of the Jewish (Third) Republic, and the secularization of French schools. Borrowing from Drumont, his anti-Semitic heirs would refer to France's suffering in World War I and then again in the collapse of 1940 as the reproduction of the Jewish ritual murder on a national scale.[26]

Drumont's *La France juive: Essai d'histoire contemporaine* (1886) contributed more than any other French writing to the mobilization of French anti-Semitism at the time of the Dreyfus Affair. Drumont's central theme was that the Jews, members of a primitive and despised religion and an inferior race, had made themselves the masters of France. For Drumont, the Jewish drive to world domination grew out of Jewish religious teachings. *La France juive* employed references to every form of anti-Semitism, including the medieval myths of Jewish collective responsibility for the murder of Christ, Jewish betrayal of Christ, the identification of Jews with the Devil, and Jewish involvement in the ritual murder of Christians. Drumont was not shy regarding a remedy to France's Jewish Problem. Beyond the restoration of legalized ghettos, expropriation of excessive Jewish wealth, and expulsion,[27] Drumont called for the reinstitution of the yellow badge worn during the Middle Ages.[28]

The Catholic Church in France played an active role in the perpetuation of traditional religious anti-Semitism during the nineteenth century. Churchmen aimed their venom specifically at the Jewish Talmud, which they saw as a work of anti-catechism and the inspiration for alleged Jewish vices. Father Louis Chiarini's *Théorie du Judaisme* of 1830 offers a prime example of the attributed pernicious nature of the Talmud. The mid-nineteenth-century French Catholic church sanctioned works such as Joseph Mery's *La Juive au Vatican* and Father

---

[26] Arthur Hertzberg, *The French Enlightenment and the Jews* (New York, 1968), 35–36; Birnbaum, *Anti-Semitism*, 112, 178; Michel Winock, *Nationalism, Anti-Semitism, and Fascism in France*, trans. Jane Marie Todd (Stanford, 1998), 88, 90.

[27] Drumont's advocacy of Jewish expulsion from France found support in allied quarters. The Assumptionist newspaper *La Croix*, in the early 1890s, advocated both emigration of Jews and expulsion of Jews, as were occurring in Russia. In 1891, Laur, a deputy in the French National Assembly, proposed the expulsion of Jews from France. The proposal, along with a proposal to expel the Jewish Rothschilds from France, received votes from thirty deputies in the National Assembly (Wilson, *Ideology*, 676–77).

[28] Wilson, *Ideology*, 511, 541, 674–76; Katz, *Prejudice*, 295.

Charles Guenot's *La Vengeance d'un juif*. The works focused on the nefarious nature of Judaism, particularly Jewish cruelties and Jewish responsibility for the murder of Christ.[29] The principal vehicle for the transmission of the Catholic Church's anti-Semitism during the late nineteenth century was *La Croix*, the daily newspaper of the Assumptionist fathers. *La Croix* held considerable influence among the Catholic faithful in France. Its daily circulation reached 180,000 copies in 1893, making it the second most popular anti-Semitic daily in France, after Drumont's *La Libre parole*. In fact, its circulation was double that of the popular *Figaro* and *Le Rappel*. In 1894 alone, 104 provincial supplements of the newspaper were published, and more than two million copies of various *La Croix* publications were distributed. Also in 1894, with the Dreyfus Affair beginning to cast its sordid shadow on France, *La Croix* declared that Dreyfus's exhortation of "*Vive la France*" at his public degradation at the Paris *Ecole Militaire* harkened back to Judas Iscariot's kiss of Jesus. The newspaper was strongly supportive of Edouard Drumont and became the first newspaper to review Drumont's rabidly anti-Semitic *La France juive* in 1886. In April 1898, at the height of the Dreyfus Affair, *La Croix* circulated an anti-Semitic pamphlet entitled *Le Complot Juif* (The Jewish Conspiracy) containing the Jewish plan of world domination. In this pamphlet, the Jews are accused of planning a war against the Catholic Church in order to destroy Christianity. Jews are further portrayed as controllers of the press, the economy, and government, as well as corrupters of values and disseminators of revolution and socialism. What motivated Jews to pursue such pernicious acts? According to the pamphlet, the Jews were acting upon the promise to Abraham to reign over the earth. *La Croix* referred to the Jews as the "deicide people" in a published article in November 1890.[30] Though *La Croix* toned down its religious attacks on Jews after the Dreyfus Affair, at certain intervals the paper could be counted on to find Jewish misdeeds at the heart of detected Christian misfortunes, as in the early months of the Spanish Civil War, when *La Croix* claimed that Jews sent by Moscow were instructing the Spanish "Reds" on techniques to murder priests, monks, and nuns.[31]

---

[29] Pierre Pierrard, *Juifs et catholiques français: D'Edouard Drumont à Jacob Kaplan 1886–1994* (Paris, 1997), 21.

[30] Wilson, *Ideology*, 206–07, 542, 603–04; Byrnes, *Antisemitism*, 194–97; Rubenstein, *After Auschwitz*, 51.

[31] Eugen Weber, *The Hollow Years: France in the 1930s* (New York and London, 1994), 204.

Complementing the role played by such organized church publications as *La Croix* in keeping alive the medieval legends of Jewish infamy were the occasional Sunday sermons. Particularly instrumental in the French countryside, where few Jews resided, these sermons occasionally resurrected the images of Ahasuerus (*le Juif errant*), the ritual murderers, and the avaricious Jew and, especially around Easter, reminded the faithful of the unregenerate nature of the Jews, while invoking the age-old brandishment of *Oremus Pro perfidis Judaeis* (Let us pray for the perfidious Jews).[32]

Since the sermons and writings of the early Christian fathers, Jews had been depicted as destroyers of Christianity. French anti-Semites saw the hand of Jews in what they perceived as the dismantling of Christian social and family values during the Third Republic (1871–1940). In the minds of many French anti-Semites, Christian France was constantly under siege by Jews and Freemasons. That the law governing divorce in France had been proposed in 1884 by Alfred Naquet, a Jew, ignited an anti-Semitic eruption. Drumont remarked that divorce is "une ideé absolument juive." Further linking Jews to the breakup of the family and an attack on Christian social values in the eyes of many French anti-Semites was the publication in 1907 of a book entitled *Du Mariage* by the future French prime minister Léon Blum, in which Blum, a Jew, appears to advocate premarital sex.[33] Louis Massoutié, a rabid anti-Semite, further claimed the Blum advocated in his book that younger females should seek older (and more experienced) male lovers for premarital sexual experience in order to ensure a better marriage.[34] In the mid-1930s, Blum's Popular Front would come under attack by Christian anti-Semites for its overtures toward modifying the laws regulating church influence within the schools in Alsace and Lorraine and for its alleged plans to replace the *Code Civil* with the Talmud.[35]

The French Catholic Church justly perceived its authority over educational matters as declining in the second half of the nineteenth century. The principal assault on the Catholic Church's control of primary

[32] Michael Burns, "Boulangism and the Dreyfus Affair 1886–1900." In Strauss, ed., *Hostages of Modernization*, vol. 3/1, 527; Weber, *Hollow*, 204.

[33] Birnbaum, *La France*, 76–78; Lindemann, *Esau's*, 214; Ralph Schor, *L'Antisémitisme en France Pendant les années trente* (Paris, 1992), 175–76; Winock, *Nationalism*, 90–91; Wilson, *Ideology*, 673.

[34] Louis Massoutié, *Judaisme et Marxisme* (Paris, 1939), 129–34.

[35] Birnbaum, *La France*, 76–78; Schor, *L'Antisémitisme*, 177–79.

education occurred between 1879 and 1886 with the introduction of the Ferry Laws. This legislation sought to dislodge church control over public education and to introduce a secular-republican education. In the eyes of the church, behind the despised legislation calling for the separation of church and state was a Jew, Paul Grunebaum-Ballin, a member of the French Conseil d'Etat and spokesperson for the French church-state separation law. Also, Camille Sée, a Jew and a former member of the French Conseil d'Etat, had played an instrumental role in the establishment of high schools for French females that would exclude religious education and was thereby blamed for altering the French family and perverting young French women. During the 1890s, calls for the exclusion of Jews from teaching in French schools came from *La Croix* and the anti-Semitic Congress of Lyon.

Exposition of medieval tales of Jewish crimes did not rest solely with the presses of the conservative right and the Catholic Church. At times, the political left jumped into the fray and opportunistically exploited these Jewish myths. One such notable case comes from Georges Sorel, the well-known revolutionary-syndicalist, who between 1911 and 1913 published *L'indépendence*. Within the issues of *L'indépendence*, we find Sorel recounting the crimes of the Jews, including that of ritual murder.[36]

French literature played its role in the perpetuation of the medieval myths of the avaricious Jew, the Jews as the people of Satan, and the Christ killers. Among some of the more popular French writers of the nineteenth and early twentieth centuries invoking these myths in their works were des Mousseaux, Proudhon, Toussenel, Ohnet, Bourget, Vogue, Goncourt, La Tour du Pin, Adam, Champsour, and Rosny (the elder). For instance, Gougenot des Mousseaux's influential book *Le Juif, le judaisme et la judaisation des peuples chrétiens* highlighted the accusation that Jews are deicide people and consumers of Christian blood, and alleged that the Kabbala promotes the worship of Satan and that Kabbalist Jews aim to institute the reign of the anti-Christ in union with the Freemasons. Des Mousseaux claimed, moreover, that the Jewish Talmud wills its followers to cheat and kill Christians. After the publication of his book, des Mousseaux received from Pius IX the Cross of Commander of the Papal Order.[37]

---

[36] Sternhell, "Roots," 127.
[37] Wilson, *Ideology*, 256–57, 543–45; Winock, *Nationalism*, 89–90; Schor, *L'Antisémitisme*, 10; Kertzer, *The Popes*, 128.

## GERMANY

The German-speaking populations of Central Europe were hardly immune to the mythology of Christian anti-Semitism during and after the Protestant Reformation. Popular images of the Jews as deniers of Christ, pariahs and a demonic people, perpetrators of ritual murder, and agents of the Antichrist were firmly rooted among Germans as among other European Christians. The myth of Ahasuerus, the wandering Jew, had gained wide currency in sixteenth-century Germany. During the Protestant Reformation, Martin Luther had turned against the Jews and preached a virulent anti-Semitism that highlighted Jewry's irredeemable corruption.[38] In 1710, the respected German scholar Johann Andreas Eisenmenger published a major scholarly study, *Entdecktes Judenthum* (Judaism unmasked), in which he gave credence to the ages-long anti-Jewish myths of the desecration of the Host and the ritual murder of Christians. Eisenmenger supported his charges by drawing upon actual passages from Jewish texts, including the Talmud and Jewish rabbinical literature.[39]

Eisenmenger's *Entdecktes Judenthum* served as a major source of religious anti-Semitism among Catholic writings in Germany during the nineteenth century. Both Rittter de Cholwa Pwlikowski's book *Hundert Bogen aus mehr als fünfhundert alten und neuen Büchern über die Juden neben den Christen* and August Rohling's pamphlet *Der Talmudjude* drew heavily upon Eisenmenger, as did the assaults by two mid-nineteenth-century notable German theologians, Sebastian Brunner and Bishop Konrad Martin. Both Brunner and Martin cautioned their faithful about the perils of the Talmudic Jews.[40] German Catholic Church antipathy toward Judaism had an additional source in the late nineteenth century. In particular, some in the German Catholic Church saw the hand of the Jews in Bismarck's anti-Catholic church policies of the *Kulturkampf*. Bismarck had empowered Heinrich von Friedberg (Jewish origin) to execute the decrees of the *Kulturkampf* and had appointed von Friedberg's brother, Emil, to the position of minister of justice in 1879. Both legislators in the Catholic Center Party and writers for Catholic Church newspapers, they cited the presence of prominent Jews in the National Liberal Party (one of the main political voices against the German Catholic Church) and

[38] Weiss, *Ideology*, 22–25; Birnbaum, *Anti-Semitism*, 12.
[39] Katz, *Prejudice*, 19–20; Weiss, *Ideology*, 31–32.
[40] Helmut Berding, *Moderner Antisemitismus in Deutschland* (Frankfurt, 1988), 91; Langmuir, *History*, 326.

used anti-Semitism to mobilize support against Bismarck's anti-Catholic campaign. At times, popular Catholic anti-Semitism in Germany boiled over. Two notable cases surrounded popular religious accusations of Jewish ritual murder. Unsolved local murders led to the Jewish ritual murder allegations in the predominantly Catholic Rhineland town of Xanten in 1891 and in the largely Catholic West Prussian town of Konitz in 1900.[41]

German Protestant theologizing did not refrain from occasional assaults on Judaism. Luther had undoubtedly supplied the German Protestant Church with ample explosives. Conway states that attacks on Jewish materialism and intellectualism became commonplace in Protestant sermons during the Weimar era and that the Protestant press frequently caricatured the Jews as corrupt and degenerate and accused them of seeking to destroy traditional Christian morality within Germany.[42] Conway implies, moreover, that both German Protestant and German Catholic anti-Semitism during the Weimar era derived not solely from religious but also from racist sources.[43] The German Protestant Church demonstrated a stronger preference than the German Catholic Church for Hitler's Nazi Party.[44] Among the most ardent clerical supporters of the Nazi Party was Joachim Hossenfelder, founder of the fervently anti-Semitic German Christian Church in 1932. The German Christian Church referred to its followers as "the storm troopers of Jesus Christ."[45] The darkest chapter in the contemporary history of both German Churches vis-à-vis the issue of anti-Semitism is the relative silence on the part of Protestant and Catholic leadership towards the Nazi treatment of German Jews. The courageous resistance to Nazism exhibited by Protestant leaders such as Martin Niemoeller and Dietrich Bonhoeffer and the opposition to Nazism shown by the Catholic archbishop of

---

[41] Lindemann, *Esau's*, 122; David Blackbourn, "Roman Catholics, the Centre Party and Anti-Semitism in Imperial Germany." In Paul Kennedy and Anthony Nicholls, eds., *Nationalist and Racialist Movements in Britain and Germany before 1914* (London and Basingstoke, 1981), 114; Langmuir, *History*, 326; Byrnes, *Antisemitism*, 81.

[42] J. S. Conway, "National Socialism and the Christian Churches during the Weimar Republic." In P. D. Stachura, ed., *The Nazi Machtergreifung* (London, 1983), 140–41.

[43] Ibid.

[44] Eric Johnson, *Nazi Terror: The Gestapo, Jews, and Ordinary Germans* (New York, 1999), 223–24.

[45] Ibid., 223.

Muenster, Clemens August Graf von Galen, or the criticism expressed by Pope Pius XI in his well-known *Mit brennender Sorge* in March of 1937, while significant, constituted rare acts of defiance to Nazi anti-Semitism by leaders of both the Protestant and Catholic Churches.[46] Much has been written about the silence of the Protestant and Catholic leadership regarding the Holocaust. The present study will not delve into this specific issue, except to say that where the churches had taken a firm and public stand against Nazism, as exemplified clearly in the churches' victory in 1941 in halting the Nazi euthanasia program, the Nazi leadership appeared to pay heed and change course.

## GREAT BRITAIN

Although the last barriers to Jewish emancipation fell in Great Britain in 1858 with Jewish eligibility to serve in Parliament, and in 1871 with the passage of the Promissory Oaths Act admitting Jews to high offices, noticeable traces of the religious anti-Semitic tradition were to be found in English literature and the press. The character of the miserly, avaricious, deceitful, cunning, or vengeful Jew figures in Shakespeare's Shylock, Scott's Rebecca, and Dicken's Fagin. On the eve of the twentieth century, lesser-known British novelists invoked medieval Jewish stereotypes that included Jews as the anti-Christ, devil figure, and usurer. Among these writers were T. Kingston Clarke, Marie Corelli (also very active in the anti-alien movement in the early 1900s), Frank Harris, James Blyth, Violet Guttenberg, and Guy Thorne.[47] Popular British newspapers could also be counted on to keep alive the negative Jewish stereotypes. For instance, the *Daily Mail*, Britain's most widely circulated daily newspaper in the first decades of the twentieth century, published a number of serialized novels, including Edgar Joyce's 1899 *House of Hate*, B. L. Farjean's 1900 *Pride of Race*, and Pierre Costello's 1907 *A Sinner in Israel*, in which Jews were portrayed as cunning, excessively proud, or avaricious.

---

[46] Ibid., 212–13, 222–23; Kershaw, *Popular Opinion*, 274–75.

[47] Bryan Cheyette, "Jewish Stereotyping and English Literature 1875–1920: Towards a Political Analysis." In Tony Kushner and Kenneth Lunn, eds., *Traditions of Intolerance: Historical Perspectives on Fascism and Race Discourse in Britain* (Manchester and New York, 1989), 26–27; John M. Efron, *Defenders of the Race: Jewish Doctors and Race Science in Fin-De-Siecle Europe* (New Haven and London, 1994), 34–35.

Vestiges of traditional religious anti-Semitism surfaced within some circles of the British press during the "Eastern Crisis" of 1875–78. The particular incident that launched the anti-Semitic tirade appears to have been the alleged Turkish massacre of Bulgarian Christians. During the Eastern Crisis, Disraeli, the British prime minister at the time, placed apparent British national interests ahead of the interests of European Christianity. Though a converted Christian, Disraeli's Jewish background nevertheless gave some critics of his policies, including the former British prime minister Gladstone, the fodder to accuse Disraeli of invoking his supposedly ancient Jewish enmity toward Christianity and his alleged friendship for the non-Christian Turks in the formulation of his policies for Great Britain.[48]

Traditional religious anti-Semitic motifs mixed with racial anti-Semitic ones in the programs of early twentieth-century British anti-Semitic political movements. In one such case, John Henry Clarke, champion of homeopathics and notable member of the anti-Semitic movement the Britons, cautioned that international Jewish finance aimed at the overthrow of Christian civilization in England and that the disease of "Germanism" was carried by the ubiquitous parasite of the "wandering Jew."[49]

### ROMANIA

Religious anti-Semitism found a home in both the Roman Catholic Church and the Orthodox Church. In Romania, the Orthodox Church stood supreme. As early as the seventh century, the Orthodox Church's *concile* in Trullo promised severe punishment to Christians who accepted the treatment of Jewish physicians, and beginning in the fourteenth century, the deicide accusation pervaded official documents issued by the Orthodox Church. A Wallachian code of 1652 threatened excommunication to Romanian Christians who failed to abide by strict segregation vis-à-vis the Jews, and the church admonished its faithful that sexual contact with Jews would call down the wrath of God.[50] Romania's

---

[48] David Feldman, *Englishmen and Jews: Social Relations and Political Culture 1840–1914* (New Haven and London, 1994), 97–103, 120.

[49] Gisela Lebzelter, "Anti-Semitism – a Focal Point for the British Radical Right." In Paul Kennedy and Anthony Nicholls, eds., *Nationalist and Racialist Movements in Britain and Germany before 1914* (London and Basingstoke, 1981), 96–97.

[50] Andrei Pippidi, "The Mirror and Behind It: The Image of the Jew in the Romanian Society." *Shevut*, vol. 16, 1993, 80.

relative economic and social backwardness likely contributed to the lingering of religious anti-Semitism in the country well into the twentieth century. While in Western Europe the influence of the Christian churches had waned significantly by 1879, in Romania, by contrast, the authority of the Romanian Orthodox Church held firm, especially outside of the principal urban areas. Writing in 1891, Moses Schwartzfeld, a respected Romanian Jewish intellectual, attributed a significant role to the anti-Semitic legacy of the Orthodox Church in shaping popular anti-Semitic views. Schwartzfeld pointed to the church-inspired folk literature, found in proverbs, songs, superstitions, and anecdotes, depicting Jews as a cursed people and a bloodthirsty and rapacious people commanded by Satan.[51]

Traditional religious anti-Semitism in Romania contributed significantly to Romanian persistence in refusing to grant civil rights to its Jewish inhabitants. While many non-Romanian ethnic groups, such as the Greek minority, resided in Romania during the nineteenth century, only Jews were barred from naturalization on the basis of their non-Christianity.[52] As early as 1866, efforts of Romanian Jews to gain emancipation ran aground. Article 7 of the 1866 Romanian Constitution, by specifying that only foreigners of Christian faith could become naturalized Romanian citizens, issued in an era of civil limitations for Romanian Jews.[53] In return for recognition of Romania's independence, the leading European powers at the Congress of Berlin between 1878 and 1879 pressured the Romanian government to recognize the rights of all its inhabitants regardless of ethnic origins or religion.[54] In 1879, the Romanian Assembly debated the question of Jewish civil rights and ultimately refused to acquiesce to the request of the Western nations participating in the Congress of Berlin to recognize the rights of Jewish inhabitants.[55] The revision of Article 7 (removing religion as a basis for Romanian citizenship) angered many inside and outside the Romanian

---

[51] Jean Ancel, "The Image of the Jew in the View of Romanian Anti-Semitic Movements: Continuity and Change." *Shevut*, vol. 16, 1993, 41.

[52] Irina Livezeanu, *Cultural Politics in Greater Romania: Regionalism, Nation Building and Ethnic Struggle, 1918–1930* (Ithaca and London, 1995), 192; Volovici, *Nationalist*, 4–5.

[53] Livezeanu, *Cultural*, 197; Keith Hitchins, *Rumania 1866–1947* (Oxford, 1994), 16–17; Carol Iancu, *L'émancipation des Juifs de Roumanie (1913–1919)* (Montpellier, 1992), 22.

[54] Almog, *Nationalism*, 42.

[55] Iancu, *Juifs*, 24.

parliament.[56] However, the revision of Article 7 was still used to block Romanian Jews from obtaining full civil and political rights. Only after considerable debate in March 1923, as a result of the post–World War I peace treaties from which Romania acquired Hungarian Transylvania, Austrian Bukovina, and Russian Bessarabia, did Romania accede to the Allies' demand to emancipate its Jews.[57]

Between 1879 and 1939, well-known and respected Romanian intellectuals played pivotal roles in the spread of anti-Semitism and frequently criticized Judaism on a religious basis, although racial hatred of Jews frequently peppered their writings as well. Among the most prominent Romanian intellectuals invoking anti-Semitic religious stereotypes of Jews were Vasile Conta, Vasile Alecsandri, Cezar Bolliac, Mihai Eminescu, Ioan Slavici, Bogdan Petriceicu Haşdeu, V.A. Urechia, Alexandru D. Xenopol, Nicolae Iorga, Alexandru Cuza, N. Istrati, and Nicolae Paulescu.[58]

Vasile Conta, a deputy in the Romanian parliament and an eminent philosopher, in a speech to the Romanian parliament debating Jewish civil rights in September 1879, warned those in attendance that the Jews, the enemies of Christianity, had selected Romania to build their long-awaited Palestine, as foretold in the Jewish Talmud. Conta noted that the supreme aim of the Jews, formulated in the Bible and Talmud, was to enslave all other people to the Jewish people in order to secure the rule of the entire world by the "yids."[59] In 1922, Nicolae C. Paulescu, a scholar and well-known professor of physiology at the medical school of Bucharest, predicted a conflict between the forces of "Godly Christianity" and "Devilish Judaism" and feared that the Jews would try to exterminate the native Romanians as they had conquered the Russians.[60]

During the interwar period, religious anti-Semitism could still be used to mobilize the populace to take action against Jews. The highly popular Alexandru Cuza, a professor of political economy, a former president of the Romanian Chamber of Deputies, and the founder of the rabidly anti-Semitic League of National Christian Defense (LANC),

---

[56] Hitchins, *Rumania*, 16–17; Iancu, *Juifs*, 26.

[57] Ezra Mendelsohn, *The Jews of East Central Europe between the World Wars* (Bloomington, 1983), 184; Butnaru, *Silent*, 34.

[58] Oldson, *Providential*; Vago, "Traditions," 110; Volovici, *Nationalist*, 14.

[59] Volovici, *Nationalist*, 14.

[60] Ibid., 28–29.

in his lectures and writings frequently assailed the Jews for a host of crimes, including being murderers and betrayers of Jesus Christ, Bolshevik pagans, and consumers of Christian blood. Between 1899 and 1928, Cuza published five anti-Semitic Christian works in which he claimed that the Jews were both programmed and commanded by their religion to dominate the world. For Cuza, the Jewish religion contained a secret code commanding Jews to undermine Christian societies, particularly Romania. Cuza mainly targeted the Old Testament and the Talmud, attacking the divinity and universality of the Jewish God and accusing the sacred texts of the Jewish religion of espousing hatred for other nations. Cuza lambasted the Talmud for what he claimed was its message of world domination concealed in the two supposed appendices to the Talmud, the Cahal and the Freemasonry. The Talmud came under additional assault by Cuza's LANC in 1927, with a published accusation that the Talmud instructed Jews to employ Christian blood for Jewish religious rites. Cuza's anti-Semitism embodies both religious and quasi-racial foundations. While traditional religious anti-Semitism held that Jewish absolution could come about through baptism and conversion, Cuza advocated that Jewish repulsiveness emanated from Jewish contaminated blood and from the Jewish commitment to their God's mission of destroying Romania and its culture. Thus, for Cuza, conversion to Christianity would not free the Jews from their demonic faith.[61]

Additionally, Romanian Orthodox Church figures contributed to popular anti-Semitism through sermons and actions. In 1926, N. Georgescu, director and seminary priest in the Bessarabian town of Edinita, led a demonstration of students through the town shouting, "Down with the kikes" and "Death to the kikes," as he urged peasants to burn Jewish houses.[62] In 1934, in a debate between Mircea Eliade, a popular intellectual in Corneliu Zelea Codreanu's anti-Semitic League of the Archangel Michael, and C. Racoveanu, a so-called Romanian expert on Christian Orthodox issues, Racoveanu, citing the Gospels (John 7:24), claimed that the Jews were damned forever for being and remaining Jewish. Eliade, also employing the Gospels (John 39:44), challenged the Orthodox Church's representative's interpretation, suggesting that the Jews were condemned forever not because they remained Jews or refused to accept Christ as the Messiah, but rather because they were the

[61] Ancel, "Image," 47–51.
[62] Livezeanu, *Cultural*, 125–27.

"children of the Devil."[63] And finally, on the eve of World War II, the
patriarch of the Romanian Orthodox Church, Miron Cristea, together
with the Romanian minister president, met with Wilhelm Fabricus, the
Nazi German ambassador to Bucharest, in an effort to request an end
to the apparent German policy of support for Romania's Iron Guard. In
the discussions, the patriarch and minister president were reported to
have praised the anti-Semitic actions of Nazi Germany and expressed
their preference for a similar policy in Romania.[64]

## ITALY

Traditional religious anti-Semitism in Italy has its beginnings nearly
two thousand years ago in Rome. Josephus, the Roman historian, observed a population of roughly eight thousand Jews residing in Rome in
4 B.C.E. Religious anti-Semitism had ebbed and flowed in Italy from the
time that Christianity became the official religion of the Roman Empire
in the fourth century to King Victor Emmanuel II's signing of a Royal
Decree in 1870 extending civil rights to the Jews of Rome and the closing
of the last ghetto in Rome. (The Law of March 29, 1848, granted Jews
equal status in other Italian provinces between 1848 and 1860.) Relative religious toleration of Jews flourished during the Italian Renaissance
and the Napoleonic era but was followed by protracted periods of religious repression, such as the sixteenth-century Counter-Reformation.
In Italy, the Counter-Reformation produced the establishment of the
first ghettos for Jews and church-inspired destruction of sacred Hebrew
works, such as the church-authorized public burning of Hebrew books,
including hundreds of copies of the Talmud, in Bologna in 1553. The
Restoration, coming on the heels of the French Revolution and the
Napoleonic era, which had freed Italian Jews from the ghettos and proclaimed equal rights for Jews, ushered in a period of reaction marked by
restoration of medieval laws pertaining to Jews and the return of Jews to
the ghettos.[65] As late as 1799, Jews were victims of pogroms in northern
and central Italy. Rossi reports that in August 1799, pogroms against

---

[63] Ancel, "Image," 56.
[64] Theodore Armon, "The Economic Background of Antisemitism in Romania between the Two World Wars: C. Z. Codreanu and the Jewish Trade, 1918–1940."
SHVUT, vols. 1–2, nos. 17–18, 1995, 329–30.
[65] Zuccotti, Italians, 12–15; Mario Rossi, "Emancipation of the Jews in Italy." Jewish
Social Studies, vol. 15, April 1953, 129–34; Attilio Milano, Storia degli ebrei in Italia
(Turin, 1963), 351–54; Kertzer, Kidnapping, 15; Kertzer, The Popes, 66.

Jews erupted in the Marches, Tuscany, and Piedmont. In addition to the extensive property damage resulting from these pogroms, thirteen Jews were murdered in the Senigallia ghetto, and twelve Jews were burned alive in Siena.[66]

One of the more infamous examples of nineteenth-century Italian religious anti-Semitism was the Mortara Affair of 1858. Secret baptisms of Jews were common occurrences in Italy as late as the 1850s. The most publicized case of a coerced christening was that of Edgardo Mortara, eleven months old, the son of Momolo and Marianna Mortara of Bologna. When the baptism reached the attention of the Dominican Father Feletti, in June 1858, he decreed that the child be taken from his parents by papal police and placed in a Catholic foundling home. Pleas to return the child to his parents from the family of Edgardo Mortara, from Jewish groups throughout Europe, and from representatives of Austria-Hungary, England, France, and Prussia fell on deaf ears. Not even the intervention of Napoleon III and Franz Josef could persuade Pope Pius IX to alter the Holy See's decision to approve the abduction of the child and his conversion to Christianity.[67] *La Civiltà Cattolica*, the most influential of all Catholic journals and the unofficial organ of the papacy, had launched a defense of the Catholic Church's abduction of Edgardo Mortara and blamed Jewish control of the foreign press for mobilizing international opinion against the Holy See. *La Civiltà Cattolica* claimed further that Edgardo Mortara had been saved from his cruel Jewish parents and provided with the spiritual and physical protection of the church.[68]

Popularization of the myths of Jewish crimes against Christians survived into the nineteenth century in Italy. Kertzer observes that, with the nurturing of the Catholic press, parish priests, and sermons, the notion that Jews regularly captured Christians in order to drain their blood was widespread in Italy at the time of the Mortara Affair.[69] In fact, two years

---

[66] Rossi, "Emancipation," 114.

[67] Kertzer, *Kidnapping*, 33–34; Rossi, "Emancipation," 129–30. The only positive outcome of the international pressure on the Holy See to reverse its decision in the Mortara Affair was the agreement that at the age of maturity (twenty-one years) Edgardo would be allowed to visit his natural father and decide which religion to follow. That at age twenty-one Edgardo chose to be Catholic was not surprising, given that the church had educated him in Catholicism with the desire that he be ordained a priest. Edgardo went on to become an eminent prelate of the Roman curia (Finzi, *Anti-Semitism*, 26).

[68] Kertzer, *Kidnapping*, 56, 78, 115, 135.

[69] Ibid., 137–38.

before the outbreak of the Mortara Affair, a Jewish merchant in northeastern Italy was arrested and charged with the crimes of kidnapping
and draining blood from a twenty-three-year-old Christian servant for
religious purposes.[70] The charge of ritual murder gathered steam during
the Mortara Affair. *La Civiltà Cattolica* had since its origination in 1850
focused largely on Jewish misdeeds. During the Mortara Affair, the journal had invoked the "blood libel" allegation by asserting that there was
irrefutable proof of Jews seizing Christian children for the purposes of
extracting their blood. As late as 1893, this same journal published a
series of articles purporting to reveal the existence of the long-standing
Jewish practice of taking Christian blood for religious purposes. Joining the *La Civiltà Cattolica* in the accusation of Jewish ritual murder,
*Il Cattolico*,the Genoan daily, published an article in January 1859 entitled "The Horrendous Murder of a Child." The paper reported that
while the liberal press was castigating the Pope for the Holy See's role
in the Mortara Affair, it ignored the commission of a horrible ritual
murder of a Christian boy performed by a Jew in the Moldavian town of
Folkchany. Ultimately, the boy's (Christian) uncle was found guilty of
the murder.[71]

The Roman Catholic Church served as the major purveyor of anti-
Semitism in Italy before 1938.[72] Clerical anti-Semitism in Italy had
roots in the traditional religious leitmotifs but also in the beliefs that
Italy's Jews had wholeheartedly embraced the successful movement for
Italian unification (perceived by the church as antithetical to its interests) and that they advocated a Jewish national home in Palestine.
Motivated largely by self-interest, the Italian Jewish community had
welcomed and contributed greatly to the mid-nineteenth-century movement to unify Italy – a fact that did not go unnoticed by the Italian
Catholic Church. Like the Catholic Church in France, which unfa-
vorably identified Jews with the Third Republic, the Italian Catholic
Church saw the subversive hand of the Jews – seeking to undermine traditional Christian values – behind the drive for Italian unification and
the establishment of the detested liberal state. The idea of a Jewish
homeland in Palestine caused special anxiety within the Vatican, for

[70] Ibid.
[71] Ibid., 136–38.
[72] Mario Toscano, "L'uguaglianza senza diversità: Stato, società e questione ebraica
nell'Italia liberale." In Mario Toscano, ed., *Integrazione e Identità: e'sperienza ebraica
in Germania e Italia dall'Illuminismo al fascismo* (Milan, 1998), 213.

the official Roman Catholic position held that the Jews must accept the word of Christ and convert before they would be able to return to the land of Israel.[73]

The Catholic Jesuit journal *La Civiltà Cattolica* spearheaded the clerical anti-Semitic campaign during the last half of the nineteenth century and the first part of the twentieth century. Pope Pius IX had agreed to a proposal pushed by Father Antonio Bresciani (the author of the immensely popular novel *L'Ebreo di Verona*) and other leading Jesuits in 1850 to launch a journal to oppose the Italian secular press. The Pope handpicked the staff of *La Civiltà Cattolica* and placed Father Bresciani at the journal's helm. Throughout its history, *La Civiltà Cattolica* popularized myths of Jewish world conspiracy and alleged Jewish efforts to undermine Christian society, but at the same time, the journal condemned the use of violence against Jews.[74] Attacks on the Talmud were a regular feature in the editions of *La Civiltà Cattolica*. In its attempt to clearly extricate Christianity from its Jewish roots, *La Civiltà Cattolica* claimed that the modern Jewish religion is based not on the Bible but on the anti-Christian Talmud. In an article in 1886, *La Civiltà Cattolica* claimed that by their promulgation of brotherhood and peace, the Jews sought to exterminate Christianity and institute their messianic kingdom as prophesized for them in the Talmud.[75] *La Civiltà Cattolica* took an active part in the anti-Dreyfus campaign in Italy, claiming that the Dreyfus case was actually a conspiracy contrived by the Jewish plutocracy, with help from the Freemasons, Protestants, socialists, and anarchists, to undermine Catholic and French interests. The Jesuit journal added that Jewish leadership of the plot derived from the Jewish ambition to dominate the world. To counter the conspiracy, the journal proposed the passage of an international law granting Jews the status of foreigners or guests, rather than citizens.[76] The 1890s were difficult years for Italy in light of economic crises, labor unrest, and the country's

---

[73] Milano, *Storia*, 356–57; Maurizio Molinari, *Ebrei in Italia: un problema di identità (1870–1938)* (Florence, 1991), 91.

[74] Lynn M. Gunzberg, *Strangers at Home: Jews in the Italian Literary Imagination* (Berkeley, 1992), 65–67; Gadi Luzzatto, "Aspetti dell'antisemitismo nella 'Civiltà cattolica' dal 1881 al 1903." *Bailamme*, vol. 1, no. 2, December 1987, 128–29.

[75] Luzzatto, "Aspetti," 128–29; Kertzer, *Kidnapping*, 138; Molinari, *Ebrei*, 91–92.

[76] Besides *La Civiltà Cattolica*, the clerical press published G. Spadolini's *L'opposizione cattolica da Porta Pia al '98*, which during the Dreyfus Affair indulged in a profession of anti-Semitism (John A. Thayer, *Italy and the Great War: Politics and Culture, 1870–1915*, Madison and Milwaukee, 1964, 423).

colonial setback in Africa. In a series of famous articles in the 1890s, *La Civiltà Cattolica* laid blame for these problems on the Jews and called for the appropriation of Jewish wealth as a solution to the Jewish Problem. The view that Jews adhered to Freemasonry and played an instrumental role in the Risorgimento was widely shared within Catholic circles. That the mayor of Rome during the early 1900s was Ernesto Nathan, a prominent Jew and leader of the Italian Freemasons, did little to dissuade the church of the link between Jews and Freemasonry as well as the tie between Jews and other anti-clerical and radical movements. As elsewhere, religiously inspired anti-Semites in Italy accused the Jews of playing a consequential role in the secularization of elementary and secondary education. In Italy, the Catholic Church had controlled the curriculum in schools until the passage of the Credaro Laws in 1910 and 1911.[77] During the interwar period, the Catholic Church increasingly highlighted the purported link between Jews and revolutionary unrest. In the aftermath of World War I, Pope Benedetto XV and his secretary of state, Cardinal Gasparri, praised Monsignor Jouin, curator of Sant'Agostino in Paris and founder of the *Revue Internationale des Sociétés Secretès*, for his Italian translation of the notorious anti-Semitic *Protocols of the Elders of Zion*.[78] Moreover, at the time of the Spanish Civil War, *La Civiltà Cattolica*, along with the Catholic University of Milan's journal, *Vita e Pensiero*, sought to warn its readers of the pernicious role played by Jewish Bolshevism in its efforts to destroy Christian Europe.[79] Relatedly, Father Agostino Gemelli, founder and rector of the Catholic University of the Sacred Heart in Milan and later president of the Pontifical Academy of Sciences, in a published review in *Vita e Pensiero* in which he commented on the suicide of Felice Momigliano, a prominent Italian Jewish intellectual, wrote, "would not the world be a better place if, together with positivism, socialism, free thought and Momigliano, all the

---

[77] Emilio Gentile, "The Struggle for Modernity: Echoes of the Dreyfus Affair in Italian Political Culture, 1898–1912." *Journal of Contemporary History*, vol. 33, no. 4, 1998, 499; Andrew M. Canepa, "The Image of the Jew in the Folklore and Literature of the Postrisorgimento." *Journal of European Studies*, vol. 9, 1979, 260–61; Molinari, *Ebrei*, 92; Renzo De Felice, *Storia degli ebrei italiani sotto il fascismo* (Turin, 1993), 32–35, 40.

[78] Jouin also authored the highly anti-Semitic *La judeo-maçonnerie et la révolution sociale* and *La judeo–maçonnerie et la domination du monde* (De Felice, *Storia*, 43).

[79] De Felice, *Storia*, 42–43; Canepa, "Image," 260–61; Gentile, "Struggle," 499; Zuccotti, *Italians*, 34; Michaelis, *Mussolini*, 6–9; Molinari, *Ebrei*, 91–92.

Jews who continue the work of those who crucified our Lord were to die as well? It would be a liberation."[80]

How successful the campaign carried out by groups within the Catholic Church was in terms of winning adherents among Italy's predominantly Roman Catholic population is virtually impossible to gauge. Michaelis claims that the Catholic press' anti-Semitic campaign served to further isolate the Catholic Church from the mainstream of Italian life, although Finzi asserts that the Catholic Church's centuries-old dissemination of negative Jewish stereotypes may have indirectly contributed to the apparent acceptance by the majority of Italians of the fascist regime's anti-Jewish legislation in 1938.[81] However, the Italian Catholic Church consistently rejected both violence against Jews and anti-Semitic arguments based on biological or anthropological foundations. As late as 1938, Pope Pius XI spoke out against racial anti-Semitism, noting its inconsistency with Christian teaching and Italian culture.[82] Nonetheless, the Catholic Church in Rome refused to abandon its long-standing belief in the religious and moral danger posed by Judaism to Christian society and continued to allow the injunction of *Oremus pro perfidis judeis* at the beginning of the ceremonies of Holy Week.[83] With the ascension of Eugenio Pacelli (Pope Pius XII) to the Holy See in 1939, the tradition of religious anti-Semitism would hardly be threatened.[84]

In stark contrast to the writings of famous scholars in England, France, Germany, and Romania, well-known scholarly figures in late nineteenth-century and early twentieth-century Italy rarely took up the themes of Jews and Judaism.[85] However, religious anti-Semitism as a theme found favor in Italian popular literature. The widely circulated

---

[80] Finzi, *Anti-Semitism*, 98–99.

[81] Meir Michaelis, "Fascist Policy toward Italian Jews: Tolerance and Persecution." In I. Herzer, ed., *The Italian Refuge: Rescue of Jews during the Holocaust* (Washington, DC, 1989), 34; Finzi, *Anti-Semitism*, 106.

[82] De Felice, *Storia*; Adriana Goldstaub, "Rassegna Bibliografica Dell'Editoria Antisemita nel 1938." *Rassegna Mensile di Israel*, vol. 54, 1988, 409–433; Kertzer, *The Popes*.

[83] Finzi, *Anti-Semitism*, 106.

[84] Gene Bernadini, "The Origins and Development of Racial Anti-Semitism in Fascist Italy." *Journal of Modern History*, vol. 4, September 1977, 435–36; Kertzer, *The Popes*.

[85] One notable exception to this in Italy is Francesco Coppola. Coppola authored a number of articles dedicated to Maurras, a well-known leader of the French Action Française movement, espousing religious anti-Semitic ideas (Thayer, *Italy*, 213).

and highly popular 1850 novel *L'ebreo di Verona* (The Jew of Verona), by Antonio Bresciani, helped to shape fictional religious anti-Semitic writings for decades in Italy. At least seventeen editions of Bresciani's novel appeared, in addition to English, French, German, and Portuguese translations. Bresciani, who played an instrumental role in the launching of *La Civiltà Cattolica*, incorporated a number of religious anti-Semitic themes in his novel. The context for the novel is the revolutionary upheavals in Italy and Europe during the period 1848–49. The novel portrays European Jews motivated by anti-Christian sentiments (the anger of Judas) as a driving force behind revolutionary upheaval and liberalism. In particular, the novel's chief protagonist, a Jew named Aser, is depicted as a revolutionary Mazzinian and a descendant of a Jewish banking family who wanders (notions of Ahasuerus, the wandering Jew) Europe promoting subversive and revolutionary causes, while taking advantage of his family's international contacts. In the end, Aser undergoes an internal struggle and is successfully transformed. He converts to Christianity and forsakes subversive and revolutionary causes.[86]

Other well-known Italian novelists employed unfavorable religious anti-Semitic motifs in their works. Carlo Varese's *Sibilla Odaleta* invoked the ritual murder allegation and pointed to a Jewish undermining of society from within. Giuseppe Alessandro Giustina's *Il Ghetto* (1881), though certainly not overtly anti-Semitic, represents Jews as generally superstitious, treacherous, and venal. The widely read Carolina Invernizio's[87] *L'orfana del ghetto* (1887) depicts Jews as morally and spiritually inferior. The ritual murder theme is also present in Invernizio's novel. Her Jewish characters seek vengeance, thirst for hatred, and act with tremendous tenacity, vindictiveness, and malice. Invernizio presents the God of Israel as a merchant God with whom one can bargain. One of the characters in *L'orfana del ghetto* alleges that the Jews are masters of the world, controlling commerce and industry. For Invernizio, the Jewish religion perverts the Jews, and only conversion to Christianity can save them.[88]

Religious anti-Semitic themes continued in the writings of twentieth-century Italian novelists. Papini's *Gog* emphasized the role Jews have

---

[86] Gunzberg, *Strangers*, 67–68, 75–76, 89, 228.

[87] Carolina Invernizio was one of Italy's leading novelists during the last years of the nineteenth century. Her *L'orfana del ghetto* went through seven editions and was reprinted in 1975 (Gunzberg, *Strangers*, 198–206; Canepa, "Image," 269).

[88] Canepa, "Image," 265–69; Gunzberg, *Strangers*, 168–84, 198–206.

played as purveyors of anti-Christian revolutionary doctrines (e.g., Einstein, Freud, and Marx) and as worshippers of the idol of money. Papini goes further to reiterate Jewish responsibility for the murder of Christ and the undermining of Christian philosophy. Papini saw conversion to Christianity as a solution to the Jewish Problem but held out little hope of its success, because Jews lacked sufficient modesty and refused to renounce their love of money and power.[89]

## RELIGIOUS ROOT: THE ENLIGHTENMENT CRITIQUE

With the advent of the Enlightenment, religious anti-Semitism took on a new leitmotif emanating, interestingly, from the attacks leveled on the Jewish religion by such eminent secularists as Voltaire, Diderot, Montesquieu, von Dohm, and d'Holbach. As secularists, these philosophers in opposing Judaism did not resort to the ancient religious charges of Jews as Christ killers or Christ rejectors. Rather, in their critique of the roots of Christianity, they condemned Judaism for remaining a fossilized religion, persisting in a self-image of its special "election," and upholding antiprogressive beliefs. In this way, the Enlightenment may have contributed to modernizing and secularizing anti-Semitism.[90] During the nineteenth century, many secularists felt betrayed by Jews, who, in their eyes, failed to abandon their distinctive beliefs and practices after having been emancipated and granted civil rights. Whereas traditional religious anti-Semitism appealed largely to a less-educated public, the secularist critique attracted a more highly educated following.

One could interpret the products of Enlightenment thinking in both positive and negative terms for European Jewry. On the positive side, the Enlightenment stood for the rationality of human nature, natural rights, the principles of the social utility of knowledge, and, quite importantly, the opening up of careers to talent. In rejecting the Christian doctrine of original sin that saw human nature as essentially sinful, which had dominated Western civilization for centuries, the Enlightenment posited instead that human nature was essentially rational and that human

---

[89] Gunzberg, *Strangers*, 253–56.

[90] Hertzberg, *French Enlightenment*; Efron, *Defenders*; Weiss, *Ideology*; Pulzer, *Jews*; Weinberg, *Because*; Katz, *Prejudice*; Pauley, *Prejudice*; Wistrich, *Antisemitism*; Steiman, *Paths*; George L. Mosse, *Germans and Jews: The Right, The Left, and the Search for a "Third Force" in Pre-Nazi Germany* (New York, 1970); Ruether, "Theological"; Winock, *Nationalism*.

beings had the capacity to choose between good and evil. The adoption and institution of many of these principles considerably served the interests of Jewish emancipation and Jewish social mobility in the nineteenth century.[91] While the Enlightenment advocated Jewish emancipation, it envisioned equally the disappearance of Jewry. Many of the most prominent thinkers of the European Enlightenment firmly believed that Jewish distinctiveness would disappear once the barriers to Jewish emancipation were eliminated. As the German thinker Christian Wilhelm von Dohm stated in his 1781 treatise, *Ueber die Buergerliche Verbesserung der Juden* (On the civil improvement of the Jews), the supposed moral corruption of the Jews was attributable to the oppressed conditions under which they for centuries had lived. Alter the conditions under which Jews live, and Jews will shed their negative habits and turn into good citizens, von Dohm asserted.[92] In particular, breaking down the walls of the ghettos and dismantling the hold of Talmudic Judaism that had governed life in the Jewish communities would pave the way to terminating the depraved moral, spiritual, and intellectual conditions of European Jewry. Enlightenment thinkers ascribed to the relativist insight that environment and historical experience essentially conditioned human beliefs and behavior and that nothing in the human mind or culture was innate. Both Montesquieu and d'Holbach held that Jewish negative characteristics were attributable to environment and that changing their environment would change their character. Von Dohm thought that if Jews could be shepherded away from their traditional commercial endeavors and directed toward activities such as farming and the crafts, they could become moral men.[93]

For the philosophers of the Enlightenment, climate or environment encompassed as well a people's cultural setting, and thus they frequently cited the importance of education in altering behavior and beliefs. In the particular case of the Jews, many saw what they perceived as the intolerant and unyielding character of the Jewish religion as a chief obstacle preventing the full assimilation of Jews. Diderot, the great French Enlightenment thinker, remarked that the establishment of the separate Jewish nation was to be found in the religion of the Jews. Katz observes that, in the view of the deistic literature of the Enlightenment, Mosaic

---

[91] Steiman, *Paths*, 94, 97.

[92] Steiman, *Paths*, 98; Mosse, *Germans*, 39.

[93] Hertzberg, *French Enlightenment*, 276; Steiman, *Paths*, 102; Mosse, *Germans*, 41; Ruether, "Theological," 42.

law has set the Jewish people apart from others through its adherence to isolationist and exclusionist practices. Jewish dietary practices made it difficult for Jews to eat with others, and Jewish law forbade Jews and Christians to intermarry. Jewish writings further reinforced the separation of Jews and non-Jews through their insistence that the Jews were specifically selected as God's chosen people and thus, in the eyes of many non-Jews, afforded the Jews a spiritual status superior to the rest of humanity. Common among adherents to this thinking was the idea that Jewish social isolation and special status served as the source of the alleged Jewish double standard of morality: Jews would behave ethically in their dealings with fellow Jews but were held to no such obligations in their dealings with Gentiles.[94] Moreover, as Rubenstein notes, the Jewish religious claims of being God's chosen people and the special object of God's concern in history did little to mitigate Christian antipathy toward Jews.[95]

For many of the Enlightenment thinkers, attacks on the Mosaic foundation of Judaism had an additional purpose. In their struggle against traditional beliefs (e.g., Christian beliefs), Enlightenment thinkers such as Diderot felt the need to undermine the wellspring of Christianity (as well as Islam), which led them in the direction of assailing the Talmud and the Old Testament of the Jews. While the giants of the Enlightenment were scornful of Christian scholasticism, they found Jewish scholasticism, notably the Talmud, obtuse and highly preposterous. A scholarly testament to the struggle against this form of traditionalism was Denis Diderot's Encyclopedia. Between 1751 and 1772, Diderot published seventeen large volumes of this momentous work. In the volumes of the Encyclopedia, Judaism received harsh treatment for its promotion of the antisocial behavior of Jews and for its contribution to Christianity. According to Diderot, within Judaism one finds a confused mix of revelation and reason, nurturing fanaticism, and blind allegiance to authority. Two contributions of Judaism were ignorance and ancient superstition. The notable French philosopher d'Holbach referred to the Talmud and other significant rabbinical writings as cabalistic interpretations, old wives' tales, and fables. For Diderot, Mirabaud, and other Enlightenment writers, Jews could become citizens only if they abandoned their religious faith. The disappearance of the Jew as a Jew was seen as necessary to the complete emancipation and assimilation of

---

[94] Katz, Prejudice, 56.
[95] Rubenstein, After Auschwitz, 13.

European Jewry.[96] It is not surprising that Jewish reluctance to accept
the offers of emancipation and cultural assimilation may have partly
resided in the perception that the assimilation espoused by Enlightenment thinkers would lead in reality to conversion to Christianity, the
presiding religious faith of Europe.[97]

In considering the writings of the major figures of the Enlightenment
regarding the Jews, there is some debate between the majority interpretation, which views the alleged negative characteristics of Jews as
unfixed and thereby subject to emendations in time and circumstances,
and the minority or absolutist interpretation, which sees the supposedly
negative traits of Jews as a permanent part of their nature and thereby
resistant to change.[98] Unlike many of his fellow Enlightenment philosophers, Voltaire failed to accept the argument that people were products
of their historical experience and social conditioning when it came to
discussing the Jews. The essential character of Jewish people had already
taken shape and had thus become innate, according to Voltaire.[99] For
Voltaire, the prospect of changing the Jew's alien nature was unpromis-
ing. Voltaire ascribed the alleged Jewish negative characteristics (e.g.,
usury, cheating, superstition) to innate Jewish traits. By virtue of its
alien nature, the Jewish character was both bad and innate in the mind
of Voltaire.[100] For some scholars, Voltaire's antipathy toward Judaism
went beyond attacking Judaism as a source of Christianity. Voltaire did
not limit his venomous barbs to the Jews of antiquity but also leveled
attacks on the contemporary Jews of Europe. To this end, Voltaire diverged from other Enlightenment critics of the Jews by suggesting that
he would not be surprised if some day the Jews became deadly to the

---

[96] Hertzberg (*French Enlightenment*, 312) asserts that Diderot envisioned that the
job of freeing the Jews of their ignorance and ancient superstition would be much
more difficult than freeing the Christians (and maybe impossible). In Diderot's
view, the Jew's religion and character were one. Hertzberg believes, moreover,
that this point of view was shared by Voltaire and d'Holbach as well.

[97] Steiman, *Paths*, 93–94; Ruether, "Theological," 42-43; Hertzberg, *French Enlightenment*, 309–12; Katz, *Prejudice*, 29–31; Pulzer, *Jews*, 3; Winock, *Nationalism*,
134; Lindeman, *Esau's*, 42.

[98] Katz, *Prejudice*, 56.

[99] It should be noted that Voltaire did not interpret Jewish nature as racist in any
biological sense, but rather as an outcome of the essential qualities of Jewish
civilization (Steiman, *Paths*, 102).

[100] Weiss, *Ideology*, 43; Steiman, *Paths*, 102; Hertzberg, *French Enlightenment*, 286;
Weinberg, *Because*, 67–68.

human race.[101] Nevertheless, convinced that their religious justification for continued existence had been discredited, Voltaire had little doubt that Jews would disappear when their specialized economic functions as merchants, brokers, and traders were no longer required by other nations. In this way, Voltaire anticipated the Marxian view that, as a socio-economic group defined by its economic function, the Jews would eventually disappear, as other nations came to possess their own commercial agents.[102]

Voltaire throughout his writings portrays the Jews of antiquity as a people religiously, socially, ethically, culturally, and politically deficient. What Voltaire had to say about the Jews carried considerable weight, given his stature as indisputably the greatest of all Enlightenment rationalistic authors and philosophers. Voltaire's anti-Semitic writings – supplying the essential ingredients of the rhetoric of secular anti-Semitism – would arm nineteenth- and twentieth-century enemies of the Jews with an arsenal of arguments qualitatively different from the traditional religious accusations dominating Western civilization before the Enlightenment.[103] Yet even more pernicious for Jews was the legacy established by Voltaire (and those Enlightenment thinkers upholding the absolutist interpretation), which, by depicting the so-called negative Jewish character as rooted in an alien nature, laid a cultural foundation upon which racial anti-Semitism of the mid to late nineteenth century sprung to life.[104]

Jews were becoming full-fledged citizens in much of Europe as the nineteenth century unfolded. However, full emancipation did not automatically produce full assimilation. The hopes of those eighteenth-century secularists, assured that Jews would abandon their distinctive behavior once they were granted citizenship, dimmed. While many European Jews converted to Christianity, and others abandoned traditional Jewish practices, the majority continued to uphold Jewish beliefs and practices, convinced that adopting full citizenship need not require forsaking one's religion. However, in the minds of many nineteenth-century cynics, the Jews had failed to honor their part of the bargain: in exchange for legal emancipation, a total assimilation into the

---

[101] Hertzberg, *French Enlightenment*, 300; Weinberg, *Because*, 67–68. See especially Voltaire's 1771 *Lettres de Memmius à Cicéron*.
[102] Steiman, *Paths*, 106; Katz, *Prejudice*, 47.
[103] Katz, *Prejudice*, 41–43; Hertzberg, *French Enlightenment*, 10–11, 285–86.
[104] Steinman, *Paths*, 102.

dominant culture. While Jews were outwardly professing to be good Frenchmen or good Germans, their critics felt that the Jews remained imprisoned within their exclusive and antisocial ghetto mentality. For how else could one explain the Jews' steadfast attachment to their special religious beliefs and practices? Thus, the secularist critique continued into the nineteenth and twentieth centuries. Among a large number of nineteenth and early twentieth-century scholars, an understanding of the particular paradox of Jewish assimilation lay in the persistence of a singular Jewish culture.

### FRANCE

Having, to a large extent, originated in France among the eighteenth-century Enlightenment thinkers, the secularist critique of Judaism influenced subsequent generations of French writers. Within the French intellectual community, the secularist critique flourished prominently in the camp of the political left until the Dreyfus Affair. We too often think that anti-Semitism emanates from the political right. A myopic view of anti-Semitic political rhetoric – one that would begin with the advent of the twentieth century – would obviously produce such a conclusion. A longer view of the history of anti-Semitism would certainly lead us to question placing anti-Semitism squarely at home on the political right. In fact, from the time of the French Revolution (1789) to the unfolding of the Dreyfus Affair (1890s), anti-Semitism seemed equally at home on the political left.[105] The Voltairian anti-Semitic secularist legacy had found a voice among leftists as early as the French Revolution. During the French Revolution, the issue of Jewish citizenship reached the National Assembly. The delegates, after considerable heated debate, ultimately granted French Jews the right of citizenship. Count Stanislas de Clermont-Tonnerre, a deputy in 1789 to the National Assembly, took the side of equal rights for Jews. Clermont-Tonnerre proposed that the Jews should be granted everything as individuals but nothing as a nation. In other words, in exchange for citizenship, Jews should abandon all claims to national, communal, and judicial separateness.[106] Opposing Clermont-Tonnerre's declaration of equal rights for Jews, leftist deputies from eastern France (notably Alsace, with its relatively large Ashkenazic Jewish population) spoke energetically against

[105] Wilson, *Ideology*, 333–34.
[106] Efron, *Defenders*, 18.

Jewish emancipation. These deputies, who were joined by deputies from other regions of France, invoked a Voltairian indictment of Jews, citing the irretrievably alien character of Jews as well as the parasitic nature and inutility of Jewish trades. For these leftist opponents of Jewish civil rights, the Jews were followers not just of another religion but of a quite particularistic religion that would never allow them to become fully integrated members of a single French nation. As France at this time was besieged by both internal and external enemies, these leftist opponents questioned the ability of Jews to defend the French nation, which to them amounted to the true test of citizenship. They opined that Jews would have difficulty serving as soldiers because they would not eat food or drink wine produced by Gentiles, would not work or fight on their Sabbath, and would not wear the same clothes as non-Jewish soldiers.[107]

The Enlightenment critique of Judaism continued to pervade the political left during the nineteenth century.[108] It became part of the anti-Jewish writings of French socialists such as Fourier, Proudhon, Leroux, Blanqui, Valles, Regnard, Tridon, Chirac, and Toussenel. If we could point to one single work that stood out within the pantheon of nineteenth-century French socialist writings that reflected the socialist anti-Jewish feeling, it is Alphonse de Toussenel's *Les Juifs rois de l'époque: histoire de la féodalité financière* (The Jews, kings of the epoch) in 1845. For Toussenel, behind the despoilation and ravaging of the pristine French countryside, the establishment of ugly industrial cities, and the ruination of the traditional artisanal trades were the foreigners, especially Jews. The alien nature produced by centuries of historical-cultural conditions made Jews contemptuous of the honest, hardworking French peasant and artisan, and unsympathetic to the natural beauty of France.[109] While Toussenel was cursing the Jews for the destruction of rural France, other French leftists pursued the Enlightenment anti-Jewish

---

[107] Hertzberg, *French Enlightenment*, 9–10, 366–67; Winock, *Nationalism*, 133–34; Lindemann, *Esau's*, 46–47.

[108] Even prominent French Jews who ascribed to neither the French left nor the French right could at times criticize their fellow Jews for adherence to an antiprogressive and antisocial religious tradition. Solomon Reinach, a well-respected French Jew of the late nineteenth century, chastised his religious brethren for upholding a backward and ritualistic religious tradition that isolated them from others in society at a time when the progress of science was bringing humans closer together (Lindemann, *Accused*, 62).

[109] Wilson, *Ideology*, 333–34; Lindemann, *Accused*, 81–82; Lindemann, *Esau's*, 221–22.

thrust that Judaism had to be undermined for its role in having given birth to Christianity. Here, we find the militant, atheist, and anticlerical "Hebertists" of the late Second Empire (1860s) – student followers of Blanqui who railed against God and Jews.[110]

The Dreyfus Affair signaled a shift within the left vis-à-vis public condemnations of Jews and Judaism. In light of the virulent anti-Semitism emanating from the far right at the time of the Dreyfus Affair, the importance assigned to Emile Zola's famous letter and trial, and the active role of Juarès, the prominent French socialist, in the campaign for a new trial for Dreyfus, the left changed course. By 1911, it had become common at annual French socialist conferences for leaders to denounce anti-Semitism and anti-Semites.[111] Leftist anti-Semitism after the Dreyfus Affair would attenuate significantly, although left-wing anti-Semitism in France never completely died out. A number of prominent French leftist after the 1890s, such as Paul Faure, Georges Sorel, and Maurice Thorez, would occasionally resort to anti-Semitic utterances. Among these leftists, Sorel probably stands out. The famous revolutionary-syndicalist played an instrumental role in the establishment in 1911 of the national-socialist review *L'indépendance*, which published some of his anti-Semitic pieces, such as one equating France's struggle against the Jews with the struggle in the United States against the "Yellow Peril."[112]

---

[110] Winock, *Nationalism*, 134; Wistrich, *Antisemitism*, 47–48.

[111] Winock, *Nationalism*, 144; Robert Soucy, *French Fascism: The First Wave, 1924–1933* (New Haven and London, 1986), 15; Eugen Weber, *Action Française: Royalism and Reaction in Twentieth-Century France* (Stanford, 1962), 72.

[112] Birnbaum, *La France*, 53; Weber, *Action Française*, 74. Also, Sternhell ("Roots," 121–25) agrees that the French left, for the most part, distanced itself from overt anti-Semitic utterances after 1898. He does, however, point out that leftist anti-Semitism remained within the nonconformist wing of socialism between 1898 and 1914. The nonconformists, including Herve, Sorel, and Berth, felt that mainstream socialists such as Millerand, Briand, and Viviani had betrayed the revolutionary goals of the proletarian movement and made peace with liberal and bourgeois democracy. For other examples of persisting leftist anti-Semitism, see the following: In 1898, *Humanité nouvelle*, the French socialist journal, published a translated version of Karl Marx's famous anti-Semitic *Zur Judenfrage*, and additionally in a series of clearly anti-Semitic articles praised the anti-Jewish demonstrators in France as heirs to the revolutionary tradition of 1789. In 1920, the official organ of the Communist Party, *Humanité*, and the Radical Party's *Oeuvre* joined an anti-Semitic chorus castigating Eastern European Jewish refugees in Paris for turning the city into a "nest of microbes." And shockingly, during Blum's Popular Front, a number of delegates from the SFIO, which Blum had led for so many years, accused Blum and his fellow Jewish

Leftist anti-Semitism in France, as elsewhere, emanated not only from the Enlightenment secularist critique but also from racial and economic roots. We shall have an opportunity to revisit leftist anti-Semitism later.

But it would be unfair to conclude that the secularist critique in France resided soley within the French left. The theme of Jewish intolerance caught the attention of the eminent nineteenth-century French scholar Ernst Renan. In Renan's highly influential work of 1863, *Life of Jesus*, Jesus is portrayed as a critic of the dogmatism and intolerance of the Old Testament. Renan's *Life of Jesus* is reported to have been the second most widely read book in France at the time, after the Bible. The book sold 100,000 copies in its first few months and was quickly translated into ten different languages. Renan praises Christianity as universal and the eternal religion of humanity and castigates Judaism for its tribalistic, narrow, intolerant, and antisocial tendencies. Five years after the publication of Renan's *Life of Jesus*, Louis Jacolliot would pick up the themes of Jewish intolerance and rigidity in his *Bible dans l'Inde*, which went through eight editions. Jacolliot denigrated the Jewish Old Testament as a collection of superstitions and characterized Moses as a fanatical slave.[113]

## GERMANY

Within the German speaking zones of Europe, the secularist interpretation of Jewish particularism found favor among many intellectuals. Despite the views of Weiss and Davidowicz, who have argued that the secular liberalism emanating from the Enlightenment had limited influence on the evolution of religious anti-Semitism in Germany compared to England, France, and Scotland, it appears that the Enlightenment commentary on Jewish particularism had its adherents.[114] Some German thinkers, such as Lessing and von Humboldt, embraced the contractual view of the Enlightenment, believing that Jews, if granted equality,

Popular Front members (Jules Moch and Salomon Grumbach) of pushing France into an antifascist war. The implication was clear that it was their "Jewishness" that led them to behave as they did (Byrnes, *Antisemitism*, 117–25; Weber, *Hollow*, 103; Birnbaum, *Anti-Semitism*, 209–15).

[113] Mosse, *Final Solution*, 129–30; Leon Poliakov, *The Aryan Myth: A History of Racist and Nationalist Ideas in Europe*, trans. Edmund Howard (New York, 1971), 208–09; Lindemann, *Esau's*, 87.

[114] Weiss, *Ideology*; Lucy S. Dawidowicz, *The War against the Jews, 1933–1945* (New York, 1975).

would abandon their particularistic behavior and attitudes.[115] Other German writers took a more pessimistic view of Jewish assimilation. For them, a systematic understanding of Jewish religious texts provided the keys to Jewish particularism. Karl August von Hase's 1829 *Life of Jesus* and David Friedrich Strauss's 1835 *Life of Jesus* provide notable examples of scholarship identifying the causes of Jewish intolerance and narrow particularism in the unbending application of law in biblical Judaism. In these works, Jesus is portrayed as a critic of the dogmatism and intolerance of the Old Testament. While von Hase and Strauss drew from the Old Testament to support their arguments, August Rohling's 1871 *Talmud-Jude* enlists the Jewish Talmud in his efforts to explain Jewish particularism. Rohling held academic positions as a professor of Catholic theology and, subsequently, as professor of Semitic languages at the German University of Prague. In Rohling's work, the Talmud instructs Jews to treat Christians as servants and permits Jews to violate Christian women and charge Christians exorbitant rates of interest on loans. Furthermore, Rohling remarked that the Talmud laid out a program of Jewish world domination. Not surprisingly, Rohling volunteered his services as an expert witness for the prosecution in the infamous Hungarian ritual murder trial at Tisza-Eszlar in 1883. Rohling testified that Jews were commanded by their religious texts to perform such practices as ritual murder.[116]

During the second half of the nineteenth century, several prominent German intellectuals would question the commitment of German Jews to forsake their historical particularism and to integrate themselves into the German national community. Among this group of German intellectuals, Heinrich von Treitschke, the celebrated German historian, stands out. Treitschke, in a series of articles between 1879 and 1880 in the prestigious *Preussische Jahrbücher*, questioned the Jews' willingness to abandon their parochial allegiances and their desire to assimilate fully into German society. Treitschke, along with Richard Wagner and Paul de Lagarde, urged German Jews to accelerate the pace of their assimilation into German society.[117] Even German liberals, such as Theodor Mommsen, Rudolf Virchow, and Johann Gustav Droysen, who by no means shared the overall politically conservative viewpoints of

---

[115] Levy, *Downfall*, 9.
[116] Mosse, *Final Solution*, 129–40; Lindemann, *Esau's* 87.
[117] Donald L. Niewyk, "Solving the "Jewish Problem" – Continuity and Change in German Antisemitism 1871–1945." *Leo Baeck Institute Year Book*, vol. 35, 1990, 338; Byrnes, *Antisemitism*, 81; Lindemann, *Esau's*, 131–36.

Wagner, de Lagarde, and von Trietschke, pointed to the persistence of Jewish particularism as a barrier to full assimilation. The German liberal stand found voice in an article in the *Kölnische Zeitung*, the National Liberal Party's newspaper. The newspaper called on German Jews to prove themselves worthy of full membership in the German nation by abandoning their allegiance to the Progressive party, Zionism, and the Parisian-based *Alliance Israelite Universelle*.[118] Beyond alleged Jewish support for these particular organizations, German liberals urged Jews to abandon ritual practices that distinguished Jews from other Germans. Included here were the Jewish sabbath, circumcision, special dietary laws, and the kosher slaughter of animals.[119]

Much like their counterparts in France, German nineteenth-century socialists embraced the Enlightenment attacks on the Jewish Old Testament and the Jewish origins of Christianity. Bruno Bauer and other "Young Hegelians," heavily influenced by the Voltairian rebuke of Jewish particularism, condemned Judaism as both a fossilized and an antiprogressive belief system. They argued that Jews must be denied emancipation unless they abandon their exclusionist and particularist essence. For the "Young Hegelians," Jewish irrational and persistent attachment to absurd rituals and taboos indicated that the Jews refused to accept equal membership in the human family. Karl Marx fully embraced the Voltairian critique of his fellow "Young Hegelians" and denigrated Judaism for its antisocial essence. Marx's chief statement on the Jewish religion appeared in his 1844 essay *Zur Judenfrage* (On the Jewish Question). Though his essay dealt largely with the economic role of Jews as moneymakers, he chastised Judaism as a reactionary religion that promoted such antisocial behaviors as parasitism and clannishness. In particular, Marx suggested that the secular basis of Judaism was practical need and self-interest. Nevertheless, Marx was a firm advocate of Jewish emancipation in that it fit into his dialectical materialist model of social change. For Marx, Jewish emancipation was consistent with the principles of bourgeois society, but Judaism and Jewish particularism would inevitably disappear in the new socialist order. Marx bequeathed an ambivalent position on Judaism to his socialist followers – a position that greatly shaped leftist anti-Semitism for generations.[120]

---

[118] Niewyk, "Solving," 339.

[119] Ibid.

[120] Robert S. Wistrich, *Socialism and the Jews: The Dilemmas of Assimilation in Germany and Austria-Hungary* (Rutherford, NJ, 1982), 19–30; Lindemann,

Ferdinand Lassalle, the founder and president of the General Association of German Workers and, like Marx, descended from a Jewish lineage, stood out as a harsh critic of Jews. Karl Kautsky, editor of the Social
Democratic Party's journal *Neue Zeit*, which was generally sympathetic
to Jewish rights, cited Jewish self-segregation, failure to assimilate, and
stubborn attachment to a distinctive religion, customs, and language
as motivating factors in the mob attacks on Russian Jews in the hor-
rific Kishinev pogrom of 1903.[121] Unrivaled among German socialists
for vituperative anti-Semitism was Eugen Duehring. Duehring's widely
read 1880 *Die Judenfrage als Rassen-Sitten-und Kulturfrage* (The Jewish
Question as a question of race, manners, and culture) gave an ideological foundation to the racial struggle against Jews and Judaism. We will
have the occasion to examine Duehring's contributions to racial anti-
Semitism later; here we focus on Duehring's secularist attack on Judaism
and his place in the pantheon of leading German anti-Semitic socialists.
Duehring, a lecturer in philosophy and economics at the University of
Berlin, asserted that the renewal of German culture required a firm dis-
avowal of the Old and New Testaments and a total emancipation from
the Judeo-Christian yoke. Moreover, he presented a model of German
socialism in which he advocated a national self-sufficiency that was the
antithesis of the Jewish socialism of Marx and Lassalle.[122] Duehring's
anti-Semitic writings (and most definitely his attack on Marx) spawned
Engel's direct rebuke of Duehring in his *Anti-Duehring* and may have
contributed greatly to the German Social Democratic movement's shift
away from anti-Semitism.[123]

### GREAT BRITAIN

The dichotomization of the backward/particularistic Judaism and the
modern/universalist Christianity found a favorable reception in Great
Britain. Baden Powell, philospher, theologian, and professor of geom-
etry at Oxford University, published his *Christianity without Judaism* in
1857. In order to uphold the integrity of Christianity, Powell sought to

Esau's, 161; Massing, *Rehearsal*, 159; Byrnes, *Antisemitism*, 115–17; Niall Ferguson, *The World's Banker: The History of the House of Rothschild* (London, 1998),
464.

[121] Jack Wertheimer, *Unwelcome Strangers: East European Jews in Imperial Germany*
(New York and Oxford, 1987), 39–40.

[122] Mosse, *Final Solution* 165; Wistrich, *Socialism*, 48–54; Berding, *Moderner*, 146f.

[123] Wistrich, *Socialism*, 48–50.

undermine the Mosaic foundations of the Hebrew Old Testament. In Powell's account, the Old Testament writings, based largely on outdated theistic thinking, presented a particularistic and nonobjective account of the physical world. Furthermore, the roots of Jewish intolerance and anachronistic and antisocial behavior (e.g., circumcision and prohibitions on intermarriage) were to be found in the Old Testament. Mathew Arnold, the most celebrated Victorian Hellenist, presented in his 1869 *Culture and Anarchy* a systematic comparison of Hebraism and Hellenism in which he stressed the former's pursuit of conduct and obedience and its subjugation of freedom of spirit and intellect. The well-known British historian Goldwin Smith echoed the depiction of the superiority of the Christianity over Judaism as a declaration of humanity and universalism in an essay published in the *Contemporary Review* in February 1878. In Goldwin Smith's semiscientific essay, he asserted that Judaism constituted the highest level reached by a tribal religion.

Employing interpretations of Hebrew texts to support arguments about the distinctiveness of Jewish behavior found adherents outside of mainstream British academia. As the last half of the nineteenth century unfolded, British Evangelical theology increasingly emphasized the arrested development of Judaism and portrayed the Judaism of the Old Testament as a religion of prohibition, punishment, and particularism. Thus, not surprisingly, in 1887, the *Saint James Gazette*, commenting on the lack of assimilation of recent Jewish immigrants in Great Britain, concluded that Jews could never become fully assimilated in England, for they refused to abandon their Hebrew ways.[124]

Like the left in France and Germany, the British left played a central role in the popular dissemination of anti-Semitism in late nineteenth- and early twentieth-century Britain.[125] Rubinstein points to three principal sources of British leftist anti-Semitism. The three sources of opposition to Jews are Jewish claims for a corporate national identity (Jewish homeland), Jewish involvement in capitalism and British imperialism, and the Jewish attachment to an antiprogressive and primitive religion.[126] The lion's share of British leftist anti-Semitism was of the economic variety. The socialist left in Great Britain, from the time of Karl Marx and Friedrich Engels, had targeted the "capitalist Jew" and

---

[124] Feldman, *Englishmen*, 83–91, 294.

[125] Holmes, *British*, 24; W. D. Rubinstein, *A History of the Jews in the English-Speaking World: Great Britain* (New York, 1996), 112–13.

[126] Rubinstein, *History*, 219–20.

the "Jewish gold international." We will examine much of the socialist left's economic anti-Semitism later, in the discussion of the economic root of anti-Semitism. Nonetheless, hints of a secular critique of Judaism and Jews resided with the British left. Beatrice Potter Webb, the highly popular late Victorian and Edwardian novelist and social observer, linked the extreme instrumentality of Jewish social behavior and Jewish world-liness to a Jewish intellect conditioned by centuries of Talmudic study. And during the interwar period, the prominent Fabian intellectual H.G. Wells blamed anti-Semitism substantially on the particular Jewish attachment to the concept of the Jews as "chosen people."[127]

## ROMANIA

As elsewhere in nineteenth-century Europe, well-known and respected Romanian intellectuals played pivotal roles in the spread of anti-Semitism and frequently criticized Judaism from a secularist basis. Con-stantin Stere (1865–1936) picked up on Voltaire's criticism of Judaism as antiprogressive. For Stere, Judaism's archaic nature inevitably led to conflict with modern cultures. Judaism turned Jews into an autonomous social and political group opposed to all innovation and marked by a fe-rocious and fanatical exclusiveness. Stere noted further that Jews would have to renounce their culture and abandon "the stranglehold of the Talmud" in order to integrate successfully into a universal culture. Yet Stere believed that Jews would resist assimilation because it would lead to the disappearance of the Jews as a distinctive cultural type.[128] Nicolae C. Paulescu claimed in 1922 that Jews, instinctively acquisitive, sought to rule over others and planned to obtain world power. According to Paulescu, the Talmud instructed the Jews toward these objectives. For Paulescu, the doctrine of the Talmud and the institution of the Cahal re-vealed the means by which the Jews would secure world domination and exterminate other peoples.[129] Besides intellectuals, the perception of Jewish separateness influenced the thinking of prominent Romanian statesmen. Mihail Kogălniceanu, a late nineteenth-century Romanian foreign minister, fretted publicly about the unassimilated character of the hordes of Jews emigrating to Romania from Russia. Kogălniceanu,

---

[127] Feldman, *Englishmen*, 83–91, 294; Rubinstein, *History*, 220–22.
[128] Volovici, *Nationalist*, 35–36.
[129] Ibid., 29.

relatively moderate in terms of his anti-Semitic views, called upon Romania's Jews to embrace assimilation.[130]

Whereas the literature on British, French, and German anti-Semitism displays ample evidence of a leftist anti-Semitism in those societies during the nineteenth and early twentieth centuries, I could find no evidence of a leftist-inspired anti-Semitism in Romania before the Holocaust. If indeed the Romanian left shunned anti-Semitic declarations before the Holocaust, this may largely be attributed to the late development and weakness of the Romanian left and to its unmistakenly foreign and Jewish makeup. As we will see in the discussion of the political root of anti-Semitism, Jews and non-Romanians dominated the Marxist left in Romania virtually from its origins in the last decade of the nineteenth century to the outbreak of World War II.

## ITALY

Widespread acceptance and use of the Enlightenment critique emphasizing the ritualistic and antiprogressive character of Judaism never materialized in Italy to the extent that it did north of the Alps. Italian Jews for the most part wrote and spoke in the various Italian dialects, and Italian Jewish orthodoxy was markedly less rigid than in most other European countries. Hughes ascribes the failure of the Jewish Reform movement to catch on in Italy during the nineteenth and twentieth centuries to the assimilationist and yielding attitudes of Italian Jews.[131] One possible measure of the assimilationist attitudes of Italian Jewry is the high rate of mixed marriages between Jews and non-Jews. Steinberg observes that a 1938 census report documents that 43.7 per cent of Italian marriages involving Jews were marriages in which one partner was not Jewish. According to Steinberg, the rate of intermarriage involving Jews was markedly higher in Italy than it was elsewhere in Europe.[132] But it would be wrong to assume that the Enlightenment opprobrium of Judaism had no adherents in Italy. In the last decades of the eighteenth century, Italian adherents of the "*illuministi*" movement, such as G. B. G. d'Arco, Pietro Regis, Giovanni Antonio Ranza,

---

[130] Oldson, *Providential*, 101–09.

[131] H. Stuart Hughes, *Prisoners of Hope: The Silver Age of the Italian Jews 1924–1974* (Cambridge, MA, 1983), 9–11.

[132] Jonathan Steinberg, *All or Nothing: The Axis and the Holocaust 1941–1943* (London and New York, 1990), 222–23.

and Giuseppe Compagnoni, while favoring the Enlightenment's call for
the emancipation of Jews, noted the obstacles to integration presented
by Jewish intolerance and antisocial behavior, which they attributed
to the dogma and rituals of the Jewish religion. Decades later, in the
poems (*Sonetti Romaneschi*) of the mid-nineteenth-century Roman poet
G. G. Belli, we find Voltairian anti-Semitic notions of Jewish elitism,
clannishness, and exclusionism.[133] During the Risorgimento, an anti-
clerical anti-Semitism found favor in the works of a group of Italian
writers, including della Gattina, Ellero, Ferrari, and Guerrazzi. And in
the post-Risorgimento period, Giosuè Carducci claimed in his *In una
chiesa gotica* (1876) that the Judeo-Christian tradition, rooted in the
Jewish ethos, had destroyed the joy, beauty, and freedom embodied in
the Aryan Greco-Latin nature. Carducci's attack on the Jewish foundation of Western Christian culture was part of a larger campaign against
organized religion and in support of paganism.[134]

In comparison to the political left's embrace of anti-Semitic rhetoric
in France, Germany, and Great Britain, the Italian left rarely took
up the anti-Semitic banner. Antonio Gramsci, Italy's greatest Marx-
ist intellectual, echoing sentiments expressed earlier by the renowned
Italian political philosopher Benedetto Croce, attributed the absence of
Italian anti-Semitism to the highly successful assimilation of Jews in
Italy. Italian national unification had made Italian Jews part of the nation in the same way that it had made Italians out of the inhabitants of
Piedmont and Naples, according to Gramsci.[135] Scattered leftist anti-
Semitic rumblings seem to have surfaced during the Dreyfus Affair. To
that end, Gentile reminds us that before the publication of Zola's famous letter defending Dreyfus, the Italian socialist movement, through
its newspaper, *Avanti!*, claimed that the Dreyfus Affair was a plot hatched
by rich French Jews.[136]

Figure 2.1 presents the results of an examination of religious anti-
Semitic acts in the *American Jewish Year Book* and religious anti-Semitic
attitudes in the five principal European daily newspapers between 1899

---

[133] Gunzberg, *Strangers*, 28–30, 112.
[134] Canepa, "Image," 264; Gunzberg, *Strangers*, 168–84. Also, Canepa ("Image,"
269–70) implies elsewhere that in the years between Italian unity and World
War I, anti-Semitism, deriving from a notion of Judaism's inferior religious status
and from alleged negative Jewish traits such as venality and coarseness, was more
widespread in Italy than is generally assumed.
[135] Gunzberg, *Strangers*, 55.
[136] Gentile, "Struggle," 499–500.

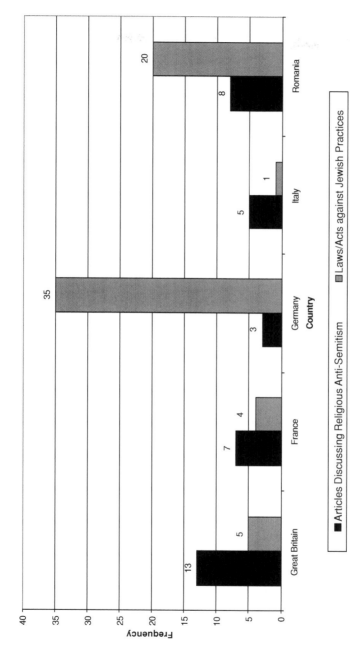

Figure 2.1. Newspaper articles discussing religious anti-Semitism and laws/acts against Jewish practices by country, 1899–1939. *Note:* Articles are taken from the fifteenth day of the month for every month between 1899 and 1939. Articles were taken from the *Daily Mail* in Great Britain (N = 299), *Le Petit Parisien* in France (N = 199), *Berliner Morgenpost* in Germany (N = 269), *Corriere della Sera* in Italy (N = 101), and *Universul* in Romania (N = 136). Laws and acts against Jewish practices were obtained from the volumes of the *American Jewish Year Book* (see category 5 in Table 1.1).

and 1939. Not surprisingly, the overall number of newspaper articles coded as religious anti-Semitic is relatively low. Traditional religious anti-Semitism had lost much of its appeal by the twentieth century, especially in Western Europe. Regarding religious anti-Semitic acts, we find higher numbers in Germany and Romania and the lowest count in Italy. In the case of Germany, fourteen of the religious anti-Semitic acts reported occurred between 1933 and 1939.[137]

Of the four principal roots of Jewish hatred, the religious root has been with us the longest. The traditional form of religious anti-Semitism – based on the role Jews played in the crucifixion of Christ, the failure of Jews to accept Jesus as the Savior, and the popular negative Jewish stereotypes – gained momentum during the European medieval period. With the onset of the European Enlightenment in the late eighteenth century and the gradual waning of the authority of traditional religious beliefs, a new form of anti-Semitism, based on a supposedly more systematic and scientific study of religion, appeared. The Enlightenment critique of Judaism tended to attract a better-educated following than traditional religious anti-Semitism. The secular prejudice focused on Jewish particularism deriving, in the view of the proponents, from the distinctive Jewish culture. Adherents of the secular critique differed on the question of whether Jews could break free from their cultural inheritance and successfully assimilate into Gentile society. Whether one drew upon the traditional religious prejudice against Jews or used the secular argument, the common assumption held that once Jews converted to Christianity or abandoned the Jewish faith, the "Jewish Problem" would disappear. However, as the nineteenth century unfolded, a new form of anti-Semitism emerged that would not see conversion or rejection of the faith as a sufficient solution to the "Jewish Problem." For among the followers of this new form of anti-Semitism, Jews constituted a separate and pernicious race, and only through enforced social isolation or physical removal could the problem of the place of Jews in society find a resolution. We now turn to the second principal form of anti-Semitism, the racial root.

---

[137] Approximately two-thirds of the newspaper articles coded as religious anti-Semitic focused on criticisms of Jewish practices or beliefs. The remaining one-third of the articles dealt with claims that Judaism threatened Christianity. We found no articles associating Jews with anti-progressive beliefs. Furthermore, we found no significant differences in reportage on religious anti-Semitism between the principal and secondary newspapers within each of the five countries.

# CHAPTER THREE

# THE RACIAL ROOT

During the latter half of the nineteenth century, Jews were increasingly depicted as members of a unique race rather than as members of a separate religious group. Spurred on by European colonialism, nationalistic fervor, and fear of immigration, the new science of race dug deep roots into European mass culture. "Scientific racism," or "race science," referred to the ideology that differences in human behavior derive from inherent group characteristics, and that human differences can be demonstrated through anthropological, biological, and statistical proofs.[1] During the nineteenth century, race science rose and gained respectability. To assert that race science won wide acceptability by no means overstates the case. Between 1870 and 1940, race science was not merely the ideology of an extremist fringe of rabid anti-Semitic demagogues. The belief in the existence of separate races and that fundamental differences among races derived from physical and psychological attributes was shared by all social classes and ethnic groups, including well-educated Jews.[2] Proponents of racial theory held a firm belief that there are inexorable natural laws, beyond the control of humans, governing individuals and cultures. Arguments that territorial national sovereignty should be based on a culturally identifiable nation and that the superior cultures of Europe had the right and duty to colonize non-European areas of the world found justification in scientific racism.

The impact of scientific racism on European Jewry would be profound, for race science permitted anti-Semites to attire their hatred of Jews in

---

[1] Efron, *Defenders*, 3.
[2] Ibid., 176.

the disguise of science.[3] By drawing upon the contributions of a number of scientific and social scientific fields, race science gained a high degree of intellectual credibility and social acceptability. In particular, scientific racism benefited from the emergence of modern anthropology, Darwinian biology, and the science of eugenics.[4] Employing theories and evidence (oftentimes statistical evidence) from these new scholarly fields, an array of scholars and writers challenged the Enlightenment commitment to human equality and proposed that there are inherent qualitative differences among races and that there exists a natural hierarchic order of races.[5]

The science of anthropology, which gained the status of an independent science around 1860, stressed the division of human groups by the physical and cultural attributes of their members. Anthropologists sought to classify human groups through the methods of observation, measurement, and comparison. Mid-nineteenth-century anthropologists borrowed from earlier advances made in physiognomy, phrenology, and craniology. These sciences offered anthropologists means to distinguish among human groups on the basis of facial and cranial features. The pioneering work of Paul Broca, professor of clinical surgery and founder of the Anthropological Society in Paris in 1859, helped to pave the way for the linking of craniology and anthropology. Broca had argued that, through the measuring of human skulls, scholars could describe human groups and evaluate their relative worth. What began as a taxonomic

---

[3] Efron, *Defenders*, 3; Wilson, *Ideology*, 494. Discrimination against Jews by virtue of race has roots in late fifteenth- and early sixteenth-century Spain. Spanish statutes relating to the "purity of blood" (*Estatutos de limpieza de sangre*) were used against "new Christians," who were converted Spanish Jews or converted Moors. Both converted Jews and Moors were said to belong to an inferior race and accused of constituting a foreign body in Spanish society. The Spanish statutes prevented anyone with Jewish ancestry from holding prominent positions within Spanish society (Poliakov, *Aryan*, 327; Wistrich, *Antisemitism*, 36–37; Kertzer, *The Popes*, 207; Carroll, *Constantine's Sword*, 360–61).

[4] Efron, *Defenders*, 3; Arendt, *Origins*; Wilson, *Ideology*; Bernstein, *Hannah*, 79; Massing, *Rehearsal*, 82.

[5] Efron, *Defenders*, 175; Massing, *Rehearsal*, 82; Poliakov, *Aryan*, 255–64; Mosse, *Germans*, 53; Fein, "Explanations," 18. Mosse (*Final Solution*, 3) believes that the contributions from late eighteenth-century evangelism and pietism helped to shape nineteenth-century racism by their emphases on intuition, instincts, and the emotional life of the "inner man."

description eventually evolved into the scientific construction of a racial hierarchy.[6]

Even before Charles Darwin's scientific undertakings, biological terminology had begun to find its way into racist and nationalist discourse. During the late eighteenth century, intellectuals began to employ the organic analogy. The organic analogy envisioned society as a living organism involving a mutuality of dependence and interdependence among parts and the whole. Late eighteenth- and early nineteenth-century European romanticism applied the organic analogy to the concept of the nation. Eventually, some nationalists would use the romanticist concept of the nation to purport that the presence of foreigners constituted a grave threat to the health of the nation.[7] The concepts of "natural selection," "the survival of the fittest," and "biological heritage of humans" put forward by Charles Darwin in his 1859 classic work, *Origin of Species*, were not inherently racial. However, Darwin's theories were appropriated and, in many instances, distorted by racist thinkers in order to validate a series of claims, including that there exists a natural inequality of human groups, that society is an arena of biological struggle, and that the nation is the chief inculcator and vehicle of racial development. For instance, racial thinkers employed Darwin's conjecture about the extinction of less improved forms to make claims about the prospects for inferior races and changed Darwin's assertion of the importance of *environmental* factors in the evolutionary process to the decisive role of *heredity* to explain natural selection and variation of species.[8]

The third principal intellectual or scientific contribution to racial theory came from eugenics. Francis Galton, a cousin of Charles Darwin and the founder of the science of eugenics, published his *Hereditary Genius* in 1869. Coining the term "eugenics" (from the Greek "good in birth" or "noble in heredity"), Galton claimed that, like physical qualities, intelligence was a product of heredity. From his observations of

---

[6] Poliakov, *Aryan*, 264; Stephen Jay Gould, *The Mismeasure of Man* (New York, 1981), 82–84; Mosse, *Final Solution*, 2–3; Steiman, *Paths*, 132; Efron, *Defenders*. Mosse (*Final Solution*, 2–3) notes that though the new science of racism drew on anatomical measurements, observations, and comparisons of human groups, these factors increasingly lost ground to an aesthetic criterion of beauty derived from ancient Greece.

[7] Steiman, *Paths*, 122.

[8] Steinman, *Paths*, 132; Mosse, *Final Solution*, 72–73; Richard M. Lerner, *Final Solutions: Biology, Prejudice, and Genocide* (University Park, PA, 1992), 11–13.

the variation in abilities and talents of different families, he devised a numerical scale, which he claimed would allow science to rank the major races. He proposed that by creating policies based on his quantitative measurements, nations could successfully develop the capacity to breed highly gifted humans. Galton was keenly interested in social salvation and proposed that maintaining a healthy and strong society would require the altering of the relative fertility of good and bad stocks in the community. He encouraged governments to pay attention to the civic worth of the progeny and to discourage high birth rates among the unfit races or the degenerate breeding stocks. Galton's notions of racial hygiene and breeding had gained widespread scientific respectability throughout Europe and the United States by the time of his death in 1911.[9] Though Galton's science of eugenics was meant to have application for all races, Galton did, according to Gilman, imply that the Jewish race constituted a lower strain and that Jewish genius was, in reality, craftiness rather than intelligence. In his 1892 Presidential Address to the International Congress of Demography, Galton proposed that restrictions on Jewish and Chinese immigration to the West would have a salutary effect on the evolution of the human species in that part of the world.[10]

With the notable exception of Galton's derogatory remarks about Jews and Chinese, the science of eugenics did not provide a full-blown theory defining race and did not specify which were the superior and inferior races. The evolution of a comprehensive race science benefited not only from the merging of eugenics with European anthropological notions of the hierarchy of races and biological Darwinian concepts of "survival of the fittest" and "natural selection," but also from the impact of a rising nationalism, a frenzied European colonialism, and massive immigration.[11]

With the awakening of national consciousness throughout the mid nineteenth century, European nationalism became fused with racism. The eighteenth-century Enlightenment focused attention on the concept of the nation. The French Revolution's Declaration of Universal Rights called for the rights of life, liberty, and the pursuit of happiness

[9] Poliakov, *Aryan*, 291–92; Lerner, *Final Solutions*, 11–13; Mosse, *Final Solution*, 73–75.

[10] Sander L. Gilman, *Smart Jews: The Construction of the Image of Jewish Superior Intelligence* (Lincoln and London, 1996), 39.

[11] Higham, *Strangers*, 149–57.

and for equality before the law for all citizens of the nation. However, as the nineteenth century unfolded, advocates of nationalism turned away from the cosmopolitanism of the Enlightenment and asserted that rights were national and would be guaranteed only for those who belonged to the *culturally identifiable nation*. Emphases on a common history, shared language, and shared emotions increasingly defined a nation, and during the nineteenth century, these emphases tended to be strongest in those societies seeking national unification, such as Germany and Romania, or in those societies having recently experienced a national humiliation, such as France.[12] The philosophical writings of Johann Gottfried von Herder, the great late eighteenth-century German thinker, are crucial to the linking of the nation to a shared culture and language. For Herder, the nation is distinguished by the inner spirit of the people (*Volksgeist*) expressed through culture and language. Herder's writings spurred a gen-eration of philologists and German Romanticists who sought to trace the linguistic origins of European peoples. Among the major conclusions of these early nineteenth-century philologists and Romanticists was that at the foundation of Western languages lay the ancient Indian language of Sanskrit. Sanskrit, which was claimed to share structural similarities with German, Greek, and Latin, was said to have been brought to Europe by the migration of ancient Aryan tribes. The term Aryan derived from the Sanskrit word for "noble."[13] In time, a shared language, culture, and history arose as chief markers of both nation and race. The national community soon became synonymous with the racial community, and Europeans increasingly identified themselves less as members of *Homo Europeus* and more as members of a French, German, or Slavic race.[14] It should be noted that the concept of race in the nineteenth and early twentieth centuries frequently encompassed supranational boundaries. For example, within Europe and the United States, racial thinking in-cluded occasional references to the Alpine, Mediterranean, and Nordic races.[15]

The rise of northern Europe as a world power and its resulting rule over the indigenous peoples outside of Europe gave enormous credibility

---

[12] France suffered a major trauma from its catastrophic and sudden military defeat at the hands of Prussia in 1870–71.

[13] According to Mosse (*Final Solution*, 39), this marks the first appearance of the term "Aryan" in European intellectual discourse.

[14] Bernstein, *Hannah*, 79, 180; Mosse, *Final Solution*, 33–39; Lindemann, *Esau's*, 85–86.

[15] Higham, *Strangers*, 149–57.

to the existence of racial hierarchies. As northern European states extended their rule into Africa, Asia, Oceania, and the West Indies, travel to and knowledge of these less developed regions of the world increased. But how did the nation states of Western Europe justify the subjugation of these lands and people? The answer took the form of extending "civilization" to primitive peoples. In other words, it was the mission of the nations of Christian Europe – with their superior faith – to aid in the development of those less fortunate societies. To Europeans, the fact that it was Christian Europe civilizing non-Europeans, rather than the reverse, could be explained only by the racial superiority of Christian Europeans.[16] But European countries varied in terms of their colonial reach. Belgium, France, Great Britain, the Netherlands, Portugal, and Spain were early colonizers. Among them, Great Britain and France benefited the most in the scramble for colonies in Africa and Asia. Late national unification hindered German and Italian colonialism. Germany entered the colonial race relatively late, acquiring colonies in 1884 in parts of the Cameroons, East Africa, and southwest Africa and establishing a colonial base in China in 1897. Italy grabbed Libya and parts of Somalia late in the nineteenth century but suffered a military setback in its attempt to capture Abyssinia (Ethiopia) in 1896. Romania had no colonies, for it lacked the resources to establish overseas colonies and was preoccupied with reannexing bordering territories having sizable Romanian populations.

In terms of race science, where did the Jews reside? Race science took no definitive stance on the place of Jews within a racial hierarchy. Moreover, at times Jews were alternately referred to as members of a particular race and as members of various races.[17] Also, it would be

---

[16] R. W. Connell, "Why Is Classical Theory Classical?" *American Journal of Sociology*, vol. 102, no. 6, 1997, 1522; Poliakov, *Aryan*, 225; Mosse, *Final Solution*, 12–13; Steiman, *Paths*, 130; Efron, *Defenders*, 28; Dilip Hiro, *Black British White British: A History of Race Relations in Britain* (London, 1991), 5; Lebzelter, "Anti-Semitism," 92.

[17] Discussions of a Jewish race surface at least as early as the European Enlightenment. Wilhelm Christian Dohm, the famous German Enlightenment thinker, at first considered the Jews to be of Asiatic origin but by 1781 had declared them to be white and capable of enlightenment. At the end of the eighteenth century, Johann Kaspar Lavater, in classifying human faces, failed to distinguish significantly between Christian Europeans and Jews by giving the Jews aquiline noses and pointed chins (Mosse, *Final Solution*, 14). Perhaps this benign treatment resulted partly from ignorance of Jews, for most European Jews lived behind ghetto walls at the time of the Enlightenment.

incorrect to assume that *all* racial scientists were anti-Semitic. In fact, anti-Semitism found no home in the writings of the best known mid-nineteenth-century racial theorist, Count Arthur de Gobineau. In his widely read *Essay on the Inequality of Human Races*, Gobineau wrote of three principal races: black, white, and yellow. Gobineau considered the white race to be superior to the black and yellow races. In contrast to the other two major races, the white race was blessed with the two critical elements of civilization, a religion and a history, according to Gobineau. Drawing on the research of the early nineteenth-century philologists, Gobineau asserted that the white race had originated in Asia and had eventually divided into the Ham (Hamites), Shem (Semites), and Japheth (Aryan) branches. Over time, through conquest and expansion, the Hamites and the Semites (to a lesser degree) had saturated themselves with black blood. The sons of Japheth (Aryans) remained pure until the early Christian era, but then, through their expansion, experienced some race mixing. Applying the laws of "historical chemistry" to the races, Gobineau concluded that the mixing of races inevitably leads to a weakening of each strain and ultimately to self-annihilation. Proponents of racial anti-Semitism would appropriate Gobineau's general assertions of racial degeneration and the fall of civilization to their own attacks on the allegedly pernicious role that Jews played in national degeneration in Europe.[18]

Gobineau was not the only prominent racial scientist who refused to embrace anti-Semitism. The influential scholar René Taine, whose 1863 *Histoire de la littérature anglaise* did much to provide currency to race as a tool in sociohistorical studies, refrained from employing anti-Semitism.[19] And as George Mosse has forcefully argued, many racial biologists in England and Germany rejected anti-Semitic claims of Jewish racial inferiority. Alfred Ploetz, the principal founder of racial biology in Germany, considered the majority of Jews to be Aryans, and Fritz Lenz, a prominent leader of the German Society for Racial Hygiene, spoke to the incompatibility between fanatical anti-Semitism and racial hygiene.[20]

---

[18] Poliakov, *Aryan*, 233–37; Mosse, *Final Solution*, 55–56; Dimont, *Jews*, 320.

[19] Wilson, *Ideology*, 472–73.

[20] Mosse, *Final Solution*, 80–82. Further, Mosse (*Final Solution*, 82) points to a sea change regarding the compatibility of a fervent anti-Semitism and racial hygiene occurring after 1935 in Germany in the publications of the German *Journal for Racial and Social Biology*.

How is it, then, that anti-Semitism became increasingly interwoven with racial thinking? By themselves, the advent of European colonialism and the project of national unification could hardly constitute a fertile context in which racial anti-Semitism would flourish. Moreover, before 1881, the relatively small Jewish population of Western Europe seemed, in the minds of many Gentiles and Jews, to be on the road to assimilation. This was, however, about to change with the westward march of Russian and Eastern European Jewish immigrants. The wave of Eastern European and Russian Jewish immigration fueled a firestorm of racial anti-Semitism.

As late as 1900, a preponderant majority of the 10.6 million Jews throughout the world were Ashkenazim residing in East Central Europe.[21] The term "Ashkenazi" comes from the Hebrew word for German. The Ashkenazim had from the Middle Ages spoken Yiddish, a language derived from German. In addition to the Ashkenazim, there were Oriental and Sephardic Jewish branches. Oriental Jews, comprising less than five percent of the world's Jewish population, resided largely in the Near East (Asia Minor, Babylon, the former Persia, and parts of Syria), while the Sephardic Jews lived along the Mediterranean coast and, to a large extent, had settled in Spain since the Mohammedan period. After 1492, nearly one-quarter of a million Sephardic Jews left Spain to settle in the Balkans, Italy, and North Africa. The term "Sephardic" originates in the Hebrew word for Spain, "Sephard." The separate branches also differed from one another by virtue of ritual, dress, and language.[22]

Occasional migrations or forced relocations of Ashkenazic Jews had occurred between 1750 and 1850, with Bukovina, northeastern Hungary, Moldavia, and the Pale of Settlement serving as the principal settlements. One of the largest forced resettlements of Jews took place between 1795 and 1835 with the establishment of the Pale of Settlement within the czarist Russian Empire. Ruppin adds that roughly one-quarter of a million Jews emigrated from East Central Europe between 1800 and 1880.[23] But events beginning in 1881, primarily within

---

[21] There seems to be no consensus about the percentage of Ashkenazim. Paul Robert Magocsi (*Historical Atlas of East Central Europe*, Seattle, 1993, 107) cites seventy percent, although Ruppin (*Jews*, 9–10) refers to roughly ninety percent.

[22] Magocsi, *Atlas*, 107–09; Ruppin, *Jews*, 9–10. With the exception of Yemeni Jews, Oriental and Sephardic Jews share a similar liturgy.

[23] Ruppin, *Jews*, 45–46.

the Russian Empire, would turn the stream of Ashkenazic emigration into a flood. The events that sparked the beginnings of the massive Jewish emigration occurred in April and May of 1881 in the wake of the assassination of Czar Alexander II. The assassins belonged to the revolutionary Narodnaya Volya terrorist group. Among the plotters was the Jewish-born Gessia Gelfman. Gelfman's Jewish background and participation in the assassination may have ignited the ensuing anti-Jewish outburst. Between April 15 and 16, a violent pogrom aimed at Jews and at Jewish property erupted in Elizabethgrad and spread quickly throughout southwestern Russia, engulfing the cities of Kiev, Kishinev, Odessa, and Yalta. During 1881 alone, more than two hundred pogroms took place in Russia. The authorities generally stood by, refusing to protect the Jews. In 1882, the Russian government instituted the anti-Semitic "May Laws" restricting Jewish residential, educational, and professional access. Substantial anti-Jewish violence erupted again from 1902 to 1906, apparently directed by state authorities. In one particular murderous pogrom in the Bessarabian capital of Kishinev, lasting two days during Passover, forty-five to fifty Jews were murdered and nearly fifteen hundred Jewish residences were destroyed and looted.[24]

The Russian pogroms of the 1880s and the 1900s marked a first major wave of Jewish emigration from East Central Europe. The breakup of the Habsburg, Hollenzollern, and Romanov empires at the end of World War I would usher in a second wave of emigration, followed by a third wave during the 1930s in the wake of Hitler's rise to power in Germany. In the aftermath of World War I, with the emergence of new states in East Central Europe and the fighting between Bolshevik and anti-Bolshevik forces in the former Russian empire, anti-Jewish pogroms erupted in Galicia, Hungary, Poland, the Ukraine, and Russia. Marrus mentions that between 1917 and 1921, anti-Jewish violence resulted in thousands of Jewish deaths and massive destruction of Jewish property.[25] As in the previous decades, a multitude of Ashkenazic Jews in these affected regions of East Central Europe fled westward. After a relative calm in the 1920s, the Jewish refugee flood would again pick up with the imposition of anti-Jewish legislation in Nazi Germany during the mid-1930s. Between 1933 and 1939, a large proportion of Austrian and German Jews emigrated to France, the Netherlands, the United

---

[24] Rubenstein, Auschwitz, 100; Rubinstein, History, 94–95; Byrnes, Antisemitism, 88–90; Feldman, Englishmen, 127–28; Finzi, Anti-Semitism, 54–55.

[25] Marrus, Unwanted, 61–63.

Kingdom, and the United States. In contrast to the two earlier waves, Germany and eventually Austria no longer served as destination points for these Jewish refugees, whose ranks would contain highly assimilated and long-time residents of the German Reich.

In the wake of the anti-Jewish violence and governmental restrictions, Jews began to flee westward. Between 1881 and 1899, Jewish emigration from East Central Europe climbed from a yearly average of 3,000 a year to 50,000. Yearly averages jumped to 135,000 between 1900 and 1914. Jewish emigration would fall during World War I but gather momentum after 1920. In 1921, more than 140,000 Jews emigrated from East Central Europe. With the imposition of immigration restrictions in the United States during the mid-1920s, the yearly average of Jewish emigration declined to around thirty to forty thousand. The rate would rise once again after 1933, with the rise of Nazi Germany's anti-Jewish campaign. The lion's share of the emigrating Ashkenazic Jews eventually settled in North and South America. However, many of those who would ultimately find their way to the Americas transited Western European countries like Germany, Great Britain, and the Netherlands, while others chose Western Europe as their final destination.[26] Where did these Jews settle in Western Europe and what impact did they have on Jewish-Gentile relations?

Ruppin notes that roughly 80,000 foreign Jews settled in France between 1881 and 1930, while Schor observes that some 150,000 Jews, mostly from East Central Europe, took up residence in France between the two world wars.[27] By 1939, the Jewish population of France, which had hovered around 50,000 in 1872 and had comprised between 80,000 and 90,000 in 1900, had reached 300,000, or 0.7 percent of the total French population.[28] Eastern European immigrant Jews tended to settle in Paris, particularly in the third and fourth districts (*arrondissements*).[29] In 1935, nearly 80 percent of the foreign Jews in the Paris region came from Eastern Europe.[30]

In 1871, the Jewish population of the new German Reich stood around 512,000, or 1.25 percent of the total population. By 1910, the

---

[26] Ruppin, *Jews*, 45–46, 62; Marrus, *Unwanted*, 36–37; Pauley, *Prejudice*, 23–26.

[27] Ruppin, *Jews*, 62; Schor, *L'Antisémitisme*, 14.

[28] Ralph Schor, *L'opinion française et les étrangers 1919–1939* (Paris, 1985), 182; Friedlaender, *Nazi Germany*, 220; Byrnes, *Antisemitism*, 92–93; Marrus, *Politics*, 30; Weber, *Hollow*, 102.

[29] Schor, *L'Antisémitisme*, 14; Marrus, *Politics*, 34.

[30] Friedlaender, *Nazi Germany*, 220.

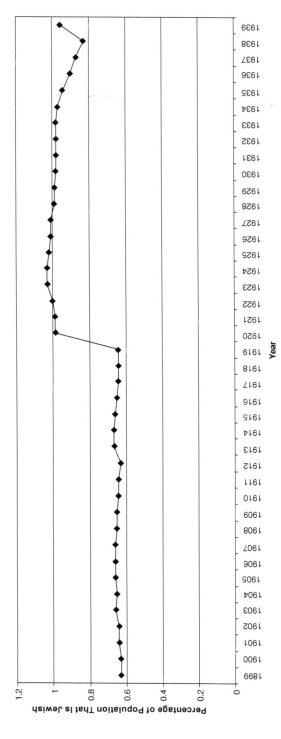

Figure 3.1. Jewish population in Great Britain, France, Germany, Italy, and Romania (combined) by year, 1899–1939. *Note:* The *American Jewish Year Book* furnishes annual figures for the Jewish population within each country between 1899 and 1939. The volumes of the *American Jewish Year Book* also provide estimates for country populations beginning in 1914. For years prior to 1914, country population figures were obtained from Mitchell (1992). The figure depicts the percentage of the total population that is Jewish for a given year. The spike in Jewish population in 1920 mostly reflects Romania's acquisition of Bessarabia, Bukovina, and Transylvania after World War I.

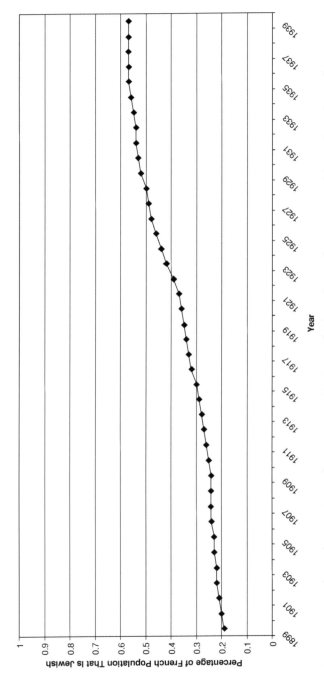

Figure 3.2a. Jewish population in France by year, 1899–1939. *Note*: The figure depicts the percentage of the total population that is Jewish for a given year in France. *Source*: *American Jewish Year Book*.

German Jewish population had climbed to 615,000, or 0.95 percent of the total population.[31] The increase came largely from the immigration of Eastern European Jews. Wertheimer notes that the Ost-Juden or Eastern European Jewish population of the German empire rose from 16,000 in 1880 to 70,000 in 1910, while Ruppin observes that between 1881 and 1930 more than 100,000 Eastern European Jews settled in Germany.[32] The rise in the Eastern European Jewish population in Germany resulted principally from a German labor shortage during World War I (Jewish workers from the occupied territories during World War I transferred to the German Reich) and the outbreak of violent pogroms in Poland, Russia, and the Ukraine between 1918 and 1921.[33] Moreover, by virtue of Germany's defeat in World War I, Poland annexed the former eastern German provinces of Posen, parts of Upper Silesia, and West Prussia. A large proportion of the Jews residing in these former German provinces made the decision to resettle in the newly established Weimar Germany. The immigrant Eastern European Jews settled principally in Germany's large urban areas, as demonstrated by the dramatic increase in the Jewish population of Berlin, which in 1871 was roughly 47,500, but had skyrocketed to more than 181,000 by 1925. In 1925, the roughly 564,000 Jews in Germany made up 0.9 percent of the total German population.[34]

Between 1880 and 1918, the Jewish population of the British Isles rose from 60,000 to close to 300,000. The increase came predominantly from mass emigration out of the Russian Pale of Settlement. The passage of the Aliens Act in 1905 slowed, but did not end, the flow of Russian and Polish Jews into the United Kingdom. Jewish immigration into Britain picked up again between 1933 and 1939, with the admittance of between 50,000 and 60,000 Jewish refugees from the Nazi Reich. By 1939, the Jewish population had grown to 350,000, or slightly more than

---

[31] Wistrich, Socialism, 58.

[32] Wertheimer, Unwelcome, 79; Ruppin, Jews, 62.

[33] Both Ascheim (Steven E. Ascheim, "The Double Exile: Weimar Culture and the East European Jews, 1918–1923." In M. N. Dobkowski and I. Wallimann, eds., Towards the Holocaust: The Social and Economic Collapse of the Weimar Republic, Westport, CT, 1983, 228) and Friedlaender (Saul Friedlaender, "Political Transformations during the War and Their Effect on the Jewish Question." In Strauss, ed., Hostages of Modernization, vol. 3/1, 150–64) remark that by 1922 at least half of the population of Eastern European Jews who had entered Germany during World War I had departed.

[34] Wertheimer, Unwelcome, 81; Ruppin, Jews, 23, 63–64; Ascheim, "Double," 228. Friedlaender, "Political," 151.

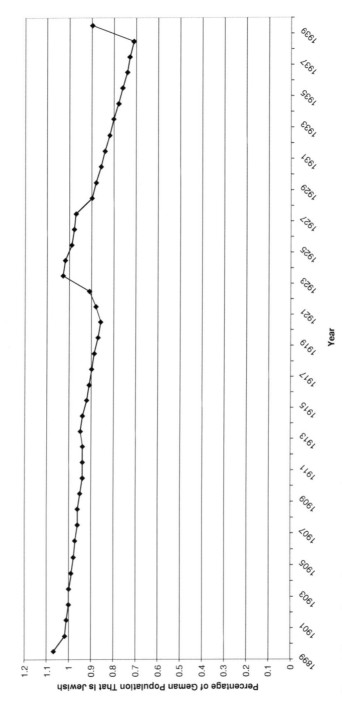

Figure 3.2b. Jewish population in Germany by year, 1899–1939. *Note:* The figure depicts the percentage of the total population that is Jewish for a given year in Germany. The increase in Jewish presence in 1939 largely reflects Germany's annexation of Austria with its large Jewish population. *Source: American Jewish Year Book.*

0.7 percent of the total population of the United Kingdom. The Eastern European Jews settled largely in London and in provincial cities such as Birmingham, Glasgow, Leeds, Liverpool, and Manchester. In particular, of the 350,000 Jews in the British Isles in 1939, 230,000 resided in London, and of those, 150,000 had settled in London's East End.[35]

Among the five countries included in this study, Romania varies from the others in terms of its history of Jewish emigration and immigration. The other countries in this study – with the exception of Germany after 1933 – served primarily as recipients of emigrating Jews during the late nineteenth and early twentieth centuries. As was the case in Russia, Romania's refusal to grant its Jews full legal rights, its benign neglect of anti-Semitic outbursts, and the country's relatively few economic opportunities led to a steady westerly flow of Jewish emigrants. The Romanian Jewish population, which had numbered 265,000 in 1882 (5.3 percent of the total population), had declined to roughly 240,000 by 1912 (3.3 percent of the total population). Close to 52,000 Jews exited Romania between 1899 and 1907.[36] However, a high birthrate among its Jewish population and a constant influx of Jews from the neighboring Russian and Habsburg Empires (Galicia) insured that Romania's Jewish population fell less than expected.

The new Jewish immigrants who came largely from Russia and the Habsburg Empire differed in dress, language, and customs from the more assimilated Sephardic Jews who had heretofore populated the Old Kingdom. The new Jewish immigrants typically settled in the towns of Moldavia, where they made up 32 percent of the urban population. For instance, Jews comprised 42 percent of the population of Iasi (Jassy), the largest Moldavian town. By contrast, outside of Moldavia, the Jewish urban proportion was significantly lower, as seen in the case of Braila (14 percent) and Bucharest (13 percent).[37] In 1930, the Jewish population in the new Romania had skyrocketed to more than 750,000 (4.2 percent of the total population) compared to roughly 240,000 (3.3 percent of the total population) in 1912.[38] These new Jews were typically Ashkenazic. Within the new Romanian provinces, Jews constituted 10.8 percent of the Bukovinian population and 7.0 percent of

---

[35] Wistrich, *Antisemitism*, 104; Holmes, *Anti-Semitism*, 13; Feldman, *Englishmen*, 157; Field, "Anti-Semitism," 295; Rubinstein, *History*, 103; Sherman, *Island*, 264–65; Robert Skidelsky, *Oswald Mosley* (New York, 1975), 393–94.

[36] Ioanid, *Holocaust*, xxi; Hitchins, *Rumania*, 165–66.

[37] Hitchins, *Rumania*, 164; Iancu, *L'émancipation*, 18; Ruppin, *Jews*, 64.

[38] Ioanid, *Holocaust*, xxi.

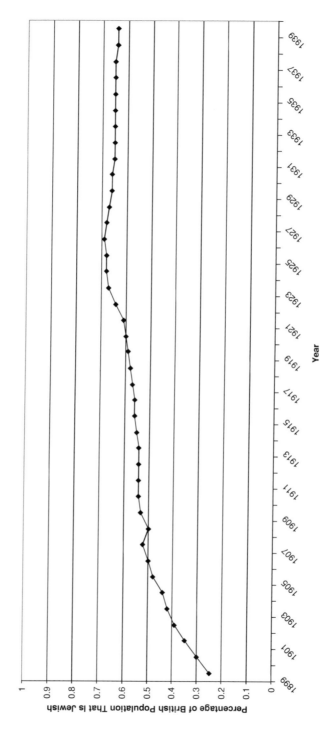

Figure 3.2c. Jewish population in Great Britain by year, 1899–1939. *Note*: The figure depicts the percentage of the total population that is Jewish for a given year in Great Britain. *Source*: *American Jewish Year Book*.

the Bessarabian population. The Jewish urban population in the new provinces was even greater, with Jews comprising 30 percent of the urban Bukovinian and 27 percent of the urban Bessarabian population.[39] The nearly 300 percent increase in Jewish population during the interwar period should be viewed as part of a larger trend in which the proportion of ethnic Romanians diminished substantially vis-à-vis non-Romanians.[40]

The Jewish community of Italy, numbering approximately 34,000 in 1861, rose to nearly 40,000 by 1911, or 1.15 Jews per 1,000 inhabitants, and climbed to more than 54,000 by 1931. By virtue of its location and relatively low level of economic development, Italy did not attract the attention of East Central European Jews in a way that France, Germany, and Great Britain did at the turn of the century. Furthermore, the Ashkenazic Jews of East Central Europe may have preferred destinations in which an established Ashkenazic settlement already existed – immigrants tend to select destinations where family and friends reside. The Jews of Italy were largely descendants of the Sephardic strain that had settled in Italy after the fifteenth-century expulsions. Before 1919, natural increase from birthrates accounted for much of the growth in Italy's Jewish population. Between 1871 and 1900, roughly 4,000 foreign Jews entered Italy, and the majority of these were Sephardic Jews originating in other Mediterranean countries. During the first two decades of the twentieth century, a more diverse group of approximately 1,500 foreign Jews, comprising both Sephardic and Ashkenazic branches, entered Italy.[41] Foreign Jewish immigration did, however, play a larger role in Italy between 1921 and 1938, with the entry of roughly 9,000 foreign Jews. After 1933, more than 15,000 foreign Jews entered Italy, with the largest proportion coming out of Germany and Austria. By 1938, the foreign Jews comprised nearly one-quarter of the total Jewish population of Italy.[42]

[39] Hitchins Rumania, 338.

[40] Livezeanu, Cultural, 9–10.

[41] Sergio Della Pergola, "Precursori, convergenti, emarginati: trasformazioni demografiche degli ebrei in Italia, 1870–1945." In Ministero per I Beni Culturali E Ambientali Ufficio Centrale per I Beni Archivistici, ed., Italia Judaica: Gli ebrei nell'Italia unita 1870–1945 (Rome, 1993), 53–54.

[42] Della Pergola, "Precursori," 76; Canepa, "Christian-Jewish," 24; Klaus Voigt, "Jewish Refugees and Immigrants in Italy, 1933–1945." In Herzer, ed., Italian Refuge, 141–42; Cecil Roth, The History of the Jews of Italy (Philadelphia, 1946), 527; Ruppin, Jews, 26.

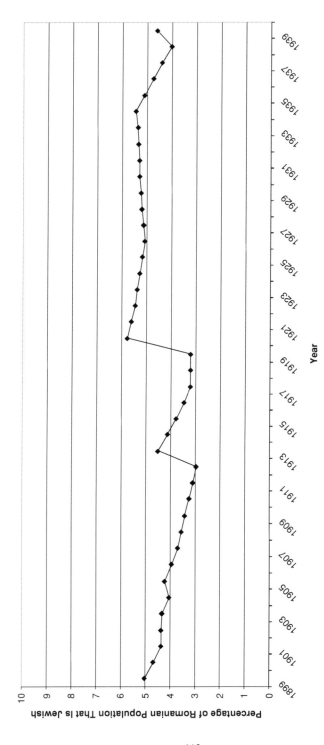

Figure 3.2d. Jewish population in Romania by year, 1899–1939. *Note:* The figure depicts the percentage of the total population that is Jewish for a given year in Romania. The spike in Jewish population in 1920 mostly reflects Romania's acquisition of Bessarabia, Bukovina, and Transylvania after World War I. *Source: American Jewish Year Book.*

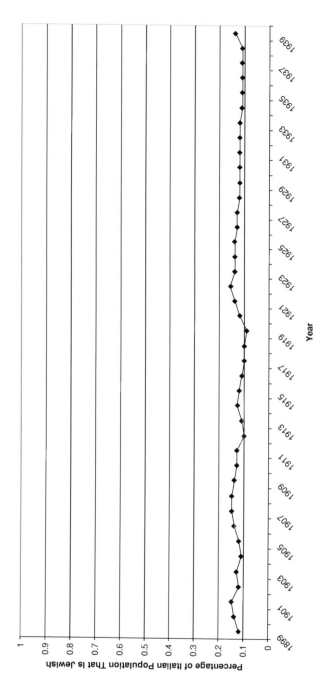

Figure 3.2e. Jewish population in Italy by year, 1899–1939. *Note:* The figure depicts the percentage of the total population that is Jewish for a given year in Italy. *Source: American Jewish Year Book.*

It was not simply the sudden and dramatic increase in the Jewish population, but perhaps more the strange customs and appearance of the Eastern European Jews or Ost-Juden that affected the racial perception of Jews in the West.[43] For the most part, these newly arrived Ashkenazic Jews from East Central Europe had come out of an isolated premodern civilization in which they had shown little interest in adopting the host culture. The Eastern European Jews and their Western European co-religionists differed significantly. In contrast to Western European Jews, the Eastern European Jews were typically less assimilated, more predisposed toward the Yiddish language and religious orthodoxy, less likely to intermarry and maintain a low birthrate, and more likely to hold lower-middle-class or proletarian jobs and to support Zionism or socialism. Alderman's explanation of possible causes of the August 1911 anti-Semitic riots in South Wales presents us with an illustrative case of the wide divide existing between the assimilated Western European and unassimilated Eastern European Jews and how that cleavage affected Jewish and non-Jewish relations. Alderman contrasts the earlier Jewish community of South Wales, comprising Jews born and educated in the mining towns of South Wales and speaking fluent English or Welsh, to the newly arrived Jews from Eastern Europe – speaking little English, pursuing the trades of peddling and shopkeeping, and rarely mixing with people outside their group. To the native Welsh, the Eastern European Jews remained foreigners and interlopers, according to Alderman.[44]

The depiction of the Eastern European Jews as fanatical, backward, superstitious, and unenlightened emanated from both non-Jewish and Jewish quarters. Whether it was due to their physical appearance, spoken language, religious orthodoxy, class background, or political orientation, the arrival of masses of non-assimilated Jews often created an embarrassment for the established Jewish communities throughout Europe. Assimilated Western Jews were proud of their achievements and social mobility and perceived correctly that the swelling population of Eastern Jews had reinforced negative Jewish stereotypes among Europe's non-Jewish

---

[43] This is not to imply that Gentile preference for Sephardic or highly assimilated Ashkenazic Jews dates from the late 1800s. The origins of this preference date back to earlier centuries. Hertzberg (*French Enlightenment*, 1) observes that the makers of the French Revolution had ordered that the Portuguese, Spanish, and Jews of the Avignon region should enjoy citizenship rights twenty months before the granting of these same citizenship rights to the Ashkenazic Jews of Alsace, Lorraine, and Metz.

[44] Geoffrey Alderman, "The Anti-Jewish Riots of August 1911 in South Wales." In Strauss, ed., *Hostages of Modernization*, vol. 3/1, 375.

population.[45] Both Soucy and Schor assert that even one of France's
most prominent Jews, the Baron Robert de Rothschild, publicly expressed concern about the left-wing political behavior of many of the
newly arrived Jews from the East and their failure to assimilate into
French culture.[46] Throughout the last decades of the nineteenth century and well into the twentieth century, the mainstream press frequently
reinforced the distinction between the more acceptable assimilated
Western European Jew and the less acceptable unassimilated Eastern
European Jew. For instance, Jewish-born Marcel Proust (his mother's
side) is referred to as a French novelist, and Jewish-born Maurice Ravel
as a French composer, while Stavisky, a Jew of Russian origin at the
center of a highly publicized French governmental scandal in the mid-
1930s, is referred to as a Jew.[47] Much the same occurred elsewhere, as
the British press would often lavish praise upon such well-known and
assimilated Jewish families as the Isaacs, Montefiores, Solomons, and
Rothschilds, while heaping scorn upon and citing the religious background of recent Russian Jewish immigrants residing in London's East
End. To conclude that the dramatic upsurge in Eastern European Jewish
immigration drastically transformed the image of the Jew in the West
is to state the obvious. The concern raised by Eastern European Jewish
immigration is reflected both in the volume of laws and acts dealing
with Jewish immigration and in newspaper coverage. Figure 3.3 shows
the number of articles referring to Jewish immigration from my sample of
the principal European dailies between 1899 and 1939. The *Daily Mail* of
Great Britain surpassed the other national newspapers in both coverage
of Jewish immigration and in calls for limiting Jewish immigration.

In the context of a spreading European colonialism, rising nationalism, and Eastern European Jewish immigration combined with the
emergence and popularization of the new science of race, racial anti-
Semitism gained adherents throughout the nations of Europe. For many
of those embracing racial anti-Semitism, Jews should no longer be considered simply as a minority with their own religious beliefs, rituals, and

---

[45] Mendelssohn, *Jews*, 6–7; Wertheimer, *Unwelcome*, 148, 161; Lindemann, *Esau's*,
51; Feldman, *Englishmen*, 6–7.

[46] Soucy, *French Fascism*, 79; Schor, *L'Antisémitisme*, 301–04. Robert de Rothschild
also expressed anxiety concerning the entry of German-Jewish refugees, for
he feared, like other French Jews, that given France's high unemployment in
the 1930s, increased Jewish immigration might spark heightened French anti-
Semitism, and that German Jews tended to display typical German arrogance
(Schor, *L'Antisémitisme*, 301–304).

[47] Steiman, *Paths*, 108.

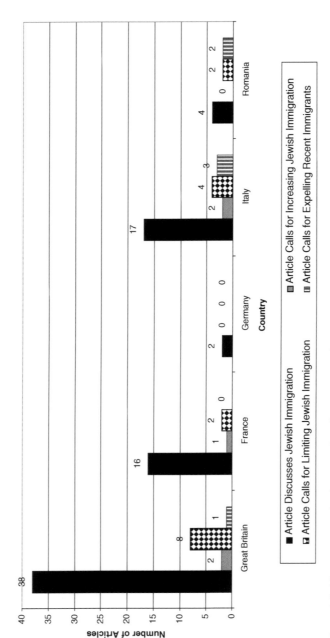

Figure 3.3. Newspaper articles discussing Jewish immigration by country, 1899–1939. *Note:* Articles are taken from the fifteenth day of the month for every month between 1899 and 1939. Articles were taken from the *Daily Mail* in Great Britain (N = 299), *Le Petit Parisien* in France (N = 199), *Berliner Morgenpost* in Germany (N = 269), *Corriere della Sera* in Italy (N = 101), and *Universul* in Romania (N = 136).

customs within the national territory of established nations. In the new thinking, Jews constituted a separate race, and, as a race, the Jews were inferior to Aryans but also the most dangerous of the inferior races.[48] Next, I highlight the contributions of some of the more prominent racial anti-Semites in France, Germany, Great Britain, Romania, and Italy, whose publications and political movements nurtured the racial root of anti-Semitism in Europe before the Holocaust.

### FRANCE

Racial anti-Semitism erupted in France during the Dreyfus Affair. However, a foundation for French racial anti-Semitism had been established much earlier. We have previously encountered the secular anti-Semitism of the early French socialists Charles Fourier, Alphonse Toussenel, and Pierre-Joseph Proudhon. Proudhon clearly held great distaste for European Jewry. Proudhon's anti-Semitism embraced religious, economic, and racial forms. He was one of the earliest writers to refer to the Jews as "the race of Sem." He attributed Jewish antiproductive and parasitic behavior to race and referred to the Jews as the enemy of humanity, calling for either their repatriation to Asia or their extermination.[49]

---

[48] Gavin I. Langmuir, "Toward a Definition of Antisemitism." In Helen Fein, ed., *The Persisting Question: Sociological Perspectives and Social Contexts of Modern Antisemitism*, vol. 1. (Berlin and New York, 1987), 86.

[49] Finzi, *Anti-Semitism*, 20; Stephen A. Schuker, "Origins of the 'Jewish Problem' in the Later Third Republic." In Frances Malino and Bernard Wasserstein, eds., *The Jews in Modern France* (Hanover and London, 1985), 148–49; Lindemann, *Esau's*, 166–67; Byrnes, *Antisemitism*, 117–25. According to Wistrich (*Antisemitism*, 47–48), although much of the French left embraced the Voltairian secular critique of Judaism, some currents of the French left, notably the Blanquist movement, endorsed elements of Renan's counterposition positing the superior Aryan race (deriving from the genius of Rome and Greece) and the inferior Semitic race (endowed with the mercantile spirit of exploitation). Also, racial anti-Semitism gained a number of adherents within the French anarchist left during the last quarter of the nineteenth century. Among the most prominent of these racial anti-Semitic anarchists were Gustave Tridon, Albert Regnard, and August Hamon. Tridon, the author of *Le Molochism Juif*, pleaded for an Aryan victory over the Jews to save Western civilization and referred to the Jews as an omnivorous race sacrificing humans to its gods. Regnard lauded the Aryans and denigrated the Jews in his book *Aryens et Semites, Le Bilan du Judaisme et de Christianisme*, while Hamon speculated about the contrasting structure and substance of the Aryan and Jewish brains (Judd L. Teller, *Scapegoat of Revolution*, New York, 1954, 140–41).

No French intellectual contributed more to the development of French racial anti-Semitism than the eminent French thinker Ernst Renan.[50] In several of Renan's works, including his *Etudes d'histoire religieuse*, *L'Avenir de la Science*, *Life of Jesus*, and *Ecclésiastes*, Jews figure prominently. In the mid nineteenth century, Renan, along with Christian Lassen, was among the first to popularize and contrast the Semites (Jews) and the Aryans (Indo-Europeans).[51] In Renan's classification of races, based largely on linguistic criteria, blacks and Native Americans constituted inferior races, while Aryans and Semites comprised superior races. Within the superior races, Aryans stood clearly above Semites. Once the Semitic race had passed the Old Testament to the Indo-Europeans, the Aryans eclipsed the Semites. What the Semites lacked, the Aryans held in abundance. The Aryans possessed creative ability, discipline, and a capacity for independent political organization. For Renan, all the great military, political, and intellectual movements in world history belonged to the Aryans. The Semitic race possessed particular negative qualities. In contrast to the Aryan race, the Semitic or Jewish race worshipped money and was primitive, unimaginative, sensuous, and subjective. Renan added that the Jews had fulfilled an unwholesome social function and performed largely a parasitic and exploitative role throughout their history.[52]

Renan's racial anti-Semitism seems mild when compared to the racial anti-Semitism of Edouard Drumont, the dean of late nineteenth-century French anti-Semitism. During the 1880s and 1890s, no French writer did more to galvanize the French anti-Semitic movement than Drumont. There is little doubt that Drumont was a racial anti-Semite, given his

---

[50] A number of scholars, including Wistrich (*Antisemitism*, 47), Birnbaum (*La France*, 138–39), and Wilson (*Ideology*, 470–71), assert that it is incorrect to assume that Renan was an anti-Semite. Wistrich and Wilson claim that Renan's characterizations of the Semitic race pertained to ancient Jews and did not apply to modern assimilated Jews. Birnbaum and Wilson see Renan's contributions to the science of race being appropriated by anti-Semites such as Drumont, who ignored Renan's caveats and qualifications.

[51] Though "Semitic" properly refers to all the peoples of the Near East who spoke Semitic languages, it was largely synonymous in the European context with Jews.

[52] Shmuel Almog, "The Racial Motif in Renan's Attitude to Jews and Judaism." In Shmuel Almog, ed., *Antisemitism through the Ages*, trans. Nathan H. Reisner (Oxford, 1988), 270–73; Birnbaum, *La France*, 138–39; Katz, *Prejudice*, 136; Poliakov, *Aryan*, 208–09; Schor, *L'Antisémitisme*, 10; Wistrich, *Antisemitism*, 47.

firm conviction that the "Jewish Problem" was a racial problem and could be solved only by removing Jews and Jewish influence from France. Drumont's two-volume *La France Juive*, published in 1886, sold more than 100,000 copies in its first year and soon became the most widely read book in France. By 1914, *La France Juive* had gone into its two hundredth edition. Additionally, the widely circulated French newspaper daily *Le Petit Journal* published Drumont's book in installments. The first volume entails Drumont's depiction of the idealistic, heroic, earnest, and chivalrous Christian Aryans and the scheming, deceitful, and greedy Semites. According to Drumont, it was among the Aryans that the notions of liberty, justice, and good attained their fullest development. In Drumont's *La France Juive*, the attack on Semites extends beyond alleged Jewish failures to match Aryan genius and creativity. Drumont distinguishes between the handsome Aryan and the Jew with his hooked nose, eager fingers, and unpleasant odors. He notes, further, that the Jews are by nature spies, traitors, criminals. and carriers of diseases. The Jews have gotten away with their crimes because of the inadvertent tolerance and disinterest of Aryans. In Drumont's thinking, Jewish racial inferiority did not translate into Jewish weakness. Drumont believed that the Jews, by virtue of their racial purity and ability to live in all climates, presented a grave threat to Christian Aryans. He bolstered his claims of the Jewish threat by exaggerating the Jewish population of France. In *La France Juive*, Drumont asserted that there were more than 500,000 Jews in France, while there were in reality roughly 50,000 Jews in France in 1872.[53] This paradox of Jewish racial inferiority and Jewish dominance is clear in the title of Drumont's *La France Juive*, as Drumont cleverly chose this title to warn Christian France of Jewish control over French financial and governmental institutions. Drumont would not be alone among racial anti-Semites who popularized the paradox of Jewish racial inferiority and Jewish power in the decades leading up to the Holocaust.

Drumont's *La France Juive* catapulted the writer to the position of France's number one anti-Semite during the late 1880s and 1890s. In 1892, Drumont launched his widely read anti-Semitic daily newspaper,

[53] Byrnes, *Antisemitism*, 92, 137–39, 152–53; Roger Eatwell, *Fascism: A History* (New York, 1996), 24; Wilson, *Ideology*, 457; Poliakov, *Aryan*, 281; Richard I. Cohen, "The Dreyfus Affair and the Jews." In Almog, ed., *Antisemitism through the Ages*, 301; Marrus, *Politics*, 30; Jean-Yves Mollier, "Financiers juifs dans la tourmente des scandales fin de siècle (1880–1900)." *Archives Juives*, vol. 29, no. 2, 1996, 66.

*La Libre Parole*. The newspaper, whose motto was "La France aux
Français," quickly reached a circulation of 200,000 in 1893 and reigned
as the leading anti-Semitic daily in France until 1905. Drumont's *La
Libre Parole* lasted until 1924 but would reappear under the editorship of
Jacques Ploncard in 1928. Through the daily columns of *La Libre Parole*,
Drumont unleashed a continual barrage against Jews. Every catastrophe
that had befallen France had Jews behind it. During the Dreyfus Affair,
Drumont's *La Libre Parole* championed the cause of the anti-Dreyfusards
and advocated the execution not only of Dreyfus, if found guilty by a
military tribunal, but also of number of leading Jewish financiers.[54] For
Drumont, the execution of Jewish financiers would serve as a deterrent
to other Jews.[55]

Drumont's anti-Semitic crusade, bolstered by the Dreyfus Affair, inspired countless anti-Semitic movements throughout France during the
1890s.[56] Among the more notable national French anti-Semitic movements were Drumont's La Ligue antisémitique de France, La Ligue antisémitique française, L'Union nationale, La Ligue de la Patrie française,
La Jeunesse antisémite et nationaliste, Les Amis de Morès, and La
Fédération nationale antijuive. Three of these anti-Semitic movements,
La Ligue antisémitique française, L'Union nationale, and La Jeunesse
antisémite et nationaliste, enjoyed considerable success at mobilizing
anti-Jewish sentiment in France during the Dreyfus Affair. Founded by
Jules Guérin, the militant and violence-prone La Ligue antisémitique

---

[54] Drumont linked Dreyfus's treachery to the Jewish plot to dominate France
(Cohen, "Dreyfus," 301).

[55] Wilson, *Ideology*, 173, 205, 677–78, 733–34; Birnbaum, *Anti-Semitism*, 86; Katz,
*Prejudice*, 300.

[56] Obviously, French anti-Semitism did not confine itself solely to anti-Semitic
leagues and newspapers. During the first few months of 1898, in the midst of
the notorious Dreyfus Affair, anti-Jewish riots occurred in approximately seventy
French towns, and anti-Jewish pogroms took place in French Algeria. In Algiers,
the leader of the French Algerian racist movement, Max Régis, was elected mayor
and called upon Algerians "to water the tree of liberty with Jewish blood" (Mosse,
*Final Solution*, 160). In January 1898, more than 150 French elected deputies
supported a bill calling for the removal from public jobs of those French citizens
who could not document three generations of ancestors born in France. Moreover,
in the 1898 French national legislative elections, twenty-two self-declared anti-
Semitic deputies won election. In February of 1899, sixty-five French deputies
proposed a bill to the French National Assembly to rescind the political clauses
of the *Cremieux Decree* of 1870 that had naturalized Algerian Jews (Mosse, *Final
Solution*, 160; Wilson, *Ideology*, 733–34). For a superb examination of French
anti-Semitism at the time of Dreyfus, see Wilson's *Ideology*.

française drew much of its support from the French capital and organized demonstrations against Jewish-owned department stores. L'Union nationale, established in 1893, organized active cells in thirty-five separate French *départements*. This highly racist anti-Semitic movement called for the removal of Jews from public life and at its meetings frequently resorted to calls for "La France aux Français" (France for the French) and "Mort aux Juifs" (Death to the Jews). In 1901, La Jeunesse antisémite et nationaliste sponsored a large anti-Semitic congress in Paris with the goal of creating a single anti-Jewish national party. Drumont was elected as one of the honorary presidents. The congress adopted "Down with the Jews" and "France for the French" as its two principal slogans.[57]

In the pantheon of late nineteenth-century French racist anti-Semitic writers, Drumont was certainly the foremost popularizer of the Aryan myth; however, Drumont lacked the pedigree of a major French intellectual or novelist. The same could not be said of others who contributed to French racial anti-Semitism. Maurice Barrès, founder of French integral nationalism (*nationalisme intégral*), was a luminary among late nineteenth-century French conservative-nationalist novelists. In his numerous writings, Barrès frequently contrasted the antinationalist qualities of the Semitic race with the nationalist traits of either the Gallic or Indo-European race. The alleged mismatch between Jews and nationalism became a central theme of Barrès' anti-Semitic contributions. Barrès' existential and historical construction of nationality included requirements of generations of continual residence in the country and a particular attachment to the country's past. For Barrès, the majority of French Jews were recently naturalized citizens and lacked ties to France's historic soul. In Barrès' nationalist view, the Jews were not French but alien invaders and potential traitors to France. In January 1890, Barrès wrote that if the Semitic race continued to battle against the Gallic race, the Semites could one day vanish in a bloody race war. Barrès, like so many of his contemporaries, saw the Prussian defeat of France of 1870–71 as a great humiliation and believed that the defeat resulted in large part from the pollution of the true Gallic race by foreigners. The Dreyfus Affair ignited this sentiment for Barrès and others.[58]

---

[57] Birnbaum, *La France*, 233; Pierre Birnbaum, "Affaire Dreyfus, culture catholique et antisémitisme." In Michel Winock, ed., *Histoire de l'extrême droite en France* (Paris, 1993), 88–89; Wilson, *Ideology*, 58–59, 733–34.

[58] Wilson, *Ideology*, 380, 458, 678; Birnbaum, *La France*, 10–11; Massing, *Rehearsal*, 80.

Jules Soury's *Campagne nationaliste* impressed Barrès in its examination of the evolution of the irreconcilable cleavage in France between Semites and Aryans. Soury wrote of the eventuality of a racial and religious war between Semites and Aryans. Soury's racial point of view led him to claim during the Dreyfus Affair that the biological differences between Semites and Aryans resulted in divergent reactions to particular diseases.[59]

Like Drumont, Wilhelm Marr in Germany, and Karl Pearson in Great Britain, Vacher de Lapouge portrayed the Jews as an inferior race and yet a dangerous rival to the Aryans. In his 1899 book, *L'Aryen, Son Rôle social*, De Lapouge's conception of race approximated Gobineau's, in that De Lapouge equated the superior Aryan race with *Homo Europeus* or Christian Europeans. Employing Darwinian biological notions, De Lapouge asserted that the inferior Jewish race constituted a threat to the survival of the Aryan race. The Jewish race was particularly dangerous for its own consciousness of race. The depiction of Jews in De Lapouge's book emphasizes the lack of scruples and values, particularly in commercial dealings. For example, De Lapouge's observes that unlike the Jews, Aryans are guided by values when they pursue business endeavors. In the final battle between Jews and Aryans, De Lapouge predicted that the Jews would go down to defeat because they had no spirituality, lacked a political instinct, and were unable to fight.[60]

In terms of French anti-Semitism, when we think of Emile Zola, the great French novelist, we naturally consider him a major opponent of anti-Semitism and associate his name with the defense of Alfred Dreyfus. In the midst of the campaign against Dreyfus, Zola had the courage to publicly and vigorously confront those French institutions to whom Dreyfus's Jewish background was sufficient reason to convict him of treason. However, rarely noted is that several of Zola's novels, including *Au Bonheur des Dames*, *Son Excellence Eugène Rougon*, *L'Argent*, and *La Débacle*, contributed to the propagation of common negative racial stereotypes of Jews.[61] The point here is that racial stereotyping of Jews was fairly common throughout Europe between 1879 and 1939 and that seeming philo-Semites were themselves not immune from expressions of racial anti-Semitism.

---

[59] Birnbaum, *La France*, 10–11; Wilson, *Ideology*, 458.
[60] Mosse, *Final Solution*, 58–60; Poliakov, *Aryan*, 281.
[61] Wilson, *Ideology*, 474–75.

Although the anti-Semitic wave in France subsided in the aftermath of the Dreyfus Affair, Drumont's crusade against the Jews, lodged largely in inflammatory racial rhetoric, found a home with the founders of the French royalist and Catholic L'Action française. Under the directorship of Charles Maurras and Léon Daudet, L'Action française mounted a campaign aimed at strengthening integral nationalism. The leadership of L'Action française between 1899 and 1939 comprised numerous academics, journalists, playwrights, and artists. For Maurras, unquestionably the guiding figure of the movement, a key pillar of integral nationalism was anti-Semitism. The L'Action française movement purported that the Jews would always remain as foreigners even if they repudiated their religion, because their ethnic identity could not change. Maurras and his supporters claimed that for France to become once again truly Catholic, Christians would have to be educated to the threat posed by Jews, and they would have to possess the will to impose special treatment on the Jews, including a restriction on Jewish immigration and naturalization, a ban on Jews in public employment, the withdrawal of full citizenship from Jews, and the restoration of the Jewish ghetto or the expulsion of Jews from France.[62]

Regardless of the efforts launched by the anti-Semitic L'Action française, French racial anti-Semitism remained relatively subdued during the first two decades of the twentieth century.[63] Perhaps nothing better captures the decline of French anti-Semitism during this period than the public praise offered to French Jewry for their show of patriotism in the victorious war against archenemy Germany between 1914 and 1918 by the well-known and committed anti-Semite Maurice Barrès. The honeymoon would not last long, however; French racial anti-Semitism would again pick up steam during the 1920s and explode after 1933. A number of factors contributed to the upswing in French anti-Semitism, including the Depression of the 1930s, the growth of the political left, the state of Franco-German relations, and the influx of tens of thousands of Jewish refugees fleeing anti-Semitism in Central and Eastern Europe.

[62] Katz, *Prejudice*, 300; Birnbaum, *Anti-Semitism*, 234–35; Sternhell, "Roots," 115; Wistrich, *Antisemitism*, 129–200.

[63] In the early years of the twentieth century, there were, nevertheless, some notable racially inspired anti-Semitic assaults on Jews in France apparent in the efforts of the Camelots du Roi and in the writings of Ernest Psichari, Henri Massis, and Romain Rolland. Rolland's widely circulated ten-volume *Jean Christophe* highlighted the shamelessness of the Jewish race (Sternhell, "Roots").

During the 1920s, the anti-Semitic torch in France continued to be carried by Maurras and Daudet, particularly through their newspaper, *L'Action française*. Daily circulation of the newspaper ranged between 50,000 and 100,000 during the interwar period. Illustrative of Maurras's and Daudet's anti-Semitic campaign are some prominent articles in *L'Action française*. The immigration of Eastern European Jews into France in 1920 incited Maurras to write on March 9, 1920, about the dangers for France of this Jewish inundation. According to Maurras, "[C]omme la forêt de Macbeth, on peut dire que les immenses ghettos de l'Europe centrale sont en marche dans la direction de Paris. Ce seront de nouveaux bohémiens dans nos murailles et de nouveaux microbes pathogènes, politiques, sociaux et moraux." Daudet lashed out at the alleged Jewish sponsorship of socialism in a lead article in the July 4, 1920, edition of *L'Action française*. Attacking the speech to the French National Assembly given by a leading socialist and Jew, Léon Blum, Léon Daudet begins the article with a negative racial caricature of Blum: " . . . ce petit juif, si curieusement ethnique, avec son nez effilé et droit entre ses yeux mauvais, se montre onctueux, sucré et bénin, comme celui qui à une lorgnette a placer . . . C'est un étonnant specimen de spinoziste dégénéré, tombé de l'optique, ou des pierres fines dans l'agio. Il se dégage de ses petites manières, tout à coup, quelque chose de froidement féroce. L'usurier qui hait sa victime apparaît dans la fifille déchaînée." Further on in the article, Daudet attempts to explain why the Jewish race aspires to lead the proletariat in revolution: "Ceux de sa race ont toujours se mettre en actions et obligations révolutionnaires à long terme les revendications du prolétariat."

A list of prominent racial anti-Semites in France during the 1920s would certainly include the author Urbain Gohier. Gohier would gain attention for his widely popular French translation of the "Protocols of the Elders of Zion" during the early 1920s. Like many of his contemporaries, Gohier represented the Jews as a separate and unassimilable race. Gohier also wrote *La terreur juive* (The Jewish terror), in which he picked up on Drumont's warnings of an impending danger from the Jewish threat. Gohier portrayed the Jews as a resolutely nationalist and homogeneous nation of twelve million that, while dispersed worldwide, is unified in the pursuit of universal domination.[64] *L'Action française* was not France's only major anti-Semitic newspaper during the 1920s.

---

[64] Winock, *Nationalism*, 82–83.

In 1928, the rich perfume magnate Francois Coty launched his antifor-
eigner and virulently anti-Semitic newspaper *L'Ami du Peuple*. Coty's
newspaper attained a circulation of 800,000 in 1928 and reached one
million by 1930.[65] Racial anti-Semitism in the 1920s cultivated roots
within French academia as well. Berillon, a major figure in French psy-
chotherapy and a professor of psychology, authored *Les caracteres na-
tionaux, leurs facteurs biologiques et psychologiques* in 1920, in which he
warned against the dangers of racial mixing, most notably about the peril
of racial mixing involving inferior and dangerous races. Berillon writes:
"C'est dans la pureté de la race que résident les éléments essentiels de
la conservation des peuples. . . . Les croisements avec les races hostiles
ont pour effet de dissocier les caractères héréditaires et d'en provoquer
la dégénérescence. Il convient donc de protéger la race contre les im-
mixtions étrangères et de s'opposer aux croisements avec les individus
de race inférieure ou antagoniste."[66]

In many ways, anti-Semitism in 1930s France rivaled that of the
Dreyfus era of the 1890s.[67] Some of France's greatest intellectuals contributed to the dissemination of racial anti-Semitism during the decade
of the 1930s. There were those whose work reflected negative Jewish
stereotypes: André Gide, François Mauriac, Romain Rolland, Paul
Morand, Paul Léautaud, Marcel Jouhandeau, Marcel Arland, Jacques
Feyder, and Edmond Jaloux. There was also a group whose writings
explicitly depicted the Jews in racial terms and portrayed the Jews
as a threat to French society: Georges Bernanos, Pierre Drieu de la
Rochelle, Jean Pluyette, Maurice Bardèche, Jean Giraudoux, Maurice
Blanchot, and most significantly, Robert Brasillach and Louis-Ferdinand
Destouches (Céline).[68] Jean Pluyette's 1930 *La doctrine des races et la
sélection de l'immigration en France* employed a version of racial theory
to claim that the inequality among civilizations derives from a natural inequality in human intellectual aptitude. According to Pluyette,

[65] Schor, *L'Opinion*, 179.

[66] Ibid., 179–80.

[67] Marrus and Paxton (*Vichy*, 48–49) suggest that French xenophobia and anti-
Semitism had reached the point during the decade of the 1930s that few political
or intellectual leaders felt comfortable in launching a defense of the Jews or,
particularly, an argument in favor of increased Jewish immigration.

[68] Weber, *Hollow*, 102–03; Marrus and Paxton, *Vichy*, 43–46; Schor, *L'Opinion*,
180; Friedlaender, *Nazi Germany*, 211–13; Winock, *Nationalism*, 275–76; Alice
Kaplan, *The Collaborator: The Trial and Execution of Robert Brasillach* (Chicago
and London, 2000).

the differences in aptitude correspond clearly to ethnic differences, and, among all races, the north European possesses the highest aptitudes. One year later, Georges Bernanos wrote *La Grande Peur des biens pensants*, in which he lauded the high priest of French anti-Semitism, Drumont. His book espoused the claim that the values of Christian civilization and the organic unity of the French nation were being corrupted by rising Jewish domination. During the late 1930s, Robert Brasillach, editor-in-chief of the popular anti-Semitic and fascist newspaper *Je suis Partout*, published a series of articles calling for the implementation of racial laws against the Jews. In 1939, Brasillach, in a malicious subterfuge to circumvent the intent of the *Loi Marchandeau* to curb inflammatory writing, entitled his weekly "Letter to a Provincial" in *Je suis Partout* "The Monkey Question." Kaplan states that the message of "The Monkey Question" was clear: Jews are not citizens, but animals.[69]

The theme of the Jewish threat to French civilization from increasing immigration found a home in the writings of Jean Giraudoux, the famous French dramatist, and Pierre Drieu de la Rochelle. Giraudoux's *Pleins pouvoirs* purported that the French racial stock was being threatened by hordes of Eastern and Central European ghetto Jews descending upon France. These Jewish barbarians inclined toward lawlessness, and their corruption undermined the native French artisanal traits of precision, perfection, and trust, according to Giraudoux. Giraudoux called for the establishment in France of a Ministry of Race. If you thought that Giraudoux's comments about Jewish immigrants would make him the *bête noire* of French society, you might want to rethink that position, given that Edouard Daladier, the French premier, appointed Giraudoux to the post of minister of public information shortly after the publication of *Pleins pouvoir*. Drieu de la Rochelle's 1939 novel, *Gilles*, dwelled cynically on the decline of European civilization, pointing to the invasion of millions of foreigners, Jews, halfbreeds, blacks, and Asians into his beloved France. Although Drieu de la Rochelle sought to discourage all foreign immigration into France, other writers and scholars differentiated between Jewish and non-Jewish foreigners. Among them, Georges Mauco, author of *Les Etrangers en France: Etude géographique sur leur rôle dans l'activité économique*, and France's leading ethnologist René Martial argued that France desperately needed immigrants because of the human losses in World War I and a low birth rate. However, they claimed that the race of East European Jews was undesirable because

[69] Kaplan, *Collaborator*, 23–24.

their admittance would not answer France's deficiency of rural and urban workers and, furthermore, that these Jews were hardly assimilable and highly quarrelsome and likely to participate in smuggling, fraud, and unfair competition. Similar sentiments about East Central European Jews emanated from representatives of the French government in late 1938 and early 1939 in the midst of Germany's annexation of parts of Czechoslovakia. Caron reports that French government officials, while stressing France's need for certain kinds of foreign workers, argued that an infusion of foreign Jews would exacerbate racial relations in France. This occurred at a time when those attempting to reach France were largely Jews in grave danger.[70] Other authors, such as Georges de la Fouchardiere in his 1938 book, *Histoire d'un petit Juif*, lamented that parts of Paris resembled villages in Bukovina, Carpathia, or Palestine, inundated with small Jews with frizzy hair, playing in polluted streams.

Not surprisingly, the theme of a Jewish invasion of France also captured the attention of French journalists in the 1930s. Two newspapers, *Candide* and *Je Suis Partout*, focused on the threat to France's racial purity brought on by the influx of Eastern European Jews into France. *Candide* referred to Paris as "Canaan-on-the-Seine," while *Je Suis Partout* warned of the Jewish invasion of France. Even the prestigious daily newspaper *Le Temps* appeared to sound an alarm by featuring a series of articles by Raymond Millet in the spring of 1938 on the supposed Jewish invasion of France.[71]

Yet in terms of literary reputation and Jewish hatred, none of these writers could match the much-celebrated Céline, born Louis-Ferdinand Destouches. Céline was one of France's greatest twentieth century novelists, and his works were widely read. Céline had fought bravely in World War I and had suffered grave wounds. After World War I, he had worked

---

[70] Vicki Caron, "The Antisemitic Revival in France in the 1930s: The Socioeconomic Dimension Reconsidered." *The Journal of Modern History*, vol. 70, March 1998, 61.

[71] Weber, *Hollow*, 105; Marrus and Paxton, *Vichy*, 52–53; Schor, *L'Opinion*, 180; Friedlaender, *Nazi Germany*, 211–13; Birnbaum, *La France*, 44; Caron, "Antisemitic," 52–56; Schor, *L'Antisémitisme*, 92. That the head of the French government between 1936 and 1938 was Léon Blum provided French anti-Semites ammunition to charge the Jewish prime minister with the crime of altering France's racial balance by increasing the rate of naturalization of foreign Jews. In fact, the naturalization of foreign Jews did increase to 15,000 for 1936 and 17,000 for 1937 (Schor, *L'Antisémitisme*, 177–79).

as a hygienist, practicing on the outskirts of Paris, where he witnessed the deleterious effects of severe alcoholism on the French working class. When the French Popular Front came to power, under the leadership of the French Jewish prime minister Léon Blum, and pushed through legislation shortening the work week to forty hours, Céline had found his explanation for the declining health of French workers. It was the Jew who, by providing workers with more leisure time to drink alcohol, had infected the healthy body of France.[72] Friedlaender refers to Céline's 1937 novel *Bagatelles pour un massacre* as the most vicious anti-Semitic vilification in modern Western literature, apart from outright Nazi productions.[73] Though the book vilifies Jews for trying to get France into a war with Hitler's Gemany and for disseminating communism, it clearly highlights racial themes. In Céline's view, the Jews possess a permanent and immutable character, rendering them unable to adopt French moral values. As a solution to the "Jewish Question," Kingston asserts that Céline regarded the exclusion of Jews to be synonymous with their extermination.[74] What is perhaps the most startling fact about the publication of Céline's rabidly anti-Semitic work was the public reaction to it. No less a distinguished literary luminary than André Gide gave the book a favorable review in the *Nouvelle Revue Française*.[75]

That *Bagatelles pour un massacre* failed to elicit a negative popular and literary reaction reflects the inroads that racial anti-Semitism had made in French society during the 1930s. Support for this claim is evident in Birnbaum's research.[76] According to Birnbaum, in the French *departements* of Aude and Eure where Léon Blum and Pierre Mendez-France (both Jewish) ran for National Assembly seats, the opposing political parties and the editor of a principal local newspaper employed racial arguments against them. The arguments emphasized that these candidates benefited from an international cartel of powerful Jews and that both belonged to a race that did not work the land. Displeased by Blum's election as a deputy from Aude, Joseph Caillaux commented that Blum "did not have enough soil on the sole of his shoes."[77]

[72] Winock, *Nationalism*, 276–78.
[73] Friedlaender, *Nazi Germany*, 212–13.
[74] Paul J. Kingston, *Anti–Semitism in France during the 1930s: Organizations, Personalities and Propaganda* (Hull, 1983), 128–29.
[75] Winock, *Nationalism*, 275–78; Kingston, *Anti-Semitism*, 128–29; Friedlaender, *Nazi Germany*, 212–13.
[76] Birnbaum, *Anti-Semitism*, 142.
[77] Ibid., 130.

In addition to the role played by a sizable group of France's inter-war intellectuals in the popularization of racial anti-Semitism, anti-Semitic newspapers and political parties also contributed to the rising anti-Semitic campaign.[78] I have already mentioned the royalist and anti-Semitic *L'Action française*. There were, however, several other highly anti-Semitic newspapers garnering wide circulation during the 1930s. Among those were *L'Ami du Peuple*, *Gringoire*, *Au Pilori*, *La Vieille France*, and *Je suis Partout*. In an April 15, 1938, editorial in *Je suis Partout*, Robert Brasillach called for an "anti-Semitism of reason" rather than one of instinct and proposed the adoption of a *statut des juifs*. For Brasillach, the *statut des juifs* would effectively consider the Jews to be a foreign people with a special legal status. Treating Jews as foreigners and imposing the strictest hurdles to Jewish naturalization would insure the national security and independence of France.[79] Many of these anti-Semitic newspapers were directly associated with anti-Semitic political movements such as La Solidarité française, Le Francisme, Le Parti populaire français, Le Rassemblement antijuif de France, Le Grand Occident, and L'Ordre national. Membership in these anti-Semitic groups typically ranged from 10,000 to more than 150,000. Some of the better known anti-Semitic political agitators during the 1930s were Jacques Doriot, Marcel Bucard, Jean Renaud, Henri Coston, Jacques Ploncard, Jean-Charles Legrand, Pierre Clementi, Jean Boissel, and Louis Darquier de Pellepoix.[80] Among elected deputies to the French National Assembly, Xavier Vallat stands out for his pronounced anti-Semitism. Vallat, well-known for his public display of disrespect in the National Assembly upon Léon Blum's appointment in 1936 to head the French government, had on an earlier occasion placed the infamous Stavisky scandal in a racially anti-Semitic context. The *Journal Officiel*, the official record of the French National Assemby, contains Vallat's remarks on January 29, 1934, in which Vallat emphasized the Eastern European Jewish origins of Stavisky and his fellow conspirators. Vallat stated: "J'ai été extrêmement frappé par la lecture des noms des prévenus ou des inculpés dans les affaires pour lesquelles la bande

---

[78] Schor's (*L'Antisémitisme*, 28) empirical examination of anti-Semitic publications during the 1930s points clearly to a significant growth in the frequency of anti-Jewish publications between 1930 and 1939. By Schor's account, while 19.6 percent of the decade's anti-Semitic publications appeared between 1930 and 1933, 47.0 percent surfaced between 1937 and 1939.

[79] Marrus and Paxton, *Vichy*, 43–44.

[80] Schor, *L'Opinion*, 621; Schor, *L'Antisémitisme*, 29.

Stavisky était poursuivie en 1926: Stavisky dont le père venait d'Odessa;
Zweifel qui venait de Lituanie; Smilovici, Margaritopol, Davidovici,
Popovici, Transparidesco et Johanid qui venaient de Roumanie. Si l'on
ajoute à cela les scandales des affaires Poullner, Costachesco, Danowsky,
Moeller, vous voudrez bien constater que dans ces deux listes il n'y a
pas beaucoup de gens nés en Auvergne, en Savoie ou en Bretagne."[81]
By 1939, racial anti-Semitism had made major inroads into the French
popular consciousness.

GERMANY

What becomes clear from this examination is that racial anti-Semitism
attracted adherents across the social spectrum in France before 1939.
France hardly stood alone in terms of the presence of widely held racial
anti-Semitic attitudes. Certainly, the racial root of anti-Semitism had
its proponents in Germany in the late nineteenth and early twentieth
centuries. The early nineteenth-century German Romanticist Friedrich
von Schlegel, comparing the languages and cultures of ancient India
and Europe, claimed to have found structural similarities between Sanskrit and German, Greek, and Latin. He referred to German, Greek, and
Latin as "Aryan" languages carried to Europe by Aryan tribes. Schlegel
contrasted the creativity within Aryan languages with the static nature
of non-Aryan languages.[82] Schlegel's writings can in no way be considered anti-Semitic. It was Christian Lassen, Schlegel's student and
successor at the University of Bonn, who, like his more famous contemporary Ernst Renan in France, had in his massive study of language
contrasted the superior Aryans to the inferior Semites. In contrast to
the creative Aryans, imbued with a sense of balance and harmony and
an appreciation of the beauty of the natural world, Lassen portrayed the
Semites (including Arabs and Jews) as a people devoid of self-control
and possessed by unbridled egoism. Lassen's writings drew considerable
attention in racist circles and heavily influenced a generation of German
racist scholars, propagandists, and writers.[83]

France had its Drumont, but Germany had Marr. Wilhelm Marr, a
journalist, probably did more than anyone else in the last quarter of
the nineteenth century to popularize racial hatred of Jews in Germany.

---

[81] Schor, *L'Antisémitisme*, 96.
[82] Lindemann, *Esau's*, 85–86.
[83] Ibid., 86.

Marr, generally recognized as the inventor of the term "anti-Semitism," published his *Der Sieg des Judentums über das Germanentum* (The victory of the Jews over the Germans) in 1879. His book became a best-seller in Germany, going through twelve editions in its first year. Interestingly, the title of Marr's work, much like the title Drumont chose for his anti-Semitic book, conveys the image of a Jewish triumph over Aryan people. Both Drumont and Marr likely believed that such titles would arouse forceful responses from their non-Jewish audiences. The Jews, by Marr's account, during a period of eighteen hundred years had gained control over German commerce, arts, and media and had corrupted German civilization. The Jews had triumphed not through their armies but through their unique spirit. Germans had, owing to their own negligence, fallen victim to the Jewish spirit and had become "jewified." He cautioned against both hating individual Jews and seeing the Jewish problem as a religious one. Marr totally dismissed traditional religious anti-Semitic claims of deicide and ritual murder.[84] While he denigrated alleged Jewish attributes of exploitation of others and disinclination toward real work, he extended praise to the Jews for their strong family life. Central to Marr's thesis is the argument that Jewish behavior derives from the essence of Jewish racial nature. For Marr, the Jews are a racially determined group unable to alter their ways and properly assimilate into German society. Unlike French Huguenots or Slavic people, who Marr held could assimilate into German society, Jews, by virtue of their toughness and desire to dominate, could never become Germans. Marr changed the perception of Jews in German society from that of a weak group to one holding substantial power. His book proposed that only by a separation of races could Germany solve the "Jewish Problem."[85]

[84] Marr was not the first major German writer to suggest that the "Jewish Problem" was racial rather than religious. In 1861, Johann Nordmann published *Die Juden und der Deutsche Staat* (The Jews and the German state), in which he proposed that the Jews belonged not only to a separate religion or church but also to a particular racial type. Nordmann suggested, moreover, that like Jewish physical features, particular "Jewish thinking" belonged to the category of Jewish racial traits (Berding, *Moderner*, 145–46).

[85] Weiss, *Ideology*, 97; Steiman, *Paths*, 152; Lindemann, *Esau's*, 128–30; Pauley, *Prejudice*, 28–29; Grosser and Halperin, *Anti-Semitism*, 219–20; Eatwell, *Fascism*, 28. Weiss (*Ideology*, 98) seems to imply that Marr's anti-Semitism, by stressing the destructive, evil, and unalterable nature of Jewish behavior, contains a seed of genocide. According to Weiss, Marr's racial anti-Semitism led directly to the death camps. I cannot agree with Weiss's assessment, as I find no evidence that Marr ever called for more than the separation of Germans from Jews. Moreover,

Among late nineteenth-century German intellectual anti-Semites, Paul de Lagarde and Julius Langbehn attracted considerable attention. Lagarde, a prominent professor of Asian studies, authored *The Religion of the Future* and the widely read *German Essays*, two highly anti-Semitic works. Langbehn's anti-Semitic *Rembrandt as Educator* went through forty editions in two years. Lagarde referred frequently to the biological nature of the Jews, who threatened the German "*Völk*" community. He equated the Jewish threat to the threat of infestation by diseased bacilli or infected vermin. Both Lagarde and Langbehn called for a German racial resurrection and advocated the destruction of European Judaism. Lagarde observed that one exterminates rather than argues with threadworms and bacilli.[86]

As I have already suggested, the political left did not shy away from the occasional anti-Semitic barb, and at times, notably before 1900, leftist anti-Semitic rhetoric contained racial overtones. Earlier, we encountered the secular anti-Semitism of the German socialist Eugen Duehring; here, we take up his contributions to racial anti-Semitism. Duehring espoused a biological worldview, in which the Nordic-Germanic race constituted the superior race. To regain its true racial nature and achieve its rightful place as a superior race, the Nordic-Germans must rid Germany of the Jews by means of racial war, if necessary. Jewish depravity, according to Duehring, emanated from the Jewish racial character, and there was no sin for which the Jews were not responsible. He proposed the institution of special laws governing Jews and the removal of Jewish influence from German education, press, business, and finance.[87]

Building on the theme of race war, Houston Chamberlain published in 1900 his landmark work on race, *The Foundations of the Nineteenth Century*. Chamberlain's widely popular book, written in a relatively accessible style, found a favorable reception among intellectuals as well as among political and literary elites. The book's admirers included Winston Churchill, D. H. Lawrence, Albert Schweitzer, and George Bernard Shaw.[88] In many respects, this work interwove religious,

Marr's proposed solution to the so-called Jewish Problem hardly differed from those of racial anti-Semites outside of Germany.

[86] Poliakov, *Aryan*, 307–09; Weiss, *Ideology*, 136–39; Levy, *Downfall*, 32; Lerner, *Final Solutions*, 27–28.

[87] Berding, *Moderner*, 146; Pauley, *Prejudice*, 29–30; Wistrich, *Socialism*, 53–54; Mosse, *Final Solution*, 165.

[88] Lindemann, *Esau's*, 351–53.

economic, political, and racial themes. Chamberlain employed the concept of race to explain the rise and fall of civilizations. If for Marx the concept of class determined human history, for Chamberlain the key causal factor in human history was race. Not only did race offer the key to interpreting history, Chamberlain believed that racial struggle and interaction constituted the driving forces in human history. Race shaped the political and ideological battles of the past, present, and future. Chamberlain's racial anti-Semitism in his *Foundations* is not the rabid race hatred of a Lagarde or Langbein; it is subtle and symbolic. In Chamberlain's racial mysticistic study, the Germanic races embody the greatest degree of vitality and creativity by virtue of the interbreeding among the different Aryan branches – the Celts, Slavs, and Teutons. Among the contributions to civilization emerging from the creative nature of the Aryan race are the sciences of botany, chemistry, mathematics, and physics, In contrast, the Jewish race's lack of creativity derives from its incompatible mixing of Aryan Amorites, Semitic Bedouins, Hittites, and Syrian racial strains.[89] Chamberlain pitted the creative Teutonic race against the uncreative Jewish race in a war of competing cultures and principles. Woodroffe notes that, for Chamberlain, the Jewish culture represented the false gods of Marxian socialism, liberalism, international finance capitalism, materialism, and Judaic Catholic Christianity.[90] Pursuing a line similar to that of Drumont and Marr, Chamberlain argued that the Jews, although inferior in intelligence and numbers and in spite of their persecution, had successfully asserted their domination over the Celts, Slavs, and Teutons and that they, the Jews, threatened to destroy Western culture and civilization. Chamberlain pointed to Jewish domination in the fields of commerce, government, science, the arts, and literature as indicators of Jewish paramountcy.[91] Chamberlain's monumental study would become one of the potent molders of racial anti-Semitism, both inside and outside of Germany during the first third of the twentieth century.

Wilhelm Marr had alluded to an association between Jewish economic dominance and race in 1879. The association became a principal

[89] Steiman, *Paths*, 165; Lindemann, *Esau's*, 351–52; Woodroffe, "Racial," 145; Mosse, *Final Solution*, 107.

[90] Woodroffe, "Racial," 152. Additionally, Steiman (*Paths*, 165) remarks that in the *Foundations*, Chamberlain claimed that Jesus was Aryan and that the church founded in his name had been corrupted by Semitic influences.

[91] Steiman, *Paths*, 165; Lindemann, *Esau's*, 351–52; Woodroffe, "Racial," 145; Poliakov, *Aryan*, 516–19.

theme of works by the German political scientist Otto von Boenigk and the eminent German sociologist Werner Sombart.[92] Boenigk had argued in his 1893 *Grundzuege zur Judenfrage* that for Germans work was a duty and a calling, but for Jews a means to an end. He proposed further that the Jewish predisposition to amassing excessive wealth, pursuing materialism, and exhibiting crooked business dealings could not be altered; it was part of the Jewish racial nature. Sombart, in his 1911 *The Jews and Modern Capitalism*, linked a Jewish racial character (including a calculating nature) to the Jewish creation of capitalism.[93]

Chamberlain's racial anti-Semitism did not draw upon the new sciences of biological Darwinism and eugenics. At about the time Chamberlain published *The Foundations of the Nineteenth Century*, several members of the German scientific community began to employ notions from these new sciences to explain the alleged racial differences between Germans and others.[94] In 1895, the notable German physician and eugenicist Alfred Ploetz published his *The Excellence of Our Race and the Protection of the Weak*. As a genetic determinist, Ploetz presented a case for the evolutionary superiority of the Aryan race, arguing that both positive and negative traits are rooted in genes, and thus that only genes furthering positive attributes should be reproduced. Ploetz viewed the higher birth rates among the poor and the racially inferior as principal obstacles to the racial health of Germany. Relatedly, he advocated biological and medical intervention to preserve racial purity and to halt racial degeneration. In light of the threat of racial degeneration, Ploetz formulated a policy he termed "racial hygiene." Ploetz's racial hygiene called for a revision in medical thinking that would have physicians, in caring for patients, place the health of the entire

---

[92] Linking Jews to particular economic behaviors had earlier roots in German literature. Though neither Gustav Freytag's 1855 novel *Soll und Haben*, nor Wilhelm Raabe's 1862 novel *Hungerpastor*, proposed a racial explanation for Jewish economic practices, they both claimed that the lack of a certain spiritual impulse among Jews nurtured a particular Jewish materialism and a sober rationalistic mind (Mosse, *Germans*, 37).

[93] Niewyk, "Solving," 340; Poliakov, *Aryan*, 286.

[94] Much of the German eugenic thinking, as well as similar thinking in Great Britain, Scandinavia, and the United States, had been informed by the pioneering work in eugenics of Galton. Also, even before the turn of the century, calls arose for the German government to make notice of Darwin's theory, as it might apply to the struggle for existence between a productive Germanic-Aryan race and a parasitic Semitic race. O. Beta's book *Darwin, Germany and the Jews*, published in 1876, advocated scientifically justified anti-Jewish legislation (Poliakov, *Aryan*, 294).

race ahead of the concerns of individuals. Wilhelm Schallmayer, a eugenicist and a member of the Monist League, took Ploetz's proposal of
medical intervention a step further. In 1903, Schallmayer proposed that
the medical community consider withholding medical care for the genetically inferior. He believed that the process of natural selection had
lost its ability to maintain the racial purity of the nation.[95] Many of
Ploetz's racial notions found a home in his journal, *Archiv fuer Rassen-
und Gesellschaftsbiologie*, and in his International Society for Racial Hygiene, of which he served as president.[96] As mentioned earlier, Ploetz did
not originally classify the Jews as an inferior race; rather, he placed the
Jews (to whom he attributed an Aryan descent) at the top of his racial
scale. However, later in life his views changed, and only non-Jewish
Germans remained at the racial pinnacle.[97]

Echoing themes similar to those of Ploetz, Ernst Haeckel, a renowned
biologist, firmly held that the genetic or biological health of the German
people was threatened with racial degeneration. Drawing upon biological Darwinistic notions, he posited that if genetically inferior races were
protected from the rigors of natural selection, a biological degeneration
of society would occur. He argued for the implementation of programs
of "negative" and "positive" eugenics in order to preserve the superiority
and purity of the German people. Negative eugenics entailed limiting
the breeding of racially inferior human stocks, while positive eugenics fostered the selective breeding of racially superior human stocks. In
order to gain scientific and political support for his social Darwinistic
thinking, Haeckel would go on to organize the Monist League.[98]

It does not appear that Jews figured centrally in the racial writings
of Ploetz and Haeckel. However, in the context of the popularization
of Marr's, Duehring's, and Chamberlain's racial anti-Semitic arguments
and the increasing flood of eastern European Jewish immigration, it was
only a matter of time before Darwinian biological and eugenic reasoning began to apply themselves to the "Jewish Question." And indeed,
German race scientists, such as Eugen Fischer and Fritz Lenz, eventually

---

[95] Lerner, *Final Solutions*, 28–30.
[96] In 1924, the International Society for Racial Hygiene would become the
German Society for Racial Hygiene (Stefan Kuehl, *The Nazi Connection: Eugenics, American Racism, and German National Socialism*, New York and Oxford,
1994, 19).
[97] Poliakov, *Aryan*, 294–98.
[98] Lerner, *Final Solutions*, 23–27.

appropriated genetic thinking and applied it to the Jews even before
the rise of national socialism in Germany. Fischer, who would become
a teacher at the Kaiser Wilhelm Institute for Anthropology, Eugenics,
and Human Heredity, published in 1914 *The Problem of Racial Crossing
among Humans*. Fischer linked particular alleged Jewish racial features,
such as a large or hooked nose, to recessive genes. Thirteen years later,
Lenz, coeditor of the major German journal for racial hygiene and a
firm proponent of a policy of procreation of "hereditarily worthy" people, claimed in his *Outline of Human Genetics and Racial Hygiene* that
by virtue of their genetic makeup, Jews could never become Germans
even if they authored books on Goethe. It should be noted here that the
Nazis were not the originators of a genetic determinist ideology, nor did
such an ideology attract adherents solely in Germany.[99]

Not unlike the situation in France, political movements and parties in Germany picked up the racial anti-Semitic theme beginning in
the last quarter of the nineteenth century. Between 1879 and 1898,
several anti-Semitic movements and parties emerged in Germany, and
a number of them succeeded in getting candidates elected to the
German Reichstag. Among the best-known anti-Semitic groups were
the Christliche-Soziale Partei, Antisemitenliga, Soziale Reichspartei,
Deutscher Volksverein, Deutsche Reformpartei, and the Deutsche
Antisemitische Vereinigung. In 1889, these parties joined together to
form the Deutschsoziale Partei. The year 1879 in Germany witnessed
not only Marr's popular anti-Semitic publication, but also the rise to
prominence of Adolf Stoecker, imperial court chaplain and anti-Semitic
leader of the Christian Social Party (Christliche-Soziale Partei).[100] In
a major speech delivered at his party's rally on September 19, 1879,
Stoecker, combining religious and racial arguments, warned against the
growing power of Germany's Jews. For Stoecker, the Jews were a state
within a state and a separate tribe within a foreign race, pitted against
both Christianity and Germany's Teutonic nature. Stoecker, believing
that Jews were bound to behave as they did, held out little hope that
the Jews could change and become good Germans.[101]

One year later, the Soziale Reichspartei (Social Reich Party), under
the stewardship of Ernst Herici, gained significant attention through

---

[99] Efron, *Defenders*, 19; Kuehl, *Nazi Connection*, 17; Lerner, *Final Solutions*, 31.
[100] The Christian Social Party was originally called the Christian Social Workers'
Party.
[101] Massing, *Rehearsal*, 285–86.

its promotion of the "Anti-Semites Petition." The petition indicted the Jews as an "alien tribe," seeking to dominate the Aryan race. The petition demanded that the German chancellor, Bismarck, place limits on Jewish rights in Germany, exclude Jews from positions of high governmental authority, and curb the flow of Jewish immigration into Germany. Within its first year of circulation the petition obtained more than 265,000 signatures.[102]

Otto Boeckel was certainly among the best known anti-Semites in Germany during the 1880s and 1890s, both as a popular politician and as author of the widely sold 1885 book, *The Jews: The Kings of Our Times*. Boeckel campaigned indefatigably on the theme of an anti-Jewish program in the rural areas of the German state of Hessen and won election to the Reichstag. He referred to the Jews as an ancient and tenacious race of parasites and exploiters dominating the banks and cattle markets. He echoed the charge that Jews comprise an alien race, thinking and acting differently from Aryans, and that baptism and mixed marriages would not bridge the irreconcilable gap between the Jewish and German nations. Much like his mentor, Wilhelm Marr, Boeckel linked Jewish activities to racial corruption. Boeckel's efforts, most notably as leader of the Peasant League of Hessen, enabled him to play a critical role in the politics of Hessen for several years.[103]

The 1893 Reichstag elections marked a significant victory for Boeckel and Germany's anti-Semitic parties. Sperber reports that between the elections of 1890 and 1893, the vote for the conservative and anti-Semitic parties climbed from 14 percent to 17 percent.[104] In particular, Sperber notes that the vote for the anti-Semitic parties rose from 50,000 in 1890 to 270,000 in 1893 and credits the aggressive racist campaign launched by the anti-Semites for the rise in electoral support.[105] With sixteen representatives in the 1893 Reichstag, the

---

[102] Hans-Ulrich Wehler, "Anti-Semitism and Minority Policy." In Strauss, ed., *Hostages of Modernization*, vol. 3/1, 30; Levy, *Downfall*, 21–23; Lindemann, *Esau's*, 14.

[103] Mosse, *Final Solution*, 166–67; Niewyk, "Solving," 354; Weiss, *Ideology*, 100–01.

[104] Jonathan Sperber, *The Kaiser's Voters: Electors and Elections in Imperial Germany* (Cambridge, 1997), 217. In the 1893 Reichstag, candidates elected on an anti-Semitic platform frequently joined the Conservative Party's Reichstag group (Massing, *Rehearsal*, 229–30).

[105] Sperber, *Kaiser's*, 217.

anti-Semites formed their own independent parliamentary group.[106] Among those racial anti-Semites elected to the Reichstag in 1893 was Hermann Ahlwardt. Ahlwardt gained a seat in the Reichstag from a rural district east of Berlin. In his attacks on Germany's Jews, Ahlwardt invoked racial reasoning, and on a number of public occasions, he called for the extermination of Jews. In a major speech before the German Reichstag on March 6, 1895, Ahlwardt laid out the racial case against Germany's Jews. He cited the irreconcilable differences between the racial traits of the Jews and the Teutons and claimed that studies have shown that the innate racial characteristics of the Jews, acquired over thousands of years, have made it impossible for Jews to change their nature. In one of the more memorable passages from his speech, Ahlwardt posited that, just as a horse born in a cowshed is still no cow, a Jew born in Germany is still a Jew. The cardinal difference between Jews and Teutons, according to Ahlwardt, is that Jews, unlike Teutons, do not ascribe to a culture of labor but rather to a culture of appropriation and exploitation. Ahlwardt went on in his speech to discuss how, after a period of twenty years, even Germany's Polish guests begin to resemble Germans, while after seven to eight hundred years, the Jews in Germany continue to stand out as separate race, refusing to immerse themselves into the cultural soil of labor.[107]

Parliamentary anti-Semitism in Germany began to wane after 1898, as candidates running on a clearly anti-Jewish program failed to garner sufficient votes. Radical racial anti-Semitism between 1898 and Germany's defeat in World War I found a voice, however, in the writings of a group of anti-Semitic polemicists, including Theodor Fritsch and Heinrich Class, and in various fringe movements, such as the Thule Society. Fritsch had gained prominence earlier through the publication in 1893 of his widely circulated *Anti-Semitic Catechism*, which was reprinted after 1896 as *The Handbook of Anti-Semitism*. Before World War I, Fritsch kept up his anti-Semitic tirade through his journal, *Hammer-Blaetter für deutschen Sinn*. Among other themes, Fritsch stressed that Germans

---

[106] Massing, *Rehearsal*, 71; Hajo Holborn, *A History of Modern Germany 1840–1945* (Princeton, 1982), 321. One outcome of the growing popularity of the anti-Semitic wing in German politics may have been the German government's decision during the 1880s and 1890s to conduct mass sweeps to force out the growing alien population in Germany's largest urban areas. While not the only target of the government anti-alien campaign, Russian Jewish immigrants did figure predominantly (Wertheimer, *Unwelcome*, 62).

[107] Massing, *Rehearsal*, 300–05; Weiss, *Ideology*, 104.

should not mix with Jews in order to keep their blood pure. Heinrich Class's chief contribution to racial anti-Semitism was his 1912 book, *If I Were Kaiser*, in which he lays out his radical solution to Germany's so-called Jewish Question.[108] During World War I, the Thule Society advocated a German rebirth and a halt to the degeneration of the German "*Völk.*" In order to accomplish these goals, the Thule Society called for the relentless eradication of the Hebrew race and the termination of racial interbreeding. In the aftermath of Germany's defeat, the Thule Society joined with other anti-Semitic groups, claiming that the national enemy of the creative Germanic race is the parasitic and capitalistic Jewish race.[109]

The impact of several major national traumas in Germany, including the sudden military surrender in 1918, the toppling of the Hohenzollern Empire, the rise of the "red menace" on German soil, and two severe economic collapses (1922–23 and 1930–32), contributed greatly to a period of heightened anti-Semitism during the interwar period. Recently arrived Eastern European Jewish immigrants, whose numbers had climbed precipitously between 1914 and 1922, became a principal focus of an organized campaign of anti-Semitic vitriol, particularly during the economic crisis of 1922–23. Kauders reports that the *Sueddeutsche Mittelstandszeitung* of Nuremberg in April 1922 compared Germany's Ost-Juden to fleas and lice and warned Germany's assimilated Jews to distance themselves from their Eastern European co-religionists. Kauders notes, further, that in late October 1923, the newspaper *Deutscher Tag* referred to Eastern Jewry as vermin and parasites sucking the blood out of the German economy and called for their expulsion from Germany.[110] One month later, Germany's first twentieth-century pogrom erupted in a section of Berlin heavily populated by Eastern European Jews. The *Scheunenviertel* pogrom lasted three days and involved looting of Jewish property and violence, primarily directed against Eastern European Jews.[111]

After World War I, Germany witnessed the spawning of new racist, anti-Semitic parties and movements. Adolf Hitler's German National

---

[108] Weiss, *Ideology*, 106; Levy, *Downfall*, 260–61.

[109] Jay Hatheway, "The Pre-1920 Origins of the National Socialist German Workers' Party." *Journal of Contemporary History*, vol. 29, no. 3, July 1994, 452–54.

[110] Anthony Kauders, *German Politics and the Jews: Duesseldorf and Nuremberg 1910–1933* (Oxford, 1996), 95–96.

[111] Ascheim, "Double," 236.

Socialist Workers' Party is certainly the best-known of these racist anti-Semitic movements, although in the immediate aftermath of World War I, groups like the Pan German League, Reichslandbund, the German Racist League for Defense and Attack, the Voelkischer Schutz-und Trutzbund, and the Thule Society attracted sizable popular support.[112] The German Workers' Party (Deutsche Arbeiterpartei) or DAP, the forerunner of the Nazi Party, sprang out of the chaos surrounding Germany's collapse at the end of World War I. The DAP was formed on January 5, 1919, in Munich under the leadership of Anton Drexler and Karl Harrer. Over the span of a few years, the German Workers' Party grew in size, attracting a heterogeneous following. One of the party's early recruits was Adolf Hitler. In a short time, Hitler made his presence felt, becoming the party's most popular orator.[113] Between 1920 and 1921, Hitler established his complete authority over the party. He added the words *National Socialist* to the party's name and adopted the swastika as the party's symbol and flag, and in February 1920, the party issued its official twenty-five points program. In all, four of the twenty-five points applied directly to Jews. Point 4 stated that only those of German blood were considered *Volksgenossen*, and only *Volksgenossen* could be German citizens. Point 6 of the party program called for the exclusion of Jews from public offices in the German Reich, including offices at the local and state levels. Point 7 addressed the right to deport members of foreign nations (the NSDAP considered German Jews to be foreigners). Point 23 advocated the policy of barring Jews from journalism. Other points in the party program implicitly attacked Jews or Jewish interests, including the call to abolish the "thralldom of interest," confiscation of war profits, nationalization of syndicates and trusts, and prohibition of land speculation.[114]

Under Hitler's leadership, the Nazi Party before 1923 became a rapidly growing Bavarian regional folk (*voelkisch*) movement, although Hitler's initial attempt to seize power in Bavaria by means of a coup collapsed in November 1923. During Hitler's brief 1924 imprisonment in Landsberg Prison for his part in the failed coup, the Nazi Party fell into disarray. Hitler refounded the Nazi Party in February 1925, two months after his release from prison. Later that year, the Nazi Party replaced its "putschist"

---

[112] Weiss, *Ideology*, 223–24.

[113] F. L. Carsten, *The Rise of Fascism*, 2nd ed. (Berkeley, 1980), 95.

[114] Johnson, *Nazi*, 87; H. L. Lebovics, *Social Conservatism and the Middle Classes in Germany, 1914–1933* (Princeton, 1969), 206.

strategy with a strategy to gain power electorally, while establishing the foundations for a national organization. Between the reconstitution of the Nazi Party in 1925 and Hitler's appointment as chancellor in January 1933, Hitler would remain the undisputed leader of the Nazi Party.

The NSDAP electoral strategy hit a major roadblock in the general elections of 1928. The Nazi Party polled a meager 2.5 percent. In contrast to the disappointing showing at the polls, the party's recruitment of new members was extremely successful: membership grew from 27,000 members in 1925 to 108,000 in 1928.[115] The electoral fortunes of the party rose in 1929, as evidenced by strong showings in state and local elections in Schleswig-Holstein, Lower Saxony, and Baden. The first major Nazi electoral breakthrough occurred in the general elections of September 1930. The NSDAP (Nazi Party) received 6,400,000 votes, or 18.3 percent of the total, and gained 107 seats in the Reichstag. As a result, the party was second only to the Social Democratic Party (SPD) in the size of its delegation. After the general elections of July 1932, the NSDAP replaced the SPD as the largest political faction in the Reichstag, with 230 seats. In the July 1932 election, the NSDAP received 13,750,000 votes, or nearly 38 percent of the total. In light of the tremendous popular backing for the NSDAP, President Hindenburg changed his thinking about a Hitler-led government and appointed the Nazi leader chancellor of Germany on January 30, 1933.

Once in power, the Nazi leadership drafted a set of policies based on its racial anti-Semitic ideology that served systematically to disenfranchise the country's Jewish population and to convince them to emigrate. The Civil Service Law of April 7, 1933, coming less than three months after Hitler's ascension to power, called for the removal from their posts of those Jewish civil servants who had not served at the front in World War I. This law included the "Aryan clause" that approved the forced retirement of Jewish judges, teachers, and other Jewish professionals. On September 15, 1935, at the Nazi Party's annual gathering, Hitler announced the party's infamous Nuremberg Laws. The Nuremberg Laws included the "law for the protection of German blood and honor and the Reich Citizenship law." Among other things, these laws provided a legal definition of a Jew and a set of policies restricting physical relations between Jews and Aryans (e.g., sexual contact between Jews and non-Jews and Jewish hiring of non-Jews for domestic help). In November of 1935, the Nazi government followed up on its Nuremberg Laws with

[115] Carsten, *Rise*, 130.

a law specifying in more detail the Nazi definition of a Jew. The "first regulation to the Reich Citizenship Law" distinguished between a pure Jew (*Volljuden*) and part Jew (*Mischling*). The category of pure Jews comprised those with three or more Jewish grandparents. In subsequent legislation, the Nazi regime distinguished between *Mischling* of the first and second degree. A first degree *Mischlinge* had two Jewish grandparents, while a second degree had only one Jewish grandparent. The year 1938 was a particularly harsh one for Jews in Germany. During the months of June and July 1938, measures to prohibit Jewish doctors and dentists from treating Aryan patients and bans on Jewish lawyers representing Aryan clients were enacted. In August 1938, the Nazi regime passed a regulation (that would take effect on January 1, 1939) governing Jewish first names. Parents of newborn Jewish children were obliged to select names from a prescribed list of easily recognizable Jewish names. The new law also required Jewish men and women whose first names were not on the approved list to take a new Jewish first name – Israel for males, Sara for females. Any failure by a Jew to provide his or her new Jewish first name in official dealings could result in severe sanctions for that individual.[116]

Racial anti-Semitic thinking was clearly a cornerstone of Nazi Party ideology and policy. From Lucy Dawidowicz to Daniel Goldhagen and John Weiss, many scholars have asserted that racial anti-Semitism shaped Hitler's worldview, forming the matrix of his ideology and the ineradicable core of National Socialist doctrine. Racial anti-Semitism is indeed present in many early Nazi writings. For instance, Alfred Rosenberg, a rabid anti-Semite and editor-in-chief of the *Voelkischer Beobachter*, the major Nazi Party newspaper, wrote in his widely read commentary on the *Protocols of the Elders of Zion* that Jewishness was unequivocally a racial condition. In Nazi propaganda, Jews were portrayed as the mainstays and chief beneficiaries of exploitative capitalism, the principles advocates of Marxist socialism and internationalism, and the major instigators of a worldwide conspiracy to destroy German and Aryan racial interests.[117] Nevertheless, as I have argued elsewhere – in contrast to Dawidowicz, Goldhagen, and Weiss – we err if we attribute

---

[116] Johnson, *Nazi*, 90–117.

[117] B. Miller Lane and L. J. Rupp, *Nazi Ideology before 1933: A Documentation* (Austin, 1978), xiii–xv; Sarah Gordon, *Hitler, Germans and the "Jewish Question"* (Princeton, 1984), 53–54; K. D. Bracher, *The German Dictatorship: The Origins, Structure, and Effects of National Socialism*, trans. J. Steinberg (New York, 1970).

the Nazi Party's electoral popularity solely to its professed anti-Semitism. Prior to 1933, the Nazi Party's anti-Semitism lacked originality and showed strong similarities to many other Weimar political parties. Nazi anti-Semitism borrowed heavily from the political writings and speeches of Adolf Stoecker, Hermann Ahlwardt, and Otto Boeckel in Germany, Georg von Schoenerer and Karl Lueger in Austria, Edouard Drumont and Maurice Barrès in France, and Henry Ford in the United States.[118] Furthermore, in the world of Weimar politics, the Nazis did not have any ideological monopoly on anti-Semitism and xenophobia. Anti-Semitic utterances found a home among Weimar political parties other than the NSDAP. While it should come as no surprise that the more conservative parties, the German Nationalist People's Party (DNVP) and the German People's Party (DVP), frequently employed racial anti-Semitic rhetoric, the German left could also be counted on to tap into anti-Semitism when they had the opportunity.

During the interwar period, both the German Catholic and Protestant Churches were not immune to anti-Semitism. Protestant theologizing frequently included racist anti-Semitic caricatures. Jews were depicted as corrupt and degenerate and eager to destroy German Christian morality. From their pulpits, some Protestant clergy attacked Jews for their alleged intellectualism and materialism. Conway observed that the Catholic Church was not exempt from anti-Semitism, either. In those Catholic areas that had recently experienced an influx of Eastern European Jews, the Catholic Church had, on occasion, seen fit to target Jews.[119] My general point is that racial anti-Semitic thinking was

---

[118] William I. Brustein, *The Logic of Evil: The Social Origins of the Nazi Party, 1925–1933* (New Haven and London, 1996); William I. Brustein, "Who Joined the Nazis and Why?" *American Journal of Sociology*, vol. 103, no. 1, July 1997, 216–21. My view of the lack of originality in Nazi racial anti-Semitism differs from Friedlaender's (*Nazi Germany*, 86–87). Friedlaender characterizes Nazi anti-Semitism as embodying elements of both a vision of the mythic dimensions of the race and the sacredness of Aryan blood and a more traditional religious vision. Friedlaender refers to this kind of anti-Semitism as "redemptive anti-Semitism." Friedlander writes: "Redemptive anti-Semitism was born from the fear of racial degeneration and the religious belief in redemption: The main cause of degeneration was the penetration of the Jews into the German body politic, into German society, and into the German bloodstream. Germanhood and the Aryan World were on the path to perdition if the struggle against the Jews was not joined; this was to be a struggle to the death. Redemption would come as liberation from the Jews – as their expulsion, possibly their annihilation."

[119] Conway, "National," 140–41.

deeply embedded in interwar Germany, and by itself cannot explain the phenomenal popularity of the German Nazi Party. Nazism, while not eschewing anti-Semitism, benefited greatly from the popularity of other critical factors, not least the party's economic programs.[120]

## GREAT BRITAIN

As the British colonial empire expanded during the nineteenth century to include large portions of sub-Saharan Africa and the Indian subcontinent, racial thinking gained popularity in Great Britain. By mid nineteenth century, British scholarly and popular writings made use of racial taxonomies and spoke of the superiority of the Anglo-Saxon race. In these writings, Jews, for the most part, played a marginal role and received relatively benign treatment, perhaps reflecting the paucity of Jewish settlement in the United Kingdom before 1881 and British anthropological and ethnographic preoccupation with the non-Caucasian peoples of the far-flung British Empire.[121] Interestingly, to explain Britain's relatively low level of racial anti-Semitism, both Efron and Mosse cite the frequent and intimate contact of the British with non-Caucasians and the relative absence of Jews in mid-nineteenth-century Britain. They contrast this to continental Europe, where infrequent exposure to non-Caucasians and the presence of larger Jewish populations resulted in continental Europe's greater preoccupation with racial anti-Semitism.[122] As Mosse asserts for the societies of continental Europe, "the highly visible Jews took the place of blacks, as the 'foils' of race."[123] This claim, however, has never been subjected to empirical verification and does not sufficiently explain variation in racial anti-Semitism within the societies of Europe. Moreover, contact with non-Caucasians and the lack of a major Jewish demographic presence before 1900 did not prohibit French scholars and publicists from embracing racial anti-Semitic thinking.

Scientific racism, and in particular racial anti-Semitism, did find favor in mid-nineteenth-century Great Britain among some prominent intellectuals. In 1850, the famous Scottish anatomist Robert Knox published his major work, *Races of Men*. In his attempt to explain the revolutionary

---

[120] See Brustein's *Logic*.
[121] Efron, *Defenders*, 34–35.
[122] Ibid.; Mosse, *Final Solution*, 70.
[123] Mosse, *Final Solution*, 70.

upheavals of 1848 and to show that racial conflict rather than class conflict is the foundation of revolutionary upheaval, Knox identified the Jews as the racial enemy of the Saxons. He wrote disparagingly of alleged Jewish physical features and focused inordinately on the racial basis of the peculiar Jewish occupational structure. Knox pointed out that Jews were neither craftsmen nor tillers of the soil and lacked ingenuity and a love of the arts. In contrast to the superior Saxon middle classes – depicted by Knox as industrious, thoughtful, clean, punctual, and neat – the Jewish bourgeoisie was scheming, cunning, and usurious.[124]

Knox was certainly not the only prominent British intellectual of the mid to late nineteenth century to employ a form of scientific racism to explain differences between Jews and non-Jews. The celebrated Victorian Hellenist Matthew Arnold, in his *Culture and Anarchy*, published in 1869, offered a systematic comparison of Hebraism and Hellenism. Arnold ascribed to Hebraism the attributes of good conduct and obedience, and to Hellenism the distinctive feature of freedom of spirit and intellect. It was the science of race, Arnold proffered, that furnished the key to understanding the superior genius and history of the Indo-European people – a people that included the English.[125]

British racial anti-Semitism benefited from a series of events during the last quarter of the nineteenth century, among which the "Eastern Crisis" and the Boer War loom large. During the "Eastern Crisis" of the late 1870s, British foreign policy, under the stewardship of Prime Minister Benjamin Disraeli, sought to prevent the total collapse of the faltering Ottoman Empire in the hope of preventing the Russian Empire from spreading its influence into the region. Many in Great Britain opposed Disraeli's policies in light of the alleged Turkish massacre of Bulgarian Christians. Disraeli's Jewish background armed several of his critics with a rationale for his decision to support the non-Christian Turks. Not least among Disraeli's opponents were two notable British historians, Goldwin Smith and E. A. Freeman. Goldwin Smith, a professor of modern history at Oxford, invoked Jewish racial exclusiveness as the motive force behind Disraeli's affinity for Turkish interests. Smith went on to argue that neither Disraeli nor Anglo-Jewry could be considered British patriots by virtue of their Jewish origins. In an essay published in the February 1878 volume of the *Contemporary Review*, Smith claimed that Judaism is a religion of race rather

---

[124] Mosse, *Final Solution*, 67–69; Efron, *Defenders*, 47–53.
[125] Feldman, *Englishmen*, 87–88.

than a form of religious nonconformity. Judaism, for Smith, constitutes the highest level achieved by tribal religion. To Judaism's narrowness, Smith contrasted Christianity's superior universality and humanity. The distinctive character of Jews is rooted not in Judaism's theological tenets but in the racial character of Jews, according to Smith. Furthermore, Smith alleged that for the Jews, the Gentile is not simply different by his or her religion but by blood as well. Citing the Jewish racial character, Smith questioned the fitness of Jews as citizens of Great Britain. Smith continued his racial attack on British Jews in an article entitled "The Jewish Question," which appeared in the 1881 edition of the *Nineteenth Century*. In this article, Smith accused Anglo-Jewry of egotistical exclusiveness and separateness and charged that the Jews consider their race superior to all others. Years later, Smith, a major opponent of the Boer War (1899–1902), would accuse Anglo-Jewish capitalists of having been the hand behind British involvement in the war.[126]

Disraeli's political prominence and the "Eastern Crisis" may have also rekindled E. A. Freeman's racial anti-Semitism. Freeman's *The Ottoman Power in Europe* employed racial theories to explain the positions adopted by Disraeli and the Anglo-Jewish community in England. Freeman saw the common oriental identity shared by Jews and Muslim Turks, at variance with the Christian identity, behind Disraeli's assumed Hebrew policy. Freeman's racial thinking was largely rooted in philology; he emphasized the decisive role of language as the determinant of race. However, one of his important contributions to racial thinking was his noting that the association of language and race was reinforced and modified through culture. By allowing culture to modify the link between language and race, Smith could conveniently distinguish between the less desirable Indian branch and the more desirable Aryan branch (e.g., Teutons, Celts, and Slavs), although both Indian and Aryan branches belonged to the common Indo-European language group. Europeans were, thus, distinguishable by virtue of their community of languages *and* their common civilization based on a shared classical and Christian heritage. The Jews, by virtue of their not belonging to the Indo-European language group and their lacking Christian culture, possessed a distinctive nationality and a religious particularity, and, consequently, stood outside of the wider European family of Christian nations.[127]

---

[126] Feldman, *Englishmen*, 90–91, 97–101; Holmes, *Anti-Semitism*, 11–12; Rubinstein, *History*, 109–10.

[127] Feldman, *Englishmen*, 90–92, 101.

Not only did Disraeli serve as a foil for British racial anti-Semites, his popular novels may have also unintentionally contributed to the popularization of racial anti-Semitism in Great Britain in the mid nineteenth century. Before his ascent to the position of prime minister, Disraeli had achieved a prominent reputation as a novelist. In his 1844 novel *Coningsby*, based largely on his affectionate representation of the Rothschilds, he portrayed a secret and vast Jewish power seeking to achieve world domination. Disraeli invoked the concept of race in ascribing to the Jews such alleged Jewish traits as the taste for power, particular racial pride and sense of superiority, and clandestine and mysterious behavior. Though he was a converted Christian, Disraeli's Jewish ancestry provided ammunition to racial anti-Semites, who could now claim that the racial foundation of Jewish arrogance and the drive for world power had been confirmed by a renowned Jew.[128]

Disraeli's rise to power and the "Eastern Crisis" had provided the context for an outburst of racial anti-Semitism in Great Britain during the mid-1870s and early 1880s. The Boer War and the sudden increase of Eastern European Jewish immigration into England in the late Victorian and Edwardian periods sparked a new anti-Semitic outbreak at the turn of the century.[129] The alien character of the Jews became a theme in the writings of adherents of both the British left and right. In my examination of the economic root of anti-Semitism, I will examine in greater detail the contributions of the renowned intellectual and novelist Beatrice Potter Webb, who was also the wife of the famous British Fabian Socialist Sidney Webb, and the anti-Semitic bestowal of the famous leftist economist J. A. Hobson. Suffice it to say that Beatrice Potter Webb summoned a racial conceptualization to ascribe to the Jews, both native born and foreign born, a superior intellect and a flexible morality, which gave them a certain propensity to acquire wealth and property and to exploit the less-cunning Gentiles.[130] Likewise, Hobson, in his 1891 book *Problems of Poverty*, ascribed the Jewish pursuit of profit and the exploitation of others to the absence of social morality

---

[128] Lindemann, *Esau's*, 76–77.

[129] Reflecting the heightened anti-Semitism during the later Victorian Age was the anti-Semitic propaganda surrounding the dissemination of the malicious rumor that Jack the Ripper, the Whitechapel murderer, was a Jew. Whitechapel, part of London's East End, served as one of the chief repository for Eastern European immigrant Jews (Lebzelter, "Anti-Semitism," 93–94).

[130] Lindemann, *Esau's*, 365–66.

among Jews.[131] Once again, Hobson would target Jews in his 1900 publication *The War in South Africa*, where he claimed that a small group of international financiers, German in origin and Jewish in race, had masterminded British imperialist policy in South Africa. Leftist anti-Semitism in Britain at the turn of the century drew support from other quarters as well. *Justice*, the official newspaper of the British Social Democratic movement, attacked Jewish involvement in high finance by emphasizing that the "bestial behavior" of a certain group of rich British Jews harmed the entire Jewish race. John Burns, a Liberal-Labor member of the House of Commons, in his scathing commentary on Jewish influence on British policy in South Africa, invoked alleged negative Jewish attributes of cowardliness and physical unsightliness.[132]

At the other end of the political spectrum, Arnold White and Joseph Bannister couched their anti-Semitism in the language of race. Arnold White's *The Modern Jew*, published in 1899, alleged that the Jews, unsuccessful at assimilating into British culture, had, through their ability to control influential administrative positions, achieved authority over the English race. White charged the Jews with creating a state within the state and drew attention to the absolute solidarity of world Jewry and its immense power, which he claimed constituted a threat to British international interests.[133] Two years after the publication of White's *The Modern Jew*, Joseph Bannister authored his maliciously biased *England under the Jews*. Recalling the rabid racial anti-Semitism of Lagarde and Langbein, Bannister referred to the Jews as a pestilence, a poison, a deadly bacillus, a parasite, and a beast of prey and implied that the health of the British nation necessitated the removal or elimination of the Jews. Bannister was particularly incensed about the influx of foreign Jews, which he warned had turned Britain into the dumping ground of foreign Jewish parasites – all of whom were thieves, swindlers, perjurers, sexual perverts, forgers, usurers, and blackmailers.[134]

As we witnessed in the cases of France and Germany, the last quarter of the nineteenth century saw the rise of anti-Semitic political movements and parties. In both France and Germany, these anti-Semitic political formations frequently relied on racial arguments. The rise of organized British anti-Semitic movements and parties occurred somewhat later

---

[131] Holmes, *Anti-Semitism*, 20–21.

[132] Lebzelter, "Anti-Semitism," 94–96; Rubinstein, *History*, 111–13.

[133] Lebzelter, "Anti-Semitism," 95–96.

[134] Field, "Anti-Semitism," 298; Lebzelter, "Anti-Semitism," 93.

and, with the exception of Oswald Mosley's British Union of Fascists, failed to achieve the degree of popularity experienced in France and Germany. The list of principal anti-Semitic groups in Great Britain included the British Brothers' League, the Britons, the Imperial Fascist League, the British Fascists, and the British Union of Fascists. These movements endeavored to mobilize support for their anti-Semitic positions through public meetings, marches, and sales of their newspapers. The best known anti-Semitic newspapers were *The British Guardian*, *The Fascist*, *British Fascism*, *Blackshirt*, and *Action*. The earliest of the British anti-Semitic groups was the British Brothers' League (BBL), founded in 1901 in the East End of London by William Evans Gordon. By 1902, the BBL had a following of nearly 45,000, drawn largely from the non-Jewish population of London's East End. The BBL sought to put pressure on the British government to halt the influx of poor foreign Jews into Great Britain. Gordon, who became known as the "father of the Aliens Bill," referred to the type of aliens reaching the British Isles from the Russian empire as "refuse" and not of the material to make good British citizens.[135] In these efforts, the BBL succeeded; in 1905, the British parliament passed the Aliens Act, putting into place Britain's first restrictive immigration policy.[136] Though the Aliens Act did not mention Jews outright, it was clear to most observers that the purpose of the act was to halt the flow of Eastern European Jews into Great Britain.[137] Regarding the Aliens Act of 1905, Winston Churchill aptly remarked that it appealed to the "insular prejudice against the foreigners, to racial prejudice against the Jews, and to labor prejudice against competition."[138]

The Britons, clearly more racially anti-Semitic than the BBL, emerged on the British scene in 1918. Henry Beamish founded the Britons in 1918 and would continue as the movement's president until

---

[135] Israel Finestein, *A Short History of Anglo-Jewry* (New Haven, 1957), 138; John Garrad, *The English and Immigration: A Comparative Study of the Jewish Influx 1880–1910* (London, 1971), 38; Lebzelter, *Political*, 8; J. Green, *Social History of the Jewish East End in London 1914–1939* (New York, 1991), 445.

[136] In 1919, the British government instituted another Aliens Act, which further tightened controls on non-British Empire immigration into the British Isles. Jewish immigration between 1919 and 1933 slowed significantly (Rubinstein, *History*, 274–75).

[137] Tony Kushner, *The Persistence of Prejudice: Antisemitism in British Society during the Second World War* (Manchester and New York, 1989), 10–11.

[138] Garrad, *English*, 142.

his death in 1946. Membership in the Britons was limited to so-called pure-blooded Aryans. Beamish and his movement resolved to warn the world of the Jewish menace and to rid Great Britain of its Jews by forcing them to return to Palestine. In 1923, leaders of the Britons put forward the idea of Madagascar as a Jewish homeland; an island homeland would better ensure the isolation of the Jews. Race figured predominantly in the Britons' propaganda. For the Britons, one cannot be at the same time a member of the Jewish and English races. Moreover, the "Jewish Problem," according to the propaganda of the Britons, was largely a racial and not a religious one. The organization called for strict restrictions on immigration and for prohibiting citizens born to non-British parents from voting and holding public office. Beamish strove to disseminate the Britons' racial anti-Semitism through the movement's publications. Among those publications were Beamish's 1920 *The Jew's Who's Who*; the Victor Marsden translation of the infamous *Protocols of the Learned Elders of Zion*; Lord Sydenham's *The Jewish World Problem*; and such journals as *Jewry uber Alles*, *British Guardian*, and *The Investigator*. *The Investigator* appeared first in 1937 and displayed the swastika and the motto "For Crown and Country, Blood and Soil."[139] Both Eatwell and Lebzelter observe that by the 1930s many members of the Britons advocated the extermination of the Jews as a solution to the "Jewish Problem."[140]

In the spring of 1929, Arnold Leese founded the Imperial Fascist League (IFL) and began publishing its journal, *The Fascist*. Leese, a veterinary surgeon, claimed that the Jews were responsible for all the corruption and evil existing in the world. Leese attributed to the Jews responsibility for Freemasonry, communism, capitalism, and unemployment. Race thinking was central to the platform of the IFL. Leese asserted that race served as the basis of all politics and claimed that the Aryan and Jewish races were locked in a battle for control over the world. Leese called upon the "noble" Aryans to rid the world of the Jewish pollution in order to preserve civilization and frequently referred to Jews as a "negroid tribe." Like Beamish, Leese supported a plan to relocate the Jews to Madagascar, but in the 1930s he suggested, as a way to rid the world of the Jewish menace, forcible sterilization and mass murder by the lethal chamber.[141]

---

[139] Lebzelter, *Political*; Robert Benewick, *Political Violence and Public Order* (London, 1969), 42–43; Roger Eatwell, *Fascism: A History* (New York, 1996), 225–26.
[140] Eatwell, *Fascism*, 226; Lebzelter, *Political*, 65.
[141] Rubinstein, *History*, 204; Benewick, *Political*, 44–46; Holmes, *Anti-Semitism*, 164; Green, *Social*, 77; Field, "Anti-Semitism," 299.

A forerunner to Mosley's British Union of Fascists was the British Fascists. Anti-Semitism, while present, did not play as central a role in the ideology and programs of the British Fascists as it did for Beamish's Britons and Leese's IFL. The party sought to mobilize popular support principally through the publications of its papers, *Fascist Bulletin* and *British Fascism*. The British Fascists included calls for the removal of Jews from public posts, the revocation of Jewish citizenship, and the termination of Jewish domination over British financial, political, industrial, and cultural interests. The British Fascists additionally alleged that Jews were responsible for the spread of communism and that German Jews ran the government of the Soviet Union.[142]

The largest and best-known of Britain's fascist and anti-Semitic movements between the wars was the British Union of Fascists (BUF), led by Sir Oswald Mosley. Official estimates put the movement's membership at roughly 500,000 in 1934. In its early days, the BUF refrained from anti-Semitism and included among its members some Jews.[143] However, within its ranks, the BUF contained a number of prominent anti-Semites such as William Joyce, John Beckett, and Arthur Keith Chesterton, who may have eventually been partly responsible for the BUF's embrace of anti-Semitism. Signs of an emerging anti-Semitism first appeared in a front-page article in November 1933 in the movement's newspaper, *Blackshirt*. The article accused Jews of controlling British newspapers, international finance, and politics and spoke of a Jewish aim to achieve world domination. The article alleged that British Jews were using their influence for the benefit of their race as opposed to the interests of the British. Jews, especially recent immigrants to the East End of London, were singled out as perpetrators of unpalatable crimes and antisocial behavior. The major publications of the British Union of Fascists advocated a policy of segregation and deportation of Jews, although the BUF's leading newspaper, *Blackshirt*, left open the possibility of more radical solutions in its October 31, 1937, edition. The October 31 edition noted that before long, science might provide the means to fully rid England of the Jewish pest.[144]

---

[142] Kenneth Lunn, "The Ideology and Impact of the British Fascists in the 1920s." In Tony Kushner and Kenneth Lunn eds., *Traditions of Intolerance: Historical Perspectives on Fascism and Race Discourse in Britain* (Manchester and New York, 1989), 150–51; Benewick, *Political*, 29–37.

[143] Skidelsky, *Mosley*, 380; Lebzelter, *Political*, 109; Eatwell, *Fascism*, 235.

[144] Mandle, *Anti-Semitism*, 44; Skildelsky, *Mosley*, 342–44, 380; Lebzelter, "Political," 416–20; Holmes, *Anti-Semitism*, 180–82; Green, *Social*, 460; Eatwell, *Fascism*, 235–36. Tony Kushner ("The Paradox of Prejudice: The Impact of

By 1936, Joyce and Beckett had persuaded Mosley to adopt a more virulent anti-Semitism and to focus the attention of the BUF on the slum-ridden East End of London. To that end, Mosley organized several meetings and marches in the predominantly Jewish East End of London, culminating in the violent clash between the Blackshirts and Jews in the well-known "Battle of Cable Street" in early October 1936. The East End of London figured as well in Mosley's political plans in 1937. London's East End, while home to a large, relatively unassimilated Jewish population, also contained a sizable non-Jewish working-class population that had exhibited noticeable sympathy toward anti-Semitic rhetoric since late in the nineteenth century. The British Union of Fascists decided to run candidates in the March 6, 1937, elections in three electoral districts of the East End of London (Shoreditch, Limehouse, and Bethnal Green North-East). Anti-Semitism figured predominantly in the BUF's campaign, most notably in the Shoreditch race, where the rabidly racial anti-Semite William Joyce ran. The BUF included in its electoral campaign attacks on Jewish international finance, Jewish support for communism, Jewish control of the established political parties, and Jewish ownership of property and business in the East End. The BUF obtained 14 percent of the popular vote in Shoreditch. The BUF's best electoral showing occurred in the Bethnal Green district of the East End, where the two BUF candidates combined to win 23 percent of the popular vote. In none of the districts did the BUF candidates win election.[145]

Racially tinged anti-Semitic rhetoric did not confine itself solely to the publications of the marginal radical anti-Semitic and fascist movements in Great Britain. Mainline newspapers could be counted on to fuel the flames of racial anti-Semitism. An illustrative case can be gleaned from the prestigious London newspaper *The Times*, which published a series of articles under the heading "Alien London" in the autumn of 1924. One of these articles, published on November 27, 1924, and dedicated to the settlement of Jews in London's East End, stated: "They stand aloof – not always without a touch of oriental arrogance – from their fellow citizens. They look upon us with suspicion and a certain

Organized Antisemitism in Britain during an Anti-Nazi War." In Kushner and Lunn, eds., *Traditions of Intolerance*, 78–79) reminds us, however, that calls for the extermination of Jews by Mosley and the BUF were rare. More common was the demand that Jews and foreigners be expelled from Great Britain in order to remove alien influences and to free the national race consciousness.

[145] Mandle, *Anti-Semitism*, 56–58; Skildelsky, *Mosley*, 393–94, 408–09; Eatwell, *Fascism*, 235–39.

contempt. Mixed marriages between orthodox Jews and Gentiles are forbidden. These people remain an alien element in our land."[146]

## ROMANIA

In the case of Romania, the spread of racial thinking certainly had more to do with nation building and fear of continuing immigration of Russian and Galician Jews than with a need to legitimate a Romanian colonialism. Unlike France, Germany, Italy, and the United Kingdom, Romania undertook no foreign colonial adventures during the nineteenth and twentieth centuries. Given Romania's relatively late independence; its sensitivity to the perception of the great powers' intrusion into Romanian domestic matters; and its less-than-cordial relations with neighboring Austria-Hungary, Bulgaria, the Ottoman Empire, and Russia, fervent nationalism held a paramount place within Romanian society. Moreover, strong nationalism often begot suspicion of resident ethnic minorities. After independence, Romanian nationalists strove to define which groups belonged to the Romanian nation. For many Romanians, resident Jews were racial outsiders who, even with conversion, could never become full members of the Romanian nation.

Romanian racial anti-Semitism before the Holocaust rarely drew upon the burgeoning race science emerging in Western Europe. For instance, Nagy-Talavera posits that the racial form of anti-Semitism failed to excite Romanian anti-Semites as it did their counterparts in Western Europe.[147] Why? We saw, notably in the cases of Britain, France, and Germany, that racial science furnished an explanation for superior industrial and cultural development and a justification for colonial enterprises. Romania, by contrast, was economically underdeveloped relative to the big powers of Western Europe and, given the absence of a colonial empire, had no need to justify its domination over colonial peoples. To say that Romanian racial anti-Semitism seldom made use of race science is not to say that Jews were depicted favorably or as racial equals. For Oldson, racial anti-Semitic thinking peppered the writings and speeches of some of Romania's most respected and influential intellectuals between 1879 and 1914. Oldson characterizes the hostility displayed by

---

[146] David Cesarani, "Joynson-Hicks and the Radical Right in England after the First World War." In Kushner and Lunn, eds., *Traditions of Intolerance*, 128.

[147] Nicholas M. Nagy-Talavera, *The Green Shirts and the Others: A History of Fascism in Hungary and Rumania* (Stanford, 1970), 332.

Romanian intellectuals toward Jews as unique vis-à-vis the hatred directed toward other ethnic minorities in the new nation. Underlining the potential impact of the intellectuals' anti-Semitism on the Romanian masses, Oldson notes: "If men of such stature and talent thought this way, if they equated anti-Semitism with being Romanian and with the fundamentals of the nation's heritage, we cannot be surprised at the continuing impact they have had."[148]

Among the well-known Romanian intellectuals who voiced concern over the threat that Jews presented to Romanian national culture were poets Vasile Alecsandri, Cezar Bolliac, and Mihai Eminescu; literary critic Titu Maioerescu; historians Bogdan Petriceicu Hasdeu, V. A. Urechia, Alexandu D. Xenopol, and Nicolae Iorga; politicians Mihail Kogălniceanu and Ion Heliade-Rădulescu; scientists N. Istrati and Nicolae Paulescu; economists Pop Martian and A. S. Aurelian; philosopher and professor of law Vasile Conta; and political economist Alexandru Cuza.[149]

Racial anti-Semitism was certainly discernible in the anti-Semitism of these intellectuals. In our earlier discussion of religious anti-Semitism, we encountered the anti-Semitism of Nicolae C. Paulescu, a well-known professor of physiology at the medical school of the University of Bucharest, co-founder of the anti-Semitic National Christian Union, and co-publisher of the anti-Semitic newspaper *Apărarea Națională*. During the 1920s, Paulescu had asserted that Romania faced a conflict between "Godly Christianity" and "Devilish Judaism." Paulescu also employed racial arguments in his anti-Semitism in that he claimed that the "Jews are a race ruled by two essential passions: the instincts of domination and ownership." He noted, furthermore, that the four vices of rousing, lechery, greed for riches, and vanity all had Jewish origins. Paulescu proffered that the sole panacea for Romanians, given the Jewish threat, consisted of a steadfast anti-Semitism. Paulescu based his racial anti-Semitism on what he referred to as philosophical physiology. For Paulescu, the doctrines of the Talmud and the Cahal revealed the means by which the Jews would secure world domination and exterminate other peoples.[150]

Among late nineteenth-century intellectual anti-Semites, Mihail Eminescu and Vasile Conta loom large, thanks in large part to their

[148] Oldson, *Providential*, 99–101.
[149] Oldson, *Providential*; Vago, "Traditions," 110; Volovici, *Nationalist*, 14.
[150] Volovici, *Nationalist*, 28–29; Livezeanu, *Cultural*, 265–66; Ancel, "Image," 47.

stellar reputations as scholars. Eminescu, a journalist and the national poet of Romania, is frequently referred to as "Romania's Shakespeare." This late nineteenth-century literary luminary did much to give legitimacy to a racial anti-Semitic bias in Romania. His writings became part of the curricula in Romanian schools and universities and stood on the shelves of Romania's intelligentsia. Eminescu accused the Jews of corrupting the native culture wherever they gained the rights of citizenship and of being too consumed with their own racial identity to commit themselves to the Romanian nation.[151] Vasile Conta, a professor of law and an elected deputy to the Romanian parliament, is considered the most important Romanian philosopher of the late nineteenth century. Volovici notes that Conta was the true founder of Romanian ideological anti-Semitism. In a well-publicized speech to the Romanian parliament debating Jewish civil rights in September 1879, Conta invoked "the principles of modern science" to oppose Jewish rights. For Conta, race contributed to the basis of a nation, and Jews could never become members of the Romanian nation, even through conversion to Christianity or intermarriage. Conta claimed that "[t]he Yids constitute a nation that is different from all the other nations, and they are their enemies. . . . They [Jews] were descendants of a single race, which has always kept itself pure. . . . The supreme aim of Jews, formulated in the Bible and Talmud, was to enslave all the other people to the Jewish people in order to secure the rule of the entire world by the yids."[152]

After 1900, the dissemination of racial anti-Semitism continued as a theme in the works of a new generation of Romanian intellectuals, including the two luminaries Nicolae Iorga and Alexandru Cuza. Nicolae Iorga's name belongs to the long list of prominent Romanian intellectuals who either led the anti-Semitic crusade or jumped onto the anti-Semitic bandwagon before the Holocaust. Iorga's influence on Romanian anti-Semitism is profound, given his standing as a renown professor of history at the University of Bucharest, a member of the Romanian Academy, an elected deputy to the Romanian parliament, and of the post of prime minister. In 1895, Iorga, along with Alexandru Cuza and Jean de Biez, founded the International Anti-Semitic Alliance and in 1906 began to publish the anti-Semitic newspaper *Neamul Românesc*. Iorga equated true Romanian nationalism with anti-Semitism. The highly influential Iorga considered Jews as commercial

[151] Oldson, *Providential*, 115–20.
[152] Volovici, *Nationalist*, 14.

vampires and parasites and argued that Romanian Jews did not belong to one of the "healthy races" because of Jewish exploitative activities and the lack of attachments to Romanian cultural and historical heritage. He claimed that the Jews were largely responsible for the miserable plight of Romania's peasantry and accused the Jews of acting as the agents in order to propagate the "Germanization" of Romania. Iorga called for a Romania for the Romanians and only for Romanians.[153]

For the first four decades of the twentieth century, Cuza was indisputably Romania's most radical intellectual anti-Semite and, among Romanian anti-Semites, came closest to laying out a Romanian science of race. Cuza, a professor of political economy and law at the University of Iasi and a former president of the Romanian Chamber of Deputies, founded the International Anti-Semitic Alliance along with Iorga and Jean de Biez in 1895 and contributed to well-known Romanian anti-Semitic publications such as *Neamul Românesc* and *Apărarea Națională*. Among Cuza's anti-Semitic publications was his 1910 monograph *The Reduction of the Christian Population and the Increase in the Number of Kikes*.[154] Cuza, unlike the majority of Romania's intellectual anti-Semites, advocated a "science of antisemitism" deriving from a synthesis of history, anthropology, theology, politics, political economy, and philosophy. Influenced by the racial theories of H. S. Chamberlain, Cuza's new science of anti-Semitism led him to claim that Jews constituted an inferior alien race incorporating particular physical and moral characteristics that made them inassimilable into other populations. In contrast to the Romanian race, the Jewish race lacked seriousness, clarity, and precision of expression.[155] Cuza claimed that through the application of the new science, he had discovered a practical solution to the "Jewish Problem" – that is, the elimination of the Jews from society, which would serve to terminate their unnatural and parasitic presence and help to ensure the peace of all nations.[156]

Cuza's science of anti-Semitism would become the cornerstone of his Christian Nationalist Defense League (LANC) party program and be instrumental in the shaping of the extreme philosophy of Corneliu Codreanu and his fascist Iron Guard.[157] A forerunner of Cuza's vehemently

---

[153] Oldson, *Providential*, 132–35; Butnaru, *Silent*, 25.
[154] Butnaru, *Silent*, 25.
[155] Vago, "Traditions," 112, 118; Volovici, *Nationalist*, 26.
[156] Volovici, *Nationalist*, 26–27.
[157] Ibid.

anti-Semitic LANC was the National Democratic Party (co-founded in 1910 by Cuza and Iorga). The party's program called for the total elimination of Jewish influence from the social, economic, cultural, military, and political life of Romania.[158] Cuza's LANC got off the ground in 1923. Cuza selected the swastika as a symbol for his movement.[159] Expanding upon the platform of the National Democratic Party, the LANC incorporated a more radical anti-Semitism, including the abrogation of political rights for Jews and the expulsion of Jews who had entered Romania after 1914.[160] *Apărarea Națională* became the official newspaper of the LANC movement. In 1935, the aging Cuza merged the LANC with Octavian Goga's National Agrarian Party. For Cuza, minimal electoral successes in the elections of 1927 (1.90 percent), 1931 (3.89 percent), 1932 (5.23 percent), and 1933 (4.47 percent) led him to seek an alliance in order to enhance the electoral prospects of his party.[161] Octavian Goga, a well-known poet and a member of the Romanian Academy, founded the National Agrarian Party in 1932. Pronounced anti-Semitism seems not to have played a dominant role in Goga's political thinking before 1932. Shapiro believes that Goga's post-1932 anti-Semitism derived largely from Goga's perception that former Hungarian Jews residing in Romanian Transylvania supported a "Magyarization" of Transylvania.[162] The new party took the name National Christian Party, or PNC. With the merger, the new National Christian Party held eighteen parliamentary seats, and the swastika became the party's symbol. The program of the PNC opposed liberalism and Marxism, while favoring nationalism, Christianity, and the constitutional monarchy. Regarding Romania's Jews, the party platform called for the expulsion of those Jews who had entered Romania after 1918, either themselves or their ancestors. The remaining Jews would have to observe a strict *numerus clausus* and would be excluded from all public offices.[163] Like many of the radical political parties and movements of the interwar period, the PNC supported its own paramilitary units.

---

[158] Iancu, *Les Juifs*, 227–29.

[159] Paul A. Shapiro ("Prelude to Dictatorship in Romania: The National Christian Party in Power, December 1937–February 1938." *Canadian-American Slavic Studies*, vol. 8, no. 1, Spring 1974, 50) observes that Cuza had been using the swastika as a symbol for his anti-Semitic movements as early as 1910.

[160] Volovici, *Nationalist*, 26–27.

[161] Hitchins, *Rumania*, 403–04; Shapiro, "Prelude," 49.

[162] Shapiro, "Prelude," 49.

[163] Shapiro, "Prelude," 51; Hitchins, *Rumania*, 404.

The PNC's paramilitary unit took the name "Lancieri." The blue-shirted Lancieri members engaged in numerous violent acts against Romania's Jewish population between 1935 and 1937.[164]

Among Romania's anti-Semitic movements, Corneliu Zelea Codreanu's Iron Guard is clearly the best known. Codreanu, inspired by the teachings of Cuza and Iorga, had during the 1920s been a follower of Cuza's LANC and had played an important role in LANC's student organizations. By 1927, relations between the seventy-year-old Cuza and his young disciple had badly deteriorated in disputes over the means and goals of LANC. In the same year, Codreanu founded the Legion of the Archangel Michael, which became the Iron Guard in 1930. The Legion's uniform consisted of a green shirt, Sam Browne belts, and black trousers inserted into high leather boots. The Legion maintained its own salute, imitating the Roman gesture, and published its own newspaper, *Pământul Strămoşesc*. Codreanu sought to mobilize followers around the themes of a revolutionary movement of Christian rejuvenation, anti-Bolshevism, anticapitalism, and anti-Semitism. The Iron Guard ideology held that while Romanian values embodied faith, hard work, patriotism, cleanliness, and spiritual purity, Jewish characteristics included loudness, greed, uncouthness, and pornography. Codreanu opined further that the Jews were sucking the Romanian lifeblood and poisoning the Romanian spirit, and that the "Jewish Problem" could only be resolved by removing the Jews from Romanian life. For Codreanu, the Jews were Romania's curse, and his movement set out to rid Romania of Jews while openly calling for the destruction of the Jews.[165] During one of the Legion's first party conferences in Oradea in December 1927, Jewish synagogues in the vicinity were sacked and burned, and Jewish property was pillaged.[166] By 1930, the Iron Guard was active in both university settings and rural areas within the newly acquired territories. In one incident in the Romanian town of Borşa, the Iron Guard is believed to have inspired a major anti-Semitic attack by armed peasants against the town's population of 4,000 Jews.[167]

In order to gauge the popularity of the brand of radical racially inspired anti-Semitism of Cuza, Goga, and Codreanu, we can look to the

---

[164] Shapiro, "Prelude," 51.
[165] Fischer-Galati, "Fascism," 165; Shapiro, "Prelude," 49; Mendelsohn, *Jews*, 203–04; Bela Vago, *The Shadow of the Swastika* (Farnborough, 1975), 22–23; Butnaru, *Silent*, 45; Wistrich, *Antisemtism*, 146; Mosse, *Final Solution*, 197–98.
[166] Butnaru, *Silent*, 45.
[167] Livezeanu, *Cultural*, 291–92.

December 1937 Romanian national elections. In December 1937, the Iron Guard and the PNC ran separate slates of candidates in the national election. Together, the two anti-Semitic parties captured nearly 25 percent of the popular vote and 105 seats in the Romanian parliament. In the national elections of December 20, 1937, six major political parties ran candidates. Both the Iron Guard and the PNC made anti-Semitism a central theme of their campaigns. The Iron Guard, with 15.58 percent of the vote, came in third among the parties, and the National Christian Party, with 9.15 percent of the vote, finished fourth. Shapiro, in studying the results of the 1937 election, notes that the voting patterns for each of the anti-Semitic parties were not overlapping but rather geographically complementary.[168] The combined vote of the two anti-Semitic parties ranged from a high of 32.1 percent in Bukovina to a low of 18.6 percent in Transylvania.[169] The Goga-Cuzist PNC and Codreanu's Iron Guard did not cooperate during the election. In fact, their paramilitary groups clashed on a number of occasions before the election.[170] Though the combined PNC and Iron Guard vote failed to account for an electoral majority in the December 1937 election, King Carol II nevertheless, on December 28, 1937, brought into power Europe's second overtly anti-Semitic government, headed by Goga. On January 21, 1938, the King and Goga approved a measure calling for a mandatory review of the citizenship of Romanian Jews. On February 27, 1938, the Romanian parliament ratified a law to define membership in the Romanian nation based on blood. The new law offered a legal distinction between Romanians "by race" and Romanians "by residence."[171]

Romanian racial anti-Semites did show a preference for the Sephardic over the Ashkenazic Jews. The Romanian historian Alexandru D. Xenopol distinguished between the French, Italian, and Spanish Jews, all of whom had learned the language of their host countries, and the Romanian Jews, who, even after generations of residence, continued to misuse Romanian and preferred to express themselves in "the intolerable jargon of Jewish-German." [172] Eminescu claimed that the Spanish and

[168] Shapiro, "Prelude," 65.
[169] Ibid., 59.
[170] Ibid.
[171] Ioanid, *Holocaust*, 18–19.
[172] Oldson, *Providential*, 128–29. According to Oldson (*Providential*, 128–31), Xenopol seems to fluctuate between a religious and a racial critique of Jews. On the one hand, he summons Romania's Jews to seek baptism and to intermarry to accomplish assimilation, while on the other hand, he claims that Romania's

Polish Jews had little in common, while Hasdeu opined that Romanians admired the occasional cultured Romanian Jew.[173] Interestingly, it was not uncommon to hear prominent Romanians suggest a preference for awarding civil rights to the more-assimilated Sephardic or "Spanish" Jew while steadfastly refusing civil rights to the less-assimilated Ashkenazic or "Galician-Russian" Jew. The fact that Romania's Sephardic Jews tended to reside in Wallachia, while the Ashkenazic Jews lived in Moldavia and later in the newly acquired provinces of Bessarabia and Bukovina, may help to explain regional variation in Romanian anti-Semitism as well as the greater survival rate of Wallachian Jews vis-à-vis non-Wallachian Jews during the Holocaust.[174] For anti-Semites, the Ashkenazi Jews of Bessarabia and Bukovina, rather than the Sephardic Jews of Wallachia, more clearly embodied the negative Jewish stereotype (orthodox, Yiddish-speaking, long hair, and curled sideburns).[175] The Romanian preference for Sephardic Jews surfaced in an interview given by the newly appointed prime minister of Romania on January 10, 1938. In his interview with the French newspaper *Paris Soir*, Octavian Goga spoke of his preference for the olive-skined, black-eyed, reasonably fine-featured Jews of the Old Kingdom, who had descended from Spanish Jews of the fifteenth century, while denigrating the horde of "barbaric" Jews in the recently acquired Romanian provinces, who had originated in Poland and Russia and whose dominant features included slanted eyes, flattened faces, and reddish skin.[176] Regarding the

---

Jews constitute a foreign enemy rather than a religious enemy and that the likelihood that Jews would abandon their traditional ways and assimilate into the Romanian national culture was minute.

[173] Oldson, *Providential*, 144–45.

[174] Oldson, *Providential*, 4; Mendelsohn, *Jews*, 173–74; Iancu, *L'Emancipation*, 18; Ioanid, *Holocaust*, 13. Also, Ioanid (*Holocaust*, 13) observes that the Jews of Wallachia were largely of both Sephardic and Ashkenazic backgrounds. However, he emphasizes that in contrast to the Jews of Moldavia, the Wallachian Jews had established themselves in Wallachia in earlier times and were typically more assimilated than the Jews of Moldavia. Moreover, Leon Volovici has suggested to me that Ashkenazic and Sephardic Romanian Jews tended to specialize in different professions. Ashkenazic Jews were more likely than Sephardic Romanian Jews to be inn-keepers and sellers of spirits – occupying professions that produced heightened tensions with non-Jewish Romanians. Thus, according to Volovici, the overrepresentation of Ashkenazic Jews in certain professions elicited greater antipathy toward them.

[175] Fischer-Galati, "Fascism," 158–59.

[176] Ioanid, *Holocaust*, 18–19.

Romanian role in the regional pattern of Jewish victimization during the Holocaust and, more specifically, the higher survival rate of Jews residing within Wallachia, Oldson observes that "[t]hey did not butcher or allow Germans to take the bulk of their own Jews."[177] By contrast, the high level of Jewish victimization in Transylvania may be attributed to the general perception that Transylvanian Jews (particularly in the northern regions of Transylvania) preferred Magyar over Romanian culture, which rendered them suspect (like Bessarabian and Bukovinian Jews) to many Romanian anti-Semites.[178]

National insecurity certainly contributed to anti-foreign sentiment and, particularly, to anti-Semitism in pre–World War I Romania. Romanian national insecurity did not wane during the interwar period, and thus, not surprisingly, anti-Semitism remained a potent force. The creation of a "Greater Romania" after 1919 – with the annexation of Bessarabia, Bukovina, and Transylvania, with their large non-Romanian populations – and the post-1919 awareness of Hungarian and Russian irredentist claims prompted a full-scale campaign to Romanize the new territories and heightened suspicion of possible "fifth column" ethnic minorities. In 1919, Ion Brătianu, the Romanian prime minister, informed President Woodrow Wilson that the influx of inassimilable Russian and Ukranian Jews into Romania was not unlike the "Yellow Peril" confronting the United States.[179]

Given Romania's history of repression of Jews and its reluctance to grant Jews citizenship, it should come as no surprise that Jews in Romania resisted Romanian acculturation. Mendelsohn notes that, according to the 1930 census, 728,115 of the 756,930 Jews in Romania claimed Jewish rather than Romanian nationality.[180] Reluctance among many of Romania's Jews in the newly acquired provinces to embrace sufficiently Romanian culture may have fueled Romanian insecurity and resentment of Jews during the interwar period. This reluctance needs to be addressed against the backdrop of the Romanian perception that Jews had demonstrated little resistance to embracing Magyar and German language and culture.[181] Consistent with the claim that Jews had failed to embrace Romanian culture is Nagy-Talavera's assertion that Romanian Jews in 1940 celebrated the Soviet Union's annexation

---

[177] Oldson, *Providential*, 4.
[178] Fischer-Galati, "Fascism," 160.
[179] Marrus, *Unwanted*, 64.
[180] Mendelsohn, *Jews*, 180.
[181] Lindemann, *Esau's*, 312.

of Bessarabia and northern Bukovina and Hungary's annexation of
Transylvania.[182]

Racial anti-Semitism failed to gain a significant foothold in Italy before
1938. The context in which the science of race in general, and racial
anti-Semitism in particular, seemed to flourish elsewhere in Europe failed
to take shape in late nineteenth- and early twentieth-century Italy.[183]
Italy's relatively late colonial adventures in Libya, Eritrea, and Somali
failed to elicit a rationalization for colonial conquest based, as elsewhere
in Western Europe, on the "white man's burden" or the superiority of
the Aryan or Anglo-Saxon races. Italian intellectuals and politicians
turned to a demographic argument – namely that conquest provided
an outlet for Italy's excess population – to justify Italy's need to gain
colonial possessions. Moreover, leading Italian anthropologists such as
Enrico Morselli claimed that the inhabitants of Italy's African colonies
belonged to the white race.[184] A context to nourish the growth of racial
anti-Semitism differed in other important respects in pre-Holocaust
Italy. Whereas the wave of Ashkenazi and Yiddish-speaking Eastern
European and Russian Jews appeared to swamp Great Britain, France,
Germany, and Romania after 1881, relatively poor and geographically
remote Italy experienced very little Jewish immigration before the mid-
1930s. Throughout the period, Italy's Jewish population grew slowly and
retained its highly assimilated character.[185] I shall return to the subject
of the high level of Italian Jewish assimilation below.

The particular character of Italian nineteenth-century nationalism,
in addition to Italy's colonial experience and Jewish immigration, may
have contributed to a context in which racial anti-Semitism fell short.

---

[182] Nagy-Talavera, *Green Shirts*, 320–32.

[183] Ballinger (Pamela Ballinger, "Submerged Politics, Exhumed Pasts: Exodus, Collective Memory, and Ethno-National Identity at the Borders of the Balkans."
Ph.D. diss. Johns Hopkins University, 1998, 115) appears to offer a dissenting
opinion on the lack of Italian racial or ethnic prejudice. While Ballinger agrees
that racial anti-Semitism lacked a popular basis in Italy, fascist mistreatment of
the subject peoples of Italy's African empire (black Ethiopians) and the Balkans
(Slovenia and Croatian Slavs) showed that Italians were not immune from ethnic, racial, and national chauvinisms.

[184] Canepa, "Christian," 27–28.

[185] Roth, *History*, 475; Canepa, "Christian," 17.

Canepa notes that Italian nineteenth-century nationalism differed from the nationalisms emerging elsewhere in Europe in that Italian nationalism until 1938 embraced a more universalistic concept based on cultural criteria rather than racial or *voelkisch* criteria.[186] Regarding the Jews, many Italian nationalists never lost sight of the contributions of Italian Jews to Italy's long struggle for national independence between 1815 and 1870. Moreover, Italian patriots, such as Massimo D'Azeglio, in writing about the "Jewish Question" in 1848, stressed the linking of Jewish emancipation and regeneration to the unification of Italy.[187]

Despite the less-than-fertile soil for the emergence of racial science in Italy, racial thinking found some prominent Italian adherents. Within the community of late nineteenth-century Italian scholarship, the writings of Cesare Lombroso, Paolo Mantegazza, Guglielmo Ferrero, Enrico Ferri, and Alfredo Niceforo employed the new science of race to explain phenomena ranging from the alleged Jewish trait of usury to the social and economic backwardness of southern Italy. While I will concentrate on Italian racial thinking in the context of anti-Semitism, I want to emphasize that much of the interest in Italy regarding the new racial thinking surrounded differences between northern and southern Italians rather than the Jews. Both Lombroso's *In Calabria, 1862–1897* and Niceforo's *L'Italia barbara contemporanea* drew upon the new science of race to explain Italy's economic and military problems, which they attributed to the backwardness of southern Italy. Not surprisingly, Lombroso's and Niceforo's books appeared in the aftermath of Italy's startling military defeat at the hands of Abyssinian forces at Adowa. Niceforo employed his system of the classification of human types to argue that southern Italians were biologically destined to be dominated by others and that they represented a "feminine people" within the Mediterranean racial stock. He contrasted the inferior stock of southern Italy to the northern Italians, who belonged to a "masculine people" within

---

[186] Canepa, "Christian," 17.

[187] Steinberg, *All or Nothing*, 221–22. Before the fascist seizure of power in Italy, few nationalist writings invoked anti-Semitism. There were exceptions, however. A notable exception was Francesco Coppola, who in his article "Israele contro l'Italia," published in the November 16, 1911, edition of *Idea Nazionale*; his article "Nazionalismo e Democrazia," published on December 28, 1911, in *Idea Nazionale*; and his reply to his critics, "Il mio antisemitismo," published in the November 30, 1911, edition of *Idea Nazionale*, questioned Jewish attachment to Italian nationalism. Several fellow nationalists severely criticized Coppola for this expression of anti-Semitism (Thayer, *Italy*, 213, 423).

the racial family of Celts. Niceforo would publish a subsequent volume in 1901 (*Italiani del nord e italiani del sud*) extending his racial scientific claims about the differences between northern and southern Italians. In this second volume, Niceforo makes use of the cephalic index, based on the research of Giuseppe Sergi, to demonstrate scientifically that the superiority of northern Italians over southern Italians can be attributed to the longer male cranium of northern Italians.[188]

If Niceforo applied racial thinking to the southern Italians, other prominent Italian scholars sought to apply the new science of race to the Jews. Foremost among these scholars were Mantegazza, Lombroso, Ferrero, and Ferri. In 1885, Paolo Mantegazza authored three influential articles – "La questione antisemitica," "La questione è chiusa," and "La razza ebrea davanti alla scienza," – in the journal *Fanfulla della Domenica*. Mantegazza linked alleged Jewish traits of usury, worship of gold, and hypochondria to race. Much like Lombroso, Mantegazza sought to provide a scientific explanation of anti-Semitism, while at the same time opposing the persecution of Jews.[189]

Cesare Lombroso, a respected physician and criminologist and considered the most eminent figure in Italian positivism, published *L'antisemitismo e la scienze moderne* in 1894. Lombroso's work sought to explain the reasons for popular anti-Semitism and the persecution of Jews. Along with Guglielmo Ferrero, author of *L'Europa Giovane*, and Enrico Ferri, Lombroso based his arguments on both cultural and racial thinking, claiming that both Jewish attachment to antiquity and inherent Jewish traits are responsible for particular Jewish behaviors, such as the purported acquisitive instinct (*appartarsi dagli altri*). Though Lombroso considered the Jews to be more Aryan than Semitic, he was highly critical of some Jewish religious rites, including circumcision. While Lombroso invoked notions of racial science in his research, he ultimately held that the so-called Jewish Problem would disappear as Jews modernized and became more assimilated into European society.[190]

We have seen how German and British eugenicists at the beginning of the twentieth century advocated biological and medical intervention to preserve the nation's racial purity and to halt racial degeneration.

---

[188]  Thayer, *Italy*, 177–81.

[189]  Toscano, "L'uguaglianza," 220–24; Anna Rossi-Doria, "La diffidenza anti ebraica liberale e democratica." In Dataneus, ed., *L'Italia e l'antisemitismo* (Rome, 1993), 42–43.

[190]  De Felice, *Storia*, 31; Toscano, "L'uguaglianza," 220–24; Rossi-Doria, "La diffidenza," 42–43.

In Italy, the eugenics movement never attracted the kind of following that it found in northern Europe, nor did it embrace racial thinking or call for laws to enforce forced sterilization or intraracial marriage. With few exceptions, Italian eugenicists saw eugenics as a means to eradicate societal misery and to improve the quality of life. Italian eugenicists asserted that the radical and racially based Northern European form of eugenics ran counter to Italy's Latin and Roman Catholic culture.[191] The Italian eugenics movement began to develop on the eve of World War I, as the scientific contributions of Darwin and Lombroso (particularly his investigation of delinquency) gained the attention of Italian scholars. In 1912, Serafino Patellani created the first university course in social eugenics in Genoa, and shortly thereafter, Giuseppe Sergi established the Committee for the Study of Eugenics in Rome. During the early interwar period, the Italian eugenics movement was led by Ettore Levi, Achille Loria, and Enrico Morselli. Only in the latter stages of Italian fascism do we find acceptance of the more radical German/Anglo-Saxon strain of eugenics and biological racism in Italy. More specifically, in the midst of Italy's Ethiopian adventure in the mid 1930s, biological racism begins to gain favor among a small contingent of Italian racist thinkers, including Preziosi, Cipriani, Cogni, and Evola. Evola presents arguments that there is a *sangue ebreo* (Jewish blood) and that there exists an inherent opposition between the Aryan and Semitic spirits.[192]

Elsewhere in Europe before World War I, ardent nationalists frequently adopted and espoused racial anti-Semitism. In Italy, nationalist anti-Semitism before World War I constituted the exception rather than the rule. Nationalist criticism of Italian Jews, when it occurred, typically focused on the perception that Italian Jews would support the Zionist movement.[193] Those extremists – whether politicians, publicists, or writers – who welcomed racial anti-Semitism tended to employ a rather loosely defined notion of race, a notion stressing a social and nonbiological foundation and associating the Italian race with concepts like "a people of rulers."[194] Nonetheless, examples of nationalistic racial anti-Semitism in Italy before fascism do exist. As one of the earliest known and most visible cases of nationalistic Italian racial anti-Semitism, Molinari cites Francesco Pasqualigo's (Italian deputy from Veneto) 1873

[191] Roberto Maiocchi, *Scienza italiana e razzismo fascista* (Florence, 1999), 9–10.
[192] Ibid., 11–25.
[193] De Felice, *Storia*, 46, 54–55; Molinari, *Ebrei*, 25.
[194] Gunzberg, *Strangers*, 229–33.

letter to the Italian king advising the king not to accept the appointment of a Jew, Isacco Pesaro Maurogonato, as finance minister. Pasqualigo charged that since Jews comprise "a state within the state," Italy would be ill served by this appointment.[195] In the Jesuit journal *La Civiltà Cattolica*, we come across a reference to Jews as a dangerous race in its defense of the guilty verdict in the Dreyfus case in France. According to *La Civiltà Cattolica*, the "Jewish race" perpetrated the treachery of Dreyfus as part of its conspiracy against Catholic and French interests. The "Hebrews" seek to dominate the world, and the states of Europe should all agree to consider the Jews as foreigners and revoke their citizenship, according to the Jesuit journal.[196]

Also, several well-known Italian nationalistic novelists and playwrights occasionally employed notions of race and nation. Vestiges of a racially anti-Semitic portrayal emerge in the fictional work of Gabriele D'Annunzio, Carducci's heir as Italy's major poet and one of pre-fascist Italy's most famous ultra-nationalists. In D'Annunzio's 1889 *Il piacere* and his 1905 *Che l'amore*, he highlights alleged negative Jewish behavioral and physical features.[197] Here we also find the writings of Enrico Corradini and Alfredo Oriani, who employed race in the years before World War I to criticize the purported Jewish parasitic inclinations and preferences for city life.[198] The 1930s in Italy marked a dramatic rise in the quantity of racial anti-Semitism in both fictional and pseudo-scientific scholarly works. Among the many fictional works offering negative racial portrayals of Jews in the 1930s are Alfredo Panzini's *Viaggio con la giovane ebrea*, Michele Saponaro's *Bionda Maria*, Enrico Corradini's *Beniamino Nicosia*, Salvator Gotta's *Lilith* and *Il Paradiso Terrestre*, and Giovanni Papini's *Gog* and his *La leggenda del Gran Rabbino*.[199]

In light of the relative dearth of public signs of racial anti-Semitism in Italy before 1938, the publication on July 14, 1938, of the Italian

---

[195] Molinari, *Ebrei*, 37.

[196] Gentile, "Struggle," 499. Surprisingly, we might have expected to find traces of racial anti-Semitism in the writings of the ultra-nationalistic and influential journal *La Voce* during the Dreyfus Affair. This journal, edited by Giuseppe Prezzolini, frequently lavished praise on the anti-Dreyfusard and anti-Semitic French nationalist Charles Maurras, but condemned racism and anti-Semitism. Prezzolini attacked anti-Semitism as "beastly" and "vile" and praised the Jewish people as the salt of the earth (Gentile, "Struggle," 510).

[197] Canepa, "Image," 264–65.

[198] Gunzberg, *Strangers*, 228–29, 241.

[199] Ibid., 251–52.

fascist anti-Semitic "Manifesto of the Racist Scientists" (*Manifesto degli scienziati razzisti*) seems out of place to many students of Italian anti-Semitism. Much has been written about Mussolini's alleged "volte-face" with regard to anti-Semitism. Did he always harbor racially anti-Semitic views but, for opportunistic reasons, downplay them until the propitious moment? Did Hitler finally convince Mussolini of the so-called Jewish racial threat? Or did Italian anti-Semitic racism lack the biological features found in racial anti-Semitism in other European societies? All of these assertions have found support in the scholarly literature on Italian fascist anti-Semitism. Between 1922 and 1936, the official view of the Italian fascist government was that the "Jewish Problem" did not exist in Italy. During this period, Jewish rights were respected, public expressions of anti-Semitism by Fascist Party leaders were rare, and, within limits, the efforts of the Italian Zionist Federation to create a Jewish homeland were encouraged.[200] Furthermore, in their thinking about the relationship between race and nation, Mussolini and most early Italian fascists rejected the biological arguments of their German counterparts. The Italian fascist notion of nation appeared to emphasize the significance of a national unity based on a shared idea, a larger moral and spiritual concept of culture, and the importance of historical traditions. Italian fascism apparently ruled out race as a factor in the determination of nation.[201] (It should be noted that the large number of Italian Jews in the Italian Fascist Party certainly played a role in the party's public positions on Jewish issues. We will have the opportunity to discuss Jewish participation in Italian fascism when we examine the political root of anti-Semitism.) Yet Ledeen sees underneath the veneer of the benign fascist stance on Jews, a hidden residue of anti-Semitism.[202] As examples of an underlying anti-Semitism, Ledeen points to an unsigned article in the November 29, 1928, edition of *Il Popolo di Roma* attacking Italian Zionists for their dual loyalty and to the fact that throughout the

---

[200] Michaelis, *Mussolini*, 28.

[201] Risa Sodi, "The Italian Roots of Racialism." *UCLA Historical Journal*, vol. 8, 1987, 43; Michaelis, *Mussolini*, 29; Bernardini, "Origins," 433, 445. A major exception here among the early Italian fascists, according to Sodi ("Italian," 43), is Giulio Cogni, who adopted a biological definition drawing heavily upon Houston Chamberlain. Cogni published his views in *Il Razzismo*. For an excellent discussion of the writings of and the differences among Italian fascist racists during the 1930s and 1940s, see Sodi's article ("Italian," 40–71).

[202] Michael A. Ledeen, "The Evolution of Italian Fascist Antisemitism." *Jewish Social Studies*, vol. 37, no. 1, January 1975, 8–11.

1920s, several influential positions in the fascist regime were held by
such well-known anti-Semites as Roberto Farinacci, Mario Carli, and
Giovanni Preziosi.[203] De Felice opines, by contrast, that between 1919
and 1938, there was no *single* Italian fascist position on Jews but rather
many competing strains within the party.[204]

By 1936, overt signs of racial anti-Semitism began to emerge, and,
again, context appears to have played an important part in the rise
of this anti-Semitism. Italy's invasion of Ethiopia figures centrally in
Mussolini's change of heart regarding the Jews. Mussolini believed that
"international Jewry" had sided with Great Britain to oppose his invasion of Ethiopia and that both Italian Jews and international Zionists
had failed to convince the members of the League of Nations to lift the
economic boycott of Italy imposed after his Ethiopian invasion. The
Ethiopian conquest also gave prominence to the issue of race, after
the fascist government tried to prevent intimate contact between its
soldiers and Ethiopian blacks. In an attempt to preclude racial mixing
between Ethiopians and Italians, theories of race were presented that
consequently opened the door to the question of the racial identity of
Italian Jews.[205] Mussolini's fateful decision in 1936, in the wake of the
Ethiopian invasion and the commitment to aid General Franco in the
Spanish Civil War, to enter into an alliance with Nazi Germany may
have pushed him farther along the road to a more explicit anti-Semitism.
De Felice posits that the implementation of racially anti-Semitic policies resulted largely from pragmatic political factors, including Italy's
preoccupation with its new colonial empire and its intensifying, though
unequal, relationship with Hitler's Germany. For De Felice, Mussolini's
Italian racial decrees pertaining to the Jews were considerably milder
than those in Germany, and their mildness reflected the low levels of
popular anti-Semitism existing in Italy.[206] Hughes assigns greater independence to Mussolini's decision to support the implementation of
the 1938 anti-Semitic legislation. In Hughes's view, Mussolini sought to
create his own version of anti-Semitism based primarily on "creative"
or spiritualist considerations, while eschewing anthropological or biological arguments. He argues that direct pressure from Nazi Germany

---

[203] Ibid., 8–9, 11.
[204] De Felice, *Storia*, 67.
[205] Molinari, *Ebrei*, 113; Bernardini, "Origins," 440–41; Ledeen, "Evolution," 13–14;
Zuccotti, *Italians*, 34.
[206] De Felice, *Storia*. See also Ballinger ("Submerged," 113–14) for a similar reading
of De Felice.

to institute anti-Semitic policies had little or no impact on Mussolini's decision.[207]

A series of anti-Semitic articles and books preceded the publication of the "Manifesto of the Racist Scientists." Mussolini authorized Paolo Orano (a fascist member of parliament and the rector of the University of Perugia) to publish a critical analysis of the "Jewish Question" in 1937. Orano's 1937 *Gli ebrei in Italia* summarized many of the recent fascist allegations leveled against the Jews, including Jewish ties to internationalism, Zionist support for British policies in the Mediterranean, and Jewish dominance in the antifascist Popular Front in France. Orano delved deeper into the divergence between Jewish and non-Jewish Italians, pitting the Christian and fascist Italian values of idealism, faith, discipline, duty, sacrifice, and obedience against the Jewish attributes of materialism, anarchy, insubordination, and individualism. Orano charged that the Jewish people were essentially revolutionaries who sought to control and undermine the societies in which they resided.[208] In the immediate aftermath of the publication of Orano's book, the principal newspapers across Italy launched a series of articles addressing issues surrounding the "Jewish Question," followed by the publication of a series of anti-Semitic books and periodicals. Among these new anti-Semitic publications appearing in early 1938 were Giovanni Preziosi's edited volume *Italian Life*, Alfredo Romanini's *Jews, Christians and Fascism*, Roberto Farinacci's *Regime fascista*, Telesio Interlandi's *Tevere*, and Giulio Evola's *Three Aspects of the Jewish Problem*. The infamous "Protocols of the Learned Elders of Zion," which had been previously translated and published in Italian by Preziosi in 1921, was now reprinted.[209]

The Italian government began to institute bans on Jews residing in Italy before the publication of the "Manifesto." In August 1937, the government halted the admission of foreign Jews into Italian universities and banned most Jews from teaching in Italian schools.[210] The actual "Manifesto of the Racist Scientists," commissioned by Mussolini

---

[207] Hughes, *Prisoners*, 58.

[208] Bernardini, "Origins," 441–42; Molinari, *Ebrei*, 113; Alexander Stille, *Benevolence and Betrayal: Five Italian Jewish Families under Fascism* (New York, 1991), 65.

[209] Molinari, *Ebrei*, 113; Roth, *History*, 523; Meir Michaelis, "Fascist Policy toward Italian Jews: Tolerance and Persecution." In I. Herzer, ed., *The Italian Refuge: Rescue of Jews during the Holocaust* (Washington, DC, 1989), 53.

[210] Grosser and Halperin, *Anti-Semitism*, 257–59.

and signed by a group of so-called racial experts, appeared on July 14, 1938. The document contained ten alleged scientific propositions, each followed by a brief commentary. Included as racial precepts were that different races exist, that the concept of race is purely biological, that the population of Italy is of Aryan origin, that a pure Italian race exists, and that Jews do not belong to the Italian race. The "Manifesto" proclaimed further that Jews and Africans belong to extra-European races.[211] The arguments presented in the "Manifesto" appeared to contradict the traditional fascist conception of nation, which had conceived of the nation as an organic state based on historical traditions rather than racial criteria.[212] In the days and months following the publication of the "Manifesto of the Racist Scientists," a series of anti-Jewish laws and regulations were issued. The new laws contained bans on Jews' practicing certain professions and on Jews' marrying or employing non-Jewish Italians. Additionally, the laws included restrictions on Jews' owning property or businesses over a certain value, the termination of Jewish service in the Italian military and Jewish membership in the Italian fascist party, and a ban on Jewish attendance at Italian public schools. Jews (including those naturalized) who had settled in Italy or its colonies since 1919 were given six months to leave the country.[213]

A number of scholars of Italian fascism and Italian anti-Semitism have concluded that the institution of the racially anti-Semitic measures in Italy marked a significant disjunction in the modern history of Italian and Jewish relations. These scholars also question the extent to which the majority of Italians embraced fascist anti-Semitism before and during World War II. They point to the uneven enforcement and frequent disregard by the majority of Italians of the racial laws; the role that so many non-Jewish Italians played in sabotaging the efforts of fascist and German anti-Semites to impose the Final Solution on Italian Jews; the high percentage of Italian Jews who survived the Holocaust, largely through the efforts of Italians to hide them from the Germans; and the undertaking by the Italian military to block Croatian and Vichy French attempts to imprison and deport Jews.[214]

---

[211] Stille, *Betrayal*, 70; Michaelis, *Mussolini*, 152–53; Bernardini, "Origins," 445; Zuccotti, *Italians*, 35.

[212] Bernardini, "Origins," 445.

[213] Zuccotti, *Italians*, 6, 36–37; Stille, *Betrayal*, 77; Michaelis, "Fascist," 54; Roth, *History*, 527.

[214] Ballinger, "Submerged," 113–15; Eatwell, *Fascism*, 86–87.

My survey of the literature on Italian anti-Semitism clearly supports the view that, in comparison to France, Germany, and Great Britain, Italian racial anti-Semitism had minimal popular appeal in Italy between 1879 and 1939. Earlier, I suggested that the particular character of the Italian colonial experience and the highly assimilated nature of Italian Jewry may help to explain the lack of a racially anti-Semitic culture in pre-Holocaust Italy. Let me turn attention now to Italy's Jews. Jews had resided in Italy for two thousand years. Though many of Italy's Jews descended from a Sephardic background, a sizable number of Ashkenazic Jews had crossed the Alps from France and Germany from the fourteenth to the sixteenth century and settled in northern Italy. Between 1850 and 1939, the Jewish population of Italy grew from roughly 35,000 to 50,000. The Italian Jewish population throughout most of the nineteenth century comprised a slightly smaller percentage of the total population than its French equivalent, that is, one-tenth of one percent. With the notable exception of Rome, Italian Jews generally concentrated in towns and cities throughout northern Italy. In 1931, not counting Rome (12,000 Jews), the largest Jewish concentrations were found in Milan (6,500), Trieste (5,000), Turin (4,000), Florence (2,730), and Genoa (2,500). Since the mid sixteenth century, few Jews had resided in southern Italy.[215] Whether of Sephardic or Ashkenazic background, by the end of the nineteenth century, Italian Jews had assimilated into the non-Jewish society more thoroughly than Jews elsewhere.[216] Jewish ease in assimilating into Italian society was bolstered by several factors. In contrast to Jews in many parts of Europe, Italian Jews were more likely to speak the local dialect of the community. Not only did Italian Jews blend in linguistically, they mingled physically with the Mediterranean peoples of Italy. While Italian Jews affiliated with three different kinds of synagogues – Ashkenazic, Sephardic, and Italian – they generally resisted the rigid religious orthodoxy found in many Jewish quarters north of the Alps. This lack of rigidity may partially explain the failure of the Jewish reform movement to establish itself in Italy during the nineteenth

---

[215] Della Pergola, "Precursori," 70–71; Arnaldo Momigliano, *Ottavo contributo alla storia degli studi classici e del mondo antico* (Rome, 1987), 361; Hughes, *Prisoners*, 4–5; Roth, *History*, 474; Rossi, "Emancipation," 113; Lindemann, *Esau's*, 472–76.

[216] Canepa, "Christian," 14; Ivo Herzer, "Introduction." In Herzer, ed., *Italian Refuge*, 5; Roth, *History*, 474.

and twentieth centuries.[217] Indeed, the universalistic nature of Italian
nationalism, the secular ideology of the Italian state, and the complete
legal emancipation of Italian Jews after Italian national independence
facilitated the high degree of assimilation.[218] A possible measure of
Jewish assimilation was the high percentage (relative to other European
countries) of mixed marriages between Jews and non-Jews in Italy before 1938. According to a 1938 Italian census (*Demografia e Razza*),
43.7 per cent of marriages involving Jews were marriages in which either the bride or groom was not of the Jewish faith.[219] The percentage
of mixed marriages in Italy during the interwar period appears to be
significantly greater than elsewhere in Europe. De Felice observes that
the *Demografia e Razza* reported that the percentage of Jews marrying
non-Jews was roughly three times higher in Italy than in Germany on
the eve of the Nazi takeover and two times greater than in Hungary in
1932.[220]

Another sure sign of Jewish assimilation was the degree of Jewish social, cultural, and political mobility within Italy. The Jewish Italian
patriot Daniele Manin became president of the Venetian Republic
in 1848. The Italian Jew Luigi Luzzatti, having served as minister of
the treasury (on several different occasions) and minister of agriculture, became Italian prime minister from 1905 to 1911. Ernesto Nathan
served as lord mayor of Rome from 1907 to 1913, while at various junc-
tures, Sidney Sonnino (who had a Jewish father) held the positions of
Italian prime minister, finance minister, and foreign secretary. Other
prominent Italian Jews holding important government positions were
Carlo Schanzer, Leone Wollenborg, General Giuseppe Ottolenghi, and
Giacomo Malvano. In 1874, Jews comprised fifteen members of the
Italian parliament, and in 1923, eleven Jews served in the Italian
Senate. Italian Jews had volunteered in large numbers to fight on the
front in World War I, and many Jews had earned the highest military
honors during World War I. At war's end, there were at least eleven

---

[217] Stille, *Betrayal*, 25; Steinberg, *All or Nothing*, 222–23; Canepa, "Christian," 25;
Hughes, *Prisoners*, 9–11. Stille (*Betrayal*, 171–72) observes that the assimilation
of Italian Jewry was more prevalent in northern Italy and that a large proportion
of the Jews of Rome remained barely literate, deeply religious, and closely tied
to the traditions of their community.
[218] Canepa, "Christian," 17.
[219] De Felice, *Storia*, 17; Steinberg, *All or Nothing*, 223.
[220] De Felice, *Storia*, 17.

Jewish generals in the Italian army.[221] And finally, Jews comprised more than ten thousand members of the Italian Fascist Party.[222] I will have more to say about Jewish participation in Italian fascism when I examine the political root of anti-Semitism. Although there is strong evidence of Jewish assimilation in other European countries before 1939, the thoroughness of Italian Jewish assimilation and the acceptance on the part of most non-Jewish Italians of Jews as simply Italians practicing a different religious faith were exceptional.

Because it embodied the scientific spirit of the time, the racial strain of anti-Semitism appealed to a generally more educated stratum of society than the traditional religious variety. The fact that many of the scholarly proponents of racial anti-Semitism came out of the most respected ranks of society and included luminaries from science and literature certainly bolstered the popular acceptance of racial anti-Semitism. These prominent racial anti-Semites can in no way be classified as marginal or fringe figures. The advent of racial anti-Semitism handed anti-Semites a new, and more dangerous, tool to explain alleged Jewish misdeeds. Now it could be argued that Jews carried out such crimes as the ritual murder of Christian children not because they were following the dictates of their cruel religion but rather because they were evil by nature.[223] Racial anti-Semites claimed that it was scientifically demonstrable that Jews belonged to a distinct Semitic race – a race inferior to the Indo-European Aryan race – and that the Semites and Aryans were locked in conflict with one another for survival. For racial anti-Semites, Jews could never be full participants in an Indo-European nation-state by virtue of their inherent character, which derived from their race. Jews constituted a separate race with their own customs, religious beliefs, and practices in the eyes of racial anti-Semites.[224] It is worth repeating that if for religious anti-Semites, solving the "Jewish Problem" meant converting Jews to Christianity, for racial anti-Semites, resolution of the "Jewish Problem" could not be met by conversion, because Jews would always be Jews regardless of conversion. Resolution required either the isolation of Jews from Gentile society or the physical removal of Jews and the Jewish presence.

---

[221] Molinari, *Ebrei*, 71–72; Israel Cohen, "The Jews in Italy," *The Political Quarterly*, vol. 10, July–September, 1939, 4–5; Lindemann, *Esau's*, 475–76.

[222] Marrus, *Unwanted*, 280.

[223] Finzi, *Anti-Semitism*, 45.

[224] Katz, *Prejudice*, 136; Pauley, *Prejudice*, 4–5; Wistrich, *Antisemitism*, 47; Almog, "Racial," 270–73; Poliakov, *Aryan*, 281.

Moreover, my examination of the racial root of anti-Semitism takes issue with those who assert that German racial anti-Semitism was both qualitatively and quantitatively different from anti-Semitism elsewhere in Europe before 1939. Without reliable empirical evidence, I can hardly agree with Efron's conclusions regarding the uniqueness of German racial anti-Semitism. Efron has argued that in the context of racial science the Jew personified "the other" in German discourse to an extent found nowhere else in Europe, and that Jews as a race were discussed more in Germany than elsewhere in Western Europe during the late nineteenth and early twentieth centuries.[225] My examination of the racial root of anti-Semitism has shown that the pseudo-science of race attracted adherents throughout Europe, and that Jews figured predominantly in the rhetoric of race in France, Germany, and Great Britain, although racial anti-Semitism did attract scattered support in Italy and Romania. Though a cursory glance at the findings reported in Figure 3.4, depicting anti-Semitic acts and attitudes, suggests confirmation of Efron's contention, an in-depth examination of the findings raises some reservations. Of the 251 German laws or acts of discrimination listed for the 1899–1939 period, 173 happened after 1933 (Hitler's ascension to power), and all 12 of the newspaper articles from the *Berliner Morgenpost* coded as racially anti-Semitic were published between 1933 and 1939. Not to be discounted, Figure 3.4 shows that in terms of newspaper articles exhibiting a racial anti-Semitic tone, the Britain's *Daily Mail* surpassed the German *Berliner Morgenpost*.[226]

In the case of Italy, the absence of late nineteenth-century and early twentieth-century waves of Eastern European immigrants, the highly

---

[225] Efron, *Defenders*, 16.

[226] The newspaper coverage of racial anti-Semitism in Figure 3.4 is based on the results of question 19 in the coding instrument. Question 19 focuses on whether the article discusses the racial form of anti-Semitism. Question 20 addresses the tone or orientation of the article – that is, is the tone of the article unfavorable toward Jews. The data show the following for the five countries: eight of the thirty-one British articles emphasized negative racial traits of Jews, while none of the eight French articles, six of the twelve German articles, six of the eleven Italian articles, and none of the Romanian articles emphasized negative racial traits of Jews. Also, all six German articles emphasizing negative racial traits of Jews appeared between 1933 and 1939, while five of the six Italian articles emphasizing negative racial traits of Jews were published in either 1938 or 1939. For Britain, the eight unfavorable articles are scattered across the entire 1899–1939 period.

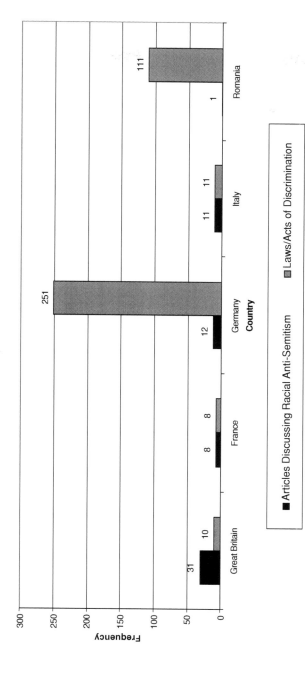

Figure 3.4. Newspaper articles discussing racial anti-Semitism and laws/acts that discriminate against Jews by country, 1899–1939. *Note:* Articles are taken from the fifteenth day of the month for every month between 1899 and 1939. Articles were taken from the *Daily Mail* in Great Britain (N = 299), *Le Petit Parisien* in France (N = 199), *Berliner Morgenpost* in Germany (N = 269), *Corriere della Sera* in Italy (N = 101), and *Universul* in Romania (N = 136). Laws/acts of discrimination are taken from the volumes of the *American Jewish Year Book* and include two categories from the typology (see Table 1.1). The first includes general laws and acts discriminating against Jews. The second includes expulsions, citizenship reversals, deportations, and laws against Jewish immigration and naturalization.

assimilated nature of Italian Jews, and Italy's relatively unsuccessful colonial experience (until 1935) likely dampened the prospects for the acceptance of racial anti-Semitism. My examination of the volumes of the *American Jewish Year Book* and the editions of the *Corriere della Sera* for the years 1899 to 1939 supports this portrait of Italy. Nine of the eleven Italian laws or acts of discrimination occurred in 1938 and 1939, while seven of the eleven newspaper articles exhibiting a racial anti-Semitic orientation appeared between 1937 and 1939. Of the four articles published between 1899 and 1937 coded as racially anti-Semitic, three discussed Jews outside of Italy. In the case of Romania, if the post-1919 annexation of territories heavily populated by Ashkenazi Jews provided fertile ground for the growth of racial anti-Semitism, Romania's lack of colonies and relatively low level of economic development probably attenuated the outlook for a full-blown racial anti-Semitism.[227]

Clearly the emergence of racial anti-Semitism marked a fundamental change in popular anti-Semitism. Yet other changes were occurring in Europe after 1879 that would bring to the fore new or remolded strains of anti-Semitism. We now turn our attention to the economic root of anti-Semitism.

---

[227] Comparing the principal and secondary newspapers in each of the five countries for 1921, 1933, 1935, and 1939, I found little variation within the British, French, Italian, and Romanian reportage regarding the number of articles discussing racial anti-Semitism. The sole exception was within the German reportage. For the selected years, the *Berliner Morgenpost* contained no articles discussing racial anti-Semitism, while the *Neueste MunchenerNachrichten* contained twelve such articles.

# CHAPTER FOUR

# The Economic Root

Over the centuries, Jews have been variously characterized as miserly, manipulators of money, ultra-materialist, and possessors of extraordinary wealth. The pervasiveness of the link between Jews and unsavory economic practices can be seen in the not-too-distant past in the usage of such unflattering verbs as "to Jew" (to cheat or to overreach) and "to Jew down" (to drive down the price unfairly by bickering) and in one of the definitions of the word "Jew" (i.e., "applied to a grasping or extortionate usurer") found in the authoritative *Oxford Universal Dictionary*, at least until 1955.[1]

The history of the economic root of anti-Semitism, while not quite as long as that of the religious root, dates back to the Christian medieval period in Europe. Warnings against middleman practices are found in the writings of early Christian fathers such as John Chrysostom and Augustine. It wasn't until the twelfth century, however, that the Catholic Church at the Lateran Council of 1139 assigned a negative significance to usury. Usury had originally referred to the cost to be paid for the use of borrowed money. In the decisions reached at the Lateran Council, usury took the meaning of charging excessive or illegal interest on a loan. The Lateran Council asserted that those who practice usury, or those who practiced it but failed to repent, would be refused a Christian burial.[2] European Jews increasingly found themselves the object of charges of usury as well as a host of other economic sins, including dishonest practices in petty commerce and secondhand trade,

---

[1] Glock and Stark, *Christian*, 109–10; Langmuir, *History*, 65.

[2] Finzi, *Anti-Semitism*, 15.

and the pursuit of parasitic and nonproductive commercial activities.[3] Why did this occur? There is no question that Jews were overrepresented as moneylenders, peddlers, and merchants in Christian Europe. Though it officially condemned usury, the Roman Catholic Church throughout the Middle Ages derived benefits from the existence of usury and from Jews as usurers. In the eyes of the church, Jews, having cut themselves off from the saving grace of Jesus Christ, were a likely group to perform the necessary but sinful practice of moneylending.[4] Moreover, the crown, cognizant of the Christian Church's prohibition against usury for good Christians, encouraged Jewish moneylending in its pursuit of its own prosperity and revenues. As the crown considered Jews its own private property, it saw fit to compel Jews to serve the role of moneylenders.[5]

Moneylending was one of the few professions open to Jews in Christian Europe. More and more, Jews were restricted to those economic activities considered the least desirable, such as moneylending, and to those that did not engender competition for Christian guilds. For instance, medieval merchant guilds successfully blocked Jews from selling their goods in shops or at the marketplace, while craft guilds prevented Jews from manufacturing goods. Ironically, before the clergy and Christian guilds successfully enlisted the support of the royal authority to restrict Jews from manufacturing activities, many early medieval European Jewish artisans had distinguished themselves as metal and gold workers, dyers of cloth, and glassblowers. Consequently, Jews were left to peddle goods in the street or countryside and to buy and sell second-hand wares, particularly clothing.[6] Prior to the Holocaust, much had been made of the fact that Jews rarely pursued the farming profession. The dearth of Jews in farming in Europe has a foundation in medieval European prohibitions against Jewish property ownership. Weiss has properly noted that land constituted a principal source of power and status in the Middle Ages in Christian Europe, and he who owned land had power over the serfs and a say in the selection of local priests.[7] The Christian Church also depended on the payment of a tithe and feared that Jewish landholders might refuse to pay the church tithe. To that end, the church strongly discouraged its faithful from selling land to Jews or

[3] Weiss, *Ideology*, 9; Glock and Stark, *Christian*, 109–10.
[4] Pauley, *Prejudice*, 3, 14.
[5] Golding, *Jewish*, 52–57.
[6] Golding, *Jewish*, 52–57; Weiss, *Ideology*, 9–12.
[7] Weiss, *Ideology*, 11–12.

offering land to Jews in exchange for their debts.[8] While Jews confronted obstacles in owning land, they were permitted and frequently encouraged by the crown or nobility to manage large estates. Especially in East Central Europe, Jews became prominent as administrators of large noble estates. Levine, who has intensively examined the economic origins of anti-Semitism in East Central Europe, observed that in 1616 more than one-half of the crown estates in the Ukraine had Jewish managers (*arendars*). The chief duty assigned to the Jewish managers was to increase the estate's revenues through more efficient collection of rents and taxes from the estate's serfs. By standing as intermediaries between the nobility and the serfs, Jews served as convenient buffers and scapegoats in times of growing economic tension.[9] By virtue of their experience as moneylenders and estate agents, numbers of Jews found employment as royal usurers of the princes, or "court Jews," and were largely responsible for managing the personal finances of the aristocracy throughout much of Europe. Illustrative of the famous "court Jews" was Joseph Süss-Oppenheimer, who, in mid-eighteenth-century Germany, arose from court agent of Duke Karl Alexander of Württemberg to the high post of privy councilor. Oppenheimer would become the *Jud Süss* of later anti-Semitic legends.[10] Even more famous than Oppenheimer, Meyer Amschel Rothschild, the patriarch of the famous Rothschild banking family, began as a court agent in 1769 to William, prince of Hessen-Kassel.[11] I will have more to say about the Rothschilds and their role in the rise of banking later.

Restrictions on Jewish employment in medieval Christian Europe tell us only part of the story of why Jews were overrepresented as moneylenders. Much has been made of the ways in which the religions of Judaism and Christianity offered contrasting views of the financial enterprise. Many Christian theologians had preached against usury from the early Middle Ages, and Christian doctrine had at the time of the Lateran Council in the twelfth century made the practice of lending money at interest a sin for Christians. A Jewish interpretation of the Old Testament prohibition on moneylending resulted in the distinction between lending among Jews and lending between Jews and Gentiles. In particular, Jews believed that the Torah gives legitimacy to usury in

[8] Ibid.
[9] Levine, *Economic*, 61–62.
[10] Ferguson, *World's*, 41.
[11] Ibid., 43.

the passage "to a foreigner thou mayest lend upon interest, but unto thy brother thou shalt not." According to this interpretation, Jews could not charge fellow Jews interest, but lending at interest to Gentiles was permissible.[12] During the twelfth century, Moses Maimonides, a great Jewish thinker, offered further support for lending at interest to Gentiles when he wrote that it is a commandment for Jews to require interest of a non-Jewish borrower. For many Jewish contemporaries of Maimonides, the act of charging Christians interest on loans would ensure that Christians and Jews would limit their interactions to business and lessen the likelihood of Jewish conversion to Christianity, which might result from more intimate and friendly relationships.[13] Levine adds that, in contrast to Christians, Jews, free from the discouragement of their religious leaders, were able during the late Middle Ages and early modern period to develop improved instruments and institutions of credit such as the *mamran* (a fully negotiable instrument of exchange developed by sixteenth-century Polish Jews).[14]

Before the nineteenth century, popular economic anti-Semitism in Europe typically embodied accusations of alleged unethical business practices in second-hand trade, petty commerce, and moneylending conducted by Jews. As the nineteenth century unfolded, economic anti-Semites would add the charge that Jews inordinately controlled the major means of production and, by virtue of this power, successfully manipulated both the domestic and foreign policies of states. The allegation of Jewish economic dominance tended to wax large during periods of economic or financial crisis that, by the last quarter of the nineteenth century, occurred periodically. How can we account for the charge of Jewish economic dominance? Though a number of Jewish families in Europe had acquired sizable fortunes before the advent of the nineteenth century – principally as court agents of aristocratic families – the myth of Jewish economic dominance truly gained widespread currency as a result of several key factors, including Jewish emancipation and European industrialization. The emancipation of European Jewry opened to Jews, previously blocked, access to higher education and the professions. More equal access to education and the professions bred increased competition between Jews and Christians, leading often to resentment. Europe's industrialization opened new domestic and global

---

[12] Glock and Stark, *Christian*, 109–10.
[13] Finzi, *Anti-Semitism*, 18.
[14] Levine, *Economic*, 130–31.

investment opportunities for entrepreneurs. Beginning around 1840, the combination of lower transport costs (helped immeasurably by the use of steamships, canals, and railways) and lower tariffs resulted in a world-wide synchronization of price movements.[15] O'Rourke and Williamson have referred to the years 1840 to 1914 as the first great globalization, thanks primarily to the exponential growth in international trade.[16] Cameron notes that by the beginning of the twentieth century, one could speak meaningfully of a world economy.[17] The removal of barriers to trade allowed capital to flow across borders, financing railways and mines in a fashion never before experienced. In fact, by 1913, one-third of British wealth was invested overseas.[18] The new investment oppor-tunities led to the accumulation of phenomenal wealth for the fledgling banking industry. Jews were well represented in the banking industry, given their prior background as moneylenders and court agents, and many Jewish families benefited greatly from the new investment oppor-tunities. This is certainly not to say that Gentile fortunes did not exist. Rather, it was the number of wealthy Jewish families in proportion to the overall Jewish population, and the concentration of Jewish wealth in a small number of arenas such as banking, that helped to cast Jewish economic dominance in a particular light. Take, for instance, the case of the state of Prussia in 1908, where it was reported that 55 of the 200 millionaires were of Jewish origin, of whom 33 had made their money in finance and banking.[19] The accumulation of extraordinary wealth, par-ticularly through profits from investment, elicited vitriolic resentment in many quarters. That several prominent Jewish families became prime beneficiaries of this new wealth gave new legs to the myth of Jewish economic dominance. No example gave more impetus to the legend of Jewish economic dominance than that of the Jewish Rothschild banking dynasty.

Put simply, for most of the nineteenth century, the Rothschilds stood atop the pantheon of banking enterprises. The family's phenomenal fi-nancial success began with Meyer Amschel Rothschild of Frankfurt,

[15] Kevin O'Rourke and Jeffrey Williamson, *Globalisation and History: The Evolution of a Nineteenth-Century Atlantic Economy* (Cambridge, MA, 1999); Rondo Cameron, *A Concise Economic History of the World: From Paleolithic Times to the Present* (New York and Oxford, 1989), 278.

[16] O'Rourke and Williamson, *Globalisation*.

[17] Cameron, *Concise*, 273.

[18] O'Rourke and Williamson, *Globalisation*; Cameron, *Concise*, 278.

[19] Finzi, *Anti-Semitism*, 57.

who, through his financial service to Prince William, elector of Hessen-Kassel during the Napoleonic Wars, and profits obtained through trade in commodities during Napoleon's continental blockade, launched the family's involvement in the banking industry.[20] The initial Rothschild fortune was accumulated through its loans to governments and speculation in existing government bonds. The Prussian loan of 1818 constituted a watershed in the history of European capital markets and led to the emergence of the international bond market, according to Ferguson.[21] The loan, put together by the Rothschilds, was a first of its kind. It was issued in London, Frankfurt, Berlin, Hamburg, Amsterdam, and Vienna, and interest was to be paid not in German Talers, but in British sterling. Ferguson points out that one of the key distinguishing traits of the Rothschild banking house, and one that hugely benefited the house vis-à-vis its financial competitors, was its multinational network. Meyer Amschel had the wisdom during the first decades of the nineteenth century to establish five distinct branches of the family firm, each headed by one of his five sons, in five major European financial centers. These were Nathan in London, Amschel in Frankfurt, James in Paris, Carl in Vienna, and Solomon in Naples. By maintaining a multinational network, the Rothschilds were in a better position to foresee events and transmit information to one another and to overcome the financial losses of an economic downturn in one country.[22] The list of financial services from which the Rothschild family accumulated its extraordinary wealth included the international bond market, bullion broking and refining, accepting and discounting commercial bills, direct trading in commodities, foreign exchange dealing and arbitrage, and personal banking services to some of Europe's best-known individuals and families.[23] By the 1830s and 1840s, the Rothschild brothers had become major industrial investors with the foresight to underwrite the construction of railway lines in France, Austria, and Germany and had acquired mines producing mercury, gold, copper, diamonds, rubies, and

---

[20] Ferguson, *World's*; Charles P. Kindlebeger, *A Financial History of Western Europe* (London, 1984), 121–22.

[21] Ferguson, *World's*, 133–34.

[22] Ibid., 3.

[23] The list of royal and nonroyal dignitaries for whom the Rothschilds provided personal banking services is too long to present. Their clients included members of the royal families of nearly every European nation, prime ministers, and well-known writers and artists. See Ferguson, *World's*, for an excellent and exhaustive study of the Rothschild family.

oil. By the late nineteenth century, the Rothschild industrial invest-ments stretched across six continents.[24] Ferguson notes that between 1815 and 1914, the Rothschild multinational partnership comprised the biggest bank in the world, and that from the mid-1820s to the 1860s, no individuals had a greater share of the world's wealth than Nathan and James Rothschild.[25] The longevity of the Rothschild banking dynasty and its ability to amass such wealth can be partially attributed to the closeness of family ties. Throughout the nineteenth century, a direct male heir of the Rothschilds led each of the five Rothschild banking houses (the Naples house closed in 1863, and the Frankfurt house ter-minated in 1901). Moreover, the Rothschild family tightly controlled the marriages of family members in order to insure that the family's wealth remained within the family. Rothschild marriages usually in-volved members of other prominent Jewish banking families such as the Montefiore family. Also, when the Rothschilds sought out other banking firms to share in the underwriting of a loan or an investment, they fre-quently turned to other Jewish banking families such as the Montefiores and Cassels in Great Britain, the Pereires, the Worms, and the Lazards in France, and the Warburgs and Bleichroeders in Germany.[26]

The Rothschilds are the best-known of the wealthy Jewish banking families before the Holocaust and may be credited with establishing a model for other Jewish banking families who emigrated from German states during the nineteenth century to establish banking institutions throughout Europe and the United States. This list would include the Openheim, Haber, Seligmann, Lazard, Reinach, Stern, Ellissen, Bischoffsheim, Koenigswarter, Hirsch, Cahen d'Anvers, and Bamberger families. Further, many of these families imitated the Rothschilds' pat-tern of selecting marriage partners for their children from within the circle of the Jewish banking group in the hope of extending their finan-cial empires across national borders. We see this pattern, for instance, in the marriage of children from the Kohns and Reinachs, resulting in the enterprise Kohn-Reinach and Company.[27] Relations among these Jewish banking families were not always amicable. Several of the fam-ilies frequently competed with one another for business. The compe-tition between the Rothschilds and the Pereires over the construction

---

[24] Ferguson, *World's*, 6–7, 276, 600; Cameron, *Concise*, 309.
[25] Ferguson, *World's*, 3.
[26] Ferguson, *World's*; Birnbaum, *Anti-Semitism*, 29; Schor, *L'Antisémitisme*, 135.
[27] Mollier, "Financiers," 70–74; Ruppin, *Jews*, 209.

of railways in Austria, Italy, and Spain has received considerable schol-arly attention.[28] Regardless of whether these Jewish banking families acted as rivals or collaborators, it appeared to many nineteenth-and early twentieth-century observers that an international Jewish banking system existed, and that at its pinnacle stood the Rothschilds. Yet the banking industry wasn't the only economic enterprise in which wealthy Jewish families appeared to dominate. Notable European Jewish families held substantial control over the department store industry, grains, the cattle trade, real estate, the fur, pearl, jewelry, diamond, and ready-made clothing trades, and perhaps most importantly, the news agencies.[29] As the institution of international finance began to take off after 1840, quick and reliable access to information and the need to communicate across borders prompted the emergence of news agencies. Between 1849 and 1851, Bernhard Wolff established a news agency bearing his name; in Berlin, Reuters, previously inaugurated in Aix-la-Chapelle, relocated to London; and Agence Havas was founded in Paris. The founders of both Wolff and Reuters were Jews.[30]

Not only did trade become global after 1840, local or national eco-nomic crises became, for the first time, worldwide. In the preindus-trial economy, abrupt price fluctuations were typically caused by nat-ural disasters such as droughts and floods and tended to be local in nature. In the new industrial economy, financial crises more often were linked to trade and became cyclical, more widespread, and increasingly severe in their impact.[31] The first major economic crisis of the new industrial economy began in 1873.[32] The crisis, referred to by many economists as the 1873 Depression, began after financial panics in New York and Vienna had spread throughout the new industrial economies. Numerous bankruptcies occurred throughout the industrial economies, with the German banking industry suffering a particularly harsh fate. The 1873 Depression unleashed a decline in prices lasting into the 1890s. Until the Great Depression of the 1930s, the 1873 Depression had itself earned the title of the Great Depression, due chiefly to its

---

[28] Kindleberger, *Financial*, 108–09.

[29] Ruppin, *Jews*, 209.

[30] Colin Holmes, "Anti-Semitism in British Society, 1876–1939." In Strauss, ed., *Hostages of Modernization*, vol. 3/1, 332–34.

[31] Cameron, *Concise*, 278.

[32] Ferguson (*World's*, 461) intimates that the 1847 economic crisis in Europe that helped trigger the 1848 European revolutions was one of the first economic crises of the new industrial economy.

severity and duration. The causes of the economic crisis are multi-faceted. One precipitant may have been the huge inflation of German credit in May 1873, resulting from French indemnity payments of five billion francs in the wake of the German military victory over France in the Franco-Prussian War. But probably more important as a contributor was the decline in prices brought about by a dramatic reduction in transportation costs. Lower transportation costs resulted from the expansion of railways into Argentina, the Ukraine, Canada, Australia, and the agricultural heartland of the United States; the use of steam-powered trans-Atlantic shipping; and the opening of the Suez Canal in 1869. Non-European-produced agricultural products, notably grains, now could compete favorably within Europe with those produced by European farmers, leading to, among other things, a fall in agricultural prices. While this may have been a boon for consumers of food, it was devastating for many farmers. A collapse in foreign investment accompanied the decline in agricultural prices. By 1878, the unemployment roll had grown to 1.2 million in the United States alone.[33] The effects of the 1873 Depression lasted throughout the 1880s and into the mid-1890s. In 1882, a financial crisis in France, occasioned chiefly by the collapse of the Union Générale Bank, contributed to a spreading recession in Germany, the United Kingdom, and the United States that lasted into 1884; a final economic plunge occurred in 1893, which lingered on for two years.[34] By virtue of technological breakthroughs in the chemical and electrical industries, the European economies then embarked on a sustained period of prosperity lasting from 1898 to 1911.[35]

With so much attention given to the devastating impact of the Great Depression of the 1930s, it is certainly understandable that the economic recessions that preceded the grand collapse, notably the decline of 1912 through 1925, have received little notice.[36] Within this recessionary period, the years 1920–21 stand out as particularly troubling. In the aftermath of World War I, prices climbed sharply worldwide as consumer

---

[33] Cameron, *Concise*, 279; James Foreman-Peck, *A History of the World Economy: International Economic Relations since 1850* (Totowa, NJ, 1983), 80–88; Angus Maddison, *Dynamic Forces in Capitalist Development: A Long-Run Comparative View* (Oxford and New York, 1991), 89–103; Lindemann, *Esau's*, 274; Katz, *Prejudice*, 247.

[34] Foreman-Peck, *History*, 174–75; Lindemann, *Esau's*, 274; Maddison, *Dynamic*, 98–99.

[35] Lindemann, *Esau's*, 274; Maddison, *Dynamic*, 104.

[36] Maddison, *Dynamic*, 104.

demand outpaced supply and then fell again as production responded in an excessive fashion. Kindleberger observes that the advent of the eight-hour workday, the spate of communist-led strikes, anxiety over the spread of Bolshevism, a hike in the hourly wage, and a rise in wholesale prices exacerbated the economic crisis of 1920–21.[37] The German economic woes would stretch into 1922 and 1923, with a precipitous fall in the value of the German mark. The German gold mark, valued at 4.2 to the dollar in 1914, had tumbled to an unbelievable 4.2 trillion marks to the dollar on November 15, 1923. Though economic growth picked up between 1925 and 1929, it varied from country to country. The German economy's dependence on short-term loans, Austria's continuing banking difficulties, and Great Britain's persistent unemployment and weakening exports hampered sustained economic growth in those countries. In fact, while France experienced an industrial unemployment rate of 3.8 percent between 1921 and 1929, the comparable rates in Germany and the United Kingdom for the same period were 12 and 9.2 percent, respectively.[38]

The boom collapsed in 1929, ushering in the greatest worldwide depression in modern history. The fall in industrial production between 1929 and 1933 has no parallel in its amplitude or international scale. Between 1930 and 1938, average rates of industrial unemployment reached 17.0 percent in the U.S., 15.5 percent in Germany, 13.7 percent in the United Kingdom, and 7.0 percent in France. Whereas the yearly percentage change in aggregate gross domestic product for the group of sixteen industrial countries was –1.0 percent in 1921, it shot to –5.7 in 1930, –6.4 in 1931, and –6.6 in 1932.[39] The Great Depression hit each of the industrialized economies, although the onset and the magnitude of the impact differed. The effects of the Great Depression were exceptionally severe for the United States, Germany, and France, while Italy and the United Kingdom suffered less from the Great Depression's repercussions. The United States, Germany, and Great Britain suffered earlier than France. For instance, the General Industrial Production Index for 1931 (with 1929 equal to 100) reached 85 in Great Britain, 79 in Germany, 74 in the United States, and 102 in France. However,

---

[37] Kindleberger, *Financial*, 331–32.

[38] Cameron, *Concise*, 351–52; Kindleberger, *Financial*, 369; Peter Temin, *Lessons from the Great Depression: The Lionel Robbins Lectures for 1989* (Cambridge, MA, 1989), 3.

[39] Temin, *Lessons*, 3; Maddison, *Dynamic*, 103, 113.

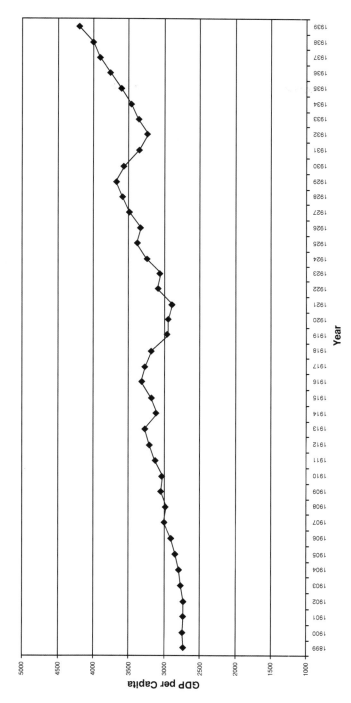

Figure 4.1. Average GDP Per capita in France, Germany, Great Britain, Romania, and Italy (combined), 1899–1939. *Note*: The GDP (gross domestic product) per capita data are in 1990 dollars and are drawn largely from Maddison (1995) and Good and Ma (1998). The GDP per capita data for Great Britain, Germany, France, and Italy are yearly for the period 1899 to 1939. For Romania, the GDP per capita figures are yearly for 1925 to 1939 but are decennial for the years prior to 1925. Where data were not available, GDP figures were interpolated based on the nearest preceding and proceeding figures.

by 1934 and 1935, when Germany and Great Britain again reached a General Industrial Production Index of 100, France, whose fall had begun later, had dropped below 100 and would not again reach the 1929 level until the eve of World War II in 1939.[40] The devastating impact of the Great Depression intensified and spread as a result of a number of poor policy decisions enacted by leaders of the major industrial nations. Countries such as the United States embraced neo-mercantilistic measures, including higher tariffs, in the hope of protecting their own economies. One result was a drastic decline in worldwide trade that hindered productivity and reduced the likelihood of a recovery. By 1931, with the collapse of Austria's largest bank, the Creditanstalt, the Great Depression engulfed the economies of East Central Europe.[41] The Great Depression lasted until the outbreak of worldwide hostilities in 1939, although both Germany and Great Britain began to rebound after 1933. Germany succeeded in raising output and eliminating unemployment during the 1930s through government spending on public works and rearmament, and Great Britain benefited from a decline in the cost of British imports, a soaring housing boom, and rising consumption levels.[42]

It was during and after these periodic recessions and depressions that attention focused on the alleged negative role that the wealthy Jewish banking houses had played in the creation of the economic crises. In contrast to earlier epochs of economic crisis during the industrial age, with the existence of multinational financial houses managing the international flows of capital and buying and selling stocks, the physical presence of Jews was no longer a necessary requisite for economic chaos in the minds of many anti-Semites. The 1873 Depression unlocked a wave of resentment against the free-market policies of the 1850s and 1860s – policies that had become associated with Jewish banking interests. The 1873 Depression also unleashed public displeasure because of the series of accompanying stock market collapses and bank failures – in which several prominent Jews had played a role.[43] The Great Depression of the 1930s evoked heightened economic antipathy toward Jews for a

---

[40] Weber, *Hollow*, 33.

[41] Maddison, *Dynamic*, 76; Angus Maddison, "Economic Policy and Performance in Europe 1913–1970." In Carlo M. Cipolla, ed., *The Fontana Economic History of Europe: The Twentieth Century, Part II* (Glasgow, 1976), 457–58; Foreman-Peck, *History*, 244.

[42] Maddison, "Economic," 463–65.

[43] Lindemann, *Accused*, 17–18; Katz, *Prejudice*, 247; Arendt, *Origins*, 35–36.

number of reasons. In a time of high unemployment, the immigration of thousands of Eastern European Jews constituted an economic threat to financially hard-pressed Gentiles. For others open to the possibility of Jewish perfidy, the Jews were seen as both manipulators and beneficiaries of the worldwide economic collapse, as foretold in the notorious but popular "Protocols of the Learned Elders of Zion."[44] We now turn our attention to the emergence of economic anti-Semitism within our five countries.

### FRANCE

Though the myth of Jewish economic dominance had manifested itself throughout Europe in the mid nineteenth century, it had sprouted particularly deep and widespread roots in France. Proponents of this myth were to be found in all social strata and in almost every political movement. As elsewhere, economic anti-Semitism in France made the most of the prominent visibility of some notable Jews in finance and commerce and of the actual or fictitious association of several Jews with highly publicized scandals in France. The waxing and waning of French economic anti-Semitism additionally seemed to reflect the health of the French economy.

There is little doubt that during the July Monarchy (1830–48) and the Second Empire (1851–70), a number of celebrated Jewish families played a central role in the modernization and industrialization of the French economy and that they benefited hugely from their involvement. James Rothschild, the youngest of Meyer Amschel's five sons, had built the French Rothschild banking house into a colossal financial empire by the mid nineteenth century and lavishly displayed his wealth through the purchase of precious art and grand estates, such as those at Ferrieres and at Les Vaux-de-Cernay.[45] James Rothschild's success in winning the concession from the government to construct the greatly prized *Nord* railway line significantly bolstered his wealth but also

---

[44] Friedlaender, *Nazi Germany*, 213.

[45] Ferguson, *World's*; Winock, *Nationalism*, 135. Also, the subject of the Rothschild fortune had figured in French literature in the 1830s with the publication of the renowned French novelist Honoré de Balzac's *The House of Nucingen*. Balzac presents his leading character, Nucingen, as a German-born banker making his fortune from bogus bankruptcies and from speculation on the outcome of the Battle of Waterloo. These were commonly held myths about the Rothschilds at the time (Ferguson, *World's*, 15).

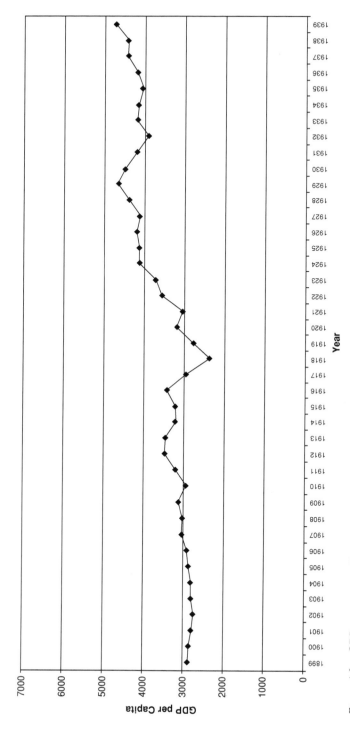

Figure 4.2a. GDP per capita in France, 1899–1939. *Note:* The GDP (gross domestic product) per capita data are in 1990 dollars and are drawn from Maddison (1995) and Good and Ma (1998).

became a catalyst for the popularization of the legend of Jewish financial dominance in France. The concession may have inspired Alphonse de Toussenel to author his starkly anti-Semitic 1845 book *The Jews, Kings of the Epoch: A History of Financial Feudalism*. Toussenel was particularly incensed by the financial terms on which James Rothschild had garnered the concession and by the fact that a Christian king (Louis-Philippe) had granted Rothschild the concession and had ennobled him as a baron. Toussenel also used the railway concession as an opportunity to cast the Jews as despoilers of France's pristine beauty.[46] Toussenel was certainly not exceptional among French leftists bemoaning the economic power of the Rothschilds. His contemporary Pierre Joseph Proudhon had accused the Rothschilds of organizing the Jewish takeover of French finance and of using their financial clout to rule France.[47]

The Rothschilds were certainly not the only highly visible wealthy French Jews at mid-century. James Rothschild's major banking and railway competitors were the Jewish Pereire brothers. Emile and Isaac Pereire, descendants of Portuguese Jews, had emerged as major competitors to the Rothschilds during the early years of the reign of Louis Napoléon. Emile, the eldest, had worked for the Rothschilds in the 1840s. With the encouragement of the emperor, Louis Napoleon, who may have been eager to free himself from his financial dependence upon the Rothschild family, the Pereire brothers established in 1852 the Société Générale de Crédit Foncier mortgage bank and the Société Générale de Crédit Mobilier, an investment bank specializing in railway finance. In 1854, the brothers tried to wrest from the Rothschilds the refunding of the French government debt.[48] That the Rothschilds and Pereires were so instrumental in the erection of the French railway network at mid-century, and in the development and expansion of French banking, solidly anchored the myth of Jewish economic dominance in the French popular imagination.

The myth of Jewish economic dominance in France received a further boost from the rise of a new group of wealthy Jewish families – many of them coming from the French banking establishment – during the Second Empire and the early years of the French Third Republic. Mollier reports that in 1865, Jews comprised 50 of the 300 principal bankers in Paris.[49] The list of key French Jewish bankers included the names

---

[46] Ferguson, *World's*, 43–54; Lindemann, *Esau's*, 221–22.
[47] Byrnes, *Antisemitism*, 117–25.
[48] Kindleberger, *Financial*, 103; Cameron, *Concise*, 30.
[49] Mollier, "Financiers," 69.

of Rothschild, Bloch, Blum, Dreyfus, Goldschmidt, Bamberger, Hirsch, Guenzberg, Reinach, Stern, Deutsch, Heine, Ephrussi, Goudchaux, Lippmann, and Bischoffsheim. Members of a number of these prominent Jewish banking families ascended to key positions in France's banking establishment. Both Michel Heine and Adolphe d'Eichtal eventually became regents of the Banque de France, and Georges May founded the Banque Internationale de Paris. Many Jews and Gentiles alike had profited immensely from France's dramatic industrial and financial expansion between 1851 and 1881, when French national income grew at a rate of 2 to 4 percent annually. France's stunning military defeat in the Franco-Prussian War of 1870–71 hardly stemmed the tide of solid economic growth.[50]

If the economic crisis of 1882 put a brake on French economic growth, it served equally to open the door to a heightened French economic anti-Semitism. The effects of the recession of 1882 lasted in France for fifteen years. The crisis began as a financial panic but was exacerbated by a two-decade-long slump in the wine and silk industries, large losses on foreign investments to governments and bankrupt railways, and a return to economic protectionism.[51] The catalyst for the outbreak of economic anti-Semitism during the crisis of 1882 seems to have been the collapse of the clerically backed Union Générale Bank. The bank's collapse proved disastrous to many small French investors. Paul Eugène Bontoux, the bank's founder and president, publicly blamed the collapse on an alliance of "Jewish finance" and "governmental freemasonry." The bank's failure evoked an anti-Semitic outcry that included Catholic journalists and socialist propagandists.[52] The Rothschild banking firm found itself at the center of the controversy, for it seemed only natural to many anti-Semites that the age-old Jewish hatred of Christians had led the chief Jewish banking house to deliberately destroy a Christian bank. No writer did more to popularize the myth that the Rothschilds had brought down the Union Générale Bank than the famous French

---

[50] Mollier, "Financiers, 69–70; Marrus, *Politics*, 36–39; Cameron, *Concise*, 236–37; Soucy, *French*, 4.

[51] Cameron, *Concise*, 236–37.

[52] Birnbaum (*Anti-Semitism*, 91) notes that the collapse of the Union Générale propelled the popularity of the anti-Semitic Catholic newspaper *La Croix*, for the collapse fit nicely into the Catholic anti-Semitic claim of the dangers of Jewish absolute power. By the end of the century, the circulation rate of *La Croix* had climbed to more than two million.

novelist Emile Zola. Ironically, Zola, who eventually became the great defender of Alfred Dreyfus, the Jewish captain, had in his novel *L'Argent* represented the collapse of the Union Générale as a victory for his character Gundermann, an enormously powerful and wealthy Jewish banker modeled on the real James Rothschild.[53] Mollier asserts that after 1882, a part of the French public was quick to see the guilty hand of Jewish financiers in every crash or scandal in France.[54]

Charges of Jewish economic machinations figured centrally in the financial collapse of the copper market in 1889 and in the Panama Scandal of 1892. In the collapse of the copper market, the director of the Comptoir d'escompte de Paris left a suicide note in which he claimed that the Rothschilds were responsible for the collapse and that he had placed documents to support the accusation in his office desk.[55] Better known is the Panama Scandal of 1892. Much of the capital for the proposed construction of the Panama Canal had been raised through the sale of shares to nearly 500,000 middle-class French citizens. When the Panama Company went bankrupt, these French citizens lost their investments. The investigations into the bankruptcy disclosed extensive bribery of parliamentary members and revealed that Jews with German origins or German-sounding names were heavily overrepresented among the intermediaries between the company's officials and the parliamentary officers. The French anti-Semitic press picked up on the Jewish role in the scandal, and the infamous Jew hater Edouard Drumont enthusiastically dwelled on the purported Jewish role in the scandal in the editions of his anti-Semitic newspaper, *La Libre Parole*. That Baron Jacques de Reinach (a Jew) had served as the principal banker of the Panama Company and that Cornelius Herz and Emile Arton (both Jews) had fled France when the news of the scandal became public afforded ample ammunition to France's anti-Semitic press of Jewish guilt. Additionally, in the opinion of many who followed the ensuing trial of the accused in 1893, the verdict failed to produce a sufficient number of convictions or harsh enough sentences. Anti-Semitic polemicists such as Drumont concluded that the trial confirmed the belief that the Third Republic remained firmly in the clutches of corrupt and unscrupulous

---

[53] Ferguson, *World's*, 782–84; Wilson, *Ideology*, 170; Byrnes, *Antisemitism*, 130–31; Marrus, *Politics*, 125; Birnbaum, *Anti-Semitism*, 91.

[54] Mollier, "Financier," 79.

[55] Ibid., 76.

Jews – many of whom, according to Drumont, were spies in the pay of Germany.[56]

The collapse of the Union Générale and French copper market and the Panama Scandal catapulted the anti-Semitic career of Drumont on the eve of the infamous Dreyfus Affair. Both Drumont's best-selling book, *La France Juive*, and his widely circulated anti-Semitic newspaper, *La Libre Parole*, made the alleged Jewish economic domination of France the central theme. *La Libre Parole* had begun publication in 1892 and devoted extensive coverage to the unfolding Panama Scandal and specifically to the purported link between "Jewish finance" and political corruption. Within two years, the paper's circulation had reached 200,000, thanks in large part to the rising tide of French anti-Semitism.[57] Drumont's economic anti-Semitic barrage went well beyond attacks on the alleged Rothschild role in the failure of the Union Générale and the association of Jews and parliamentarians in the Panama Scandal. It included denigration of the Jews as "a people who don't plant" and as the usurpers of France's historic treasures. To that end, Drumont claimed that the Jewish takeover of France was plainly visible in the degree to which Jewish financiers and their friends had gathered up the great castles and estates of France's former nobility. He asserted: "Jews, vomited from all the ghettos of Europe, are now installed as the masters in historic houses that evoke the most glorious memories of ancient France. . . . the Rothschilds everywhere: at Ferrieres and at Les Vaux-de-Cernay, in the abbey founded by Blanche of Castille . . . Hirsch, at Marly, in the place of Louis XIV; Ephrussi, at Fontainebleau, in the place of Francis I; the guano king, Dreyfus, at Pont-Chartrain."[58] In the wake of these scandals, several French literary artists took up the theme of Jewish banking domination. Chirac's *Les Rois de la République*, Corneilhan's *Juifs et Opportunistes*, and Kimon's *La politique israélite: politiciens, journalistes, banquiers* are some of the most notable examples.

---

[56] The accusation that Jewish bankers in France were in the employ of Prussia or Germany goes back at least as far as 1870–71. Mollier ("Financier," 75) observes that several non-Jewish bankers and publicists spread the false rumor that the Rothschilds had obtained the contract to raise the five billion francs required for the French reparation payments to Germany through the influence of Bismarck's Jewish banker, Bleichroeder. In reality, Thiers and Say played the decisive role in the selection of the Rothschilds (Lindemann, *Accused*, 87–88; Arendt, *Origins*, 95–97; Wistrich, *Antisemitism*, 126–28; Mollier, "Financiers," 67–77).

[57] Wilson, *Ideology*, 173; Katz, *Prejudice*, 294–97.

[58] Wilson, *Ideology*, 278.

The charge that Jews were disproportionately represented in particular professions and trades had been part of the economic anti-Semitic arsenal for centuries. Drumont was certainly not the first or the last French anti-Semite to chastise the Jews for their overrepresentation in finance and commerce. Maurice Barrès, the well-known nationalist novelist and politician, campaigned vigorously during the 1890s on the allegation that Jews possessed an anti-French nature by virtue of their distaste for manual work and honest occupations.[59] Among the complaints leveled at the so-called Jewish domination of certain professions, two in particular attracted attention during the last quarter of the nineteenth century – namely, Jewish ownership of department stores and Jewish control over the market prices of foodstuffs and raw materials. Rising resentment among small urban shopkeepers surfaced over the establishment of the new department stores and cooperatives that in late nineteenth-century Europe dotted the urban landscape. The department stores, with their vast array of low-cost products, challenged the economic viability of the small shopkeepers. The proportion of Jewish-owned department stores in France did not compare to the proportion in central Europe, but Jews became linked with this new enterprise in France as elsewhere. While such major department stores as the Grande Maison de Blanc, Galeries Lafayette, Prisunic, and Monoprix were Jewish-owned, others, like Bon Marché, the Louvre, Belle Jardinière, Printemps, Felix Potin, and Samaritaine, were not founded or run by Jews.[60]

In the minds of many European anti-Semites, Jews were strongly identified with the promotion of economic liberalism and were charged with the manipulation of currency rates and prices through perceived Jewish control over the principal financial institutions throughout the West.[61] We have seen how the phenomenal rise of the Rothschild financial house provided credibility to this charge. The accusation that Jewish finance and the Rothschilds, particularly, were responsible for the dramatic decline in the market prices of wheat and wine gained currency during the 1880s and 1890s in southern France. By the mid nineteenth century, the new national market and lower transport costs had pushed southern French agriculture toward a monoculture, the production of wine. Southern French wheat production could no

[59] Sternhell, "Roots," 108–112.
[60] Lindemann, Accused, 73; Schor, L'Antisémitisme, 136; Wilson, Ideology, 288–89.
[61] Katz, Prejudice; Almog, Nationalism; Birnbaum, Anti-Semitism; Ruppin, Jews; Arendt, Origins.

longer withstand the competition of lower-priced northeastern French, Russian, and American wheat that less expensive transportation and the removal of protective tariffs made possible. Eschewing wheat and olive cultures, southern French cultivators turned increasingly to wine, and the fate of the southern French economy became progressively tied to the future of wine. An economy relying on a single crop is, to say the least, fragile. The southern French economy was no exception. Unfortunately for the southern French vintners, the "golden era" of wine ended abruptly after 1875. The carrier of doom was a plant louse, *phylloxéra*, which attacks and kills the roots of vines. In the region of Languedoc, most severely hit by *phylloxéra*, the surface area planted with vines had fallen drastically by 1880. As wine began to regain its prominence after 1895, the vintners of southern France encountered a new threat, the inundation of less expensive Algerian and foreign wine. Now southern French vintners faced the new challenges of overproduction and underconsumption.[62]

As the market prices for their wines fell, French vintners looked to assign the blame. Why hadn't the government done more to protect them from the ravages of *phylloxéra* and the import of cheap wine? Why had the price of wine fallen so sharply? Several opportunistic anti-Semitic politicians and polemicists used events such as the collapse of the Union Générale Bank, the Panama Scandal, and the Dreyfus Affair to offer an explanation for the plight of the southern French wine producers. These anti-Semitic accounts focused largely on the purported role of Jewish finance in shaping governmental policy and manipulating the market prices of French wines. (It was common knowledge that the Rothschild family was a major investor in wine production.)[63] For one measure of how successful the allegation of Jewish responsibility for the souring economic plight of southern French agriculturalists had become, we can turn to the surprising electoral performance of anti-Semitic candidates in the 1898 French national elections. As a result of that election, twenty-two deputies identifying with the anti-Semitic program had been elected to the National Assembly. Seventeen of the twenty-two had come from rural districts.[64] One of these elected deputies, Jules Baron, from a constituency in rural western France, had included in his official program

---

[62] William Brustein, *The Social Origins of Political Regionalism: France, 1849–1981* (Berkeley, 1988), 84–85.

[63] Ferguson, *World's*, 276.

[64] Birnbaum, "Affaire," 113–14.

that he was against "the coalition of international Jewish financiers."[65] Most surprising of all was that four of the five elected deputies from the French *département* of Gers in southwestern France campaigned on an anti-Semitic program. (The fifth elected deputy, Paul de Cassagnac, did not campaign on an anti-Semitic program; however, he later joined the group of declared anti-Semites in the National Assembly.) What makes the anti-Semitic electoral tidal wave in Gers so intriguing is that few if any Jews resided in the *département*. Yet in an era of global capitalism, Jews need not be physically present in order for economic anti-Semitism to thrive. Gers vintners had suffered from both crop diseases and falling prices and may well have been responsive to charges that the Rothschilds and other Jewish financiers had manipulated the price of wine. This proposition finds support in Fitch's excellent study of the media and politics in southwestern France. Fitch finds that the anti-Semitic candidates in Gers in their appeal to rural constituents emphasized the nefarious role of Jewish financiers and represented Jews as part of a cosmopolitan force threatening the agricultural life of small farmers.[66]

Throughout my study of anti-Semitism, I have stressed that the political left was not at all immune to anti-Semitism, particularly before the Dreyfus Affair. In earlier chapters, we encountered the left's flirtation with the Enlightenment's secular critique of Jews and with forms of racial anti-Semitism. Of the four manifestations of anti-Semitism, the political left unquestionably felt most at home with the economic. In France, the writings of early socialists, including Proudhon, Leroux, Fourier, Blanqui, Valles, and Toussenel, are certainly replete with references to Jewish responsibility for the extremes of financial capitalism and to the fraudulent and parasitic economic behavior of Jews.[67] In the last quarter of the nineteenth century, a new cadre of socialists, among them Regnard, Tridon, and Chirac, carried the torch of economic anti-Semitism. Both Weber and Burns assert that before the Dreyfus Affair, the political left in France, through its host of official publications, was very probably the principal source of attacks on Jews.[68] That Jewish intermediaries had been accused of bribing French parliamentarians during the 1892 Panama Scandal afforded an opportunity for numerous leftist

---

[65] Wilson, *Ideology*, 17.

[66] Fitch, "Mass," 59–73.

[67] Schucker, "Origins," 148–49; Wilson, *Ideology*, 333–34; Mosse, *Final Solution*, 152–53; Finzi, *Anti-Semitism*, 20; Byrnes, *Antisemitism*, 117–25.

[68] Weber, *Action*; Burns, "Boulangism," 532.

political candidates to bring to light the charge of the corrupting influence of Jewish "vagabond' wealth. Some of these leftist candidates referred to the French Third Republic as the "Opportunist Republic," the "speculators' Republic," or the "Panama Republic."[69] The Dreyfus Affair is generally considered as the turning point in the marriage between the political left and anti-Semitism. Weber has remarked that the French working class at this time realized that it had no more reason to hate its Jewish exploiters than its Gentile ones.[70] However, for some socialists, the divorce had not been finalized. During the Dreyfus Affair, several socialists used the occasion to organize around the theme of economic anti-Semitism. A notable example was Jules Guérin, the leader of the Ligue Antisémitique Française (LAF). Guerin accused the Jews of controlling the three principal mainstays of the French economy: money, credit, and the transport system. He also mobilized support in opposition to the large department stores and probably encouraged adherents of LAF to boycott and attack Jewish shops and businesses.[71] While Guérin was an anti-Dreyfusard, other French socialists who were pro-Dreyfusards participated in the attack on the perceived economic role of French Jews. Jean Jaurès, the well-known French socialist leader, belongs here. In a December 1898 edition of the socialist newspaper *La Petite République*, Juarès, borrowing from the anti-Semitic prose of Fourier, Toussenel, and Proudhon, chastised the Jews for their commercial behavior, their manipulation of liquid wealth, and their formidable and disproportionate influence. In the same year, Juarès had spoken out against the Jews of French Algeria in a speech to the French National Assembly. He castigated the Jews for employing their wealth and economic power to exploit the Arab people and the French proletariat in Algeria.[72] Equally, the comments of Aristide Briand, a pro-Dreyfusard and future French foreign minister, at a debate organized by a local anti-Semitic group in Nantes in December 1898, buoyed the association of Jews with unsavory economic practices. While Briand suggested that by simply getting rid of the Jews, the exploitative nature of capitalism would not disappear, he agreed with those assembled that "Jews have proved that they are particularly rapacious."[73]

[69] Weber, *Action*, 71; Winock, *Nationalism*, 140; Wilson, *Ideology*, 333–34.

[70] Weber, *Action*, 72.

[71] Wilson, *Ideology*, 179–82.

[72] Wilson, *Ideology*, 68–69; Teller, *Scapegoat*, 146–47.

[73] Wilson, *Ideology*, 68.

The Dreyfus Affair showcased French anti-Semitism to the world, and the French left certainly helped fan the anti-Semitic flame. But as the Dreyfus Affair increasingly divided France along a number of dimensions, the left's public anti-Semitic activities subsided. The same cannot be said about the French right. On the eve of the Dreyfus Affair, Drumont enlisted the support of several notable French right-wing anti-Semites, including Jacques de Biez, Albert Millot, and the Marquis de Morès, in the founding of the French National Anti-Semitic League (La Ligue Nationale Antisémitique de France). As one of its principal goals, the Anti-Semitic League sought to combat the "pernicious influences of the Jewish-Financial Oligarchy." Again, the Rothschilds figured centrally in the anti-Semitic rhetoric of this league.[74] Throughout the Dreyfus Affair, Drumont's popular newspaper, La Libre Parole, and the clerically backed newspaper La Croix largely orchestrated the right's economic anti-Semitic campaign. For the anti-Semitic political right, Dreyfus's supposed treachery constituted evidence of an unpatriotic Jewish community willing to sell out France for the benefit of her enemies. Dreyfus acted on orders from international Jewish financiers, according to the anti-Semitic political right.

The anti-Semitic outbursts surrounding the collapse of the Union Générale Bank, the Panama Scandal, and the Dreyfus Affair occurred during the lean economic years of the 1880s and 1890s. Crop failures, bankruptcies, higher unemployment, and lower prices for agricultural goods more than likely fueled France's economic anti-Semitism. A period of economic prosperity returned to France at the end of the nineteenth century, lasting until the eve of World War I. Cameron affirms that during this period, France's rate of economic growth rivaled the prosperity of the 1815–48 and 1851–81 eras. The French economy benefited enormously from the extension of the ore fields in eastern France and from the arrival of a new stage of industrialization resulting in the new industries of electricity, aluminum, automobiles, and nickel. By 1913, the average French citizen enjoyed a material standard of living on a par with the richest nations in continental Europe.[75] Not unexpectedly, economic prosperity ushered in a relative ebbing of the economic anti-Semitic campaign in France. However, public declarations of economic anti-Semitism in France did not disappear by any means during these halcyon days. The rightist monarchist Action française movement

[74] Ibid.,171–72.
[75] Cameron, Concise, 237.

emerged in the midst of the Dreyfus Affair and would become in the years before and after World War I a leader in the promulgation of the myth of the Jewish economic threat to France. Behind the Action française's attack on Jewish economic power was the objective of weaning members of the working class away from the socialist left. Like many French rightists and nationalists, leaders of the Action française believed that anti-Semitism would serve as a unifying vehicle among France's divergent social classes. To that end, Léon Daudet identified the Jews with a list of purported enemies of the French nation and working classes. Daudet's list included bankers, creditors, union organizers, socialist agitators, and wage-squeezing employers. Daudet insisted that behind the corrupting capitalistic influence in France stood the Judeo-Masonic conspiracy.[76] Two of Daudet's well-known compatriots in the Action française, Charles Maurras and Georges Valois, joined in the assault on Jewish personal influence. In Valois's 1909 *Monarchy and the Working Class*, he stressed how the Jewish nation sought to undermine French patriotism. In his book, Valois once again returned to the economic theme of how Jews, unlike Christians, sought the quickest road to personal enrichment (e.g., through commerce, finance, politics, and civil service). Valois emphasized the purported Jewish trait of distancing themselves from tilling the soil, although they profited from those who actually worked the land. How did Jewish capitalists profit from the labor of small propertyholders? Valois unfurled the alleged Jewish strategies of pitting small property owners against the large owners and causing small property owners to become financially dependent upon Jewish capitalist financing. Valois predicted that within two generations, Jewish capitalists would successfully appropriate half of France's small farms.[77]

The economic prosperity of the "*belle époque*" was short-lived. Though emerged from World War I as one of the principal victors, the vastation, both human and physical, hampered economic growth he interwar period. Between 1919 and 1926, the value of the urrency plunged to one-fifth of its prewar value. The depreciation e French franc stimulated French exports and induced a huge w of gold, but for all those who had lent money at fixed rates of interest or signed contracts at fixed rates, the stabilization of the French franc at the new level produced considerable anguish. Moreover, the depreciation may have contributed to France's inability to pull itself

---

[76] Weber, *Action*, 72.
[77] Soucy, *French*, 152–53.

out of the 1930s Depression. The repercussions of the Great Depression were particularly harsh for France because of the country's dependence on German reparation payments. Germany's default on its reparation payments in 1931 hit France hard. The policies of Léon Blum's Popular Front government to stimulate expansion by raising wages and to reduce unemployment by reducing working hours largely backfired, for they produced a capital flight that hurt domestic investment.[78]

As the French economy encountered a series of bumps during the interwar period, economic anti-Semitism again picked up steam. French economic anti-Semitism during this period continued to focus on the alleged pernicious role of Jewish financial power. For instance, in his remarks on the significance of Mussolini's ascension to power in Italy, Léon Daudet pleaded for a strong leader to rise to power in France and redistribute the unscrupulously acquired wealth of a band of thieves and traitors to the deserving war veterans. The composition of the band of thieves and traitors became apparent as Daudet claimed that rather than Prime Ministers Millerand and Poincaré, the Jews, Rothschild, Horace Finaly (a prominent Jewish banker), and the Sassoons of London controlled France. Daudet noted additionally that he hoped that a civilian dictator, acting in the name of the king, could save France from the revolutionary menace of the Jewish and German financiers.[79] French anti-Semites had a plethora of rich Jews to castigate during the interwar period. There were of course the wealthy French Jewish bankers, including the Worms, Lazard, Louis-Dreyfus,[80] Daniel-Dreyfus, Propper, Guinzburg, Bamberg, Thalmann, Seligmann, Raphael, Stern, Heine, and Rothschild. There were also such Jews as the Kuhlmanns in chemicals, the Bloch family in the aviation industry, the Rosengarts of the Citroen automobiles, the Lip family in the watch industry, and the numerous Jewish families owning major shares in the furniture, shoe, and department store enterprises. Furthermore, in the eyes of many French anti-Semites, the rise to prominence of Léon Blum, a Jewish socialist leader, fit nicely into this view of the threat of Jewish economic power. The anti-Semitic clerical newspaper *La Croix*, in an article published in its Avignon regional edition in 1927, while reiterating Drumont's warning about the "Jewish peril," launched an assault on Blum's Jewish

---

[78] Cameron, *Concise*, 360; Maddison, "Economic," 461; Weber, *Hollow*, 26–27; Schor, *L'Opinion*, 713.

[79] Weber, *Action*, 133.

[80] Louis Louis-Dreyfus also played a dominant role in the wheat exchange (Schor, *L'Antisémitisme*, 136).

religious background and wealth, stating that being a Jew and a multi-millionaire go hand in hand.[81]

Along with the purported threat of Jewish financial dominance, interwar economic anti-Semitism focused once again on the role of Jews in French political and financial scandals.[82] The largest of these scandals was the Stavisky Affair of 1934, which seriously threatened the stability of the Third Republic. The Stavisky Affair involved criminals and parliamentarians in the floating of fraudulent municipal bonds and then an attempted cover-up of the entire affair. At the center of the controversy was Serge Stavisky, a small-time crook of Russian Jewish origin, who had somehow become a confidant of a prominent French parliamentarian. The Stavisky Affair came to a head in early January 1934 with the publication on January 3, 1934, of two letters written by Albert Dalmier, minister of colonies and a former minister of justice, recommending the fraudulent bonds, and with the mysterious death of Stavisky on January 8, 1934. It is not clear whether Stavisky actually committed suicide or was killed by French police officers pursuing him. The French press quickly jumped into the fray, exposing the allegations against a high government official and speculating on the role of foreigners, notably Jews, in the scandal.[83] The Stavisky Affair preoccupied the press and the French National Assembly throughout the first half of 1934. Much like the Panama Scandal of 1892, the Stavisky Affair nourished the accusation that Jews were inextricably linked to financial and political scandals. Stavisky's Russian Jewish background served to bolster the anti-Semitic claim that the immigration of Eastern European Jews into France had a negative effect on the French nation.

In addition to the century-old allegations of Jewish economic dominance and the Jewish role in financial scandals, we find the arrival of new economic anti-Semitic charges during the interwar period. More specifically, the rising tide of Eastern European and German Jewish immigration and the spread of Bolshevism brought about claims that recent Jewish immigrants were taking jobs away from the native French population and that rich Jewish capitalists were financing the

---

[81] Schor, L'Antisémitisme, 135–36; Jean-Marc Dreyfus, "Banquiers et financiers juifs de 1929 à 1962: transitions et ruptures." Archives Juives, vol. 29, no. 2, 1996, 90–94; Birnbaum, Anti-Semitism, 180.

[82] Dreyfus, "Banquiers," 85–86.

[83] Marrus and Paxton, Vichy, 41; Vicki Caron, Uneasy Asylum: France and the Jewish Refugee Crisis, 1933–1942 (Stanford, 1999), 44; Weber, Action, 319–24; Dreyfus, "Banquiers," 86.

Bolshevik menace. While the doors to immigrants increasingly closed in other Western nations, during the interwar period France became more and more a principal destination for political, religious, and economic refugees. But as the effects of the 1930s Depression spread and deepened in France, many voices arose blaming the economic crisis on the three million foreigners residing in France and calling for the imposition of bans on foreign immigration. In 1934, France's Radical Party proposed schemes to remedy climbing unemployment that included the phased repatriation of 800,000 foreign workers.[84] Resentment against Jewish immigration grew notably in the fields where Jewish immigrants competed with native French for jobs. After 1933, with the immigration of German Jews fleeing Nazi Germany, the resentment against Jewish economic competition reached the professions of law and medicine. Schor asserts that the consensus in France held that Jews comprised fifteen percent of those employed in the medical profession during France and thirty percent in the French *département* of the Seine.[85] Caron points to the existence of heightened levels of anti-Semitism within the French medical profession during the 1930s. In Caron's view, the high proportion of foreign students enrolled in French medical schools during the early 1930s fueled the anti-Semitism. Contributing to this wave of anti-Semitism in the medical profession was the report that one-third of foreign students studying medicine at the Faculty of Medicine in Paris were Romanians and that Jews comprised roughly 85 percent of the Romanians.[86] The high proportion of Romanian Jews enrolled in French universities resulted largely from the institution of a *numerus clausus* (quotas) in the Romanian academy and the stipulation that a Romanian secondary school diploma was the equivalent of a French *baccalauréat* degree. The campaign to restrict foreign Jewish competition in the medical profession received support from the French government. The French parliament passed on April 21, 1933, the Armbuster Law, which limited the practice of medicine in France to French citizens and required them to possess the *diplôme d'état*. Two years later, the government enacted the Nast Law of July 26, 1935, that made the practice of public medicine conditional upon a five-year waiting period for naturalized foreigners.[87] Like medicine, the legal profession experienced a

---

[84] Caron, "Antisemitic," 30–31.
[85] Schor, *L'Antisémitisme*, 149.
[86] Caron, "Antisemitic," 42–49.
[87] Caron, "Antisemitic," 42–43, 46, 49; Schor, *L'Antisémitisme*, 151–52.

marked rise in anti-Semitism during the 1930s, and native French law lobbies successfully pressured the French parliament to institute restrictions on naturalized foreigners who wished to pass the French bar.[88]

Resentment toward foreign Jewish competition arose in other professions as well. In response to a cry to protect French artisans, the government passed the Laval Law of April 5, 1935, which empowered artisan associations to impose quotas on foreign workers. The new law required foreign workers seeking employment to obtain an artisan card from the minister of labor. However, the issuance of the card became contingent upon prior approval from the local artisan association. The Laval Law did not specifically target foreign Jewish workers, but it did single out pieceworkers in the garment industry. The garment industry in the Paris region had become a site of intense anti-Jewish feelings during the 1930s, with the influx of thousands of Jewish needle and garment workers from Eastern Europe.[89] The French government enacted legislation in 1935 restricting peddling, and in 1938 instituted economic measures to halt the flow of Jewish refugees from Austria.[90]

One of the more interesting anti-Semitic myths is that rich Jews funded the Bolshevik Revolution and served as mainstays of the socialist left in Europe during the interwar period. One rationale for this myth is found in the "Protocols of the Elders of Zion," which I will explore in the next chapter. Here, I will only mention that many anti-Semites believed that rich Jewish bankers had planned and funded the downfall of the intensely anti-Semitic czarist regime and that, whether willfully or indirectly, they had prepared the ground for the (anti-Christian) Bolshevik Party's seizure of power. Moreover, anti-Semites believed that rich Jews had backed the efforts of leftist Popular Fronts throughout Europe in the hope of establishing a bulwark against the rising wave of the anti-Semitic Nazi and fascist movements.

All told, a severe economic crisis combined with relatively high levels of Jewish immigration, the notoriety of the Stavisky Affair, the perception of Jewish economic dominance, and Jewish backing of the revolutionary left afforded French economic anti-Semitism a nurturing soil in which to grow during the interwar period. We turn now to an

---

[88] Caron, "Antisemitic," 40–41.

[89] Caron, "Antisemitic," 39–40; Michael R. Marrus and Robert O. Paxton, "The Roots of Vichy Anti-Semitism." In Strauss, ed., *Hostages of Modernization*, vol. 3/1, 612.

[90] Caron, "Antisemitic," 39–40.

examination of the economic roots of anti-Semitism in Germany. We will find that many of the factors responsible for heightened economic antipathy toward Jews in France were also present in Germany before the Holocaust.

## GERMANY

We have seen how economic attitudes toward Jews in France tended to reflect the level of general economic prosperity of the population. In times of recession and depression, economic anti-Semitism grew, and in times of economic growth, it subsided. The general pattern is also true for Germany. Economic antipathy toward German Jews rose dramatically when the German economy experienced significant downswings. The principal downswings occurred between 1873 and 1878, 1890 and 1894, 1919 and 1924, and 1930 and 1933.[91] During these downswings, the charge of Jewish economic dominance held center stage.

During the first half of the nineteenth century, Jews residing in the various German states began to ascend from positions of hawkers, petty traders, usurers, and innkeepers to jobs in retail and wholesale businesses and banking. Of the fifty-two private banks in Berlin in the early years of the nineteenth century, thirty were owned by Jews. The Frankfurt Rothschilds were the most famous of the German families to rise to prominence during the first half of the nineteenth century. By 1825, the Rothschilds had established themselves as the dominant lenders to the leading powers of Europe. Two of their earliest clients were the states of Prussia and Austria.[92] As many of the German states after 1830 sought capital for industrial development, a number of other Jewish banking families climbed into the German Jewish economic elite. Among those constituting the German-Jewish banking establishment before 1871 were the Rothschilds and Gebrueder Bethmann in Frankfurt, Salomon Heine and Moritz Warburg in Hamburg, the Mendelssohns and Bleichroeders in Berlin, and Abraham Oppenheim in Cologne. Two Jewish bankers, Abraham Oppenheim and Bethel Henry Strousberg, had benefited enormously from taking the lead in financing the early construction of German railway lines after 1835. Interestingly, Bismarck,

---

[91] Hans Rosenberg, "Anti-Semitism and the 'Great Depression', 1873–1896." In Strauss, ed., *Hostages of Modernization*, vol. 3/1, 20; Maddison, *Dynamic*, 98–99.

[92] Ruppin, *Jews*, 207–08; Friedlaender, *Nazi Germany*, 77–78; Ferguson, *World's*, 142.

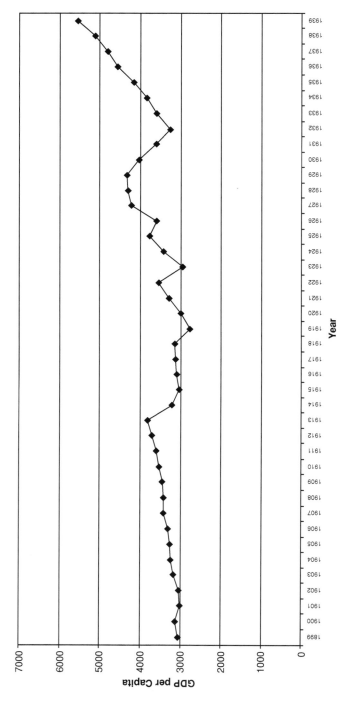

Figure 4.2b. GDP per capita in Germany, 1899–1939. *Note*: The GDP (gross domestic product) per capita data are in 1990 dollars and are drawn from Maddison (1995) and Good and Ma (1998).

the German chancellor, and Kaiser William I, the German emperor, had selected Jewish bankers to manage their own private accounts. Bismarck, upon the recommendation of the Rothschilds, chose Gerson Bleichroeder, and Kaiser William opted for Moritz Cohn.[93]

Between the establishment of the Second Reich in 1871 and the initiation of World War I in 1914, Germany experienced unparalleled economic growth. German national unity, along with an influx of five billion French francs from the French government as an indemnity payment, initiated a two-year economic boom in Germany. A total of 207 new joint stock companies came into existence in 1871, followed by an additional 479 new joint stock companies in 1872. German steel production grew at an average rate of more than 6 percent for the 1870–1913 period, enabling Germany to surpass Great Britain in steel production by 1895. Between 1883 and 1913, German net domestic product rose at an annual rate greater than 3 percent, and Germany's exports climbed from 7.4 percent of GDP in 1870 to 12.2 percent by 1913. On the eve of World War I, the unified German Empire had become the dominant industrial nation of continental Europe.[94] German Jewish financiers and bankers played a large and key role in raising the huge capital requirements for the rapid German industrial expansion after 1871, the evolution of the Berlin stock exchange, and the growth of German international investment.[95] Steiman observes that a measure of the prominence of German Jewish bankers in financing the explosive industrial expansion may be gauged by the conferral of more than 30 percent of the privy councillorships in the decade after 1879 to Jewish bankers.[96]

By the end of the nineteenth century, Jewish prominence in German banking, industry, and commerce was staggering.[97] According to Wistrich, while Jews comprised only 1 percent of the total German

[93] Kindleberger, *Financial*, 121; Ruppin, *Jews*, 208; Steiman, *Paths*, 146–47; Friedlaender, *Nazi Germany*, 77–78; Wistrich, *Socialism*, 61.

[94] Cameron, *Concise*, 240–44; O'Rourke and Williamson, *Globalisation*.

[95] Friedlaender, *Nazi Germany*, 78.

[96] Steiman, *Paths*, 146–47.

[97] The Jewish presence in the banking industry was even greater in Austria at the end of the nineteenth century. According to Friedlaender (*Nazi Germany*, 80), within the Austrian part of the Habsburg Empire more than 50 percent of the major banks were Jewish-owned, and Jews held approximately 80 percent of the key banking positions.

population, they accounted for nearly 18 percent of bank owners and directors in the German Reich and 33 percent in Berlin.[98] Ruppin's examination of the statistics shows an even greater Jewish presence. By Ruppin's account, the percentage of Jewish bank owners and directors in the state of Prussia was 43.2 percent in 1882, 37.6 percent in 1895, and 17.9 percent in 1925.[99] Jewish influence was felt equally in commerce and industry, where they held positions of prominence in roughly one-third of Germany's largest companies between 1900 and 1910.[100] Included among the wealthy and powerful German Jews – popularly referred to as the *Kaiserjuden* – at century's end were shipping magnate Albert Ballin (the founder of the German merchant marine), Emil Rathenau (originator of the German electrical industry), and the Aron Hirsch family (dominant in the German metal trade industry). German Jews were particularly conspicuous in the department store and publishing industries. The Tietz family (Hermann, Leonhard, and Oskar) owned more that thirty-five department stores; Abraham Wertheim owned one of Berlin's great department stores; and N. Israel owned Germany's largest department store between 1899 and 1914. Within the publishing industry, Leopold Sonemann founded the *Frankfurter Zeitung*; Rudolf Mosse controlled the *Berliner Tageblatt*, the *Morgenzeitung*, the *Volkszeitung*, and the *Boersenblatt*; and the Ullstein family owned the *Neues Berliner Tageblatt*, the *Abendpost*, the *Illustrierte Zeitung*, the *B.Z. am Mittag*, the *Vossische Zeitung*, and Germany's largest circulating newspaper, the *Morgenpost*. Jews were also prominent among the major editorial writers and correspondents of the most influential German newspapers. Theodor Wolff served as editor of the *Berliner Tageblatt*; George Bernhard held the position of editor of the *Vossische Zeitung*; and Bernhard Guttmann became the influential correspondent of the *Frankfurter Zeitung*.[101]

---

[98] Wistrich, *Socialism*, 61.

[99] Ruppin, *Jews*, 210.

[100] In his *Die Juden und das Wirtschaftsleben*, Werner Sombart, the noted German sociologist, pointed out that Jews constituted nearly one-quarter of the members of the boards of directors within the ten largest branches of German industy (Wistrich, *Socialism*, 61).

[101] Steiman, *Paths*, 146–48; Wistrich, *Socialism*, 61; Friedlaender, *Nazi Germany*, 77–79. Other *Kaiserjuden* included Eduard Arnhold, James Simon, Carl Fuerstenberg, Ludwig Max Goldberger, Georg Solmssen, Wilhelm Herz, Franz von Mendelssohn, Max Steinthal, Maximilian Kempner, Max M. Warburg, and Heinrich Gruenfel.

Jews were well represented among Germany's greatest fortunes. Of the twenty-nine German families in 1908 with aggregate fortunes in excess of fifty million marks, nine were Jewish. On this list, the Rothschilds (including the Goldschmidts) ranked second, the Speyers held the sixth spot, and the Mendelssohns (including the Mendelssohn-Bartholdys) ranked eighth. The German Rothschilds were worth 310 million marks alone. Jewish wealth within Germany's largest state, Prussia, in 1908 was even greater. Jews comprised 11 of the 25 wealthiest Prussians and 190 of the wealthiest 800 Prussian subjects. Of the 200 Prussian millionaires in 1908, 55 came from Jewish origins, and 33 of the 55 had made their fortunes in finance and banking.[102] The extraordinary wealth of these German Jews skewed the overall level of wealth of Germany's Jews. Werner Sombart, a prominent German sociologist at the turn of the century, calculated that Berlin's Jews, comprising roughly 5 percent of the city's population, had contributed more than 30 percent of the city's tax revenue. Sombart noted further that while the income tax per capita for the Jews of Berlin came to 357 marks, it was only 133 marks for the city's Lutherans and 111 marks for Berlin's Catholics.[103]

German Jews were also overrepresented within the German middle classes. Ruppin observed that of all gainfully employed Jews within the German state of Prussia, the percentage of Jews working in commerce was 56.6 percent in 1882 and 49.3 percent in 1925.[104] Among non-Jews, the percentages were 2.0 percent in 1882 and 10.3 percent in 1925. Jews made up roughly 22 percent of all employees in the Prussian banking and stock exchange in 1882. In Berlin in 1882 alone, Jews comprised more than 20 percent of all wholesale merchants, nearly 12 percent of all doctors, close to 9 percent of all journalists, and roughly 8 percent of all lawyers. In 1925, German Jews comprised 18 percent of all doctors, 15 percent of all dentists, and 25 percent of all lawyers in the German state of Prussia. By 1933, Jews made up slightly more than 16 percent of Germany's lawyers and nearly 11 percent of the country's physicians. We need to keep in mind that Jews comprised a little more than 1 percent of the total German population in 1933.[105]

[102] Steinberg, *All or Nothing*, 235–36; Rubinstein, *History*, 124; Finzi, *Anti-Semitism*, 57.
[103] Wistrich, *Socialism*, 59.
[104] Ruppin, *Jews*, 209.
[105] Wistrich, *Socialism*, 56–57; Ruppin, *Jews*, 219; Weinberg, *Because*, 222.

While Jews were overrepresented in Germany's upper and middle classes, they were significantly underrepresented in the fields of agricultural and industrial labor. Ruppin's examination of the German occupational structure in 1925 makes this point dramatically clear. He finds that within agriculture, forestry, mines, and mineral extraction, Jews comprised less than one-tenth of one percent of those gainfully employed, and, within metal manufactures, Jews made up slightly more than three-tenths of one percent of those employed.[106] This occupational imbalance did not go unnoticed by the purveyors of German anti-Semitism.

The Jews that were to be found in the laboring classes typically were Ostjuden or recent Jewish immigrants from Eastern Europe. In 1880, the roughly 15,000 Ostjuden accounted for 2.7 percent of the German Jewish community. By 1910, the Ostjuden population had grown to nearly 79,000, or 12.8 percent of the German Jewish community. The majority of these foreign Jews worked as petty traders (clothing, leather, tobacco, and food), hawkers, peddlers, and furniture dealers.[107]

In 1873, the German stock market crashed, ushering in a severe economic depression. The origins of the 1873 crash derive largely from the impact of a huge inflow of gold from France's indemnity payments, resulting from France's defeat in the Franco-Prussian war. The sudden influx of wealth led to inflation and considerable speculation on the German stock exchange. The crash hurt large and small investors alike throughout Germany. The crash of 1873 unleashed a spate of attacks on alleged Jewish economic dominance in Germany. Several specific factors played a role in assigning blame for the economic turmoil to the Jews. Initially, the crisis had originated with the collapse of the Austrian Creditanstalt, a Rothschild banking institution. Additionally, two Jews, Eduard Lasker and Ludwig Bamberger, had sponsored legislation in the German Reichstag liberalizing the establishment of corporations with limited liability. This led to the creation of a large number of joint stock companies, many of which had shaky financial foundations. A third contributing factor was the appearance of many Jewish-sounding names among the so-called "Stock Exchange Jews," or those who had promoted and financed the soon-to-be-insolvent joint stock companies. These specific factors should be placed in the context of the growing perception that many German Jews had disproportionately benefited from

---

[106] Ruppin, *Jews*, 142, 144.
[107] Wistrich, *Socialism*, 60; Ruppin, *Jews*, 212–13.

the remarkable economic expansion that had occurred in the various German states during the 1860s and 1870s.[108]

Otto Glagau, a Reichstag deputy, became one of the earliest to publicly blame the Jews for the crisis. He claimed that 90 percent of the bankrupt companies were controlled by Jews. *Die Gartenlaube*, a popular magazine with a circulation between 350,000/400,000 readers, published a series of articles by Glagau. In these articles, Glagau reiterated his claim about the role of Jewish speculators in the crash. Glagau invoked the particular charge that the invasion of Ostjuden from the area of Posen seeking to become rich on the German stock exchange had played a role in the crash.[109] A few years later, Adolf Stoecker, the founder of the anti-Semitic Christian Socialist Workers' Party, continued to promote the theme of a Jewish conspiracy behind the 1873 stock market collapse. Stoecker accused the Jews of worshipping gold and controlling Germany's banking, trade, and press. He warned that Germany was reaching the point where the Jews would totally dominate German public opinion and German labor, a theme already popularized by the anti-Semitic publicist Wilhelm Marr. Stoecker noted further that in order to effectively solve the "Jewish Problem," Germany's Jews would have to engage in all aspects of German labor including artisanry, factory work, and farming.[110]

The effects of the 1873 German stock market crash and the ensuing Depression eventually reached Germany's farming districts. Between 1850 and 1875, German farmers had reaped the benefits of steadily rising agricultural prices. However, the development of the railway and steamship industries led to lower transport costs and increased competition for German food producers within the domestic German market. After 1875, agricultural prices began to fall, and agricultural indebtedness rose. In the wake of the Depression, the cost of borrowing money jumped, and German farmers had difficulty paying off their debts. The rate of farm foreclosures increased greatly during the late 1870s and early 1880s. Particularly hard hit among Germany's farming community were the small livestock farmers. These farmers confronted additionally the imposition of higher tariffs on the grains used to feed their livestock

---

[108] Levy, *Downfall*, 12–13; Wistrich, *Socialism*, 51; Lindemann, *Esau's*, 106.

[109] Lindemann, *Esau's*, 119–21; Levy, *Downfall*, 13; Weiss, *Ideology*, 84; Peter Pulzer, *The Rise of Political Anti-Semitism in Germany and Austria* (Cambridge, MA, 1988), 85.

[110] Massing, *Rehearsal*, 285–86; Weinberg, *Because*, 93.

and from an outbreak of hoof-and-mouth disease that decimated the
number of livestock.[111] Anti-Semitic rural demagogues assigned blame
to the Jews. Anti-Semites strove to convince the disgruntled German
peasants that Jews were the source of their troubles by charging that
Jews were in Berlin, the government, the Reichstag, the revolutionary Social Democratic Party, the stock exchange, and even the imperial court.[112] Best known among the rural anti-Semites of the 1880s
and 1890s was Otto Boeckel. Boeckel had written his *The Jews: The
Kings of Our Times* in 1885. The book had sold in excess of 1.5 million
copies by 1909. Boeckel's book alleged that Jewish moneylenders were
behind the high interest rates charged to farmers, the low prices for
agricultural produce, and the high cost of farm equipment.[113] This anti-
Semite led the Peasant League of Hessen from 1885 to 1894. Boeckel
ran for and won a seat in the German Reichstag in 1887. Economic
anti-Semitism played an important role in his successful electoral campaign in the rural district of Marburg-Frankenberg-Kirchhain in Hesse.
He identified Ludwig Bamberger, the Jewish financier and Reichstag
deputy (also from Hessen), as a principal culprit responsible for the decline in the peasants' well-being. Bamberger, according to Boeckel, had
been one of the originators of the liberal policies so detrimental to the
economic health of Germany's small farmers and had been behind the
creation of the Reichsbank and the linking of the German currency to
the gold standard. Boeckel's attacks on Jews went beyond Bamberger.[114]
The Jews of Hessen numbered roughly 70,000 out of a total population of more than 2.8 million. The Jewish community in Hessen dated
back to the thirteenth century, and the relations between Jews and
Christian peasants had been relatively respectful before Boeckel's political campaigning. Boeckel's rural district contained a relatively dense
small-town Jewish settlement, largely consisting of cattle dealers, middlemen, and moneylenders. During the electoral campaign, Boeckel
traveled from village to village attacking these Jews and encouraging
the Christian farmers to free themselves financially from Jewish middlemen. He referred to the Jews as parasites and exploiters and offered

---

[111] Levy, *Downfall*, 49; Lindemann, *Esau's*, 152–56.

[112] Massing, *Rehearsal*, 101.

[113] Weiss, *Ideology*, 100.

[114] Boeckel, like Wilhelm Marr and "Germanicus" before him, sought to expose the
hand of the German Rothschilds in Germany's economic difficulties. Boeckel
accused the Rothschilds of cornering the world market in oil (Ferguson, *World's*,
781).

to establish "Jew-free" rural cooperatives and markets, from which Jews would be barred.[115] Some forty years later, Boeckel's notion of "Jew-free markets" became a central tenet of the Nazi Party's agrarian programs. As a Reichstag member, Boeckel continued to tie his anti-Semitism to his opposition to free trade and the liberal economic policies adopted by the German government. He founded the Central German Peasant League as a vehicle to promote his message. His league assisted the formation of a movement among small businessmen and master craftsmen in the German state of Saxony that sought to limit the entry of Jews into the crafts. At its height in 1893, Boeckel's movement had the support of eleven Reichstag deputies.[116]

Persistent problems in agriculture dampened overall German economic growth during the early 1890s. Again, as earlier, heightened anti-Semitism accompanied financial difficulties. Between 1890 and 1895, agricultural prices declined substantially. For instance, a ton of rye selling for 208 German marks in 1891 in Danzig fetched only 110 marks in 1894. The main culprit again appeared to be the opening up of new areas of grain production in the Americas and India, declining maritime freight rates, and lower tariffs. The Caprivi trade treaties of the early 1890s reduced import duties on oats from 4 marks to 2.8 marks and on barley from 2.25 to 2.0 marks.[117] The effects of the 1890s agricultural crisis spread from grain-growing to livestock-producing areas of Germany. Hoof-and-mouth disease again wrought havoc. By 1891, one-tenth of all German livestock fell victim to the disease. Two years later, a chronic shortage of feed led to a further reduction in the number of German livestock. Lower tariffs on foreign livestock products brought further pain to Germany's livestock farmers. The Caprivi trade treaties reduced tariffs on foreign oxen, calves, and fresh and prepared meat, thereby bolstering the import of foreign produce. Facing a deteriorating situation, livestock farmers assumed a heavier indebtedness. The necessity to borrow capital and to seek out credit brought them into contact with cattle dealers and money lenders, several of whom were Jewish.[118]

---

[115] Levy, *Downfall*, 49–58; Massing, *Rehearsal*, 87–88; Lindemann, *Esau's*, 152–56; Mosse, *Final Solution*, 166–67.

[116] Mosse, *Final Solution*, 166–67; Sperber, *Kaiser's*, 213.

[117] Holborn, *History*, 319; David Blackbourn, *Class, Religion and Local Politics in Wilhelmine Germany: The Centre Party in Wuerttemberg before 1914* (New Haven and London, 1980), 88–89.

[118] Blackbourn, *Class*, 88–89; Levy, *Downfall*, 51–54.

Anti-Semitic rural agitators sought to capitalize on the perception of flowering anti-Semitic resentment. The 1893 German Reichstag election marked a high point for anti-Semitic candidates. Sperber, who has examined the conservative and anti-Semitic parties in the 1893 election, claims that the anti-Semitic vote increased from 50,000 in 1890 to 270,000 in 1893.[119] Seven candidates won Reichstag seats campaigning as anti-Semites in the 1893 election. These seven deputies joined the Conservative Party caucus in the German parliament. The appearance of the Agrarian League may have had a lot to do with the stunning jump in the anti-Semitic vote. The organized and active Agrarian League threw its support to right-wing candidates advocating anti-Semitism and hostility to free trade. The League fought to force the German government to raise tariffs on agricultural goods, ease credit, and lower taxes.[120] As economic prosperity returned to Germany by the mid-1890s, the anti-Semitic parties and candidates began to recede into the background. Economic resentment surely did not disappear on the eve of the twentieth century, but it had clearly subsided, for economic prosperity and anti-Semitism failed to produce a suitable mix.

Though the anti-Semitic candidates in 1893 aligned themselves with the Conservative Party in Germany, this does not mean that the German left was bereft of economic anti-Semitism.[121] We have seen earlier that the German left had catered to both religious and racial forms of anti-Semitism. German socialists, in the last quarter of the nineteenth century, in doing battle against capitalist exploitation and government corruption, frequently resorted to the expression of economic anti-Semitic sentiments. The German left occasionally employed negative representations of Jewish moneylenders and cattle dealers in rural areas and demeaning depictions of Jewish loan sharks and Jewish opulence in urban localities.[122]

---

[119] Sperber, *Kaiser's*, 217.

[120] Sperber, *Kaiser's*, 213; Holborn, *History*, 319.

[121] In a recent book, Stefan Scheil (*Die Entwicklung des politischen Antisemitismus in Deutschland zwischen 1881 und 1912: Eine wahlgeschichtliche Untersuchung*, Berlin, 1999) notes that the left liberals and Social Democrats did not abjure from anti-Semitism during the *Kaiserreich*. Scheil advises us not simply to take the votes for anti-Semitic parties as a complete measure of the prevalence of anti-Semitic sentiments in Germany after 1870. For Scheil, anti-Semitic prejudice was pervasive throughout Germany's political culture.

[122] Massing, *Rehearsal*, 162.

Leftist economic anti-Semitism in Germany had a rich heritage. Karl Marx's writings, notably his 1844 *Zur Judenfrage*, contributed substantially to the popularization within the German left of economic anti-Semitism. Marx wrote his *Zur Judenfrage* at a time when he perceived that major Jewish banking houses, among them the Rothschilds, were financing the explosive industrialization occurring throughout Europe and acting as a principal financial pillar of the hated reactionary Metternichian Holy Alliance, which dominated Europe's political landscape from 1815 to 1848. The year 1815 marked for the political left the return of political conservatism, with the restoration of legitimist regimes in Austria, Prussia, and France. Marx's view that Nathan Rothschild served as the insurance broker for the reactionary Holy Alliance during the 1820s was widely shared by other prominent leftists.[123] Among other things, Marx asserted in *Zur Judenfrage* that huckstering is the worldly religion of the Jew and that money is the Jew's God. Marx saw the Jewish worship of money becoming the dominant thinking in the society of Christian Europe. The Jews' primary social function is money making, according to Marx. For Marx, the "Jewish Question" is the question of man under capitalism, and the solution to the "Jewish Question" required the overthrow of the capitalist system. Marx claimed further that with the elimination of the essence of Judaism – that is, huckstering – Judaism would disappear.[124] Marx's anti-Semitic legacy, notably the linking of Jews with the pernicious effects of capitalism, influenced both German and European socialists into the twentieth century. It became a theme of Werner Sombart's influential 1911 *Die Juden und das Wirtschaftsleben* (The Jews and economic life), which also linked the Rothschilds and the Jews with the creation of the modern stock exchange. Sombart, a major figure in the emergence of modern economic history, followed a year later with the publication of *Die Zukunft der Juden* (The future of the Jews), in which he depicted Jewish dominance in all aspects of German national life.[125]

During the last quarter of the nineteenth century, economic antipathy toward Jews benefited from the perception of a growing flood of foreign or Eastern European Jews entering the new Reich. An early warning of the dangers of the impending flood came from the highly prominent German historian Heinrich von Treitschke. Treitschke, who had

[123] Ferguson, *World's*, 15–16, 136; Byrnes, *Antisemitism*, 115–17.
[124] Ferguson, *World's*, 464; Massing, *Rehearsal*, 159; Wistrich, *Socialism*, 26–27.
[125] Poliakov, *Aryan*, 286; Finzi, *Anti-Semitism*, 51; Ferguson, *World's*, 781.

published the widely read *History of Germany in the Nineteenth Century* in 1879, had authored a number of influential articles in the prestigious *Preussische Jahrbuecher*. In these articles, he had cautioned his readers to take notice of the stream of Polish Jewish immigrants, who enter Germany as hustling peddlers but whose descendants will one day control Germany's stock exchange and press.[126] The outbreak of anti-Semitic pogroms in Russia in the 1880s turned the stream of Eastern European immigration into a flood. Those eastern Jews settling in Germany engaged primarily in peddling. Wertheimer observes that the occupational structure of the Jewish immigrants in Germany differed significantly from that in other Western destinations. Whereas nearly 70 percent of the Jewish immigrants in the United States and Great Britain participated in industrial labor, roughly half of the Jewish emigrants settling in Germany pursued careers in commerce.[127] Wertheimer points to the role of governmental policies, Germany's economic needs, and the predisposition of the immigrants as possible explanations for the diverging occupational structures in these countries.[128] Competition from immigrant peddlers constituted one source of friction, and competition for places in Germany's technical schools and universities became an additional arena of antagonism out of which restrictionist campaigns aimed at immigrant Jewish students emerged. Some German states during the early 1900s instituted quotas, or *numerus clausus*, on all foreigners attempting to enter German faculties, but others singled out Russian Jews. The issue became particularly acute within the faculty of medicine, where the campaign against Russian Jewish students successfully resulted in governmental decisions to reject graduates of the Russian *Realschulen*, while demanding that Russian students provide proof of study at an institution of higher learning in their home country. These decisions made it nearly impossible for Russian Jews to enter the German faculty of medicine, because the czarist regime had, through the imposition of quotas, previously closed the doors of institutions of higher learning to Jews in Russia.[129]

Germany shared in the economic prosperity of the *belle époque* stretching from the late 1890s to the eve of World War I. In an era of sustained economic growth, economic resentment against the Jews

---

[126] Weiss, *Ideology*, 87.
[127] Wertheimer, *Unwelcome*, 92.
[128] Ibid.
[129] Ibid., 34, 70.

declined. However, Germany's sudden military collapse in November 1918 ushered in a period of economic insecurity that lasted into the 1930s. And again, as before, economic antipathy toward Germany's Jews waxed and waned as the German economy oscillated between growth and decline. Unfortunately for German Jews, the nation's economy witnessed far more years of decline than growth during the interwar period. The striking magnitude of the German economic decline during the interwar years bears repeating. The value of the German gold mark in relation to the U.S. dollar, which stood at 4.2 in 1914, fell to 4.2 *trillion* in November 1923. Between 1921 and 1938, the average annual unemployment rate in Germany was 15.5 percent, compared to 7.0 percent in France and 13.7 percent in Great Britain. Between 1920 and 1938, Germany outdistanced her industrial rivals with the largest average annual decline in aggregate output. Though the German economy rebounded between 1924 and 1928, largely as a result of high investment and rapid expansion, it began to suffer again even before the disastrous collapse of the American stock market in October 1929. The particular culprit for this decline was Germany's difficulty in securing the necessary funds from U.S. lenders to finance its reparation payments to the Allies. Furthermore, the U.S. economic slump forced Germany to begin to repay its American lenders, leading to an outflow of German capital, and eventually to Germany's default on its reparations obligations and foreign debt by 1931. From 1928 to the middle of 1931, domestic imports and income declined faster than exports. Unemployment climbed from 355,000 in the summer of 1928 to 1.9 million in 1929. In 1931, the unemployment level rose to 15 percent of the workforce. The magnitude of German GDP decline between 1928 and 1938 was the greatest of the five countries in this study. In particular, Germany's percent difference between peak and trough of GDP in this period was –16.1 percent, compared to –11.0 in France, –6.1 in Italy, –5.8 in the United Kingdom, and –5.5 in Romania.[130] The economic misery hit German agriculture particularly hard. Agriculture and forestry accounted for 30.5 percent of Germany's employed population in 1925. The stabilization of the German currency in 1924 ended ten years of rising agricultural prices and set German agriculture on a path toward financial collapse. German farmers' real income increased a meager 4.5 percent, compared to the national average increase of 45 percent, between 1913 and 1928.

[130] Temin, *Lessons*, 3; Maddison, *Dynamic*, 87–89; Maddison, "Economic," 455, 460; Cameron, *Concise*, 351–52; Kindleberger, *Financial*, 306, 366.

Collapsing agricultural prices, insufficient tariff protection, and heavy borrowing resulted in a rising level of debt for many German farmers after 1924. In fact, Germany's' agricultural debt skyrocketed from zero marks in the 1923–24 period to nearly twelve billion marks (three billion dollars) by the end of 1931. High interest rates and reduced credit thwarted farmers' efforts to reduce this debt. The currency stabilization, which helped to end the German inflation of the early 1920s, tightened credit and made borrowing more expensive. Interest rates, which in 1925 were roughly twice their prewar levels, climbed steadily. Between 1925 and 1933, the cycle of crop failures, credit shortages, low prices for agricultural products, low tariffs, rising taxes, bankruptcies, and falling net profits increasingly ravaged Germany's farming community.[131]

After 1924, the fate of independent artisans and shopkeepers mirrored that of German farmers. Falling prices, shrinking markets, and expensive credit forced an increasing number of artisans and shopkeepers into heavy debt. Between 1925 and 1933, the average yearly income of the self-employed fell from 3,540 to 2,500 marks, while the income of people who were not self-employed dropped from 1,710 to 1,520 marks. Almost 50,000 business firms went bankrupt between 1930 and 1932.[132]

The deleterious effects of the interwar economic crises on Germany's working class are well known. German labor experienced a major shock between 1923 and 1924, when the reparations payment controversy and the French occupation of the Ruhr exacerbated Germany's financial situation and contributed to hyperinflation. By December 1923, more than one-half of Germany's labor force was either unemployed or underemployed. For those who had jobs, the high inflation eroded their incomes, so that real wages fell to nearly half their 1921 level. With

---

[131] G. D. Feldman, *The Great Disorder: Politics, Economics, and Society in the German Inflation, 1914–1924* (New York, 1993), 840; D. Petzina, "Germany and the Great Depression." *Journal of Contemporary History*, vol. 4, 1969, 59; Michael Kater, *The Nazi Party* (Cambridge, MA, 1983), 58; D. J. K. Peukert, *The Weimar Republic: The Crisis of Classical Modernity*, trans. R. Deveson (New York, 1989), 65; M. Sering, *Deutsche Agrarpolitik: Auf geschichtlicher und landeskundlicher Grundlage* (Leipzig, 1934), 115; H. James, *The German Slump: Politics and Economics 1924–1936* (Oxford, 1986), 258–59; David Abraham, *The Collapse of the Weimar Republic*, 2nd ed. (New York, 1986), 55, 59; Brustein, *Logic*, 64–66, 68–69.

[132] Juergen W. Falter, "Economic Debts and Political Gains: Electoral Support for the Nazi Party in Agrarian Commercial Sectors, 1928–1933." Unpublished paper presented at the eighty-fifth annual meeting of the American Political Science Association, Atlanta, Georgia, 1989, 5; Brustein, *Logic*, 73.

the revival of the German economy in 1924, due in large part to the influx of foreign capital, conditions improved dramatically for many of Germany's blue-collar workers. Unemployment among unionized workers dropped to 9 percent by May 1924 from a level of 27 percent during the previous January, and wages for both skilled and unskilled workers rose gradually. However, the halcyon days were short-lived. Beginning in 1930, unemployment among blue-collar workers skyrocketed, while wages declined precipitously. In September 1929, 17 percent of organized metalworkers were either unemployed or working part-time. One year later, that figure had jumped to nearly 45 percent. Blue-collar workers in the woodworking, clothing, leather, linoleum, and construction industries experienced a similar fate. Between 1928 and 1930, the average real wages for blue-collar laborers fell roughly eleven percent. The year 1932 brought no relief for the economic woes of blue-collar workers. Unemployment continued to climb. By summer, more than 40 percent of Germany's unionized workers were either unemployed or forced to work part-time.[133]

An upswing in economic assaults on German Jews began as early as World War I. As the war dragged on, anti-Semitic voices charged Jews with profiteering from the war economy. During the war, the appointments of Walther Rathenau (the notable industrialist) to head the War Resources Department in the War Ministry and of Max Warburg and Carl Melchior (two Jewish bankers) to manage the Central Purchasing Company provided anti-Semites opportunistic targets for the war profiteering allegation. In fact, nearly 10 percent of the directors of the war corporations were Jews. Anti-Semites often charged that Jews, while overrepresented in the Reich's wartime economy, were underrepresented at the German front. Such allegations, backed by a coalition within the German Reichstag including conservatives, liberals, and even Social Democrats, ultimately led to an official inquest into Jewish membership in the German armed forces. On November 1, 1916, the Prussian war minister issued an order to conduct a census of Jews (*Judenzaehlung*).[134] The accusation of Jewish war profiteering flourished in the aftermath of Germany's defeat and during the revolutionary upheaval between 1920

---

[133] Thomas Childers, *The Nazi Voter: The Social Foundations of Fascism in Germany, 1919–1933* (Chapel Hill, 1983), 102–03, 244; Abraham, *Collapse*, 117; Feldman, *Great*; *Wirtschaft und Statistik*, 12, (1932): 147–48, 471–73; Brustein, *Logic*, 120–23.

[134] Friedlaender, *Nazi Germany*, 74.

and 1921 and attracted support from a wide circle of groups.[135] Stoking further the anti-Semitic fire during World War I was the charge that the liberal and democratic press was controlled by prominent Jews and had harmed the German war effort. Critics pointed out that Jewish owned and managed newspapers, such as the *Vossiche Zeitung, Berliner Tageblatt, and Frankfurter Zeitung,* had advocated during the hostilities a no annexation policy and opposition to Germany's Eastern European wartime policy.[136]

The Weimar years (1919–33) hardly diminished the harboring of economic anti-Semitic resentment. During the Weimar period, many of the same charges leveled against the Jews before and during World War I retained their potency. In fact, many of the allegations against Jews grew in intensity, as many German Jews took advantage of the more open and democratic Weimar society to ascend into the upper echelons of Germany's economic, political, and cultural elites. Besides the traditional charge of Jewish economic power, there were the allegations of unfair economic competition from Eastern European Jewish immigrants and Jewish involvement in financial and political scandals[137] These accusations were hardly new, but they occurred in a context of severe economic trauma and in a climate of renewed Eastern European immigration into Germany.

Economic anti-Semitic rhetoric had established a base throughout Weimar's political culture. Between 1925 and 1933, at a time when the Nazi Party sought to build its membership base and attract a sizable electoral following, the party opportunistically employed economic anti-Semitism where and when it was thought that anti-Semitic rhetoric would work to attract support. In areas such as Middle Franconia,

---

[135] Kauders, *German,* 68.

[136] Friedlaender, "Political," 152–57.

[137] Julius Barmat, a Russian Jew, and the Jewish Sklarek brothers were involved in two of the publicized financial/political scandals of the Weimar period. In March 1927, Barmat, a Russian Jew with ties to the Social Democratic Party, was found guilty of bribing officers of the Bank of Prussia and the German postal system and sentenced to eleven months in prison. The Sklarek brothers, owners of a clothing factory, had been implicated in 1929 in the bribing of Berlin city officials and the charging of city expenses for deliveries never made. Two of the brothers had taken advantage of their membership in the Social Democratic Party to bribe members of the party serving in the city government. The German right-wing parties reveled in the publicity given to the association of Jewish illegal activities with the German left (Kauders, *German,* 126–27).

parts of Hessen and Westphalia, and stretches of the Rhineland, where anti-Semitism had a long history, the party featured its anti-Semitic propaganda. However, on numerous occasions, the party realized that anti-Semitism had potentially negative consequences for its strategy of building a mass following. Zofka's study of the Nazi Party in Swabia illustrates how the Nazis excised anti-Semitic references from their campaigning, realizing that among the local farmers, economic concerns were primary and that negative references to Jews hurt party recruitment. Zofka claims that within the farming population of the Swabian district of Gunzburg, Jewish traders were held in high esteem, and a popular expression was "Wenn kein Jude auf dem Markt ist, geht kein Handel" (If no Jew is at the market, there will be no trade).[138] Thus, the theme of anti-Semitism was suppressed in the NSDAP program when propagandizing in the Gunzburg region.[139] But there were many other instances in which Nazi Party economic anti-Semitism seemed highly suitable. From early in the party's history, Hitler had targeted what he referred to as the particular brand of Jewish capitalism. Hitler stressed that point 17 of the Nazi Party's official 1920 platform, calling for the "unremunerative expropriation of land for the common weal," applied only to land wrongfully acquired (obtained illegitimately or administered without regard for the good of the people) and primarily owned by "Jewish property speculation companies" (*juedische Grundspekulationsgesellschaften*).[140] Hilter equally sought to convince his listeners that the Nazi Party did not oppose all forms of capitalism. He distinguished between productive and unproductive capitalism. The party, Hitler argued, favored productive capitalism (*bodenstaendigen Kapitalismus*), which derived profit from one's own labor; but it disapproved of unproductive capitalism or loan capitalism, which derived profit from speculation or

---

[138] Z. Zofka, *Die Ausbreitung des Nationalsozialismus auf dem Lande* (Munich, 1979), 126.

[139] Brustein, *Logic*, 59.

[140] H. A. Winkler, *Mittelstand, Demokratie und Nationalsozialismus* (Cologne, 1972), 100; H. Gies, "The NSDAP Agrarian Organization in the Final Phase of the Weimar Republic." In H. A. Turner, ed., *Nazism and the Third Reich* (New York, 1972), 46; W. T. Angress, "The Political Role of the Peasantry in the Weimar Republic." *Review of Politics*, vol. 21, 1959, 546; D. Gessner, "The Dilemma of German Agriculture during the Weimar Republic." In R. Bessel and E. J. Feuchtwanger, eds., *Social Change and Political Development in Weimar Germany* (London, 1981), 150; Childers, *Nazi Voter*, 150; J. H. Grill, "The Nazi Party's Rural Propaganda before 1928." *Central European History*, vol. 15, 1982, 164.

"the greatest possible income with the least amount of work" and which pitted the interests of the worker against those of the employer. The Nazis incessantly associated the Jews with unproductive or loan capitalism. Also, Nazi propaganda targeted the capitalistic practices of big business, banks, the stock market, department stores, and consumer cooperatives, which the Nazis claimed hurt small businesses. Here again, the Nazi Party tacked on "Jewish" as an adjective to the many evils they attacked, as illustrated by the examples of "Jewish" exploitative capitalism, "Jewish" banks, the "Jewish" stock market, and "Jewish" department stores. By distinguishing between good capitalists and bad capitalists, the Nazis staked out their own space between the left, which was critical of all forms of capitalism, and the right, which was a staunch proponent of big business.[141]

During the agricultural crisis in the mid-1920s, the German Nazi Party gave considerable attention to the issues of agricultural prices, tariffs, credit, and taxes. Heinrich Himmler's well-known 1926 essay "Farmer, Wake Up!" offers an example of the Nazi Party leader's endeavor to link agrarian problems to the Jews. In the essay, Himmler skillfully linked the fall in agricultural prices to Jewish capitalists' control over the fertilizer and grain markets and the Weimar government's cowardice about reparations payments. According to Himmler, the end result of Jewish capitalist practices and governmental policy was that German farmers received less money for their produce and paid higher taxes. In 1927, the Nazis blamed governmental insensitivity to farmers' concerns and Jewish oligopolistic control for the flood of foreign agricultural commodities.[142]

Economic self-interest appears to have played a major role in the acquiescence of so many non-Jewish Germans to the implementation of Nazi anti-Semitic measures between 1933 and 1939. Bankier has argued convincingly that self-interest led many Germans to welcome the expulsion of Jews from employment in the universities, public service, and the professions.[143] In a time of relatively high unemployment, the sacking

---

[141] Brustein, *Logic*, 91; M. Kele, *Nazis and Workers: National Socialist Appeals to German Labor, 1919–1933* (Chapel Hill, 1972), 43; Thomas Childers, "The Social Language of Politics in Germany: The Sociology of Political Discourse in the Weimar Republic." *American Historical Review*, vol. 95, 1990; Gordon, *Hitler*, 67.

[142] H. Himmler, "Bauer, wach auf!" *Der Nationale Sozialist fuer Sachsen*, August 1, 1926; Brustein, *Logic*, 92; Lane and Rupp, *Nazi Ideology*, 94–97.

[143] Bankier, *Germans*, 69.

of Jews opened up numerous career opportunities for non-Jews. Also, the "Aryanization" of the economy that resulted in the closing of many Jewish businesses and the forced sale of Jewish property appealed to the self-interest of many non-Jewish Germans. But self-interest rather than a concern for the human rights of Jews also led many Germans to object to, or at least to ignore, some anti-Semitic measures orchestrated by the Nazi regime. For instance, the Nazi-organized boycotts of Jewish stores during the 1930s ran aground as many Germans ignored the boycotts, since they were inconvenient and impeded choice. Moreover, because they perceived that they might have to pay for the damage incurred and that they would no longer be able to shop at Jewish stores, many Germans responded negatively to Nazi-sponsored anti-Jewish violence, such as that which occurred during *Kristallnacht*.[144]

The Nazi Party possessed no monopoly on economic anti-Semitism among Weimar political parties. Though the most strident anti-Semitism erupted from leaders of the conservative Weimar parties (the German Nationalist People's Party and the German People's Party) and from the Hitler's German National Socialist Workers' Party (NSDAP), the German radical left could also be counted on to tap into economic anti-Semitism opportunistically. Kauders, in studying the political press in Nuremberg and Duesseldorf during the Weimar period, found that both the Social Democratic Party (SPD) and German Communist Party (KPD) press attacked the role of large Jewish capital and, ironically, linked Jewish capitalists to the funding of Hitler's Nazi Party.[145] A list of notable examples of leftist economic anti-Semitism during the Weimar period would include Ruth Fischer's (a Jewish Communist Party leader) speech to a student group in Berlin in July 1923, in which she castigated Jewish capitalists and proposed hanging them from lampposts. And, one month later, in a speech in Stuttgart, Hermann Remmele (a Communist Party functionary) accused Jewish cattle dealers of extracting great profits from the Stuttgart cattle market, while non-Jewish Stuttgart butchers had gone away empty-handed.[146]

None of the other four countries in this study suffered as profoundly as Germany from the severe economic crises of the interwar years. In

---

[144] Ibid.; Johnson, *Nazi Terror*, 115–16.
[145] Kauders, *German*.
[146] Donald L. Niewyk, *The Jews in Weimar Germany* (Baton Rouge, 1980), 68–69; Conan Fischer, *The German Communists and the Rise of Nazism* (London, 1991), 59–60; Brustein, *Logic*, 59.

a context marked by the disastrous effects of the hyperinflation of the early 1920s, the agricultural slump of the mid-1920s, and the Great Depression, it is not surprising that a groundswell of economic resentment against Germany's Jews arose. Jews became targets of economic resentment for many reasons, including the general perception that Jews dominated many of Germany's financial and industrial institutions and the widely held view of Jewish overrepresentation in certain professions. The recipe for the flowering of economic anti-Semitism existed outside of Germany as well. We now turn to the development of economic anti-Semitism in Great Britain.

## GREAT BRITAIN

Underlying the rise of economic anti-Semitism in Great Britain, we find, as elsewhere, the perception of Jewish economic dominance and resentment toward the economic competition resulting from Jewish immigration. And, as in France and Germany, economic antipathy toward Jews climbed in Britain during periods of economic crisis. The principal economic downturns in Great Britain occurred between the late 1870s and early 1880s, in 1907, and during the Great Depression years of the 1930s.[147] Of particular note in the case of Great Britain, it appears that the British left, at least until the early 1930s, played a pivotal role as disseminators of economic anti-Semitism.

Before 1873, Great Britain held the indisputable position of Europe's number one trading and industrial power. Between the end of the Napoleonic Wars in 1815 and the repeal of the Corn Laws in 1846, Great Britain pioneered the trade boom that culminated in the first great era of globalization (1840 to 1914). In the period from 1870 to 1913, Britain's exports climbed from 10.3 percent of GDP to 14.7 percent. In the two decades from 1850 to 1870, Britain attained its peak of industrial supremacy vis-à-vis Europe's other industrializing nations. From 1856 to 1873, the growth rate of gross national product in Britain averaged a robust 2.5 percent.[148] The industrialization of Great Britain and the financing of its expanding empire required capital investment, and prominent British Jews were among those who played a large role

---

[147] Foreman-Peck, *History,*177; Maddison, *Dynamic,* 87–89, 98–99; Cameron, *Concise,* 224; Temin, *Lessons,* 3; Walter Kendall, *The Revolutionary Movement in Britain, 1900–1921* (London, 1969), 24.

[148] O'Rourke and Williamson, *Globalisation*; Cameron, *Concise,* 224.

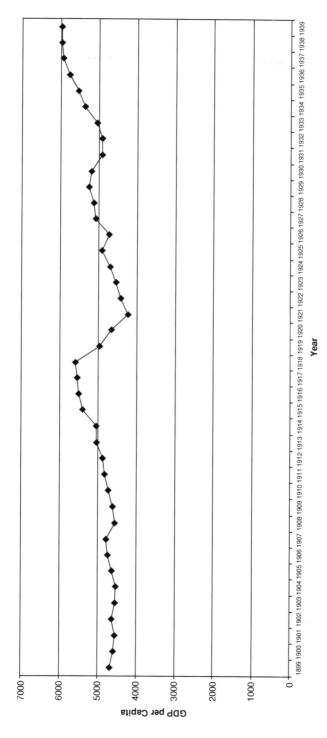

Figure 4.2c. GDP per capita in Great Britain, 1899–1939. *Note:* The GDP (gross domestic product) per capita data are in 1990 dollars and are drawn from Maddison (1995) and Good and Ma (1998).

in these endeavors. For much of the nineteenth century, the British Rothschilds were generally recognized as the preeminent Jewish family of Great Britain. Nathan Rothschild, one of Meyer Amschel's five sons, had positioned the British Rothschild financial house along with the French Rothschild house at the forefront of the family's financial empire. Between 1818 and 1832, of the value of loans to foreign governments contracted in London, Nathan Rothschild was solely responsible for 38 percent and held a share in an additional 12 percent.[149] The house of N. M. Rothschild and Sons continued its dominant position within the City's (London financial center) international finance into the third quarter of the nineteenth century. For example, the British Rothschild house was sole agent for loans valued at 10 million British pounds and served as joint agent for an additional 130 million pounds between 1860 and 1876. N. M. Rothschild and Sons also provided a loan of four million pounds to Disraeli's government in 1875 for the purchase of the Suez Canal. That the Rothschilds affixed an exorbitant interest rate, equivalent to 13 percent per annum, to the loan did little to quell negative stereotypical comments about professed Jewish avarice.[150] But the Rothschilds were not the only wealthy Jewish banking family actively engaged in the floating of government loans and prospering from investments in Great Britain's expanding commercial enterprises. Among the Jewish banking families joining the Rothschilds were the Sterns, Bischoffsheims, Cohens, Speyers, Erlangers, Lazards, Seligmans, Raphaels, and Montagus. During the second half of the nineteenth century, other prominent Jews made their fortunes chiefly in finance, principally in merchant banking and the stock exchange. These families included the Sassons, Montefiores, Mocattas, Samuels, Henriques, Goldsmids, Simons, Cassels, and the Issacs. In fact, by 1877 Jews comprised five percent of the membership of the British stock exchange.[151]

As they did elsewhere in Europe, Jews played an important role in the growing newspaper industry in Great Britain. A member of the Sasson family owned and edited the *Sunday Times* between 1893 and 1904; Harry Oppenheim stood as a major shareholder and member of

[149] Harold Pollins, *Economic History of the Jews in England* (East Brunswick, 1982), 109.

[150] Feldman, *Englishmen*, 79, 104, note 48.

[151] Feldman, *Englishmen*, 79–80; Rubinstein, *History*, 121; Pollins, *Economic*, 108; Sharman Kadish, *Bolsheviks and British Jews: The Anglo-Jewish Community, Britain and the Russian Revolution* (London, 1992), 55.

the financial group managing the *Daily News* before 1901; Harry Marks in 1884 founded and edited the *Financial Times*; the Levy-Lawson family ran the *Daily Telegraph*; Sir Alfred Mond largely funded the *Westminister Gazette*, and beginning in 1910 ran the *English Review*; and the Jewish-owned Reuter's news agency served as the principal source of information on world events for the British press.[152]

Rubinstein has provided evidence to demonstrate that Jewish economic wealth was greater in Germany than in Great Britain on the eve of World War I.[153] That is not to say the British Jews were under-represented among Britain's richest families. The percentage of Jewish nonlanded millionaires in Great Britain was 14 percent between 1870 and 1879 and 12.3 percent between 1880 and 1914 [154] These are averages; Holmes observes that British Jews constituted 16 percent of British millionaires in 1910.[155] In 1910, Jews comprised less than one percent of the British population. One difference between the wealthy German and British Jews is that while the rich German Jews made their fortunes from bases in Frankfurt, Hamburg, Cologne, and Berlin, members of the wealthy British Jewish elite built their opulence in one city, London. On the eve of World War I, Kadish observes that people occasionally referred to the rich Jewish financial elite in Great Britain as the "West End Cousinhood."[156] A further apparent divergence between wealthy British and German Jews between 1870 and 1914 is that several British Jews went from careers in finance either to the inner circle of royal power or to the government, particularly during the reign of Edward VII (1901–14). Here we find the Sassons, Ernest Cassel, Maurice de Hirsch, Edward Levy-Lawson, Felix Simon, Stuart Samuel, Edwin Montagu, Lionel Abrahams, and Rufus Issac.[157] By contrast, the inner sanctum of the German government remained relatively impenetrable to wealthy Jews.

---

[152] Holmes, "Anti-Semitism," 335.

[153] Rubinstein, *History*, 124.

[154] Feldman, *Englishmen*, 78–79; Rubinstein, *History*, 121.

[155] Holmes, *Anti-Semitism*, 109. Lindemann (*Esau's*, 241), however, suggests a larger percentage of Jews among the nonlanded millionaires in Great Britain. According to Lindemann, Jews constituted nearly 25 percent of the British nonlanded millionaires between the 1870s and the 1920s.

[156] Kadish, *Bolsheviks*, 55. The West End refers to a particular section of London, and the "cousinhood" more than likely called attention to the high degree of intermarriage within these Jewish families.

[157] Lindemann, *Esau's*, 356.

During the late Victorian and Edwardian periods, the British economy experienced a series of economic recessions. Between 1873 and 1913, the average annual rate of growth in Britain's gross national product fell to 1.9 percent from a stellar 2.5 percent in the years 1856 to 1873. Similarly, growth in Great Britain's gross domestic product for the 1873–1913 era dropped to an average annual rate of 1.8 percent from a high of 2.2 percent between 1856 and 1873. The recessions of both 1882–87 and 1907–10, marked by soaring levels of unemployment and rising interest rates, were particularly severe.[158] Not surprisingly, expressions of economic anti-Semitism became more prevalent during these intervals of economic decline. However, the association between the magnitude of economic anti-Semitism and economic decline was far from perfect in Great Britain. For instance, there is little evidence to indicate that the British economy suffered during the 1899–1903 period, yet the incidence of economic anti-Semitism appears to have climbed during those years. The likely culprit was the Boer War, which lingered on and was portrayed by many on the British left as an imperialist war spearheaded largely by international Jewish capitalists.

The economic power of British Jews became the subject of literary and scholarly critique in Great Britain certainly before the outbreak of the Boer War. The Rothschilds figure in the fictional portrayals of villainous Jewish financiers in the famous English novelist Anthony Trollope's 1875 novel The Way We Live Now, and in Charles Lever's novel Davenport Dunn. In 1887, John Reeve published his The Rothschilds: The Financial Rulers of Nations, asserting that the cosmopolitan Rothschilds, belonging to no one nationality, aspired to phenomenal wealth with little regard for the fate of friends or foes.[159] But no two scholars or novelists did more than the left-leaning Beatrice Potter (Webb) and J. A. Hobson in late Victorian and Edwardian England to popularize economic anti-Semitism. In an earlier chapter, we have encountered Beatrice Potter's and J. A. Hobson's religious and racial strains of anti-Semitism. Here, we examine their contributions to British economic anti-Semitism.

---

[158] Cameron, Concise, 224; Maddison, Dynamic, 98–99; Foreman-Peck, History, 177; Kendall, Revolutionary, 24.

[159] Ferguson, World's, 19, 789–90. The tendency to reprove Jews for the evils of capitalism in British literature continued into the twentieth century and attracted well-known writers such as D. H. Lawrence, T. S. Eliot, Ezra Pound, and Wyndham Lewis (Cheyette, "Jewish," 26–27).

Beatrice Potter's *Nineteenth Century* focused primarily on the social behavior of Eastern European Jewish immigrants in London's East End. For Beatrice Potter, the combination of superior intellect and a flexible morality among Jews culminated in an extreme form of instrumentality, allowing Jews, no matter where they resided, to amass control over money and property and, consequently, to exploit the less cunning Gentiles. In Beatrice Potter's account, considerations like personal reputation and dignity, a pride in one's labor, a tradition of integrity, and class loyalty, which shaped the economic behavior of Gentile small-scale capitalists, had little affect on Jews. Jews, by contrast, could easily succeed in business by virtue of their affinity for the production of low-quality goods and by their embrace of ruthless competition and exploitation of their employees, according to Beatrice Potter.[160] Beatrice Potter's writings contributed to the rising resentment against the immigration of Eastern European Jews into Great Britain. This was particularly true within the leftist trade union movement in its opposition to the continuing immigration of East European Jews, for continuing immigration meant for them the introduction of cheap labor into Great Britain.[161]

Hobson's principal contributions to the dissemination of economic anti-Semitism are found in three of his books. In his 1891 *Problems of Poverty*, he caricatured the Jews as the ideal "*homo economicus*" motivated to take advantage of others through the pursuit of profit. In both his 1900 *The War in South Africa* and his noteworthy 1902 treatise *Imperialism: A Study*, he assigned responsibility for the imperialist Boer War to a clique of international Jewish financiers.[162] The Boer War in South Africa evoked harsh criticism from Hobson and from the fledgling British left. As is so often the case, what triggered the outburst of criticism was a series of initial victories by the Boer forces over the British during the "Black Week" of December 1899. The highly respectable *Manchester Guardian* had sent Hobson to South Africa to report on the war. In his reporting, Hobson affirmed the existence of a Jewish imperial design, according to which, Hobson maintained, a small group of wealthy Jews, constituting

---

[160] Lindeman, *Esau's*, 365–66; Holmes, *Anti-Semitism*, 20–21; Feldman, *Englishmen*, 141–42.

[161] Anne Summers, "The Character of Edwardian Nationalism: Three Popular Leagues." In Paul Kennedy and Anthony Nicholls, eds., *Nationalist and Racialist Movements in Britain and Germany before 1914* (London and Basingstoke, 1981), 82–83.

[162] Field, "Anti-Semitism," 310–11; Holmes, *Anti-Semitism*, 20–21; Lebeltzer, "Anti-Semitism," 95–96; Lindemann, *Esau's*, 362–63.

an international clique corrupting the British press and British cabinet, had engineered the war. In particular, Hobson saw the hand of the Rothschilds and Jewish finance behind the war effort in South Africa and responsible for Britain's wrongheaded adventurism. He attacked the extensive Jewish influence within the British and Johannesburg press, which had served to arouse the British masses to support Britain's imperialistic policy in South Africa. In January 1900, Hobson published an article entitled "Capitalism and Imperialism in South Africa" in the *Contemporary Review*, in which he alleged that "the Jews are *par excellence* the international financiers." He went on in this article to lambaste the Jews for their particular brand of profit making, namely, as financial speculators. Hobson believed that prominent Jewish financiers seeking to control South Africa's diamond and gold industry had assisted Cecil Rhodes in his attempt to overturn the government of Paul Kruger, president of the Transvaal Republic. Among the Jewish financiers cited were the Rothschilds, Barnett Isaacs (alias Barney Barnato), Alfred Beit, Lionel Phillips, Sammy Marks, Isaac Lewis, Sigmund Neumann, Solly Joel, and the Albu Brothers.[163]

Several prominent British leftists shared Hobson's displeasure with British imperial policy in South Africa and with the alleged role performed by Jewish financiers in that policy. One of the most outspoken opponents of Britain's interests in South Africa and Jewish influence on governmental policy was Henry Hyndman, a socialist and head of the British Social Democratic Federation. Hyndman, on the eve of the Boer War, had chastised the "scoundrelly adventurers" – among them financiers with good old British names such as Eckstein, Beit, Solomon, Rothschild, and Joel – who had taken control of the South African Rand. He referred to Salisbury, the British prime minister, as a dupe of the "Jew clique." During the Boer War, Hyndman called the war a plot hatched by Britain's ruling classes and their masters, the capitalist Jews. Hyndman went so far as to claim that international capitalism was a Jewish invention and that the "semitic moneybags" sought to exploit the world's untapped resources.[164] During and after the Boer War, the British Social Democratic movement's official newspaper, *Justice*, served as a principal

---

[163] Rubinstein, *History*, 111; Hirschfield, "British," 108; Lindemann, *Esau's*, 359–63; Kushner, *Persistence*, 11–12; Lebezelter, "Anti-Semitism," 95–96; Ferguson, *World's*, 790.

[164] Kendall, *Revolutionary*, 32; Hirschfield, "British," 98–99; Lindemann, *Esau's*, 362–63.

disseminator of attacks on Jewish economic power in Great Britain and proposed that capitalist Jews comprised the heart and soul of the evil "gold international." The paper referred to the Boer War as the "Jew war in Transvaal" and, in its attacks on Britain's war policy, spoke of "the bestial behavior of rich Jews" and attributed to the Jews the "personification of international capitalism."[165] The leftist *Reynold's Newspaper*, edited by William Marcus Thompson, joined *Justice* in heaping scorn upon Jews for their purported role in the Boer War. Thompson, who, through his newspaper, advocated a socialist anti-Semitism, called attention to "the mean and filthy foreign Jews" and claimed that blame for popular hatred of Jews fell squarely on the Jews themselves.[166] The anti-Semitic tirade unleashed by Hobson, Hyndman, and leftist newspapers such as *Reynold's Newspaper* and *Justice* at the time of the Boer War contributed greatly to organized efforts to blame Britain's Jews for the unpopular war. For instance, in February 1900, John Burns, the Liberal-Labour MP from Battersea, in a speech before the House of Commons, accused the Jews of instigating the Boer War and of employing the British army to carry out their capitalist aims in South Africa.[167] And eight months later, the nationally representative British Trade Union Congress passed a resolution censuring British involvement in the Boer War and calling it a war to secure the gold fields of South Africa for cosmopolitan Jews, who were largely unpatriotic and belonged to no country.[168]

Economic resentment of Jews among British Gentiles derived additionally from the perceived economic threat of the thousands of Eastern European Jewish immigrants entering Britain after 1881. High unemployment during much of the 1880s dampened the reception of the host population to the arrival of new immigrants. The Ashkenazic Jews of

[165] Hirschfield, "British," 97; Kendall, *Revolutionary*, 32; Lebzelter, "Anti-Semitism," 94–95; Holmes, *Anti-Semitism*, 69. Hyndman's and the *Justice's* anti-Semitic proselytizing did not go unchallenged within the British Marxist left. Among others, Jewish socialists such as Rothstein and Joe Feinberg protested vociferously (Kendall, *Revolutionary*, 32).

[166] Hirschfield, "British," 100–01.

[167] Burns was by no means the only British MP to speak out against the so-called association between rich Jews and the Boer War. Byrn Roberts accused Joseph Chamberlain, the prime minister, of being in the hands of Jewish capitalists and foreign financiers, while Lloyd George issued negative comments about the Jewish community in Johannesburg (Hirschfield, "British," 103, 105).

[168] Rubinstein, *History*, 112–13; Hirschfield, "British," 106–07; Panikos Panayi, *Immigration, Ethnicity, and Racism in Britain: 1815–1945* (Manchester, 1994), 116; Holmes, *Anti-Semitism*, 68.

Eastern Europe settled largely in the urban centers of London's East
End, Leeds, and Manchester. The reception that many of these Jews
experienced from the native population was no different from that received today by Turkish immigrants in Germany or Denmark, North
African immigrants in France, West Asians in the United Kingdom, or
Hispanic immigrants in the United States. The rancor towards the Eastern European Jewish immigrants was particularly acute in London's East
End, where, for the most part, the impoverished indigenous population
resided in unsanitary and overcrowded housing and where work tended
to be seasonal. The new Jewish residents in the East End imbued the local
population with a host of resentments. As tenants, the Jews were accused
of abetting the acute housing shortage in the East End. As shopkeepers,
the Jews were blamed for their alleged policy of seven-day trading and
price cutting. As employers, they were charged with exploiting their
work force. As landlords, the Jews were damned for charging excessive
rents and ignoring requests for necessary repairs. And as workers, they
were despised for their willingness to work for lower wages.[169] "England
for the English" quickly gained ground as a popular slogan within the
ranks of the anti-alien movement in London's East End. Not surprisingly,
it was in the East End of London that the first overtly anti-immigrant
movement, the British Brothers League (BBL), sprang into existence.
Though the BBL emphasized the economic burden associated with the
Jewish immigration, it certainly did not refrain from identifying these
new Jews with criminal activities and characterizing them as carriers
of diseases. By 1902, the BBL counted a membership of nearly 45,000,
and three years later, the British Parliament acceded to the wishes of
the anti-immigrant lobby by passing the Aliens Bill, which drastically
curbed Jewish immigration.[170]

---

[169] Elaine R. Smith, "Jewish Responses to Political Antisemitism and Fascism in
the East End of London, 1920–1939." In Tony Kushner and Kenneth Lunn, eds.,
*Traditions of Intolerance: Historical Perspectives on Fascism and Race Discourse in
Britain* (Manchester and New York, 1989), 54.

[170] Green *Social*, 445; Holmes, *Anti-Semitism*, 13–15; Garrad, *English*, 38; Lebzelter,
*Political*, 8; Finestein, *Short*, 131; Wistrich, *Anti-Semitism*, 104–05; Eatwell, *Fascism*, 20; Lebzelter, "Anti-Semitism," 90–91. During the late Victorian and Edwardian periods, antipathy toward Eastern European immigrant Jews assumed
various expressions and forms in other parts of Great Britain. On at least
one notable occasion, anti-Jewish sentiments found violent expression. Holmes
("Anti-Semitism," 345–47) and Alderman ("Anti-Jewish," 375) attribute the
anti-Semitic riots in South Wales in August 1911 largely to the settlement in

We have seen how highly publicized financial scandals involving Jews gave impetus to economic anti-Semitism in France and Germany. Two governmental scandals taking place during the last years of the Edwardian reign had Jews as central characters and afforded Britain's anti-Semitic quarters a propitious opportunity to claim that wealthy British Jews profited from their connections and positions within the British government. The first of these scandals was the Marconi scandal, which unfolded in 1910. The Marconi scandal allegedly involved the awarding of a contract to the Marconi Company to establish wireless stations throughout the British Empire, allowing British vessels to communicate across the globe. It was affirmed that four Liberal Party ministers had profited from the issuance of the contract. Among the four were two prominent Jews, Sir Rufus Isaacs and Herbert Samuel. The disclosure that the managing director of the Marconi Company was no other than Godfrey Isaacs, the brother of Sir Rufus Isaacs (attorney general), and that Sir Rufus had purchased shares in the American Marconi Company made matters even worse for British Jews. The result of the ensuing investigation into probable conflict of interest failed to lead to the removal from office of Sir Rufus Isaacs and Herbert Samuel.[171] At about the same time, a second major scandal involving prominent British Jews in the government surfaced. The Indian silver case entailed the unorthodox and secret process by which the Jewish banking and bullion firm of Samuel Montagu obtained the rights to provide silver to the Indian government. Supposedly, Ernest Franklin, representing the Montagu firm, advised Sir Felix Schuster, chairman of the Finance Committee of the Council of India, that a large profit would result if his firm handled the transaction. Partners in the Samuel Montagu firm included such notable Jews as Sir Stuart Samuel (brother of Herbert Samuel and Liberal Party MP from Whitechapel), Edwin Montagu (permanent assistant under-secretary at the India Office), and Sir Lionel Abrahams. The presence in the Montagu firm of several prominent Jews with intimate links to members of the Liberal Party's inner circle provided British anti-Semitic circles sufficient ammunition to allege both Jewish control of the Liberal Party and the existence of a conspiracy to enrich a dominant Jewish firm.[172]

South Wales of Eastern European Jews pursuing middleman economic activities at a time of depressed economic conditions.

[171] Rubinstein, *History*, 148–49; Holmes, *Anti-Semitism*, 70–71; V. D. Lipman, *Social History of the Jews in England 1850–1950* (London, 1954), 82–83.

[172] Rubinstein, *History*, 149; Holmes, "Anti-Semitism," 331–32.

Though Great Britain emerged from World War I as a victorious
power and with its empire intact, the nation's economic expansion was
short-lived. By the beginning of 1921, the overcapitalization in several
key British industries and the return of the British currency to par had
led to an economic slump and subsequently to economic stagnation
lasting throughout much of the 1920s. Among our five countries, Great
Britain stood out during the 1920s as the nation experiencing the most
persistent economic stagnation. The problem with the British economy
centered largely on the country's depressed export trade. Between 1921
and 1929, while the industrial unemployment levels in France, Germany, and the United States averaged less than 10 percent, in Great
Britain the rate of unemployment averaged 12 percent. During the ensuing decade, the average rate of industrial unemployment in Great
Britain hovered around 15 percent, which placed British unemployment levels below those of the United States and Germany but higher
than France's.[173] These statistics are averages and do not represent sufficiently the spatial and temporal impact of the economic malaise. Hard-
est hit during the economic downturn of the 1920s were the traditional
industries, such as coal, shipping, steel, and cotton, situated particularly in the north, Scotland, and Wales. The South, and especially the
London area, suffered less due to its growing reliance on newer industries, such as automobiles, chemicals, electrical equipment, and durable
consumer goods. Moreover, the economic declines of the 1921–23 and
1929–33 periods were particularly acute. The year 1921 brought misery to workers in Britain's mines and factories. In 1921, unemployment
struck roughly one million workers, or approximately one-seventh of
the labor force. Workers during the 1920s confronted falling wages in
addition to unemployment. The chancellor of the exchequer, Winston
Churchill, proposed in 1925 to return Great Britain to the gold standard
at the pre-war parity, which resulted in a decline in prices and subsequently in wages of around 10 percent. The wage cut led to the largest
peacetime general strike in Great Britain's interwar history. At its peak,
the strike, which began on May 1, 1926, included roughly 40 percent of
British trade union members; it lasted ten days. In 1933, in the midst of
the Great Depression, Britain's unemployment rate soared to more than
23 percent of the labor force. Ironically, because Great Britain had not
experienced the economic boom of the 1920s that occurred in several

---

[173] Temin, *Lessons*, 3; Kindleberger, *Financial*, 329–31; Maddison, "Economic," 455–
56.

Western nations, the crash of 1929–33 was neither as sudden nor as sharp as it was elsewhere. Britain began to recover from the impact of the Great Depression earlier than most of the industrial nations, and by 1937, British unemployment had fallen to 10.8 percent of the insured male population. At the same time, production and foreign trade grew, and real income climbed substantially.[174] Given the strong association between economic misery and anti-Semitism, we should expect the strength of economic anti-Semitism to have been somewhat diluted in Great Britain during the 1930s, in relation to other industrial nations.

For the most part, it was the far right that picked up the anti-Semitic banner in Great Britain between the two world wars. Henry Beamish, the founder of the virulently anti-Semitic Britons movement in 1918, asserts that he became anti-Semitic as a result of his fighting in the Boer War and his resettlement in South Africa. More specifically, Beamish claims that the realization that the Jews controlled all the industries of South Africa convinced him to launch his anti-Semitic crusade.[175] Lebzelter notes rising economic anti-Semitic rhetoric from the British radical right during the economic crises of 1929–31.[176] For Lebzelter, the victory of the Labour Party in the national elections of 1929, in conjunction with the onset of the Great Depression, produced charges from the extreme right that international Jewish speculators were responsible for the financial depression, which led Britain to abandon the gold standard. During the 1930s, the message of economic anti-Semitism found a home within Mosley's rightist British Union of Fascists. In November 1933, Mosley accused the Jews of controlling the press, international finance, and the established political parties.[177] Two of Mosley's closest associates in the BUF, William Joyce and A. K. Chesterton, highlighted economic anti-Semitism in their written attacks on British Jews. In Joyce's anti-Semitic worldview, a financial/Bolshevik world Jewish conspiracy sought to destroy his beloved British Empire; he opined that the real struggle was between international Jewish finance and national socialist patriotism. Chesterton, in an article in the November 7, 1936, edition of the fascist newspaper *Action*, renewed the allegations of Jewish economic dominance. The Jews, according to Chesterton, controlled the great

---

[174] Kindleberger, *Financial*, 329–31; Cameron, *Concise*, 353–54; Maddison, "Economic," 461–62; Benewick, *Political*, 19, 85.

[175] Benewick, *Political*, 42.

[176] Lebzelter, "Political," 396.

[177] Ibid., 416.

foreign lending houses, the important branches of the retail trade, the cinema industry, and the national press. Chesterton noted further that through their large subscriptions, the Jews had a disproportionate influence over the political parties, and that they controlled the Communist Party.[178] In its electoral campaign of 1936, the BUF underscored the theme of economic anti-Semitism in London's East End. BUF speakers stressed that Jews were taking over British businesses and jobs by paying lower wages and by unfair price cutting. And much like the anti-Semitic movements on the European continent, the BUF berated the Jewish department stores. One particular target of these attacks was the Marks and Spencers department store. Marks and Spencers had started as a trestle table, selling penny goods in the Leeds market.

Mosley's followers additionally accused Jewish bakers of engaging in unfair business practices by baking on both Saturday, the Jewish Sabbath, and Sunday, the Christian Sabbath.[179] Economic anti-Semitism seemed to gather a stronger head of steam in the East End of London than it did elsewhere in Great Britain. This may be due in part to the dire economic situation of this part of London. During the 1930s, poverty and unemployment marked much of London's East End. According to the *New Survey of London Life and Labour* released in the 1930s, 18 percent of the residents of Shoreditch, 17.8 percent of the inhabitants of Bethnal Green, and 15.5 percent of the residents of Stepney lived in poverty.[180]

Economic resentment vis-à-vis the Jews emanated from other quarters besides the far right during the 1930s. In the aftermath of the Nazi annexation of Austria and the anti-Semitic violence of *Kristallnacht*, fears of Jewish refugees' swamping Great Britain and taking jobs were very likely instrumental. For instance, both the *Daily Mail* and the *Daily Express*, two of Great Britain's most popular daily newspapers, as well as the British medical profession called upon the British government on the eve of World War II not to relax the country's immigration quotas.[181] And indeed, it might appear that the British government acquiesced. Sherman points out that after the German annexation of Austria in March 1938, instructions were sent to consuls and passport control officers to apply a particular set of criteria to the aliens (Jews)

---

[178] Skildelsky, *Oswald*, 342–43, 388.
[179] Ibid., 394–95.
[180] Skildelsky, *Oswald*, 394; Benewick, *Political*, 218–19.
[181] Lebzelter, "Political," 408–09.

who were seeking admission to the United Kingdom. Underlying the government's request, according to Sherman, was the wish to prevent the emergence of serious economic and social problems in the United Kingdom that the increased immigration of Jews would produce. Included among those who should be considered unsuitable candidates for admission were small shopkeepers and retail traders; artisans; agents and middlemen; and "the rank and file" of doctors, lawyers, and dentists. Obviously, a large proportion of the Jewish refugees fleeing Austria fell into one of these designated undesirable categories. Those who were not to be refused entry included leading persons in science, medicine, or research; artists; architects; designers; and industrialists who planned to transfer their established businesses to Great Britain.[182]

All in all, economic anti-Semitism in Great Britain failed to fix itself within British society to the extent that it did in France, Germany, and Romania. This may be attributed in part to the perception that although Jews constituted a segment of the British economic elite, their presence was confined largely to banking and finance and somewhat offset by the high proportion of Gentile banking firms. Moreover, the economic downturns befalling Great Britain after 1873 appeared to be less sudden and less sharp than the downturns in Europe's other industrial powers. Given that Jews were likely to become scapegoats in times of economic crisis, the economic situation in Great Britain may not have been ripe for the kind of economic anti-Semitism that occurred elsewhere. However, the embedded character of economic anti-Semitism, largely within the culture of Great Britain's political left (at least until World War I), gave British economic anti-Semitism a special hue. This is not to suggest that the political left refrained from economic anti-Semitism in Germany, France or Italy. But in these countries, leftist economic anti-Semitism appeared to be matched by rightist economic anti-Semitism, while in Great Britain the political right tended to leave this terrain to the left. In Britain, the extreme right turned to economic anti-Semitism during the interwar period but failed to garner sizeable popular support, as can be seen in the poor electoral showings of Mosley's British Union of Fascists. What galvanized the adherents of the British Conservative and radical right parties regarding antipathy toward the Jews between the world wars was the association of Jews with Bolshevism. We will examine that alleged relationship in the chapter on political anti-Semitism.

---

[182] Sherman, *Island*, 90–91.

## ROMANIA

Economic resentment of Jews was particularly acute in Romania before the Holocaust. The belief that Jews controlled the Romanian economy and were disproportionately represented within middle-class professions held considerable appeal to many non-Jewish Romanians. The relative absence of a counterweight, in terms of an indigenous Romanian middle class before 1939, underscored these perceptions about Jews. Economic anti-Semitism in Romania would receive an additional boost from the special role that Jews performed as intermediaries between the peasants and landlords in Romanian agriculture. And finally, we will see that in Romania, as elsewhere, during periods of economic crisis, economic anti-Semitic sentiments rose sharply.

Throughout the last half of the nineteenth century and the first four decades of the twentieth century, Romania remained poor in relation to the other countries in this study. The intensive industrialization that began to spread across Western and Central Europe after 1840 hardly touched Romania. As late as 1849, approximately 8 percent of the population of the Old Kingdom of Wallachia and Moldavia was occupied full-time in manufacturing or trade. The Romanian economy relied heavily on agricultural products. Agriculture, however, was of a primitive nature, with continual usage of wooden ploughs, absence of systematic crop rotation, and a paucity of fertilizers and draught animals. In important ways, Romanian agriculture at mid nineteenth century resembled agriculture in the Rhineland and Flanders during the twelfth and thirteenth centuries.[183] Unlike the situation in France, Germany, the United Kingdom, and Italy, in Romania a large indigenous middle class failed to emerge during the nineteenth and early twentieth centuries. Precisely for this reason, the Romanian government before 1878 offered special privileges to foreign middlemen to conduct business in Romania. The presence of these middlemen foreigners (*suditi*), many of whom were Jews, elicited considerable economic resentment from the fledgling native middle class in Romania. For the most part, newly arrived Jews, Greeks, Armenians, and Bulgarians dominated traditional

---

[183] Andrew C. Janos, "Modernization and Decay in Historical Perspective: The Case of Romania." In Kenneth Jowitt, ed., *Social Change in Romania, 1860–1940* (Berkeley, 1978), 75–76.

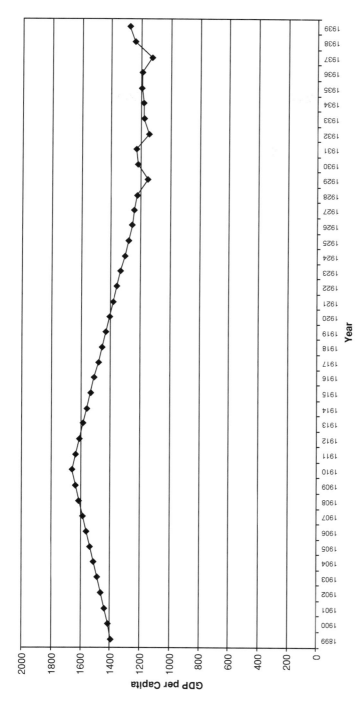

Figure 4.2d. GDP per capita in Romania, 1899–1939. *Note:* The GDP (gross domestic product) per capita data are in 1990 dollars and are drawn from Maddison (1995) and Good and Ma (1998). Romanian GDP per capita figures are yearly for 1925 to 1939 but are decennial for the years prior to 1925. Where data were not available, GDP figures were interpolated based on the nearest preceding and proceeding figures.

middle-class positions throughout much of rural Romania in the nineteenth century.[184]

Romania witnessed significant economic growth during the third quarter of the nineteenth century, due largely to its agricultural prosperity. In the 1850s, Romania emerged as one of the chief exporters of grain on the European continent, thanks to rising grain prices, international demand, completion of Romania's first railway line, and the availability of good arable land. However, with the advent of lower transportation costs in the 1870s, cheap grains, most notably from the United States, Canada, Argentina, and Russia, inundated the Romanian market. This resulted in a catastrophic fall in grain prices, making it increasingly difficult for Romanian farmers to save and to invest in efforts to modernize their agriculture. By 1887, the Romanian government was turning increasingly to protectionist policies in order to bolster the country's grain growers.[185] Nevertheless, Romania continued to depend on the export of grain into the twentieth century, with grain production accounting for approximately 85 percent of the total value of Romanian exports by the beginning of the twentieth century. In 1899, 92 percent of the Romanian grain crop was exported.[186] Because of the heavy reliance on grain production, a fall in the price of Romanian grain exports or a decline in the volume of grain exports hurt Romanian farmers, from the largest farmers to the smallest peasants. The economic crises confronting the industrial nations of Western and Central Europe and the United States in the 1870s, 1880s, 1890s, and 1930s impacted the Romanian economy, as the demand for Romanian grain dropped precipitously. Dependence on grain cultivation did not translate into relatively high agricultural yields or per capita income. Before 1914, Romanian wheat and corn yields remained 30 percent below the continental average, and with the exception of Albania and Serbia, Romania's annual per capita income (roughly $50) was the lowest in Europe.[187]

---

[184] Hitchins, *Rumania*, 16–17; Eugen Weber, "Romania." In Hans Rogger and Eugen Weber, eds., *The European Right: A Historical Profile* (Berkeley and Los Angeles, 1965), 501–02; Ioanid, *Holocaust*, xvii.

[185] J. M. Montias, "Notes on the Romanian Debate on Sheltered Industrialization: 1860–1906." In Kenneth Jowitt, ed., *Social Change in Romania, 1860–1940* (Berkeley, 1978), 58–59; Philip G. Eidelberg, *The Great Rumanian Peasant Revolt of 1907: Origins of a Modern Jacquerie* (Leiden, 1974), 32–33; Janos, "Modernization," 94–95; Hitchins, *Rumania*, 171–72.

[186] Hitchins, *Rumania*, 172.

[187] Janos, "Modernization," 96–97.

While Romanian urbanization received a boost after World War I, the 1930 official Romanian census showed that agriculture still dominated the economic landscape, with roughly three-quarters of the population making a living from the land.[188] During the interwar period, the Romanian economy experienced an initial growth spurt, thanks largely to a rise in industrial productivity. However, the growth was partially offset by declines in agriculture, brought about largely by the Agrarian Reform Act of 1923. The act led to a massive land redistribution of six million hectares (40 percent of the total arable land) among Romania's peasant proprietors. While a boon to the aspirations of a land-hungry peasantry, the land redistribution produced a decline in cereal yields, agricultural exports, and per capita farming income. The land redistribution also dashed hopes that savings from agriculture and an expected jump in peasant purchasing power would fuel Romania's industrialization program.[189] Both Weber and Butnaru believe the Agrarian Reform Act was insufficient as a means to revitalize Romanian agriculture because it failed to provide the new peasant proprietors with sufficient capital to purchase modern farming equipment and livestock. It also failed to address the problems of the peasants' lack of credit structure and their need for technical advice.[190] The high prices that peasants paid for imports, such as farming equipment and cloth, and the decline in world demand for Romanian cereals further exacerbated the perilous situation of the Romanian peasantry. The biggest beneficiaries of the Reform Act were the banks and wealthier farmers upon whom the small peasant proprietors once again became economically dependent.[191]

Prospects for economic growth dimmed further with the onset of the Great Depression (1929–33). National income in Romania dropped by 45 percent between 1929 and 1932. Romania had been the slowest of all of the Balkan states to recover from the Great Depression when the mid-1937 international economic recession struck. From a price index of 100 in 1929, the price index for Romanian agricultural products fell to 44.1 in 1934. A recovery did commence in June 1936, with the price index jumping to 64.6 and the value of Romanian exports rising by 96 percent, but the 1937 recession led to a decline in Western demand

---

[188] Livezeanu, *Cultural*, 8–9.
[189] Janos, "Modernization," 96–97, 103.
[190] Weber, "Romania," 513; Butnaru, *Silent*, 46.
[191] Butnaru, *Silent*, 46; Weber, "Romania," 513.

for Romanian products and a drop in prices. Debt per hectare of arable land climbed to 6,585 lei by 1932.[192]

Jews residing in the Old Kingdom of Wallachia and Moldavia, were overwhelmingly urban and engaged in commerce or small industry. Wallachia, with Bucharest as its capital city, had a larger native middle class than Moldavia. At the time of unification, while Jews constituted 2.0 percent of the Wallachian population, they constituted roughly 10.7 percent of the Moldavian population. Anti-Semitism displayed greater intensity in Moldavia, since the emerging Moldavian bourgeoisie found itself competing with an already-entrenched Jewish middle class.[193] Unlike the situation in much of Europe during the second half of the nineteenth century, Jewish efforts in Romania to purchase property in certain rural areas or to enter particular professions were blocked by official Romanian ordinances. For instance, prohibitions were enforced between 1866 and 1876 making it virtually impossible for Jews to buy homes, land, vineyards, hotels, or cabarets in rural areas or to work as professors, lawyers, pharmacists, or railroad employees.[194]

Throughout the Romanian countryside during the latter part of the nineteenth century, leaseholding, rather than owning, grew in importance. More than 50 percent of farms greater than 500 hectares and roughly 75 percent of farms over 3,000 hectares were leaseholds by 1900. Large-scale commercial leasing was more common in northern Moldavia, where, for example, the Austrian Jewish Fischer trust leased roughly 240,000 hectares. With easy access to Austrian bank capital, the Fischer trust succeeded in controlling both the production and distribution of grain.[195] In the years between Romanian unification and World War I, Jews remained as intermediaries (*arendasi*) between Romanian landed elites (*boyards*) and peasants. These Jewish intermediaries acted as tax collectors, fiscal agents, lessors, sellers of spirits over which the gentry held the monopoly, and distributors of manufactured goods.[196] Banned from owning land, Jews sought to lease property, which Romanian law permitted – though Jews could not lease a particular property for longer than five years. Eidelberg and Butnaru note that a number of Jews of northern Moldavia succeeded in securing loans from Austrian

[192] Shapiro, "Prelude," 68–69; Nagy-Talavera, *Green Shirts*, 278.
[193] Almog, *Nationalism*, 42–43; Janos, "Modernization," 91–92.
[194] Iancu, *L'Emancipation*, 24.
[195] Hitchins, *Rumania*, 158–59.
[196] Eidelberg, *Great*, 36–39; Ioanid, *Holocaust*, XVII.

banks in order to secure leases and, consequently, incurred the wrath of many non-Jewish tenants, who were competing with the Jews for these leases.[197] Moreover, the introduction of an additional layer between the owners and peasants resulted in higher rents for the peasants, as now both tenants and landlords exacted payments.[198] Remarkably, in 1899, Jews leased 72.4 percent of the total acreage leased by Romanian large estates.[199] Romanian nobles, according to Iancu, used Jews to block the rise of the native Romanian bourgeoisie. The role of Jews as agents of the landed elites and as lessors of major holdings employing Romanian peasants placed Jews in the position of perceived exploiters of the Romanian peasantry and, thus, contributed to the growing resentment of Jewish economic domination and exploitation.[200] At times, tensions over obtaining leases led to conflict between Jews and non-Jews, as evidenced in the summer of 1885, when Jews in the village of Brusturoasa were beaten, robbed, and forced out of the village.[201] Making matters worse for the Romanian peasantry were the fierce competition over land, as the country's population increased from 4,500,000 in 1880 to 7,300,000 in 1913, and the growing tax burden, as peasants shouldered a major portion of the costs of Romanian modernization.[202]

The Brusturoasa incident was a prelude to the major rural anti-Semitic eruption of the 1907 peasant revolt. This great peasant revolt broke out largely in northern Moldavia and was directed against both Romanian landlords and their Jewish leaseholders.[203] The violence began as peasants in the northern Moldavian village of Flaminzi protested their high taxes and their double exploitation by both their *boyard* (landed elite) and their Jewish leaseholder (the Fischer trust).[204] As the revolt intensified and broadened, many Jewish leaseholders and moneylenders were attacked.[205] From northern Moldavia, the revolt spread into Wallachia, gaining in violence.

Jewish intermediary status between peasants and elites is one factor responsible for popular economic anti-Semitism in Romania before

[197] Eidelberg, *Great*, 36–39; Butnaru, *Silent*, 20–21.
[198] Eidelberg, *Great*, 36–39.
[199] Janos, "Modernization," 92.
[200] Iancu, *Juifs*, 24–26.
[201] Butnaru, *Silent*, 21.
[202] Weber, "Romania," 508.
[203] Ibid.; Mendelsohn, *Jews*, 175; Fischer-Galati, "Fascism," 159.
[204] Butnaru, *Silent*, 27; Eidelberg, *Great*, 36–39; Iancu, *Juifs*, 36–37; Hitchins, *Rumania*, 176–77.
[205] Hitchins, *Rumania*, 176–77.

the Holocaust. Popular anti-Semitic feelings may also have been stirred by the general perception of persistent foreign meddling in Romanian affairs. For many Romanians, Jews represented a foreign and international people, and outside Jewish influence was believed to have been employed to force changes upon Romania. It is true, in large part, that Romanian independence from the Ottoman Empire was brokered by the great powers (Great Britain, Germany, Russia, France, Austria-Hungary, and Italy). The great powers made recognition of Romanian independence contingent upon the Romania's granting of civil rights to its minorities. Foreign influence was perhaps greatest in Romanian economic affairs, with foreign capital playing a significant role in the modernization of the Romanian economy after independence. According to Hitchins, foreign capital totally dominated the Romanian industries of gas and electricity, oil, sugar, metallurgy, chemicals, and forestry products before World War I. Anglo-Dutch and Belgian capital combined controlled roughly 57 percent of the capital invested in Romanian industry before World War I. For example, German, British, Dutch, French, and American capital controlled nearly 90 percent of the Romanian oil industry, while Romanian capital held 5.5 percent in 1914.[206] Foreign investment also dominated the Romanian banking system before 1914. Upon the collapse of the Hapsburg and Hohenzollern empires, Austrian and German investment in Romania was replaced by British, French, and Belgian capital. Although native Romanian capital investment in the Romanian economy continued to grow after 1918, the proportion of foreign control remained high, especially in industrial joint stock companies and banks. In fact, between the two world wars, seventeen foreign-owned banks controlled roughly one-third of all banking capital in Romania.[207] The extent of foreign investment in Romania did not change dramatically during the interwar period. Roughly 70 to 85 percent of industrial capital investment in Romania was either owned or provided by foreigners. In particular, 95 percent of electricity and gas production, 91 percent of the petroleum industry, 74 percent of metallurgy, 72 percent of the chemical industry, 70 percent of the industry linked to forestry, and 70 percent of the insurance business were foreign owned.[208]

---

[206] Ibid., 193, 188–89.
[207] Hitchins, *Rumania*, 368; Nagy-Talavera, *Green Shirts*, 255.
[208] Nagy-Talavera, *Green Shirts*, 255; Weber, "Romania," 529–30.

Fueling economic anti-Semitism was the overrepresentation of Jews in many of the professions in Romania. Ruppin reports that, on the eve of World War I, Jews were only slightly overrepresented among the professions. Yet the proportion of Jews within the different professions varied significantly. While Jews constituted more that 36 percent of doctors, veterinary surgeons, and dentists, they made up only 1.6 percent of lawyers in 1913. The variation in these proportions had much to do with whether Jewish entry was free or restricted.[209] The establishment of a greater Romania, with the post–World War I incorporation of the provinces of Bukovina, Bessarabia, and Transylvania, nearly tripled Romania's Jewish population. The Jewish population of the new provinces would continually grow, especially during the early interwar period as Jews fled the turmoil engulfing Galicia, the Ukraine, and Soviet Russia. During in the interwar period, Jews comprised between 4 and 5 percent of the Romanian population, yet held a disproportionate presence in many professions, including law, medicine, and journalism. According to the official *Bulletin périodique de la presse roumaine* of June 19, 1937, Jews made up 80 percent of the engineers in the textile industry, more than 50 percent of doctors in the army medical corps, and 70 percent of journalists.[210] Jews comprised 15 percent of all university students, although in certain academic areas, such as pharmacy and medicine, Jews made up between 30 and 40 percent of the student body.[211] Non-Jewish Romanian university students seemed particularly incensed by the disproportionate Jewish presence in higher education. Given the importance of higher education in filling positions in the elite public and private sectors, non-Jewish Romanian students sought to restrict the number of Jews entering Romanian universities.[212] In 1923, Cuza's LANC (League of National Christian Defense) pushed for legislation to tie the number of Jewish university students and Jews in the professions to the proportion of Jews in the general population. By

---

[209] Ruppin, *Jews*, 222.

[210] Livezeanu (*Cultural*, 123) finds even more pronounced Jewish representation in key professions in the newly acquired provinces. In Chisinau (Bessarabia), half the doctors and 90 percent of the dentists were Jewish.

[211] Livezeanu (*Cultural*, 87) notes that in the fall of 1926, in the province of Bukovina, the list of candidates at the baccalaureate exam included only 8.2 percent ethnic Romanians and the rest minorities, among whom Jews were heavily represented.

[212] Livezeanu, *Cultural*, 246; Mendelsohn, *Jews*, 185.

1935, such *numerus clausus* thinking was to be found in almost every Romanian political party.[213]

Jews were also reported to constitute two-thirds of the population of white-collar workers. In Bucharest alone, Jews were believed to comprise nearly 80 percent of employees of banks and commercial enterprises, 40 percent of all lawyers, and a staggering 99 percent of the brokers on the Bucharest stock exchange.[214] During the late 1930s, a Romanian government survey reported that of a total of 258,000 commercial employees in Romania, 173,000 were Jews. The survey claimed, furthermore, that 29 billion lei of the 35 billion lei invested in building construction in Bucharest between 1925 and 1926 belonged to Jews, and that of the 5.3 billion lei representing Romanian industrial investment, Jews controlled 3.7 billion lei.[215] With such statistics in hand, Romanian anti-Semites had little difficulty in making their case against Jewish domination.

The economic role of Jews in Romania became a central theme of a large number of notable Romanian intellectuals and prominent politicians during the late nineteenth and early twentieth centuries. As early as the 1870s, B. P. Haşdeu, the well-known Romanian historian and economist, warned of the dangers to Romania of dependence upon foreign capital and Jewish economic behavior. For Haşdeu and others, the interference of the Paris-based Alliance Israélite Universelle in Romanian affairs, urging foreign powers to guarantee the civil rights of Romanian Jews (as proclaimed by the Congress of Berlin in 1878), provided proof of the extent of foreign Jewish economic power. In 1886, Romania hosted the Romanian-European anti-Semitic Congress. The government of Prime Minister Ion Brtiănu granted the delegates a meeting venue in Bucharest and publicity. The congress included the participation of notable Romanian politicians and intellectuals and called for the establishment of a Universal anti-Jewish Alliance. The implementation of a universal boycott of Jewish producers, a ban on selling property to Jews, and restrictions on admission of Jews into various professions were some of the resolutions of the congress.[216] On the eve of the 1907 peasant revolt, Alexandru D. Xenopol, the famous historian, blamed

---

[213] Shapiro, "Prelude," 48; Mendelsohn, *Jews*, 185; Livezeanu, *Cultural*, 265–66.

[214] Weber, "Romania," 529–30; Volovici, *Nationalist*, 51; Nagy-Talavera, *Green Shirts*, 46.

[215] Shapiro, "Prelude," 73; Nagy-Talavera, *Green Shirts*, 46.

[216] Weber, 'Romania," 506; Iancu, *Juifs*, 220–22.

the Jews for the introduction of capitalism into Romania, the destruction and pauperization of Romania's peasantry, and the ruination of the
country's large landowning class. Jewish capitalism allegedly threatened
the very existence of the Romanian nation, according to Xenopol and
other nationalist intellectuals.[217] Both Nicolae Iorga and A. C. Cuza,
two of Romania's eminent scholars and politicians during the first four
decades of the twentieth century, stressed the negative economic influence of Jews in Romania in their writings and speeches. Cuza embraced
the economic nationalism of nineteenth-century Romanian intellectuals such as Pop Martian, Petre Aurelian, B. P. Hasdeu, and Alexandru D.
Xenopol, asserting that the solution to Romania's economic problems
lay in the expulsion of foreigners, particularly Jews, and the erection
of native Romanian enterprises. Cuza held the chair of political economy at the University of Iasi after 1901. Through his influential and
widely read nationalist newspaper, *Neamul Romanesc* (The Romanian
people), Iorga bemoaned the role that Jews played in the destruction of
the Romanian peasantry through their ownership of taverns and their
activities as usurers.[218] The desires of anti-Semitic luminaries, such as
Cuza and Iorga, to curb the alleged Jewish economic influence became
reality on December 28, 1937, with the installation of the anti-Semitic
Goga-Cuzist government, which lasted forty-four days. The revocation
of the press privileges of Jewish journalists, the ban on nearly all Jewish
newspapers, the dismissal of Jews from public payrolls, the withdrawal of
liquor licenses from Jewish proprietors, and the ban on Jews employing
non-Jewish female servants under the age of forty were among the first
measures adopted by the new government.[219]

Romanian economic anti-Semitism tended to evoke more traditional
anti-Semitic leitmotifs, such as alleged Jewish usury and avaricious
Jewish middleman practices. Romania's agrarian character and its relative lack of industrialization and capital assets resulted in the dearth of
wealthy native Jewish magnates. While there were no Romanian Jewish
Rothschilds or Bleichroeders to serve as targets for anti-Semitic venom,
there were a fair number of wealthy Romanian Jewish families before
the Holocaust. The Auschnitts owned steel factories and iron mines,
and several Jewish banks, including Marmorosh Blanc and Company,
Lobl Bercowitz and Son, Banca Moldovei, and Banca de Credit Roman,

[217] Volovici, *Nationalist*, 17; Vago, "Traditions," 109.
[218] Weber, "Romania," 509–11.
[219] Shapiro, "Prelude," 72–73.

played significant roles in the Romanian economy before the 1930s.[220] More importantly, however, numerous Romanian anti-Semites believed that wealthy foreign Jews, notably from France, Austria, and Germany, were behind the efforts of Western powers to interfere in Romanian domestic affairs, and that many of these wealthy Jews, through foreign investments in Romania, controlled the country's economy.[221] In the wake of the Great Depression, economic anti-Semitism increasingly broadened its appeal, and major political parties such as the National Liberal Party and the National Peasant Party joined the chorus calling for restrictions on Jewish capital.[222] Also, the lack of a sizeable non-Jewish middle class helped to create the perception during the interwar period that Romanian Jews, albeit well represented within the middle class, dominated Romanian commerce and the professions (e.g., banking, journalism, medicine, and the stock market).

Furthermore, unlike economic anti-Semitism in France, Germany, and Great Britain, Romanian economic anti-Semitism found no home on the Romanian political left. The low level of Romanian industrialization before the Holocaust did not beget a formative Marxist left in the country. Moreover, the Romanian left drew disproportionately from the ranks of the Jewish minority and often took up the cause of Jewish civil rights.

## ITALY

Italy became a constitutional monarchy on March 17, 1861. At that time, its level of industrial development mirrored that of Romania more than that of France, Germany, or Great Britain. In 1860, Italy possessed barely 1,100 miles of railway, and its rate of literacy for those above the age of six was 12 percent. Italy's industrialization finally took off during the 1896–1908 period, and strong economic growth, thanks largely to the injection of foreign capital from Germany, continued right up to the eve of World War I. According to the Italian Statistical Institute (ISTAT), the annual rate of increase in manufacturing production between 1896 and 1913 was a quite robust 4.3 percent, and capital formation as a whole during the first ten years of the twentieth century was

---

[220] Ioanid, *Holocaust*, xx.

[221] Indeed, the Rothschilds had taken up the cause of Romanian Jews throughout the second half of the nineteenth century.

[222] Ioanid, *Holocaust*, xvii–xix.

60 percent higher (at constant prices) than during the 1881–90 period.[223] By 1914, Italy had more than 11,200 miles of railway and a literacy rate of 62 percent for those over the age of six. These are only national averages and do not reveal the extensive regional variation within Italy. The more economically developed northern half of Italy contained the lion's share of its railways, and illiteracy among its adult population had been virtually eliminated by 1914. As Italian industrialization progressed steadily after 1896, the northern half of the country served as the locus and chief beneficiary of that industrialization.[224]

Much like France, Germany, and Great Britain, Italy suffered from the periodic economic recessions and depressions that struck the industrialized and industrializing nations of the world between 1873 and 1939. Cafagna has suggested that the 1873 crisis, while creating great difficulties (and in some cases bankruptcies) for many of the new joint stock companies and banks that had issued forth from the economic boom following the Franco-Prussian War of 1870, had not significantly affected Italian industrial growth.[225] However, the effects of the Italian agrarian crisis of 1876, brought on largely by the fall in agricultural prices, especially prices of cereals, lingered on for the next two decades. The 1880s and early 1890s saw Italy racked by a host of economic problems. The period from 1889 to 1896 is referred to as the great depression in Italy. A decline in farm prices beginning in 1882 reached alarming levels by 1890. A devastating crisis in the building industry provoked the near-collapse of the Italian banking industry. The banking crisis began in 1889 and reached the critical point in 1893 with the failure of the principal Italian banks.[226] During the depression of 1889–96, Italy failed to attract necessary foreign investment to help defray the costs of its modernization. A large share of the blame belongs to Italian governmental policies that repeatedly alienated foreign investors. Italian governmental intransigence partly contributed to the disastrous ten-year tariff war with France that lasted until 1897.[227]

---

[223] Canepa, "Christian," 23; Cameron, *Concise*, 264; Luciano Cafagna, "Italy 1830–1914." In Carlo M. Cipolla, ed., *The Fontana Economic History of Europe: The Emergence of Industrial Societies – 1*, trans. Muriel Grindrod (London and Glasgow, 1973), 297–98.

[224] Cafagna, "Italy," 279–328.

[225] Ibid., 289.

[226] Cafagna, "Italy," 294–95; Thayer, *Italy*, 57.

[227] Cameron, *Concise*, 264.

After a brief economic spurt in 1919, the Italian economy once again nose-dived. Between the first half of 1919 and the last half of 1920, the Italian lira fell from 8.05 per U.S. dollar to 24 per U.S. dollar. Moreover, wholesale prices skyrocketed from a base of 100 in 1913 to 437 in 1918 and 635 in 1920.[228] Compounding the economic woes were the rash of work stoppages in the aftermath of World War I and the fall in security prices in 1921. The number of socialist-inspired agricultural strikes in Italy increased from 10 in 1918 to 208 in 1919. The number of strikers grew from 675 in 1918 to 505,128 in 1919 and to 1,045,732 in 1920. The average strike duration increased from 4.8 days in 1918 to 6.8 days in 1919 and to 13.5 days in 1921.[229] Northern Italy experienced the largest share of agricultural strikes. In 1919, 100 of the 208 reported agricultural strikes occurred in the single northern region of Veneto; in 1921, approximately 55 percent of all agricultural strikes occurred in the three northern and central regions of Lombardy, Emilia, and Tuscany, compared to 45 percent in the remaining thirteen regions.[230] The economic boom of 1919 emboldened four of Italy's principal banks – the Banca Commerciale Italiana, Credito Italiano, Banca di Roma, and the Banca Italiana di Sconto – to loan heavily at medium and long term to Italian industry and to purchase Italian equities. But in 1921, with a steep drop in security prices, the financial health of these banks deteriorated profoundly.[231] Kindleberger notes that the economic recovery taking place in other continental European nations during the 1920s failed to materialize in Italy. Kindleberger cites Mussolini's ill-advised policies of massive revaluation of the Italian lira and the deflationary measures to achieve it as the principal culprits responsible for Italian economic stagnation before the onset of the Great Depression of the 1930s.[232] However, Maddison appears to dispute Kindleberger's claim and suggests that Italy, along with Belgium and France, benefited during the 1920s from rising prices, expansionary monetary and fiscal policy, reasonably rapid growth, and low unemployment.[233] Maddison does acknowledge that the Italian economy during the 1930s remained

---

[228] Arrigo Serpieri, *La guerra e le classi rurali italiane* (Bari, 1930), 161; Maddison, "Economic," 450.

[229] Serpieri, *La guerra*, 267.

[230] Francesco Piva, *Lotte contadine e origini del fascismo* (Venice, 1977), 95; Sepieri, *La guerra*, 270–74.

[231] Kindleberger, *Financial*, 361.

[232] Ibid., 361–63.

[233] Maddison, "Economic," 455–56.

in the throes of a severe depression. But the Great Depression was less severe in Italy than in France and Germany if we consider the percentage difference between peak and trough in the magnitude of GDP decline from 1928 to 1935. The percentage for Italy is –6.1, compared to –11.0 for France and –16.1 for Germany.[234]

Particularly in the cases of France, Germany, and Great Britain, we have seen that during stressful economic periods, prominent and wealthy Jews quickly became targets of economic anti-Semitic vitriol. Throughout much of the nineteenth century, such wealthy Jewish families as the French, German, and British Rothschilds and the German Bleichroeders served as convenient scapegoats for anti-Semites in each of the three countries. In Italy, in times of economic trouble, prominent wealthy Jews were rarely targeted. One might have thought that during the profound agrarian crisis of 1876 or the great depression of 1889–96, Jews would have become the targets of economic resentment, as they had in France and Germany. Yet that did not occur. Why? Though the Rothschilds established a branch in Naples, that branch, led by Carl Rothschild and his sons, never attained the influence of the Paris, Frankfurt, and London branches. In fact, it was James Rothschild, the head of the Parisian branch, who wielded the Rothschild influence over the Italian government during the 1850s. Two years after Italy declared itself a constitutional monarchy (1861), the Naples branch of the Rothschild house closed its doors.[235] After the closing of the Naples branch in 1863, the Rothschilds encountered a series of roadblocks in their efforts to gain contracts and concessions from the new Italian government. Camillo Cavour, the opportunistic and brilliant Italian prime minister, adeptly used the French Jewish Pereire brothers as an effective counterweight to the Rothschilds. In a number of important investment situations, Cavour favored the Pereires over the Rothschilds. By 1875, the Rothschilds had been forced to sell their prized Italian railway network, the South Austrian Lombardo Venetian and Central Railway Company, to the Italians for 750 million francs. The sale of this Italian railway network marked the virtual end of Rothschild banking interest in Italy.[236]

---

[234] Ibid., 465, 455.

[235] A negative caricature of the Rothschilds did, however, appear in G. G. Belli's 1832 *Sonetti romaneschi*. At least two of Belli's sonnets criticized the loan to Pope Gregory XVI by Karl Mayer Rothschild. That the head of the Roman Catholic Church had gone to the "Jew" Rothschild for a loan created considerable consternation for the author (Gunzberg, *Strangers*, 138–52).

[236] Ferguson, *World's*, 687–88; Cameron, *Concise*, 314; Momigliano, *Ottavo*, 366.

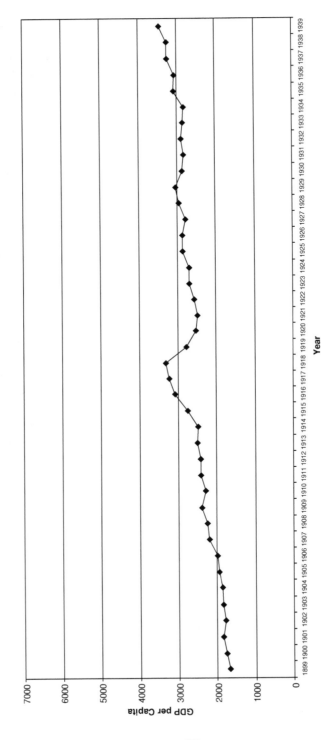

Figure 4.2e. GDP per capita in Italy, 1899–1939. *Note:* The GDP (gross domestic product) per capita data are in 1990 dollars and are drawn from Maddison (1995) and Good and Ma (1998).

During the last decades of the nineteenth century and the first four decades of the twentieth, we might have expected to find an anti-Semitic outburst when notable Jews were present in or associated with a financial/political scandal. We encountered such outbursts in France with the collapse of the Union Générale Bank and the Panama Scandal and in Germany with the 1873 crash of the stock market. It is rather surprising that in Italy during the tumultuous Bank of Rome scandals of 1893, involving a governmental investigation of large irregularities in the policies of the Bank of Rome, no anti-Semitic allegations erupted. This might be unexpected because of the revelations of serious scandals in the Jewish Pereire brothers' bank, the Società Generale di Credito Mobiliare Italiano, and the acknowledgement that a central figure in the controversy was Luigi Luzzatti, a Jew and the minister of the treasury.[237] Luzzatti would go on to become Italy's minister of agriculture and prime minister during the first decade of the twentieth century. The relative dearth of prominent Italian Jews and their high degree of assimilation into Italian society made it rather difficult for Italian anti-Semites to mobilize popular support behind a crusade to blame Jews for Italy's economic woes. Poor Jews residing in urban areas, such as the former Jewish ghetto of Rome, comprised the majority of the Italian Jewish community. Canepa has observed that as late as 1912, one-third of Italy's Jews were largely supported by private and public charities.[238]

While poor Jews constituted the majority of the Italian Jewish community, Jewish wealth and prominence were not by any means negligible within the Italian economy before the Holocaust. As it did in other continental European countries, Jewish capital in Italy played an important role in the funding of the development of Italy's economic infrastructure and in the Italian economic take-off occurring after 1898. Besides playing key roles in rural land development, the silk industry, and urban construction, Jewish families held substantial influence in the insurance business and a considerable local and regional position in banking. Italy's principal insurance company, the Assicurazioni Generali of Trieste, was founded by the Italian Jewish poet Giuseppe Lazzaro Morpurgo, and Jewish banking firms, such as Weil-Weiss and Malvano in Turin, Weil-Schott in Milan, and Treves in Venice, held key positions in the Italian banking industry. Also, Jewish families exercised vital influence in major investment banks, such as Banca Italo-Germania and the Banca

[237] Thayer, *Italy*, 57, 61.
[238] Canepa, "Christian," 21–22.

Italiana di Costruzione.[239] Italian Jews also exhibited a strong presence in a number of other professions. As elsewhere, Italian Jews were overrepresented among owners, editors, and journalists in the Italian newspaper industry, and the Jewish firms of Treves, Bemporad, Lattes, Formiggini, and Voghera stood out among Italy's major publishing houses. Vis-à-vis the general Italian population in 1911, Jews were overrepresented within the Italian civil service, law, business, and academia but underrepresented in agriculture. More specifically, while 55 percent of the Italian general population worked in agriculture, only 8.1 of the Jewish population did; and whereas a mere 5.6 percent of the Italian population engaged in commerce, 41.6 percent of Jews held positions in commerce. Interestingly, 27.2 percent of Jews worked in factories, compared to 30.2 percent for the general Italian population in 1911. In 1930, Jews comprised 8 percent of all university professors in Italy. Before World War II, prominent Jews had left their mark on twentieth-century Italian literature. Two of the best-known Italian Jewish novelists were Italo Svevo and Alberto Moravia (half-Jewish).[240] But as Roth, Steinberg, Momigliano, and Hughes have made clear, with the exception of the Italian insurance industry, Jewish ownership or control within sectors of the Italian economy remained marginal in comparison to that found in other major continental European nations, such as Germany.[241] Jewish-owned or controlled banks may have dominated particular localities or regions but rarely demonstrated international prominence. De Felice mentions that the myth of the *"banca ebraica"* (Jewish bank) surfaces at the beginning of the twentieth century in regard to the purported dominance of the Jewish-owned Banca Commerciale Italiana.[242] De Felice suggests further that the myth of Jewish high finance appealed to segments of both the Italian right and the socialist left. None of Italy's great industrial giants, such as FIAT, was Jewish-owned. Camillo Olivetti, the Jewish-born founder of Olivetti typewriters in 1911, presents the nearest approximation to an internationally known

---

[239] Ibid.; Roth, *History*, 486–87; Momigliano, *Ottavo*, 366.

[240] Gunzberg, *Strangers*, 222; Canepa, "Christian," 22; Zuccotti, *Italians*, 18; Eitan F. Sabatello, "Trasformazioni economiche e sociali degli ebrei in Italia nel periodo dell'emancipazione." In Ministero per I Beni Culturali e Ambientali Ufficio Centrale per I Beni Archivistici, ed., *Italia Judaica: Gli ebrei nell' Italia unita 1870–1945* (Rome, 1993), 123.

[241] Roth, *History*, 486–87; Steinberg, *All or Nothing*, 223; Momigliano, *Ottavo*, 366; Hughes, *Prisoners*, 23.

[242] De Felice, *Storia*, 54.

Italian industrial giant. For Roth, there were few outstanding Jewish names in industry and finance, and only a few Italian Jews successfully entered the class of the so-called international plutocracy.[243]

Thus, when Italian anti-Semites turned to an economic assault on Jews, the usual targets tended to be foreign Jews. During the infamous Mortara kidnapping case, the official church newspaper, *La Civiltà Cattolica*, blamed the alleged Jewish control over the newspapers of Europe for the criticisms of the papacy emanating from French, German, and British journalists.[244] And again during the Dreyfus Affair, the *La Civiltà Cattolica* lashed out at the purported role of the international Jewish plutocracy, which was allegedly behind Dreyfus's treachery.[245] During Italy's 1911 involvement in Libya, F. Coppola, the nationalistic and anti-Semitic publicist, published two notable articles in the Italian journal *L'Idea Nazionale* attacking the opposition of the alleged international Jewish banking group to Italian interests in North Africa and the Middle East. Coppola makes it clear in these articles that he is not referring to Italian Jews, for Italian Jews are *Italians* and support Italy's interests. He contrasts Italian Jews to their disloyal co-religionists in France, Germany, and Russia and concludes that anti-Semitism has a justifiable basis in these countries.[246] We find a further example in the 1930s, when the Italian fascist press blamed recent Jewish immigrants for a host of social and economic problems, such as increases in the housing shortage, rents, food scarcities, unemployment, crime, and crowding of schools.[247] Only rarely did Italian anti-Semites target Italian Jews, as in the case of the Italian Nationalist Association charge that the German-Jewish Banca Commerciale Italiana had a stranglehold over Italian industry and commerce;[248] but even here the emphasis is on "German-Jewish" rather than "Italian" Jews. The Banca Commerciale Italiana, founded in 1894 with a combination of German, Austrian, Swiss, and Italian capital, became an issue in 1915, when Italy joined the allies in the war against Germany and Austria. Much of the antipathy to the Banca Commerciale Italiana was directed at its director, Joseph Toeplitz. Toeplitz, who had worked at the bank since its founding in 1894, had risen to become its director in 1904. Toeplitz was of

[243] Roth, *History*, 487.
[244] Kerzer, *Kidnapping*, 135.
[245] Gentile, "Struggle," 499.
[246] Toscano, "L'uguaglianza," 231–32.
[247] Zucotti, *Italians*, 34–35.
[248] Michaelis, *Mussolini*, 6–9.

Polish-Jewish extraction and had gained Italian citizenship in 1912. In 1916, Giovanni Preziosi, in the second edition of his *La Germania alla conquista dell'Italia*, focused on Toeplitz's role in the Banca Commerciale Italiana in order to highlight the alleged German-Jewish banking dominance in Italy. And during the fascist period, Mario Carli, a fascist journalist, modeled his fictitious Jewish banking overseer, Massimiliano Lind, on Joseph Toeplitz. Like Toeplitz's, Lind's foreign origins held a central place in Carli's anti-Semitic portrayal. Despite Preziosi's and Carli's admonitions, Toeplitz would become in the aftermath of World War I one of the earliest financial backers of Mussolini's Italian fascist movement.[249] I will have more to say about the special role that Jews played in the rise of Mussolini's fascist party in the following chapter.

Popular literature remained one place in Italy where occasionally a less-than-favorable depiction of purported Jewish economic behavior or practices (e.g., legendary avarice, usury, or love of money) emerged. As was the case with the theme of religious anti-Semitism, many nineteenth- and twentieth-century Italian novelists targeted alleged unsavory Jewish economic traits. We have already encountered G. G. Belli's 1832 sonnets, in which the House of Rothschild is presented as hard-hearted and usurious. Other examples would include A. Bresciani's well-known 1850 *L'Ebreo di Verona*, Agostino della Sala Spada's 1872 *La vita: romanzo storico sociale*, G. A. Giustina's 1881 *Il Ghetto*, Cleto Arrighi's 1885 *La Canaglia felice*, Carolina Invernizio's immensely popular 1887 *L'Orfana del Ghetto*, G. Papini's 1931 *Gog*, and G. P. Callegari's 1938 *Il cuore a destra*.[250] Not surprisingly, the Jewish culprits in these Italian novels frequently had non-Italian origins. For instance, in Callegari's *Il cuore a destra*, the principal Jewish protagonist, Gabriele Gold, is portrayed as a Hungarian Jew who furtively penetrates the central Italian textile firm.[251] In short, as Gunzberg has aptly remarked, the theme of Jewish accumulation of wealth by means of avarice and usury remained in place throughout the nineteenth and into the first four decades of the twentieth century in a particular segment of Italian literature.[252]

All told, economic antipathy toward the Jews became a central component of the anti-Jewish narrative before the Holocaust. In the modern

---

[249] Gunzberg, *Strangers*, 224, 258–61; Sodi, "Italian," 46–47; De Felice, *Storia*, 46.
[250] Gunzberg, *Strangers*.
[251] Ibid., 263–68.
[252] Ibid., 226–27.

variant of economic anti-Semitism, hatred of Jews expanded beyond a dislike based on the alleged avaricious and usurious behavior of Jews to a hostility rooted in the association of Jews with the most detested features of modern capitalism. In societies such as France and Germany, where highly visible Jewish families owned or controlled major financial institutions and industries, Jews quickly became targets of economic resentment during periods of economic decline (e.g., 1873, the mid-1880s, 1893, the early 1920s, and during the Great Depression). The rise in Eastern European immigration after 1881 further exacerbated Jewish-Gentile relations, particularly among those in the host population who saw the new Jews as economic competitors or among those who perceived that the impoverished immigrants would constitute an economic burden for society. However, economic resentment toward the Jews should have varied across societies. While wealthy and powerful Jewish families were quite apparent in France, Germany, and Great Britain, they were less conspicuous in Romania and Italy. Furthermore, although the major economic crises between 1873 and 1939 struck the economies of all of Europe, the economic impact varied in duration and intensity. We should expect to find higher levels of economic antipathy toward Jews in those societies hurt most by the economic crises. Similarly, the rate of Eastern European immigration varied across European societies. Among our five countries, France, Germany, and Great Britain experienced the greatest influx of Eastern European Jews, while Italy received very few until the 1930s. The Romanian situation appears unique among the five countries in that the annexation of Bessarabia, Bukovina, and Transylvania in the aftermath of World War I increased the Jewish population nearly three-fold. The magnitude and timing of the Jewish immigration clearly should have affected the level of economic anti-Semitism within the five countries.

The findings from my examination of the volumes of the *American Jewish Year Book* and the principal European newspapers show evidence of the occurrence of and substantial variation in economic anti-Semitic acts and attitudes within the five countries. In Figure 4.3 we see that the magnitude of laws/acts characterized as economic anti-Semitic ranges from a low of 4 in France to 185 in Germany for the 1899–39 period. Germany and Romania considerably outpaced Great Britain, France, and Italy in the number of reported boycotts and laws/acts against Jewish businesses. The German laws/acts took place disproportionately after Hitler came to power: 127 of the 185 German boycotts and laws/acts against Jewish businesses occurred during the years 1933–39.

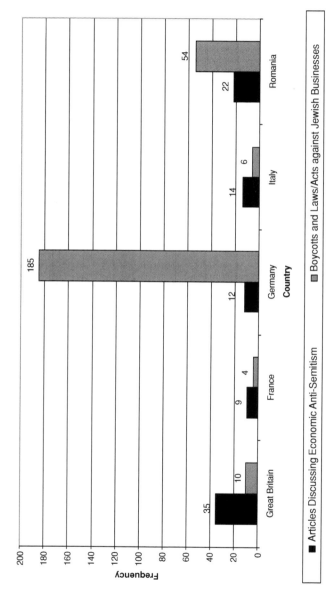

Figure 4.3. Newspaper articles discussing economic anti-Semitism and laws/acts against Jewish civil servants or businesses, 1899–1939. *Note*: Articles are taken from the fifteenth day of the month for every month between 1899 and 1939. Articles were taken from the *Daily Mail* in Great Britain (N = 299), *Le Petit Parisien* in France (N = 199), *Berliner Morgenpost* in Germany (N = 269), *Corriere della Sera* in Italy (N = 101), and *Universul* in Romania (N = 136). Laws/acts against Jewish posts or businesses are taken from the volumes of the *American Jewish Year Book* and include two categories from the typology (see Table 1.1). The first includes boycotts or strikes against Jews or Jewish businesses. The second includes laws or acts forcing Jews to leave posts or appointments or to lose businesses.

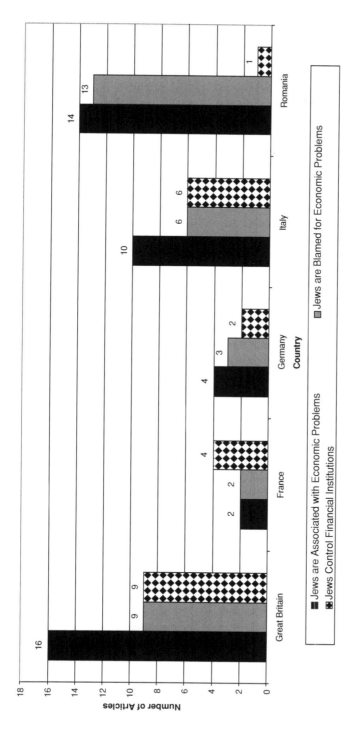

Figure 4.4. Newspaper articles discussing economic anti-Semitism by country, 1899–1939. *Note:* Articles are taken from the fifteenth day of the month for every month between 1899 and 1939. Articles were taken from the *Daily Mail* in Great Britain (N = 299), *Le Petit Parisien* in France (N = 199), *Berliner Morgenpost* in Germany (N = 269), *Corriere della Sera* in Italy (N = 101), and *Universul* in Romania (N = 136).

On the other hand, only twenty of the fifty-four reported laws/acts in Romania took place between 1933 and 1939. For Italy, the pattern observed for religious and racial anti-Semitic laws and acts appears again for economic anti-Semitic laws and acts. All six recorded boycotts and laws/acts against Jewish businesses in Italy happened between 1937 and 1939. Figure 4.3 indicates that the topic of economic anti-Semitism occupied the attention of the newspaper audience, particularly in Great Britain, Italy, and Romania, where the proportion of articles discussing economic anti-Semitism ran rather high. For instance, nearly one out of six newspaper articles from my sample of the Romanian daily *Universul* discussed issues related to economic anti-Semitism. In the case of Italy, ten of the fourteen articles appeared between 1937 and 1939. Figure 4.4 provides a more in-depth breakdown of economic anti-Semitism within the five countries. Coders were asked to code the articles on the basis of Jews' being associated with economic problems, blamed for economic problems, and being called controllers of financial institutions. The British and Romanian newspapers surpassed the others on the question of Jewish association with economic problems. However, Great Britain and Romanian reports diverged widely on culpability for economic problems. In Great Britain, slightly more than one-half of the articles associating Jews with economic problems blamed the Jews for the economic problems; in Romania, thirteen of the fourteen articles associating Jews with economic problems blamed the Jews for those economic problems. On the question of purported Jewish control of financial institutions, Great Britain's newspaper had the largest volume, with nine articles. For Romania, on the other hand, only one article discussing economic anti-Semitism claimed that Jews controlled financial institutions. The French daily newspaper, which overall contained relatively scant reportage on Jewish economic anti-Semitism, did nonetheless devote proportionately more space to the alleged Jewish control of financial institutions.[253]

[253] We have seen heretofore in this study that the preponderance of Italian anti-Semitic legislation and newspaper reportage occurs during the brief period of 1937–39. This continues to be the case with the Italian newspaper coverage of economic anti-Semitism. In short, nine of the ten articles associating Jews with economic problems, all six articles blaming Jews for economic problems, and five of the six articles associating Jews with control of financial institutions appear between 1938 and 1939. Also, examining the results of the within-country newspaper examination, I found considerable divergence between the newspapers on the questions of Jews associated with economic problems, Jews blamed

While many newspaper articles discussed economic anti-Semitism, not all displayed an unfavorable orientation toward Jews. Figure 4.5 shows significant divergence among our five countries with regard to unfavorable articles discussing economic anti-Semitism.[254] The Romanian newspaper reportage, with nineteen articles, was clearly the most unfavorable, followed by Great Britain and Italy. Surprisingly, I found only one unfavorable article in the sample of the French daily *Le Petit Parisien* for the entire forty one-year period. Assessing the findings in figures 4.3, 4.4, and 4.5, we see once again the pronounced difference between the volume of anti-Semitic acts and anti-Semitic attitudes in Germany.

In this chapter on the economic root of anti-Semitism, we have seen that throughout the period of this study Jews have frequently been accused of involvement in criminal activities such as financial and political scandals. The infamous Dreyfus Affair, the Panama Scandal, the Sklarek brothers' and the Marconi scandals are examples of some of the better-known cases. Not all the alleged Jewish involvement or association with criminal activities had economic origins; criminal activities covered a wide span, including arrest for involvement in political demonstrations and acts of violence against property and persons. Nevertheless, proponents of economic anti-Semitism frequently highlighted assumed Jewish preoccupations with money and economic power as motivating factors for the alleged Jewish association with crime. Figure 4.6 presents the results of my examination of the principal daily newspapers in the five countries for reportage on Jewish association with crime or criminal activity for the years 1899 to 1939. The findings reveal that the topic of Jews and crime captured substantial attention in the newspaper press. Roughly two-fifths of the total Italian sample of articles (39 of 101 articles) and one-fourth of the British and French total samples contained

for economic problems, and Jews accused of controlling financial institutions for the selective years of 1921, 1933, 1935, and 1939. Although the quantity of articles is quite small, the secondary newspapers – *Daily Herald*, *La Dépêche de Toulouse*, and the *Muenchner Neueste Nachrichten* – contained more articles in each of the three categories than the primary newspapers in the respective countries. *Il Messaggero* did not differ significantly from the *Corriere della Sera*, and *Lumea* possessed far fewer articles than *Universul*.

[254] My within-country comparison of newspaper reportage regarding unfavorable articles discussing economic anti-Semitism for selected years exhibited insignificant divergence. The only exception was in Romania, where for the selected years, *Universul* contained three unfavorable articles, while *Lumea* contained none.

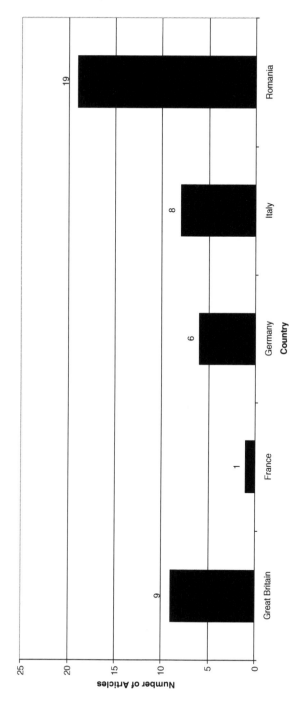

Figure 4.5. Newspaper articles discussing economic anti-Semitism in an unfavorable context by country, 1899–1939. *Note:* Articles are taken from the fifteenth day of the month for every month between 1899 and 1939. Articles were taken from the *Daily Mail* in Great Britain (N = 299), *Le Petit Parisien* in France (N = 199), *Berliner Morgenpost* in Germany (N = 269), *Corriere della Sera* in Italy (N = 101), and *Universul* in Romania (N = 136). Articles were coded "unfavorable" if the article reflected negatively on Jews, if the author's tone expressed disdain for Jews, or if the article supported actions that adversely affected Jews.

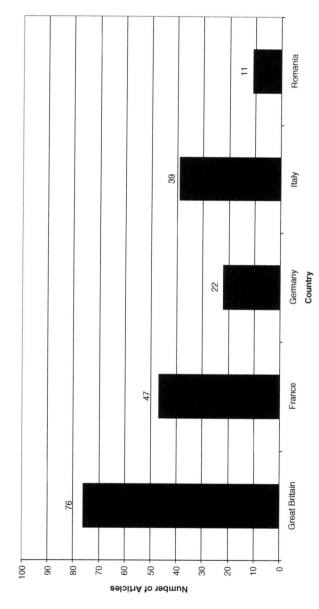

Figure 4.6. Newspaper articles associating Jews with crime or criminal activity, 1899–1939. *Note:* Articles are taken from the fifteenth day of the month for every month between 1899 and 1939. Articles were taken from the *Daily Mail* in Great Britain (N = 299), *Le Petit Parisien* in France (N = 199), *Berliner Morgenpost* in Germany (N = 269), *Corriere della Sera* in Italy (N = 101), and *Universul* in Romania (N = 136).

some reference to an association of Jews with crime.[255] The large volume of articles associating Jews with crime may appear surprising to the reader. On closer examination, many of these articles dealt with reports on criminal activities occurring in impoverished Jewish immigrant communities, such as London's East End, thus making the findings less out of the ordinary given the generally acknowledged relationship between crime and poverty.

Economic anti-Semitism is the third root of the anti-Semitic tree. We now turn to the fourth and last root of anti-Semitism, the political root.

---

[255] In the case of Germany, twenty-one of the twenty-two articles linking Jews with criminal activities appeared between 1933 and 1939. For Italy, the distribution of articles was highly bipolar: sixteen of the articles issued forth between 1899 and 1900 and nineteen between 1937 and 1939.

# CHAPTER FIVE

# THE POLITICAL ROOT

At various times throughout the modern period, the myth of a "Jewish world conspiracy" has attracted adherents. Jews have been accused of plotting to take over the world by undermining the existing social and political order. The myth of the "Jewish world conspiracy" springs from diverse sources. As one source of the myth, Yehuda Bauer has pointed to the medieval anti-Jewish Christian accusation that, as the people of the devil, Jews, like the devil, aim to control the world.[1] Others have highlighted the charge that Jews aim to avenge their century-old oppression by Christians, or the idea that Jews inherently strive for national and/or world power. Before the emergence of revolutionary socialist parties in the last decades of the nineteenth century, subscribers to the myth that the Jews covertly planned to take control of the world believed they had proof in what they perceived was the inordinate Jewish presence as "court Jews," advising and financing rulers; in the role Jews allegedly played as leaders and members of the supposedly antichurch and liberal Freemasons (a secretive international fraternity for mutual help, advancing religious and social equality); and in the establishment by prominent Jews in 1860 of the Paris-based Alliance Israélite Universelle (the first international organization to represent worldwide Jewish interests). In more recent times, Jews were assumed to be the backers or originators of radical and subversive movements whose chief aim was allegedly to bring down the reigning national political order. What supposedly attracted Jews in such large numbers to these radical

---

[1] Yehuda Bauer, A History of the Holocaust (New York, 1982), 44.

and subversive movements? According to the conventional wisdom, the Jewish predisposition toward radical and subversive movements derived from a combination of their intense internationalism – a product of the Jewish dispersion throughout the world – and from a Jewish messianism.[2]

Political anti-Semitism, defined as hostility toward Jews based on the belief that Jews seek to obtain national and/or world power, experienced a momentous upsurge after 1879 in Europe. We can largely attribute the dramatic rise in political anti-Semitism between 1879 and 1939 to the emergence and rapid development of an international socialist movement and, concomitantly, to the popularization of the notorious "Protocols of the Elders of Zion" in the aftermath of the Bolshevik Revolution. During the last half of the nineteenth century, a host of newly established political movements and parties marked the European political landscape. Many of these new political groups advocated radical programs aimed at redressing social and political inequalities. Among these new movements or parties were the socialist or Marxist groups, which steadily gained prominence in Europe after 1879. These parties were perceived to represent major threats to the interests of elite and middle-class groups as well as to the Christian religious faithful.

Socialism was disliked by many people across the social spectrum because of socialism's apparent antipathy toward religion, patriotism, and nationalism. Jews and socialism were inextricably linked in the eyes of anti-Semites, for numerous reasons. For many anti-Semites, the connection between socialism and Jews seemed real. As early as the 1880s, Drumont, the notable French anti-Semite, had linked Jews to the creation of every nefarious form of subversive internationalism, including socialism. Is it true that Jews were disproportionately represented in socialist and communist movements? The plain truth is yes, for the Jewish presence in socialist movements far exceeded the Jewish

---

[2] Jaff Schatz, *The Generation: The Rise and Fall of the Jewish Communists of Poland* (Berkeley, 1991), 38–43; Friedlaender, *Nazi Germany*, 93. Jewish messianism incorporates the objective of messianic redemption (i.e., the search for individual and societal peace, justice, harmony, and perfection) to be achieved on earth. Schatz (*Generation*, 38–43) associates the Jewish attachment to messianic redemption to a Jewish affinity for movements embodying activism and the emancipatory ideal.

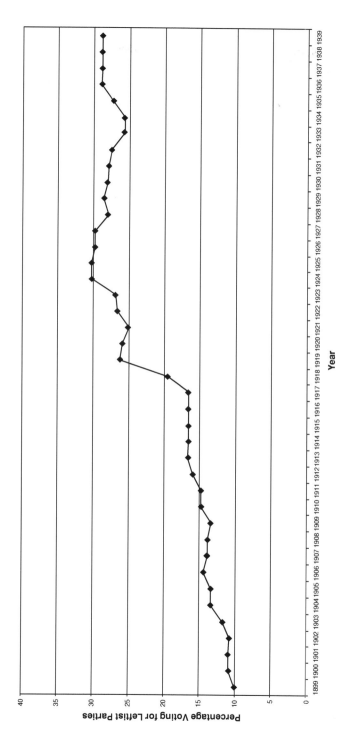

Figure 5.1. Percentage of votes cast for leftist parties in France, Germany, Great Britain, Romania, and Italy, 1899–1939. *Note:* National election results covering the period from 1899 to 1939 for the five countries have been gathered from Flora (1983), Mackie and Rose (1982), Dogan (1946), and Hitchens (1994). Electoral support for the left has been computed as the proportion of all votes cast for leftist parties. Leftist parties include social democrats, socialists, and communists. In off-election years, the figure from the most recent election year has been carried over.

percentage of the general population.[3] This does not mean that most Jews were socialists or backed socialist movements. A large proportion of the Jewish population was actively opposed to socialist and communist movements. However, in the context of a culture of church and state discrimination, many secularized European Jews became attracted to the ideals of movements such as Zionism and socialism. Jews saw in socialism a universalistic movement and a rationalistic and universalistic ideology championing humanitarianism, social and political equality, and a complete rejection of anti-Semitism.[4]

The link between socialism and Jews requires exploration. To begin with, it is worth repeating that the "red menace" – namely, the fear that a worldwide subversive communist movement sought to gain world power – had dominated Western thinking until 1989. Belief in the "red menace" reached epidemic levels in the wake of socialism's first major success, the Bolshevik Revolution of 1917, and again in the aftermath of communism's success in Eastern Europe and China after World War II. The fear of communism was undeniably real and undisputedly held center stage in the politics of the twentieth century. That prominent Jews played key roles from the beginning in the socialist and communist movements provided the European anti-Semitic crusade considerable nourishment and momentum. We begin with the claim that the two principal founders of European socialism, Karl Marx and Ferdinand Lassalle, were Jewish. Ironically, neither Marx nor Lassalle considered himself Jewish. Marx's father had converted to Lutheranism a year before the younger Marx's birth. Nonetheless, anti-Semites employed Marx's and Lassalle's "Jewishness" to connect revolutionary socialism to the Jews.

---

[3] While the thrust of my examination of the purported association between Jews and left-wing socialism focuses on Europe before the Holocaust, the accusation that Jews are predisposed to left-wing radicalism has attracted prominent adherents outside of Europe and in recent years. Two relatively recent examples are linked to the former U.S. president, Richard M. Nixon. Schatz (*Generations*, 12–13) reports that upon hearing of the riots at the 1968 Democratic national convention in Chicago, Nixon asked if all of the indicted conspirators were Jewish or only half of them. Also, in a review of tapes from the Nixon presidency released by the National Archives, President Nixon was heard telling aides that every member of the communist conspiracy in the United States during the late 1940s and 1950s was Jewish, save Whittaker Chambers and Alger Hiss, although Hiss might have been half-Jewish, according to Nixon (*Minneapolis Star Tribune*, October 10, 1999, section A, 23).

[4] Lindemann, *Esau's*, 169; Schatz, *Generations*, 50–51; Friedlaender, *Nazi Germany*, 93.

Some anti-Semitic writers, such as Massoutié, went even further and asserted that Marx's writings mirrored talmudic prophecies and that Marx's internationalist appeal coincided with the Jewish messianic tendency.[5] A more accurate interpretation of the writings of Marx and Lassalle shows that they were often harsh critics of the Jewish religion as well as of alleged Jewish economic practices. But in the eyes of anti-Semites, the fact that they descended from Jewish ancestry was sufficient reason to refer to them as Jews.

Between 1879 and 1917, the perception of a Jewish preponderant role within socialist movements began to attract attention. As early as 1879, written reports by the Prussian police had shed light on the purported link between Jews and socialism. These reports attributed Jewish financial backing to the German Social Democratic party and asserted that Jews held prominent positions in the various revolutionary parties throughout Europe. The reports supported the claim of Jewish leadership of revolutionary movements by pointing to the roles played by such alleged Jews as Karl Hirsch in Brussels, Karl Marx in London, and Leo Fraenkel in Budapest. These Prussian reports also noted that Jews comprised the majority of the members of the large revolutionary Russian nihilist movement. Support for the claim of Jewish participation in Russia's revolutionary movement came from the Russian minister of interior, who proclaimed that Jews constituted 70 percent of all political dissidents known by the Russian police operating within the Russian Empire. Relatedly, in a conversation held in 1903 between Theodor Herzl, the founder of the Zionist movement, and Count Serge Julievich Witte, a former Russian Finance minister and president of the Committee of Russian Ministers, Witte professed that in his opinion Jews made up one-half of all Russian revolutionaries.[6] While it is nearly impossible to ascertain the exact percentage of Jewish membership in pre-1917 Russian revolutionary movements, Brym, employing police statistics of arrests, has reported that Jews made up 5 percent of Russian radicals in 1875 and 38 percent in 1905.[7] He noted furthermore that in 1907, roughly 23 percent of the Russian Mensheviks and 11 percent of the Russian Bolshevik leadership were Jewish.[8] Although Brym's more reliable statistics diverge significantly from the numbers provided by Russian

---

[5] Massoutié, *Judaisme*, 138–39.
[6] Schatz, *Generations*, 12–13.
[7] R. J. Brym, *The Jewish Intelligentsia and Russian Marxism* (New York, 1978), 3.
[8] Ibid., 73.

and Prussian authorities, the evidence indicates that Jews were indeed overrepresented in the pre-1917 Russian revolutionary movement. This disproportionate representation of Jews in Russia's revolutionary movements probably contributed to the governmental and popular exaggerations about the association between Jews and subversive movements. Russian suspicions about the role of Jews in subversive actions may have been sparked initially by the investigation into the March 13, 1881, assassination of Czar Alexander II. Among those arrested as plotters was Gessia Gelfman, who was of Jewish origin;[9] Russian governmental figures did not neglect to use the occasion to highlight Gelfman's Jewish background. The perception that Jews comprised a large proportion of participants in left-wing radical movements before 1917 was not confined to the Russian Empire. Throughout Europe, the impression that Jews were radicals received widespread acceptance. I will investigate in more detail this particular impression in my examination of political anti-Semitism within France, Germany, Great Britain, Romania, and

If before 1917 acceptance of the notion that Jews were left-wing revolutionaries had resided largely with some anti-Jewish government officials and with the cadre of anti-Semitic polemicists such as Edouard Drumont in France and Wilhelm Marr in Germany, after 1917 acknowledgement of the existence of a link between Jews and revolutionary socialism reached pandemic proportions. The seizure of power by the Russian Bolsheviks in 1917, followed by a series of left-wing uprisings elsewhere in Europe in the aftermath of World War I, ushered in a wave of anti-Marxist and anti-Semitic hysteria. During the chaotic period following the end of World War I, many political leaders and major newspapers portrayed the Bolshevik Revolution and the wave of left-wing revolutionary attempts to seize power elsewhere as part of the overall Jewish plan to take control of the world. Jews were shown to have dominated the leadership of the Russian Bolshevik Party and leftist revolutionary parties in other European states. The purported link between Jews and revolutionary socialism grew ironically to include rich Jewish financiers, such as the American shipping magnate Jacob Schiff and the German banker Max Warburg. In the opinion of many in the anti-Semitic camp, wealthy Jews had engineered and funded the revolutionary movements in Russia in order to bring down the despised and intensely anti-Semitic czarist regime and to sunder the existing social order

[9] Rubenstein, *After Auschwitz*, 100.

throughout the world.[10] Much has been made of the position that Jews held in the leadership of the Russian Bolshevik Party and the fact that these Jews employed pseudonyms. The following is a partial list of the principal Russian Marxist revolutionaries, along with their real names: Trotsky (Bronstein), Steklov (Nachamkess), Martov (Tsederbaum), Zinoviev (Apfelbaum), Goussiev (Drapkin), Kamenev (Rosenfeld), Bogdanov (Silberstein), Volodarsky (Kohen), Gorev (Goldman), Parvus (Helphandt), Radek (Sobelson), and Litvinov (Wallach). A couple of years subsequent to the Russian Revolution, the archconservative British newspaper *Morning Post* published a list of the fifty most prominent Russian Bolsheviks with their aliases, real names, and "race." Among the fifty prominent Bolsheviks, the newspaper reported that forty-three belonged to the Jewish race. A similar list of leading Russian Marxists, including the claim that 95 percent of them were Jews, appeared in the book *The Causes of World Unrest*. Other contemporary sources provided lower figures for Jewish participation in the Bolshevik Revolution. In the influential and widely read book *The Makers of the Russian Revolution*, we find that among the seven principal Russian revolutionaries cited, four had Jewish backgrounds, and that roughly one-third of the top fifty Russian revolutionaries had Jewish origins.[11] Golding denies the validity of these numbers and reports that only eleven of the forty-eight members of the Soviet central government had Jewish backgrounds, and that by 1922 Jews made up only 4 percent of the membership of the Soviet Communist Party.[12] That the true figures for Jewish membership in the Soviet communist leadership and party diverged from those published in the press hardly mattered in the minds of millions of Europeans. During the "red hysteria," it was not uncommon to read that key non-Jewish Russian communists, such as Lenin,[13] Chicherin, and Lunarcharsky were also Jewish. In time, Trotsky, Zinoviev, Kamenev, and Radek became household names throughout the West, and "Jew" and "Bolshevik" became synonymous. The fact that these Jewish revolutionaries employed aliases convinced many in the West that they were deceitfully trying to hide the Jewish nature of the Russian Revolution.[14]

[10] Walter Laqueur, *Russia and Germany: A Century of Conflict* (Boston and Toronto, 1965), 74, 89–90; Massoutié, *Judaisme*, 122.
[11] Kadish, *Bolsheviks*, 35; Lindemann, *Esau's*, 430–35; Massoutié, *Judaisme*, 124.
[12] Golding, *Jewish Problem*, 102.
[13] Massoutié (*Judaisme*, 121) published the unproven claim that Lenin's maternal grandfather, Dr. Alexandroff, was Jewish.
[14] Golding, *Jewish Problem*, 102; Almog, *Nationalism*, 79.

The popular association between Jews and Bolshevism made inroads far beyond the masses of ardent anti-Semites and the uneducated. In the early 1920s, no less a figure than Winston Churchill connected the Jews to the evil Bolshevik rule.[15]

Revolutionary socialism proclaimed itself an international movement, and in the period following the collapse of the Romanov, Hohenzollern, and Hapsburg empires, revolutionary socialist movements actively sought to take power throughout Europe. Within many of these revolutionary movements, Jews played prominent roles.[16] Two of the best-known cases were Hungary and Germany. In the Hungarian "red revolution" of early 1919, led by Bela Kun (a Transylvanian Jew), 18 of the 29 members of the Hungarian Soviet Revolutionary Council had Jewish origins, while 161 of the top 203 officials in the short-lived Kun government were Jewish.[17] In the chaotic aftermath of the collapse of the Hohenzollern empire in Germany, prominent Jews played key roles in the revolutionary upheavals in Berlin and Munich. In Munich, the socialists succeeded briefly in establishing a socialist-led regime under Kurt Eisner. The list of Jews holding key positions in these German revolutionary movements included Kurt Eisner, Rosa Luxemburg, Edgar Jaffe, Gustav Landauer, Erich Muehsam, Ernst Toller, and Eugen Leviné.[18]

Even with the collapse of leftist revolutionary attempts to seize power in several European nations in the immediate aftermath of World War I, Jews continued to assert disproportionate influence within the socialist and communist parties in Europe during the interwar period. In the case of Poland, Schatz notes that the Jewish proportion of total membership in the Polish Communist Party between the world wars never fell below 22 percent, and that in Poland's large cities, Jewish communist membership typically surpassed 50 percent of the total membership. (Jews accounted for 10.5 percent of the Polish general population in 1924.)[19]

---

[15] Lindemann, Esau's, 435.

[16] Friedlaender, Nazi Germany, 214.

[17] Almog, Nationalism, 80; R.V. Burks, Dynamics of Communism in Eastern Europe (Princeton, 1961), 162; Marrus, Unwanted, 64; Massoutié, Judaisme, 126; Friedlaender, Nazi Germany, 93. Also, in Massoutie's (Judaisme, 126) highly anti-Semitic work, he observed that as in the case of Russia, many of the Hungarian Jewish revolutionaries employed pseudonyms – e.g., Pogany (Schwarz), Kunfi (Kunstatter), Vago (Weiss), Korvin (Klein).

[18] Almog, Nationalism, 79.

[19] Schatz, Generation, 76.

Schatz reports additionally that within Poland's communist youth movement in 1930, Jews comprised 51 percent of the membership.[20] Burks's
statistics corroborate Schatz's claims.[21] Burks, citing an official Polish
communist source, reports that in 1933, 26 percent of the Polish
Communist Party members had Jewish backgrounds, and that in the
Polish free election of 1922, Polish Jews were three times more likely
than Polish non-Jews to vote for communist candidates. Poland was
not the exception in terms of Jewish participation in Eastern and Central European communist movements during the interwar period. Later
we shall have the opportunity to examine the role of Jews within the
Romanian Communist Party. Though communist parties sprung forth after World War I throughout Europe, and though prominent Jews tended
to operate at the highest levels within many of these parties, there were
nonetheless some important exceptions. In contrast to the situation in
Romania and Poland, Jews were relatively absent from the leadership
of the Albanian, Bulgarian, and Yugoslavian Communist Parties during the interwar period.[22] I would speculate that the relative dearth
of Jewish domination within the interwar communist movements in
Albania, Bulgaria, and Yugoslavia (especially Serbia) can be partly attributed to the small population of Jews, but also to the greater extent of
Jewish assimilation in these three countries. While there is certainly not
a perfect correlation, Jews who experienced or perceived themselves to
experience disenfranchisement from a society had a greater likelihood
of joining a communist party. I conjecture furthermore that the relative absence of Jewish communist leadership in these three countries
contributed to lower levels of popular anti-Semitism during both the
interwar period and the Holocaust.

During the peak of the revolutionary socialist upheaval in the years
following the conclusion of World War I, political anti-Semitism received a substantial boost from the worldwide publication and translation of the infamous forgery, the "Protocols of the Elders of Zion."
The "Protocols" described an elaborate Jewish plan of world conquest
through the creation of worldwide unrest, culminating in the ascent to
world power of the Jewish House of David. In the context of World
War I and its aftermath (the collapse of the Hohenzollern, Hapsburg,

---

[20] Ibid., 85.
[21] Burks, *Dynamics*, 160.
[22] Paul Lendvai, *L'antisémitisme sans juifs* (Paris, 1971), 65–66; Burks, *Dynamics*,
159.

Ottoman, and Romanov empires and the revolutionary socialist upheavals throughout the world), the myth of a Jewish conspiracy to sow
worldwide discord for the purpose of Jewish world domination gained
currency. In particular, the Russian Revolution, by ushering in a period of European-wide revolutionary upheaval, civil war, and the birth
of an international communist movement, transformed a relatively ob-
scure pamphlet into a powerful vehicle, giving credibility to the myth
of "Judeo-Bolshevism" and linking anti-Semitism and anti-Bolshevism
for decades. [23]

In truth, the text was a forgery, based largely on two notable works
from the 1860s, Maurice Joly's *Dialogue aux enfers* and segments of Sir
John Redcliffe's (employing the pseudonym of Hermann Goedsche)
novel *Biarritz*. Joly's 1864 *Dialogue aux enfers* encompasses a satire of
the French emperor Napoleon III. The "Protocols" plagiarize nearly
word for word the fictional political speeches of Machiavelli contained
in Joly's book, in which Napoleon III conspires to dominate the world.
The actual "Protocols" substituted the Jewish elders for the French emperor. Redcliffe's 1868 *Biarritz* includes a chapter entitled "In the Jewish
Cemetery in Prague," in which a plot is hatched at midnight in the
cemetery among twelve Jewish elders, representing the various tribes of
Israel, and Ahasuerus, the wandering Jew. During this fictitious meeting, the elders conspire to garner the wealth of the world and to make
their grandsons the future rulers of all nations.[24] The "Protocols" were

[23] Richard S. Levy, "Introduction: The Political Career of the Protocols of the
Elders of Zion." In Richard S. Levy, trans. and ed., *A Lie and a Libel: The History
of the Protocols of the Elders of Zion* (Lincoln and London, 1995), 16; Pauley,
*Prejudice*, 7–9. Enhancing the credibility of the thesis of the "Protocols" among
anti-Semites was the myth that the Jews were responsible for the murder of the
Russian imperial family at Ekaterinburg during the Russian civil war. According
to the myth, among the possessions of the murdered czarina was a copy of an earlier
version of the "Protocols." According to Kadish (*Bolsheviks*, 31), Norman Cohn,
in his well-known book on the Holocaust (*Warrant for Genocide: The Myth of
the Jewish World-Conspiracy and the Protocols of the Elders of Zion* (London, 1967),
reports that the White Russian troops who discovered the murdered Russian
empress claimed that she had left clear signs that the Jews were responsible for
the murders and that the Russian Revolution marked the victory of the Antichrist
in Russia.

[24] Benjamin Segel, *A Lie and a Libel: The History of the Protocols of the Elders of
Zion*, trans. and ed. Richard S. Levy (Lincoln and London, 1995), 67; Finzi,
*Anti-Semitism*, 65; Mosse, *Final Solution*, 116–17; Wilson, *Ideology*, 409; Fried-
laender, *Nazi Germany*, 94–95; Pauley, *Prejudice*, 7–9). Also, Cohn's *Warrant for*

concocted in the mid to late 1890s by order of Piotr Rachkovsky, chief of the Paris bureau of the czarist secret police, Okhrana. The timing and location of the production of the "Protocols" is not coincidental, for it occurs at a time of heightened Russian and French anti-Semitism and the emergence of the Zionist movement. The French right aspired to link Dreyfus to an international Jewish conspiracy, while the czarist regime sought a justification for its intense anti-Semitic campaign.[25]

The "Protocols" were published for the first time in a newspaper series in Russia in 1903 and then again in 1905, as an appendix to the second edition of the Russian mystic writer Sergei Nilus's *The Great in the Small, Anti-Christ a Near Political Possibility. Notes of an Orthodox Person.* Nilus had probably been commissioned by agents of the czar to fabricate a document purporting to show the plan of Jews to conquer the world. Nilus declared that he came into possession of the "Protocols" in 1901. On one occasion, he mentioned that he had gained access to the documents thanks to the efforts of a woman who had stolen them from a prominent "elder." On a different occasion, Nilus opined that his correspondent had stealthily removed the "Protocols" from the secret vaults of the French-based Zionist headquarters. Further editions of the "Protocols" appeared in Russia in 1911 and 1912.[26] After the Bolshevik Revolution, anti-Bolshevik Russian officers brought the "Protocols" to the attention of the public in Central and Western Europe. Within a span of a few years, the "Protocols" were translated and published in several European countries and the United States.

The "Protocols" comprise basically a report written by the purported leaders of the group of the "Wise Men or Elders of Zion," describing a series of twenty-four secret meetings taking place in 1897 in Basel, Switzerland. What secrets do the "Protocols" hold? The "Protocols" entail a blueprint for Jewish world conquest – a conquest allegedly prophesized in ancient Hebrew texts. In these alleged meetings of the elders in Basel, they develop plans to incite Christians to fight against each other, to undermine the Christian world politically, economically, and morally, and to establish upon the ruins a new world state ruled by the Jews. The

---

*Genocide* includes among the sources drawn upon for the "Protocols," Gougenot des Mousseaux's *Le Juif, le Judaisme et la Judaisation des peuples chrétiens,* abbé Chabauty's *Les Francs-maçons et les Juifs: Sixième âge de l'Eglise d'après l'Apocalypse,* and his *Les Juifs nos maîtres.*

[25] Friedlaender, *Nazi Germany,* 94–95; Mosse, *Final Solution,* 118.

[26] Lebzelter, "Political," 386; Friedlaender, *Nazi Germany,* 94–95; Dimont, *Jews,* 322.

reveal that the Jews, with the help of the Jewish-dominated
, have been the source of a host of alleged evils beginning
ench Revolution, and including equality of all citizens be-
, compulsory education, freedom of conscience and religion,
freedom of the press, universal suffrage, parliamentarianism, liberalism,
socialism, anarchism, and Bolshevism. Among the purported methods
to be utilized by the elders to achieve the objective of world domination were the spread of liberalism and socialism, the control of the
press, the corruption of European women, the manufacturing of financial
crises, and the creation and support of competing political parties. If the
Gentiles discovered the plan and began to resist, the elders would blow
up the principal European capitals and infect the Gentiles with serious
diseases. With the demise of Christian rule, the House of David would
institute an absolute hereditary monarchy throughout the world, ruled
over by the king of the Jews, according to the "Protocols." What may
have convinced people who normally might have been suspicious of the
authenticity of the "Protocols" was the claim that the "Protocols" had
been authored by the Jews themselves and had fallen accidentally into
the hands of the intended victims of the Jewish plot. That the first Zionist Congress, convened by Theodor Herzl, took place in Basel in August
1897 further enhanced the claim of the genuineness of the "Protocols."
How did the intended victims learn of the alleged Jewish plot? The supposed secret Jewish plans for world conquest reached the outside world
thanks to the ingenuity of a Russian spy employed by the Okhrana who
had managed to secure a copy of the report of the Jewish elders.[27]

As preposterous as the contents of the infamous "Protocols" appear to
us today, they offered to many non-Jews an explanation and a scapegoat
for the chaos that marked Europe in the aftermath of World War I and
the Russian Revolution. For instance, the prestigious London *Times* on
May 8, 1920, in a lead article entitled "The Jewish Peril, a Disturbing
Pamphlet: Call for Inquiry," asked if the "Protocols" were authentic,
given the apparent accuracy of many of its prophecies. However, a year
later, the *Times* claimed that the "Protocols" were a forgery.[28] Not even
proof of the fallacious nature of the "Protocols" dampened interest in
them. For many anti-Semites, public disclosures of the falsity of the
"Protocols" only strengthened the belief in its authenticity. Take the

---

[27] Levy, "Introduction," 11; Segal, *A Lie*, 56–60; Golding, *Jewish Problem*, 104–05;
Mosse, *Final Solution*, 118; Pauley, *Prejudice*, 7–9; Birnbaum, *France*, 112–13.
[28] Friedlaender, *Nazi Germany*, 95.

case of the notorious French anti-Semitic Catholic prelate Monsignor Ernst Jouin, who in 1921, when confronted with evidence of the "Protocols" fakery, observed: "The Jews fight against the "Protocols," first with suppression and then with denial. That double attitude induces us to believe in the authenticity of this famous document; and, in any case, to feel absolutely certain of its veracity. Israel is entangled in its own nets."[29]

The post–World War I crisis years certainly played a key role in the phenomenal popularity and dissemination of the "Protocols." During the civil wars following the Bolshevik Revolution, anti-Bolshevik Russian emigrants brought the document to the attention of their sympathizers in the West. This may have especially been the case for Germany, where Alfred Rosenberg and Max Erwin von Scheubner-Richter – both anticommunist and anti-Semitic Baltic Germans – are believed to have deeply influenced the anti-Semitic direction of the early German Nazi Party.[30] In 1919, the earliest German and Polish editions appeared, and in 1920, we find the first English edition released in London and Boston. Shortly thereafter, French, Hungarian, Italian, and Serbian versions turn up. The famous American carmaker Henry Ford would highlight the myth of the Jewish worldwide conspiracy contained in the "Protocols" in his widely popular *Dearborn Independent* between 1920 and 1924. In Germany at the time Hitler took power in 1933, the "Protocols" had gone through thirty-three editions, with one popular edition alone selling roughly 100,000 copies. Interest in the "Protocols," and perhaps acceptance of its veracity, continued into recent times. Among the most notable instances in which the document has gained attention are President Gamal Nasser's recommendation of the "Protocols" to an eminent Indian journalist in 1958 as required reading for understanding global politics, and the decision of King Faisal of Saudi Arabia to send the "Protocols" as a gift in 1974 to Aldo Moro and Michel Jobert, the foreign ministers of Italy and France, respectively.[31]

The intensity and breadth of political anti-Semitism varied from country to country. Political anti-Semitism reached the highest levels in those countries marked by acute political instability, a powerful revolutionary socialist movement (especially one in which Jews appeared to hold important leadership roles), a sizeable presence of Russian and

---

[29] Finzi, *Anti-Semitism*, 68.
[30] Laqueur, *Russia and Germany*, Chapter 2.
[31] Finzi, *Anti-Semitism*, 62–63; Pauley, *Prejudice*, 10.

Polish immigrant Jews, and the perception of overrepresentation of Jews in key governmental positions. We now turn to an examination of political anti-Semitism in France, Germany, Great Britain, Romania, and Italy before the Holocaust.


## FRANCE

Political anti-Semitism in France before the Holocaust typically incorporated the alleged charges of Jewish control of the French state and Jewish participation in and leadership of a subversive revolutionary left. That is not to argue, however, that there were not other themes that occasionally nourished French political anti-Semitism, such as Jewish support of Zionism and internationalism and supposed Jewish complicity with France's rivals (e.g., Germany, Great Britain). As a source of political anti-Semitism, Zionism appeared to play a more pivotal role in Great Britain and Italy than in France.[32] On the other hand, the belief that Jews attached a higher priority to international Jewish matters than to perceived French national concerns remained a constant throughout the period of this study. The following instances are prime examples of cases in which critics accused prominent French Jews of subordinating French national interests to international Jewish interests. In 1840, notable French Jews such as Aldophe Cremieux and James Rothschild found themselves the subject of intense criticism for their appeal for the liberation of Jews in the 1840 Damascus Affair. Again in 1858, in the midst of the notorious Mortara Affair, prominent French Jews including Cremieux and Rothschild joined with other well-known European Jews to put pressure on the Holy See to allow the Italian Jewish boy, Edgardo Mortara, to return to his Jewish parents. The Mortara Affair inspired the establishment of the Alliance Israélite Universelle by notable Jews in Paris in 1860. Aldophe Cremieux became the organization's first president. After 1860, the Alliance Israélite Universelle worked diligently to mobilize public opinion on behalf of suffering Jews, particularly in Romania

---

[32] Instances in which political anti-Semites attempted to connect prominent French Jews to the Zionist cause were Bernard Lazare's initial embrace of Theodor Herzl's Zionist claim of the uniformity of worldwide Jewish identity and Léon Blum's public profession of adherence to the Zionist cause, as well as his role as one of the initiators of the socialist Pro-Palestine Committee (Kingston, *Anti-Semitism*, 78).

and the Russian Empire. Many French non-Jews saw the Alliance Israélite Universelle as the base of the worldwide Jewish clandestine effort to undermine Christian Europe and to dominate the world.[33]

Before the Bolshevik Revolution, Jewish domination of the French state stood as the principal political anti-Semitic leitmotif. References to exaggerated Jewish influence over French rulers were certainly not unknown during the reigns of King Louis-Philippe and Emperor Louis Bonaparte. The establishment of the French Third Republic in the aftermath of France's humiliating defeat at the hands of the Germans in 1870 catapulted the theme of Jewish political power into the popular consciousness in a qualitatively new fashion. Drumont had been one of France's first anti-Semites to lay blame for the defeat of France at the feet of wealthy and politically influential French Jews of German origin, who, he charged, had conspired with their co-religionists in Bismarck's Prussia to trample on French national interests. Drumont would again level the charge of Jewish treachery in his vitriolic accusation that the Dreyfus Affair constituted one element of the Jewish plot to sell France out to the Germans. In his immensely popular 1886 book *La France Juive*, Drumont insisted, moreover, that the Jews (including many newcomers) held disproportionate power within the French state administration. For Drumont, the Jews, by virtue of their wealth and purported influence over the Freemasons, exerted their disproportionate political influence both directly, through holding government positions, but more importantly indirectly, through the ability to control members of the French Senate, National Assembly, and ministries of the government. To cement his case against the Jews, Drumont highlighted the alleged role of Jews in the collapse of the Panama Company.[34]

Several French anti-Semitic publicists before World War I adhered to Drumont's campaign against the purported Jewish control of the French state. Among the most notable adherents were Charles Maurras and Urbain Gohier. In 1889, Maurras had charged that the Jews, by comprising "a state within the state," had successfully prevailed over the French state. Urbain Gohier, a disciple and collaborator of Drumont, also turned his attention to the alleged Jewish domination of the state in his acutely anti-Semitic work *La terreur juive*. Gohier claimed that international Jewry, by constituting a resolutely homogeneous, highly disciplined, and self-interested nation of twelve million, exercised a

---

[33] Lindemann, *Accused*, 36–39; Pierrard, *Juifs*, 24.
[34] Wilson, *Ideology*, 379–91.

preponderant influence on the governmental administrations of the various European nations. Gohier added that these particular traits of the Jewish nation have allowed Jews to achieve universal domination.[35]

By the time of the infamous Dreyfus Affair, many of France's leading anti-Semites felt no hesitation in referring to the French Third Republic as "La République juive" (The Jewish republic) and accepting Drumont's charge that, like Judas Iscariot's betrayal of Christ, the Jews of France had ill served the French nation.[36] We have already seen that several notable rich French Jews had been implicated in a number of financial and political scandals, such as the collapse of the Union Générale Bank, the crash of the copper market, and the Panama fiasco of the early Third Republic. The association of Jews with these scandals fueled the allegation of undue Jewish political influence. But this charge against French Jewry had additional sources. Among these sources was the distaste that many French conservatives, Catholics, and royalists held for the Opportunist Party, France's dominant political party during the 1870s and 1880s. The Opportunists ushered in a series of controversial reforms, and the party's leader, Léon Gambetta, had, it was commonly believed, relied on Jewish financial assistance and political advice. Among the controversial legislation approved during the era of the Opportunists were the Ferry Laws. By establishing secular control over primary education, the architects of the Ferry Laws sought to attenuate the power of the Catholic Church and political conservatives in France's extensive countryside. Many French Jews applauded the introduction of the new legislation on education, and two Jews in particular, Paul Grunebaum-Ballin and Camille Sée, were singled out as key governmental figures responsible for the new laws on primary and secondary secular-republican education. The new legislation elicited heated protest from the conservative-clerical camp and gave impetus to the anti-Semitic claim that French Jews and Freemasons had achieved a victory in their ancient crusade to destroy the foundations of Christian Europe.[37]

The Dreyfus Affair (1894–1906) unquestionably marked a high point in French anti-Semitism before the Holocaust. Attacks on Jewish property (and occasionally on Jews) blanketed the large cities and towns of

---

[35] Birnbaum, *Anti–Semitism*, 234–35; Winock, *Nationalism*, 82–83.

[36] Joining Drumont in characterizing the French Third Republic as "La République Juive" were Maurice Barrès and Charles Maurras (Birnbaum, *La France*, 61).

[37] Cohen, "Dreyfus," 301; Wilson, *Ideology*, 379, 391; Lindemann, *Esau's*, 211–14; Birnbaum, *La France*, 61–63; Almog, *Nationalism*, 46–47; Wistrich, *Antisemitism*, 126–28; Winock, *Nationalism*, 12–13; Arendt, *Origins*, 95–97.

France and French Algeria, particularly, in 1898. Moreover, French voters in unprecedented numbers turned out to elect National Assembly
deputies openly espousing anti-Semitism.[38] Antipathy toward the
French Jewish community contained religious, racial, economic, and
political features. The political attacks on Jews typically involved accusations of inordinate Jewish influence within the French State and allegations of Jewish treachery. French anti-Semites frequently portrayed
Captain Dreyfus as a pawn of the international Jewish conspiracy that
sought to enslave the French nation to its Jewish masters. Jules Baron's
(elected to the National Assembly from the western French district
of Cholet in 1898) campaign declaration that he would oppose the
coalition of Jewish financiers and Léon Borie's (elected to the National
Assembly from the southwestern French department of Corrèze in 1898)
campaign promise that he would "silence this gang of cosmopolitan Jews
who, for six months, have been attacking the French nation, slandering
the army, and causing trouble in the country generally" typified the anti-
Semitic claim of the existence of a powerful disloyal Jewish conspiracy.[39]

During the first two decades of the twentieth century, the level of
anti-Semitism abated in France. The combination of the exoneration
of Captain Dreyfus, an improving economic situation in France, and
the outbreak of World War I probably contributed to the attenuation of
French anti-Semitism. Maurice Barrès' praise of Jewish sacrifice and patriotism in World War I symbolized the new (albeit temporary) attitude
among segments of the French right during this period.[40] The respite
in French anti-Semitism was short-lived, for the Bolshevik Revolution
and the outbreak of revolutionary socialist unrest throughout Europe

---

[38] Wilson, *Ideology*; Marrus and Paxton, *Vichy*, 31; Wistrich, *Antisemitism*, 128–29;
Birnbaum, *Anti-Semitism*, 1. Also, Marrus and Paxton (*Vichy*, 31) report that
in the 1902 French national elections, fifty-nine deputies were elected under
the banner of the fervently nationalistic and anti-Semitic Ligue de la Patrie
Française.

[39] Wilson, *Ideology*, 16–17.

[40] Winock, *Nationalism*, 86; Birnbaum, *Anti-Semitism*, 116–17. After World War I,
French anti-Semites would charge, as was the case in other European countries,
that Jews had attempted to avoid service in the French army during the conflict.
The charge included the claim that French Jewish fatalities in World War I
numbered between 1,350 and 3,500 – far below the percentage of non-Jewish
fatalities. An official report released in 1938 showed that the Jewish fatality
rate (3.5 percent) exceeded the non-Jewish rate (3.4 percent) and that out of a
French Jewish population of 190,000 in 1914, 32,000 Jews served in the military
and roughly 6,500 fell in combat (Schor, *L'Antisémitisme*, 287–88).

in the immediate aftermath of World War I reignited the smoldering flame of anti-Semitism. Under the direction of such well-known French anti-Semites as Léon Daudet, Charles Maurras, and Jacques Bainville, the Action française once again picked up the anti-Semitic banner, accusing French Jewish socialist politicians such as Léon Blum, Pierre Mendes France, and Georges Mandel of passivity during World War I. At about the same time, other anti-Semitic voices joined the crusade led by the Action française. Among them we find Urbain Gohier, a former collaborator of Drumont, who charged in an August 1920 edition of the anti-Semitic review *La Vieille France* that the Alliance Israélite Universelle had orchestrated the deaths of 1.7 million Frenchmen in World War I in order to resettle more than a million Jews in France. Also in February 1920 in *La Vieille France*, Gohier published a complete French version of the "Protocols of the Elders of Zion" (*Protocoles des Sages de Sion*). The "Protocols" went through three separate editions in 1920 alone and thereafter was widely circulated and reprinted, chiefly by Monsignor Jouin, curator of Sant'Agostino in Paris and founder of the *Revue Internationale des Sociétés Secrètes*. In its editions, the French newspaper *L'opinion* summarized the subject matter of the "Protocols," while the anti-Semitic daily *La Libre Parole* serialized in roughly twenty installments its complete contents. That the highly influential British daily *The Times* eventually reported that the "Protocols" was a forgery failed to dislodge many ardent French anti-Semites from the belief that Jews and revolutionary unrest went together. As Jacques Bainville of Action française observed upon the acknowledgement of the falseness of the "Protocols," proof of the authenticity of the document is not essential, for everyone knows that the Jews are behind the Bolshevik menace.[41]

As many have suggested, the explosive popularity of the "Protocols" after 1917 can largely be attributed to the fear of the spread of revolutionary socialism and the association of Jews with revolutionary socialism. The electoral popularity of the French socialist left had risen dramatically between 1898 and 1924. In the 1898 national elections, the socialist left obtained 11.3 percent of the popular vote, while in the 1924 national elections, the socialist left vote reached 47.8 percent. The

[41] Weber, *Action*, 200–01; Birnbaum, *Anti-Semitism*, 116–17; Birnbaum, *La France*, 107–110; Schor, *L'Opinion*, 188; Michel Winock, "L'héritage contre-révolutionnaire." In Michel Winock, ed., *Histoire de l'extrême droite en France* (Paris, 1993), 45–46; Pierrard, *Juifs*, 234.

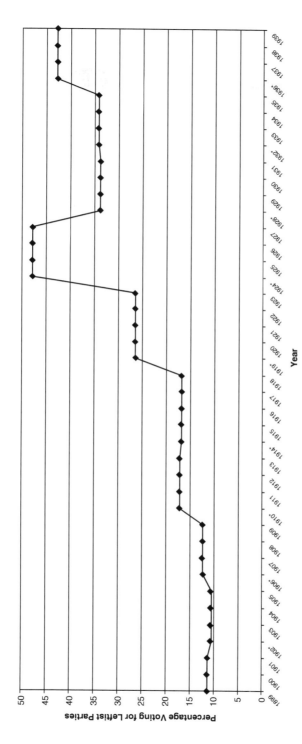

Figure 5.2a. Percentage of votes cast for leftist parties in France, 1899–1939. *Note:* Years with an asterisk are national election years. Figures are carried over in off-election years. *Sources:* Flora (1983), Mackie and Rose (1982).

French Communist Party alone won 9.8 percent of the popular vote in the 1924 elections. Between 1928 and 1936, the combined socialist left vote in France ranged from a low of 33.9 percent in 1928 to a high of 42.8 percent in 1936. The year 1936 brought the left Popular Front to power in France. In the Popular Front's electoral victory, the Socialist Party gained 19.9 percent of the popular vote, followed by 15.3 percent for the Communist Party, and 7.6 percent for the Socialist Republicans.

The notion that Jews and revolutionary socialism were inextricably linked had been advanced as early as 1886 in Drumont's *La France Juive*. Drumont had written that the Jews created socialism, internationalism, and nihilism and that the principal leaders of these movements were all Jews. Years before the "Protocols" would appear and allege that rich Jewish financiers funded revolutionary socialist movements, Drumont had asserted that Jews manipulated the socialist movement in order to achieve their own capitalist objectives.[42] Beginning in 1906, Gohier in his *Terreur Juive* made a similar case, emphasizing the Jewish role in the invention of socialism and in the financing of socialist publications. More specifically, Gohier claimed that twelve rich Jews, including Levy-Bruhl, Louis Dreyfus, Salomon Reinach, and Léon Blum, had financed the initial launching of the principal revolutionary socialist newspaper *L'Humanité*, and that the Pereire (Jewish) Bank had contributed large sums of money to another widely circulated socialist newspaper, the *Lanterne*. Thirty-two years later, the anti-Semitic journal *Je suis partout* would publish a story recirculating Gohier's profession of Jewish financing of socialism and adding that each of the twelve rich Jews contributing to the socialist journal *L'Humanité* represented one of the twelve tribes of Israel. Before the Bolshevik Revolution, the alleged role of Jewish financing of socialism found confirmation in other quarters. Georges Valois, in his 1909 *La Monarchie et la classe ouvrière*, noted that capitalist French Jews not only subsidized the socialist newspaper *L'Humanité* but also funded working-class infiltrators to undermine local French working-class organizations.[43] Let us not think that the perception that Jews and revolutionary socialism were tightly linked implanted itself solely in the minds of rabid French anti-Semites such as Drumont, Gohier, and Maurras. The accusation that Jews were behind the revolutionary socialist unrest striking Europe during the postwar years spread

---

[42] Wilson, *Ideology*, 350–51.
[43] Schor, *L'Antisémitisme*, 121; Soucy, *French*, 153.

far beyond the confines of the ultra-nationalistic anti-Semitic camp in France. The highly influential newspaper *Le Temps*, the radical socialist newspaper *L'Heure*, and several other French newspapers wrote of the prominent role Jews played in the Bolshevik Revolution. Newspapers such as *L'Ordre Public* charged that Leon Trotsky was the avenger of the Jewish people, while *La Voix Nationale* depicted the close connection between Bolshevism and Judaism as "un air de famille."[44]

During the interwar period in France, advocates of the charge that Jews were behind revolutionary socialism had no need to look beyond France's own borders to confirm their suspicions about the association. Anti-Semites could point to the leadership and the rank and file of the French socialist and communist parties. The SFIO (Section Française de l'Internationale Ouvrière), the principal French socialist movement, counted among its leaders a number of notable Jews, including Blum, Ziromsky, Moch, Grumbach, Rosenfel, Bloch, and Levy. Regarding the Communist Party, Jews never attained the positions of leadership in the French Communist Party that Jews achieved in Eastern European Communist Parties such as the Romanian Communist Party during the interwar period. But objective totals or proportions do not always dispel myths. French anti-Semites opportunistically focused their attack on the leadership role of several Russian and Polish immigrant Jews in the formation of the French Communist Party and of the left-wing labor organizations the CGTU and the CGT in the early 1920s. The list of Jews playing notable roles in the early years of the French Communist Party included Abraham Bronès, Peretz-Markich, Charles Rappoport, Marc Jarblum, and Boris Souvarine. Boris Souvarine became a particular target of the anti-Semitic press. That Souvarine adhered closely to the "Moscow" line seemed to confirm the allegation of his "foreignness" and his disloyalty to the French nation. During the late 1920s and 1930s, several immigrant Jews, among them Herman Maltchotski, Charles Aronovitch, Albert Kornfeld, and Wolf Sarabski, functioned as key organizers of revolutionary activities among newly arrived Eastern European Jewish immigrants, while diverse immigrant Jews founded radical newspapers such as *La Voix ouvrière*, *La Tribune*, *La Voix*, *L'Etincelle*, *La Vérité*, and the leftist Naie Press.[45] Eastern European Jewish immigrants could also be found among the rank and file of the various revolutionary

---

[44] Pierrard, *Juifs*; Winock, *Nationalism*.

[45] Schor, *L'Antisémitisme*, 121; Simon Cuker et al., *Juifs Révolutionnaires: Une page d'histoire du Yidichland en France* (Paris, 1987); Lindemann, *Esau's*, 435.

socialist organizations in France, as well as being mainstays within the left's voting bloc.[46] Schuker asserts that Jewish voters proved decisive in the electoral victories of ten Popular Front candidates in 1936, including seven communists from the Paris region.[47] Immigrant Russian and Polish Jewish contributions to the French revolutionary left were not solely responsible for fueling the allegation of a Jewish attachment to revolutionary socialism between the two world wars. More specifically, between 1933 and 1939, nearly 55,000 German and Austrian Jewish refugees passed through France. During their exile in France, many of these anti-Nazi Jewish refugees continued to publish scholarly articles and books that tended to harbor socialist or communist sympathies. Moreover, many of these exiled Jews, joined by their coreligionists, tried to enlist French support for boycotts of German goods as well as to stir up anti-Nazi sentiments within France. In the minds of a sizeable segment of the pacifist French population, it was particularly disturbing that recent Jewish immigrants and refugees sought to unsettle the already fragile French and German relationship. Thus, in the minds of French anti-Semites, such as the renowned writer Céline, Jews became synonymous with communists, and anticommunism became equivalent to anti-Semitism.[48]

   The electoral victory of the French Popular Front in 1936 catapulted French political anti-Semitism to center stage. No single occurrence, save the Dreyfus Affair, did more to ignite French anti-Semitism and to unite its bickering factions than the coming to power of the Popular Front, led by the Jewish socialist leader Léon Blum. Over the course of the roughly two years during which the Popular Front held power in France, venomous vitriol aimed largely at the figure of Léon Blum poured forth. The anti-Semitic press, in referring to the Blum government,

[46] Weber, *Hollow*, 107; Schuker, "Origins," 172.

[47] Schuker, "Origins," 172. The May 25, 1926, assassination in Paris of the rightist Ukrainian nationalist and military leader Semyon Petliura by Scholem Schwartzbard, a Russian-Polish Jewish poet and watchmaker, might well have served to reinforce the link between immigrant Jews and revolutionary socialist activities. It has been suggested that Schwartzbard acted on behalf of the tens of thousands of Jews murdered in the Eastern European pogroms of 1919. A French court ultimately acquitted Schwartzbard in August 1927 (Marrus and Paxton, *Vichy*, 25).

[48] Weber, *Hollow*, 104, 107; Winock, *Nationalism*, 276–78; Kingston, *Anti-Semitism*, 128–29.

frequently employed terms like *"cabinet du Talmud," "la révolution juive,"* *"la riposte du youpin,"* and *"le gouvernement du youpin-cher."*[49] For French anti-Semites, the existence of a socialist and communist presence on the margins of French politics was one thing, but the coming to power of a leftist coalition headed by Léon Blum, the bane of the anti-Semitic French right for nearly three decades, was simply too much to swallow. For many, Léon Blum's ascension to the office of premier fulfilled the dreaded prophecy of the Jewish conquest of world power laid out in the "Protocols."[50] Birnbaum opines that opposition to Blum's "Jewish origins" reached well beyond the fringes of France's anti-Semitic nationalist right. Birnbaum points to the public reaction to the encounter between Blum and Xavier Vallat, the French deputy who assailed Blum for his Jewish ancestry during Blum's swearing-in ceremony in the Chamber of Deputies on June 6, 1936. In front of the Chamber, Vallat publicly called into question Blum's rights as a Jew to serve as the head of the French government. Vallat chafed at the idea that for the first time in the history of this Gallo-Roman nation, a Jew will govern the French people. Vallat expressed his pronounced trepidation that a "subtle Talmudist," rather than a man whose roots belong to the soil, would head the French government.[51] For Birnbaum, the fact that so many deputies failed to protest Vallat's deplorable actions suggested considerable support for his scandalous behavior.[52] The hatred among many French anti-Semites and conservatives for Léon Blum reached such epidemic levels during the Popular Front that it could elicit from those quarters the popular slogan "rather Hitler than Blum." The Blum government's efforts to mobilize an anti-Fascist and anti-Nazi front fostered closer ties between France's anti-Semitic and pacifist communities. Anti-Semites and French pacifists shared the belief that the French left and French Jewry,

[49] Pierrard, *Juifs*, 258–60. Schor (*L'Antisémitisme*, 98–99) notes that Blum was not the sole target of anti-Semitic ridicule during the Popular Front. The appointment of the socialist Jean Zay (whose mother was Protestant and father was Jewish) to the Blum cabinet evoked a furious outcry from anti-Semitic and patriotic groups. It appears that Zay had written a poem in 1924 in which he blamed French patriotism for the deaths of the more than 1.5 million French soldiers in World War I. During the years of the Popular Front, Zay's poem was reprinted and widely circulated by the anti-Semitic press.
[50] Marrus and Paxton, *Vichy*, 39; Winock, *Nationalism*, 146.
[51] Friedlaender, *Nazi Germany*, 222.
[52] Birnbaum, *Anti-Semitism*, 243–44.

by preparing France for a "Jewish" war against Hitler, was once again placing Jewish interests ahead of France's national interests. The famous French anti-Semitic writer Céline held such sentiments. Céline, an honored and wounded veteran of World War I, wrote that if a new war broke out between France and Germany, it would be a war perpetrated by international Jewry for the delight of all Jews.[53]

## GERMANY

Not unlike the situation in France, political anti-Semitism in Germany before the Holocaust focused on the alleged excessive Jewish influence within the German state and Jewish participation in and leadership of a subversive revolutionary left aspiring to achieve national and world power. Although not as commonly employed as the anti-Semitic leitmotifs of undue Jewish political influence and Jewish sponsorship of revolutionary movements, the theme of Jews forming a state within a state and Jewish funding of a secret world government, referred to as the "Jewish International," occasionally surfaced.[54] This particular charge, which incorporated the portrayal of Jews as traitors to the German nation, typically found expression during periods of heightened economic or political crisis.

The charge that Jews adhered to subversive and radical movements had secured a place within a segment of the German popular consciousness decades before the establishment of the Second Reich in 1871. Like large numbers of German non-Jews, many German Jews during the pre-1848 period actively supported the radical-democratic movement within several German states in pursuit of political freedom and civil liberties. To get an impression of Jewish participation in the radical-democratic movement, one need only look at the list of prominent Jewish contributors to the most influential German radical newspaper of the 1840s, the *Rheinische Zeitung*. Besides the widely known Karl Marx (editor) and Heinrich Heine, the list included Moses Hess, Dagobert Oppenheim, Theodor Creizenach, and Andreas Gottschalk. The association of Jews with radicalism found favor with Heinrich von Treitschke, the notable nineteenth-century German historian, who referred to Heinrich Heine,

---

[53] Winock, *Nationalism*, 19–20, 276–78.

[54] Niewyk ("Solving," 348) reports that two conservative journals, *Deutsche Reich-spost* and *Der Reichsbote*, identified the Paris-based Alliance Israélite Universelle as the nerve center for the so-called Jewish International.

Ludwig Boerne, and Eduard Gans as "Oriental choir-leaders of the Revolution."[55]

The advent of revolutionary socialism and labor activism during the second half of the nineteenth century triggered an outburst of German political anti-Semitism lasting until the Holocaust. Two of the principal founders of nineteenth-century socialism, Karl Marx and Ferdinand Lassalle, were German and had Jewish backgrounds. After the deaths of Marx (1883) and Lassalle (1864), prominent Jews continued to serve in important positions within the German Social Democratic Party. Among them were Paul Singer, Eduard Bernstein, Carl Hirsch, Hugo Haase, Ludwing Frank, Max Cohen-Reuss, Berthold Heymann, Ernst Heilmann, Joseph Bloch, Georges Weill, Georg Gradnauer, Samuel Kokosky, Max Kayser, Gabriel Loewenstein, Rosa Luxemburg, and Rudolf Hilferding.[56] In addition to the fact that many Jews belonged to the Social Democratic Party, what probably made the perception of the link between Jews and revolutionary socialism more menacing to many Germans was the substantial electoral popularity of the German Social Democratic Party. The party's share of the popular vote had climbed from 27.2 percent in 1898 to 34.8 percent in 1912. Between 1881 and 1914, 43 of the 417 Social Democratic Party deputies elected to the German Reichstag were Jews, representing a rate 10 times the Jewish proportion of the German population. Anxiety about socialist popularity and Jewish presence within the socialist movement became especially apparent in the wake of the stunning SPD victory in the 1912 Reichstag elections. In these elections, the number of SPD deputies rose from 43 to 110, giving the party the largest share of seats in the Reichstag. The SPD's electoral landslide, and the fact that twenty of the twenty-five Jews elected to the Reichstag belonged to the Social Democratic Party, caused considerable consternation among Germany's anti-Semitic and conservative camps. The anti-Semitic and right-wing

---

[55] Wistrich, Socialism, 73; Pulzer, Jews, 81. Though they were referred to as Jews by anti-Semites, Heine was a convert and Marx's father had converted to Lutheranism before the younger Marx's birth.

[56] Both Lindemann (Esau's, 172) and Wistrich (Socialism, 81–82) remind us that, contrary to the conventional wisdom, the German Social Democratic Party at the end of the nineteenth century was led by three non-Jews – Bebel, Kautsky, and Wilhelm Liebknecht. Before World War I, only two Jews, Paul Singer and Hugo Haase, held positions within the highest administrative echelon of the SPD. Both Singer and Haase co-chaired (at different intervals) the SPD parliamentary group, and Haase also co-chaired the SPD party executive.

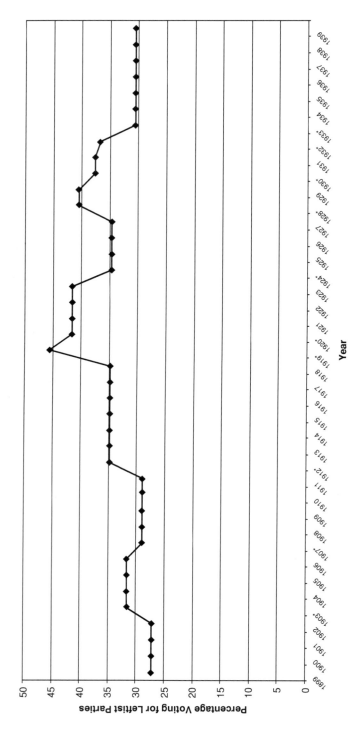

Figure 5.2b. Percentage of votes cast for leftist parties in Germany, 1899–1939. *Note:* Years with an asterisk are national election years. Figures are carried over in off-election years. *Sources:* Flora (1983), Mackie and Rose (1982).

press attacked the supposed subversive activities of "international Jewry" and dubbed the 1912 elections the "Jewish elections" (*Judenwahlen*).[57]

The association of immigrant Jews from Eastern and Central Europe with subversive revolutionary movements further enhanced German political anti-Semitism. As early as the 1880s, the association apparently caught the attention of officials in the German government. In 1884, Robert von Puttkamer, Prussia's minister of interior, justified the expulsion of Polish Jews from Berlin on the basis of their predisposition to nihilistic and social democratic ideologies. Twenty-one years later, in the aftermath of the abortive 1905 Russian Revolution, cabinet ministers in Chancellor von Buelow's government warned the German Reichstag about the subversive propensities of Russian Jewish students entering Germany. Chancellor von Buelow advised his cabinet in 1907 of the alleged political activities of immigrant Jewish students from Eastern and Central Europe who, von Buelow charged, worked on behalf of the German Social Democratic Party. That German SPD Reichstag deputies frequently spoke against restrictions on Eastern European Jewish immigration during the decade preceding World War I did little to mitigate apprehensions about a link between immigrant Jews and the German left. If German anti-Semites sought to reinforce the picture of immigrant Jews as adherents of revolutionary socialism, they had only to point to the central role that eminent Eastern European Jews played in the German revolutionary socialist movement. Within the SPD, the list of well-known Eastern and Central European Jews holding key positions included Eugene Leviné, Wilhelm Buchholz, Leo Jogisches, Karl Radek, Alexander Stein, Alexander "Parvus" Helphand, Adolf and Heinrich Braun, Max Beer, Friedrich Stampfer, and Rosa Luxemburg. Moreover, within the SPD, the Russian and Polish immigrant Jews tended to gravitate toward the party's extreme left wing. No single individual personified the purported Jewish affinity for extreme revolutionary socialism better than the renowned Polish-Jewish immigrant Rosa Luxemburg. Thus, it comes as little surprise that in the aftermath of the Bolshevik Revolution, the perception that Polish and Russian Jews fleeing the violence of anti-Semitic pogroms carried with them the "Bolshevik virus" attained epidemic proportions.[58]

---

[57] Sperber, *Kaiser's*, 258; Wistrich, *Socialism*, 75–76, 80–81; Kauders, *German*, 31, 35; Steiman, *Paths*, 161; Friedlaender, *Nazi Germany*, 75.

[58] Wistrich, *Socialism*, 82–83; Wertheimer, *Unwelcome*, 24–25, 39–40, 103–04; Blackbourn, "Roman Catholics," 119-120. Also, German and Austrian

As we have seen above, political anti-Semitism took a quantum leap after the successful Bolshevik Revolution. The disproportionate representation of Jews in the newly emerging communist movement and the spreading popularity of the "Protocols" gave impetus to the charge of a Jewish plot to sow disorder as a means to the Jewish conquest of world power. In Germany, in the immediate aftermath of Germany's surrender in November 1919, German anti-Semites quickly highlighted the disproportionate presence of Jews within the new Reich government, the revolutionary Marxist Spartacist movement, and the newly founded KPD (German Communist Party). The Council of People's Commissars governing Germany after the armistice included Jews from both the socialist and German Democratic Party (DDP) camps. Among the socialists were Otto Landsberg, Hugo Haase, Emmanuel Wurm, Joseph Herzfeld, Eduard Bernstein, and Oskar Cohn. From the German Democratic Party came Eugen Schiffer and Hugo Preuss. Preuss would subsequently craft the first draft of the new Weimar Constitution. Jews also comprised three of the four people's commissars governing the city of Berlin, while three socialist Jews – Paul Hirsch, Hugo Simon, and Kurt Rosenfeld – gained the posts of prime minister, finance minister, and justice minister, respectively, in the new Prussian cabinet. Following the national elections of January 19, 1919, in which the socialist left vote rose to 45.5 percent of the total vote, the new government under Philip Scheidemann included four Jews – Preuss, Landsberg, Schiffer (replaced by Dernburg, a Jew), and Gotheim. With the ensuing establishment of the Weimar Republic, notable Jews from the ranks of both the SPD and the DDP found themselves in important government positions. Hugo Preuss and Walther Rathenau, both of the DDP, were instrumental in shaping the early years of the Weimar Republic. Rathenau, after having organized the war economy during World War I, served as foreign minister until his assassination.

Eastern European Jews such as Rosa Luxemburg, Leo Jogiches, Eugen Leviné, and Karl Radek, along with German Jews such as Kurt Eisner, Gustav Landauer, Erich Muehsam, and Ernst Toller played pivotal roles in the revolutionary unrest of 1918 and 1919 in Germany. Kurt Eisner

---

anti-Semitic groups gave considerable attention to the fact that in 1903, Otto Weininger, an Austrian Jew, had published *Sex and Character*(*Geschlecht und Charakter*), in which he drew a connection between the absence of spirituality among Jews and a Jewish attachment to communism. By 1919, this widely read book had gone through eighteen editions (Mosse, *Final Solution*, 108–09).

proclaimed the Bavarian Socialist Republic in Munich four days before
the signing of the armistice. The Berlin-born Eisner, whom the German
right and anti-Semites referred to as a "Galician Jew," became the new republic's first prime minister and minister for foreign affairs, but he would
fall victim to an assassin's bullet on February 21, 1919.[59] On April 7,
1919, a Soviet Republic was proclaimed in Munich that included at its
helm four Jews – Ernst Toller, Gustav Landauer, Erich Muehsam, and
Arnold Walder. A second Soviet Republic succeeded the first and included among its leaders three Jews – Eugen Leviné, Tovia Axelrod,
and Ernst Toller. In Berlin, seven Jews were among the founding party
members of the Spartacists and the KPD. Four of these Jews – Rosa
Luxemburg, Leo Jogiches, Paul Levi, and August Thalheimer – were
elected to the KPD's eleven-member Central Committee. Bavaria and
Berlin were not the exceptions. We find leftist Jews taking key roles in
the revolutionary unrest in Magdeburg, Dresden, Bremerhaven, Kiel,
the Ruhr, and the Palatinate.[60] The notable Jewish presence in the
revolutionary turmoil of 1918 and 1919 and in the establishment of the
Weimar Republic was a godsend for the German anti-Semitic crusade.[61]

It would be wrong to assume that the perception in Germany of a
Jewish affinity for the revolutionary left resided solely with ardent
German anti-Semites and zealous nationalists. The notion that Jews
performed a leadership role in the revolutionary left and that many
of these Jewish socialist revolutionaries harbored antinationalist sentiments (e.g., Kurt Eisner) had spread to the general population. Kauders

[59] Eisner incurred the particular wrath of many conservatives and anti-Semites
in Germany when he published incriminating documents pointing to German
responsibility for the outbreak of World War I. He also called for Germans to con-
tribute to the rebuilding of war-torn occupied territory (Friedlaender, "Political,"
158–60; Friedlaender, *Nazi Germany*, 91–92; Weiss, *Ideology*, 215).

[60] The association of Jews with the socialist and communist parties of Germany
would continue throughout the interwar period. What is often not told is that
the Jewish presence within both movements declined precipitously after the early
1920s. For instance, Luxemburg, a co-founder of the KPD, was succeeded by Paul
Levi, who was removed, as Wistrich (*Socialism*, 88–89) points out, as a prelude to
the Bolshevization of the German Communist Party. By 1930, no Jews served as
KPD deputies in the Reichstag. Within the SPD, by the end of the 1920s Jewish
intellectuals had lost the preeminence they had held before 1914 (Wistrich,
*Socialism*, 88–89).

[61] Pulzer, *Jews*, 208–210, 264; Ascheim, "Double," 229; Weiss, *Ideology*, 215; Friedlaender, "Political," 160; Friedlaender, *Nazi Germany*, 92; Lindemann, *Esau's*,
483.

reports that in the aftermath of World War I, several regional news-papers, including the *Duesseldorfer Nachrichten*, the *Gemeindeblatt*, and the *Fraenkischer Kurier* of Nuremberg, chastised Jewish revolutionaries for their purported efforts to instigate revolutionary labor unrest both inside and outside of Germany. The Bavarian Catholic press assailed the alleged Jewish role in the Bavarian Socialist Republic. The Bavar-ian People's Party newspaper, *Bayerische Volkszeitung*, referred to Eisner as that "Galician Jew," who because of his tribal disposition has scant knowledge of the Bavarian soul. The paper claimed further that Jews comprised 80 percent of all revolutionaries.[62]

The years from 1918 to 1923 marked a new high point in German anti-Semitism. Among the anti-Semitic acts taking place between 1918 and 1923 and receiving the greatest attention were the anti-Semitic activi-ties of the Deutschvoelkischer Schutz-und Trutzbund; the assassination of Germany's Jewish foreign minister, Rathenau; Hitler's anti-Semitic campaign in Munich; and a series of violent attacks on Eastern European Jewish immigrants.[63] With the stabilization of the German mark and the quelling of attempts to seize power by the extreme right and left, Germany experienced something of a break in anti-Semitism, as evi-denced by the number of reported anti-Semitic acts and anti-Semitic attitudes. However, this respite lasted less than ten years. Though the threat of a revolutionary socialist takeover, which had seemed so likely in 1919 and 1920, dissipated, and the number of Jews serving in key govern-ment positions dropped considerably, the association of Jews with revolu-tionary socialism and with the Weimar system remained steadfast in the minds of many Germans. If German anti-Semites during the relatively tranquil years of the Weimar Republic had increasing difficulty pointing to specific Jews in key government positions or within the higher ech-elons of the German socialist and communist movements, they could always call attention to other political arenas in which Jews seemed to dominate. The arts comprised one such arena. German Jews prevailed in the field of literary criticism during the Weimar era. Friedlaender asserts that Jews comprised many of the most esteemed critics, novel-ists, poets, dramatists, and essayists in Weimar Germany. And, in par-ticular, the Jews gravitated toward the newer and more radical artistic schools, such as German expressionism and neo-objectivism, and toward left-wing political, social, and cultural criticism. For those in Germany

---

[62] Kauders, *German*, 56–58, 67, 77.
[63] Pulzer, *Jews*, 344.

seeking to find the hand of the Jews in antinationalist and leftist causes or in the threatening new modernist movements, the arts provided a convenient context.[64]

Political anti-Semitism in Germany picked up steam once again after 1930 with the onset of the Great Depression, the resurgence of Germany's Communist Party, and the growing popularity of the anti-Semitic Nazi Party. The German Communist Party had seen its share of the national vote rise from 10.6 percent in the 1928 national elections to 16.9 percent in November 1932. During the crisis years of 1930 through 1932, with skyrocketing unemployment, collapsing governmental coalitions, and incessant street battles between rightist and leftist paramilitary formations, many Germans feared a communist takeover. And in the minds of many, the link between revolutionary socialism and the Jews seemed real. In a book entitled *Communism in Germany* written by Adolf Ehrt in 1933, Ehrt referred to the Marxist Comintern as "the Jewish-Marxistic mortal enemy of the German nation." Ehrt claimed that according to published newspaper reports, Jews comprised 14 percent of the membership of the KPD and 17 percent of the SDP. Hitler's Nazi Party opportunistically capitalized on the rising fear of revolutionary socialism. Nazi speeches and writings were frequently peppered with references to the threat of communism. The "*Gefahr des Bolschewismus in Deutschland*" was dramatized in conjunction with the growth in support for the German Communist Party. Much like Mussolini's Italian Fascist Party, the NSDAP presented itself as a bulwark against the spread of communism. But in startling contrast to the Italian Fascist Party (at least until 1938), the German Nazi Party focused on the association between Jews and Marxist socialism. The NSDAP, even after forcing the socialist and communist parties to go underground after March 1933, would continue to highlight this alleged association until the final days of the Third Reich.[65]

In my discussion of French political anti-Semitism, I mentioned that during particular political, military, and financial crises, anti-Semitic groups emphasized alleged Jewish disloyalty to the national cause. For example, in the wake of France's humiliating defeat in the Franco-Prussian War of 1870, French anti-Semites accused prominent Jews of selling out French interests to the Germans. Like their counterparts in France,

---

[64] Friedlaender, *Nazi Germany*, 108–09.
[65] Brustein, *Logic*, 57; Gordon, *Germans*, 67.

German anti-Semitic groups during periods of major national turmoil engaged in the practice of labeling Jews as disloyal subjects. Hitler's anti-Jewish theory that Germany's (unexpected) surrender in World War I resulted from a "Jewish stab in the back" is the best-known example of the charge of Jewish disloyalty. The roots of Hitler's accusation can be traced back at least as far as 1915. Among the twelve Jewish deputies serving in the German Reichstag in 1915, seven (Bernstein, Cohn, Herzfeld, Hoch, Stadthagen, Wurm, and Haase) had voted against a measure to extend war credits. Jewish members of the pacifist USPD (Independent Social Democratic Party), led by Haase, not only opposed additional war credits but also disapproved of German annexation of conquered territories. That Jewish socialists such as Cohen-Reuss, Lansberg, Heilmann, and Block displayed ultra-patriotism mattered little to those predisposed to accept the charge of Jewish disloyalty. Cementing further the alleged link between leftist Jews and German pacifism, Rosa Luxemburg helped to establish in late 1915 a revolutionary Marxist antiwar group in Germany. Rumors of military shirking among German Jews were fueled by the fact that a number of Jewish parliamentary deputies and prominent Jewish revolutionaries had spoken out against the war. These rumors became sufficiently widespread that Adolf Wild von Hohenborn of the Prussian War Ministry launched a census in the fall of 1916 to assess the extent of the Jewish contribution to the German military effort and Jewish participation at the front. The results of the census were never published by the German military, but some officials in the German War Ministry leaked a rumor that the results, if made public, would be devastating to the Jews. In the aftermath of the armistice, German anti-Semitic groups picked up on the fiction of Jewish "goldbricking" and employed it in their anti-Semitic propaganda efforts. In 1932, the Central Association of German Citizens of Jewish Faith presented detailed documentation showing that Jewish participation in frontline military service equaled that of non-Jewish Germans. The report went on to demonstrate that 12,000 of the roughly 140,000 Jews serving at the front in World War I had perished. Regardless of the Jewish documentation, the myth of Jewish absence from the German war effort had already become firmly entrenched in the minds of many Germans.[66]

---

[66] Wistrich, *Socialism*, 82, 87–88; Friedlaender, "Political," 153; Strauss, "Hostages," 166–67; Friedlaender, *Nazi Germany*, 75; Lindemann, *Esau's*, 401–02.

## GREAT BRITAIN

Political anti-Semitism in Great Britain embraced themes similar to those found in France and Germany. Before the Bolshevik Revolution, anti-Semites assailed British Jews for their purported influence over the British government, their alleged lack of national loyalty, and their supposed sponsorship and participation in a conspiracy to achieve world power. After the Bolshevik Revolution, British political anti-Semitism became obsessed with the perceived link between Jews and revolutionary socialism.

In an earlier chapter on economic anti-Semitism, I pointed to the anti-Semitic charge of disproportionate Jewish influence over the British government. This charge became particularly acute during the period of Disraeli's reign as prime minister, the Boer War, and the first two decades of the twentieth century. The prime culprits targeted here were wealthy London Jewish families, including the Rothschilds, Sassons, Cassels, Hirschs, Levy-Lawsons, Simons, Samuels, Montagus, Abrahams, and Issacs. Under the government of David Lloyd George (1918–22), several prominent Jews held key ministerial appointments. Among them were Lord Reading, viceroy of India; Sir Herbert Samuel, high commissioner of Palestine; Sir Alfred Mond, minister of health; and Edwin Montagu, secretary of state for India. The presence of so many high-ranking Jews led *Blackwood's Magazine* to remark that the inscription over 10 Downing Street should read "None but Hebrews may apply."[67]

Questions surrounding a split British Jewish allegiance or divided loyalties frequently surfaced during those periods in which Jews were perceived to hold key governmental positions or to wield excessive political influence. As I have already mentioned, Disraeli's handling of the Bulgarian massacre during the Eastern Crisis elicited charges that the prime minister placed the interests of international Jewry ahead of British interests.[68] Two notable occurrences during World War I once again brought the issue of Jewish loyalty to the forefront of British popular discourse and served to reignite British anti-Semitism. Many British Jews, particularly recent immigrants from czarist Russia, did not welcome Great Britain's alliance with Russia during World War I. Anti-Russian sentiment ran high, chiefly within London's East End. In April 1916, the British government passed the Conscription Act, which called upon

[67] Rubinstein, *History*, 206.
[68] Feldman, *Englishmen*, 120.

all British male citizens between the ages of eighteen and forty-one, as well as naturalized foreigners and special categories of "friendly neutral aliens" residing in Britain, to serve in the armed forces. However, the home secretary, Herbert Samuel (Jewish), issued an exception to the Conscription Act that mainly involved Russian Jewish residents. Samuel was aware of the intense Russian Jewish dislike for the oppressive czarist regime. Samuel, along with many others within the British Jewish and non-Jewish communities, hoped that the members of the resident Russian Jewish population would disregard their antipathy toward their former homeland and volunteer for military service. Samuel's wish failed to materialize, for relatively few Russian Jewish residents joined the war effort.[69] The special exemption for Russian Jewish residents ended with the collapse of the czarist regime in February 1917. Beginning in the spring and summer of 1917, eligible alien Russian Jews had the choice of joining the British military or facing deportation to Russia.[70] Thousands of Russian Jews applied for special exemptions from military service, for reasons ranging from chronic diseases to domestic hardships. By early summer 1917, with weekly reports of mounting British casualties and stalled military advances, large segments of British public opinion began to question Jewish loyalty, and incidents of anti-Jewish hysteria erupted throughout Great Britain. British cities with sizeable Russian Jewish populations became the scenes of violent attacks on property and persons. In Leeds, anti-Semitic riots broke out between June 3 and June 17, 1917. Shouts of "kill the Jews" were reported. The chief constable of Leeds claimed that roughly three-quarters of the 1,400 Russian Jews of military age in Leeds had refused to enroll in the British armed forces.[71]

In addition to the resistance displayed by thousands of alien Russian Jewish residents to participating in the British military during World War I, the issuance of the Balfour Declaration on November 2, 1917,

---

[69] Lindemann (*Esau's*, 398–99) notes that before 1916, British Jews were overrepresented as recruits in the British war effort. Lindemann also observes that within the British Jewish community, respected leaders expressed dissatisfaction with the reluctance of Russian Jewish immigrants to serve in the military.

[70] The fact that roughly 3,000 immigrant Russian Jews opted to return to Russia rather than serve in the British military during World War I was construed by British anti-Semites after the Bolshevik Revolution as an indication of the special attachment that Jews had for revolutionary socialism (Kadish, *Bolsheviks*, 216–17).

[71] Kadish, *Bolsheviks*, 46–47, 204–06, 227; Rubinstein, *History*, 199; Holmes, *Anti-Semitism*, 128–31; Lindemann, *Esau's*, 398–99; Smith, "Jewish," 55.

raised concerns about British Jewry's loyalty to Great Britain. I will not afford much space to the complicated history and intrigues surrounding the Balfour Declaration, since they have received much attention elsewhere. The Balfour Declaration called for British readiness to help in the building of a Jewish homeland in Palestine. Rather than an expression of empathy for the Jewish people, the Balfour Declaration was largely an opportunistic political instrument conceived by the British government to influence public opinion in postczarist Russia and in the United States. It appears that several members of Prime Minister Lloyd George's cabinet (as well as Lloyd George) believed that Russian Jews wielded tremendous power in the new revolutionary government in Russia. British support for a Jewish homeland was seen as a way to coax Russian Jews into keeping Russia engaged in the war against the Central Powers. Lest we forget, the outcome of World War I was very much in doubt in 1917. An underlying British assumption was that many Russian Jews were Zionists.[72] In terms of British political anti-Semitism, the Balfour Declaration signified for many non-Jews Jewish split loyalties. Certainly thousands of British Jews gave no thought to leaving Great Britain for Palestine, but the perception that many Jews residing in Great Britain eagerly sought to resettle in a Jewish homeland was disquieting to large numbers of British citizens.

Great Britain's greatest wave of political anti-Semitism burst forth in the wake of the Bolshevik Revolution. There is no question that the British government and press became obsessed with the spread of Bolshevism and with the alleged role of Jews as sponsors of and participants in revolutionary socialism in the years following the Bolshevik Revolution. If before 1917 the association of Jews with subversive movements remained largely the concern of the extreme nationalist right in Great Britain, after 1917 this association garnered notable support across British society. We have seen in the cases of France and Germany that the charge that Jews dominated the leadership of revolutionary socialist movements and sought to achieve world power through these movements had many adherents. This particular accusation failed to attract widespread support in Great Britain before 1917. Why? A large part of the explanation may lie in British Jewry's high degree of assimilation and in the persistence of a strong current of anti-Semitism within the British left. In France, the Dreyfus Affair generally marked the abandonment of anti-Semitism by the political left, and in Germany, the

[72] Kadish, *Bolsheviks*, 145–46; Almog, *Nationalism*, 99.

formidable presence of prominent Jews in that nation's leftist movement
served effectively to mute the voice of the small group of left-wing anti-
Semites. Before 1914, one was more likely to find anti-Semitic rhetoric
issuing forth from British leftists than from British Conservatives. The
tradition of leftist anti-Semitism lingered in Great Britain into the first
two decades of the twentieth century. Certainly the influential voices of
Beatrice Potter, J. A. Hobson, Henry M. Hyndman, and William Marcus
Thompson contributed to the persistence of British leftist anti-Semitism
and probably dissuaded many impoverished East End Jews from embracing the British left. The British left, until the outbreak of World War
I, continued to target "the capitalist Jew" and the "gold international."
In particular, the British left chastised the alleged role of international
Jewry in instigating the Boer War and disapproved of the powerful in-
fluence that wealthy Jews supposedly held in the court of King Edward
VII.[73]

More than any other event, the Bolshevik Revolution heightened
anti-Jewish sentiment in Great Britain. By highlighting the role of Jews
in the Bolshevik Revolution, the British press and several well-regarded
British political figures helped to galvanize the myth of a Jewish plan
to seize world power. The myth became all the more credible in the
post-1917 context of intense anti-German feelings; growing challenges
to British imperial and colonial power in India,[74] Ireland, and Egypt;
proliferating British mining and labor agitation; the increasing popularity of the British Labour Party; and the rising incidence of post–World
War I economic dislocations. Such a series of traumatic events produced
fertile soil for a claim that some nefarious power had masterminded a
grand conspiracy against British interests. In light of the growing attention given to the association between Jews and the despised Bolshevik
movement, Jews easily became the scapegoats for many of the troubles
befalling Great Britain. Great Britain's own involvement in Russia may
have also played a part in British efforts to tie the Jews to the Bolshevik
Revolution. The British government had embarked in 1919 and 1920

---

[73] Rubinstein, History, 98; Hirschfeld, "British," 97–108; Holmes, Anti-Semitism,
    68–69; Panayi, Immigration, 116; Lindemann, Esau's, 356.
[74] Unrest in India came in handy for British anti-Semites, according to Lebzelter
    ("Political," 389). British anti-Semites pointed to Bolshevik propaganda, which
    cited India as a prime location for revolutionary upheaval, and to the fact that
    two Jews headed up India policy – E. Montagu (secretary of state for India) and
    Lord Reading (viceroy).

upon a policy to aid militarily the anti-Bolshevik "White" forces in the hope of defeating the Soviet Red Army. The White forces launched several anti-Semitic pogroms in the former Pale of Settlement. The White generals justified the pogroms as necessary to extirpate "Jewish" Bolshevism. Various British press correspondents representing conservative newspapers began to include references to the "Jewish-Bolshevik" campaign in their reports.[75] Before turning to an examination of the role played by the British press and British politicians in fanning the flames of political anti-Semitism, it is worthwhile to survey the evolution of the British revolutionary left and the role that Jews played in it.

We have seen that both naturalized and immigrant Jews in both France and Germany during the immediate post–World War I period identified increasingly with revolutionary socialist movements. In important respects, the British Labour Party differed from its continental counterparts. The British Labour Party had issued forth from the combination of three principal strands within the trade union movement: the Independent Labour Party, the Fabian Society, and the British Socialist Party. Socialist ideology appeared generally to have failed to captivate the rank and file of the pre–World War I British Labour Party to the extent that it did on the continent.[76] When Lenin criticized parts of the labor movement for displaying a trade union mentality, he clearly had in mind the pre-war British Labour movement. Though radical elements, including the South Welsh miners and the Clydeside engineers, fostered a more socialist outlook, the nonsocialist trade unionists tended to dominate the party and to move it along a "gradualist" path into the 1920s.[77] The growth in Labour Party membership and electoral support contributed to the fear of a Jewish world conspiracy and to political anti-Semitism. In the second of the two national elections of 1910, the Labour Party had garnered a trifling 6.4 percent of the total vote. By 1918, the Labour Party's electoral share had jumped to 21.4 percent, and it would continue to rise until 1929, when the party gathered a robust 37.1 percent of the vote. The electoral fortunes of the Labour Party would decline briefly in the early 1930s but rise again in the elections of

---

[75] Kadish, Bolsheviks, 10–11; Kendall, Revolutionary, 24–27; Lebzelter, "Political," 390; Almog, Nationalism, 93–94.

[76] James Jupp, The Radical Left in Britain 1931–1941 (London, 1982), 147–48, 175.

[77] Jupp, Radical, 147–48; Henry Pelling, The British Communist Party: A Historical Profile (London, 1958), 6–7.

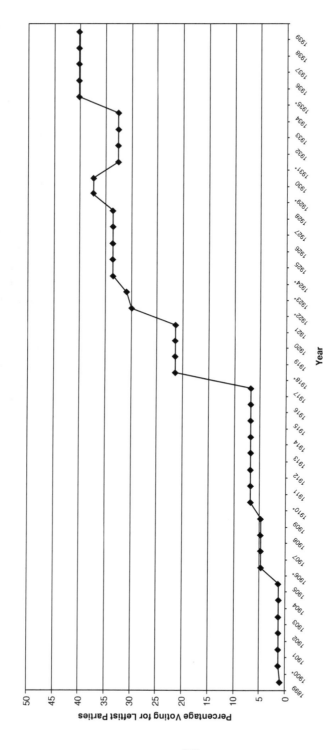

Figure 5.2c. Percentage of votes cast for leftist parties in Great Britain, 1899–1939. *Note*: Years with an asterisk are national election years. Figures are carried over in off-election years. *Sources*: Flora (1983), Mackie and Rose (1982).

1935, when the party received 38.1 percent of the national vote. The fact that in a number of elections during the early 1920s Communist Party candidates ran in districts without Labour Party opposition, and that the British Communist Party announced that several of its candidates were in fact official Labour Party nominees, reinforced the perception of a tie between the two parties. Thus, not surprisingly, the conservative mass daily the *Daily Mail* printed an editorial on November 15, 1922, entitled "Don't Forget to Vote Today: Against Socialism." The editorial stated: "We regret that the Labour Party has swung so far in the direction of Socialism, and in extreme cases even towards Communism and Bolshevism." The editorial reinforced the perception of a link between the Labour movement and communism, claiming: "The common sense of our people repudiates the socialism and the Bolshevism of the Labour leaders." By 1929, the break between the Labour Party and the Communist Party had become both official and real. However, as Kadish has aptly noted, many Conservatives failed to make distinctions among the British Labour Party, the Independent Labour Party, the British Socialist Party, and the British Communist Party and considered anyone left of the political center a "Bolshie."[78] This may help to explain why the Labour Party's impressive parliamentary victory in 1929, resulting in Ramsay McDonald's appointment as prime minister, initially sent shock waves through the British Conservative establishment, despite McDonald's gradualist approach and his harsh attacks on the British Communist Party's submissive dependence on Moscow.[79]

The two most radical political parties representing British labor were the ILP (Independent Labour party) and the CPGB (Communist Party of Great Britain). On many issues, the ILP stood to the left of the British Labour Party. For instance, whereas the Labour Party supported Britain's involvement in World War I, the ILP, along with the British Socialist Party, opposed participation. The ILP did not, however, embrace the extreme left's advocacy of the dictatorship of the proletariat or violent revolution as a means to seize power. After World War I, the ILP refused to join the Soviet Union – sponsored Comintern. The ILP contained roughly 30,000 members at the end of World War I. Membership in the ILP would decline generally during the 1920s and early 1930s, and by

---

[78] Kadish, *Bolsheviks*, 241.
[79] Richard M. Scammon, "The Communist Voting Pattern in British Parliamentary Elections." In James K. Pollock et al., eds., *British Election Studies, 1950* (Ann Arbor, 1951), 108–09; Pelling, *Communist*, 28–30; Lebzelter, "Political," 396.

1939, many ILP members had abandoned the party for the Communist Party of Great Britain. The ILP had its most impressive electoral showing in 1931, when the party received 1.5 percent of the national vote. The ILP had particular strength in Lancashire, Scotland, Wales, and Yorkshire.[80] The CPGB, from its founding on July 31, 1920, identified itself closely with the Russian Bolshevik Party. The CPGB entered its first national election in November 1922, putting forward five candidates. The party's candidates fared relatively well in the election, with J. T. W. Newbold (from Lanarkshire) winning a seat in the House of Commons, although the party's total national vote was a meager 0.2 percent. In the national elections of 1924, the CPGB presented eight candidates, and the party's candidate from the North Battersea district won his seat. Despite these electoral showings, the Communist Party of Great Britain failed to achieve the level of party membership or electoral support that the communist parties obtained in Germany, France, and Italy. For instance, in the national elections of 1929, 1931, and 1935, in which the CPGB ran a total of fifty-three candidates, only one was elected. The votes polled by the CPGB in these three elections ranged from a high in 1931 of nearly 75,000 (0.3 percent of the total vote) to a low in 1935 of roughly 27,000 (0.1 percent of the total vote). In terms of CPGB membership, the party jumped from 5,116 members in 1922 to a high of 10,730 in October 1926 but fell back again to 2,555 members in November 1930. The party's membership began to climb again in 1931 and rose dramatically between 1933 and 1939. By July 1939, the party had more than 17,000 members.[81]

We have seen that political anti-Semitism in both France and Germany benefited hugely from the sizeable Jewish presence within the French and German revolutionary socialist movements. Jews also played a significant role in the British labor, socialist, and anarchist movements. Among the many Jews affiliating with the British Labour Party during and after World World I were Oscar Tobin, Alfred Kershaw, Abraham Valentine, John R. Raphael, Isaac Sharp, and Moses Sclare. Many British Jews also contributed their time and energy to the various British socialist movements. Before 1920, such Jews as Dora B. Montefiore, J. F. Green, Theodore Rothstein, and Joe Fineberg served on the executive committee of the BSP (British Socialist Party), and Adolf Kohn,

---

[80] Kendall, *Revolutionary*, 269–73; Jupp, *Radical*, 174–78.
[81] Kendall, *Revolutionary*, 311–12; Pelling, *Communist*, 192; Scammon, *British*, 109; Benewick, *Political*, 110.

Moses Baritz, and Alf Jacobs were prominently involved in the SPGB (Marxist Socialist Party of Great Britain). Jews figured less prominently in the ILP, although Daniel Frankel, Joseph Leftwich, and Emanuel Shinwell constituted notable exceptions. The BSP tended to attract Eastern European immigrant Jews. The British Socialist Party before and during World War I became increasingly divided over the issue of foreign policy. In particular, the internationalist wing of the party held to an antiwar position and supported the efforts of the Russian Bolsheviks. This internationalist wing contained a large contingent of Jews of the former Russian Empire, such as Joe Fineberg, Boris Kahan, his sister Zelda Kahan (pseudonym Mrs. Coates), and Theodore Rothstein (pseudonym John Bryan).[82] Both Boris Kahan and Rothstein were instrumental in bringing the British Socialist Party into the fold of the Leninist Third International and in the birth of the Communist Party of Great Britain. Yet the best-known Jewish Bolshevik in Great Britain during the last years of World War I was Maxim Litvinov. Litvinov had settled in Great Britain in 1908, and between January 1918 and September 1919 he served as the semiofficial Bolshevik representative to Great Britain. Great Britain deported Litvinov to Russia in September 1919, where he eventually rose to the rank of Soviet foreign minister, a position he held until 1939. Theodore Rothstein replaced Litvinov as the chief Bolshevik representative in Great Britain.[83]

Not only did Jews maintain key roles in the revolutionary socialist movement in Great Britain after World War I, East End Jews (largely Eastern European immigrants) increasingly comprised the rank and file of the CPGB. Kadish remarks that perhaps one-third of the Britain's active communists in 1939 were Jews, while Rubinstein asserts that between 20 and 25 percent were Jews.[84] Several factors may explain the disproportionate Jewish presence within the CPGB. Many within Britain's Eastern European Jewish community had supported the Russian Revolution, in light of the czarist regime's anti-Semitic policies. During the 1930s, with the rise to power of Germany's anti-Semitic Nazi Party,

---

[82] The internationalist wing of the British Socialist Party also contained many Irish activists, such as James Connolly, Arthur MacManus, Willie Gallacher, and J. T. Murphy, who were deeply engaged in Ireland's anti-British struggle (Pelling, *Communist*, 15–17).

[83] Kadish, *Bolsheviks*, 230–41; Kendall, *Revolutionary*, 182–83, 306; Pelling, *Communist*, 15–17.

[84] Kadish, *Bolsheviks*, 246; Rubinstein, *History*, 241.

many Jews residing in Great Britain found the Communist Party's steadfast opposition to fascism and its concerted efforts to promote Jewish
concerns appealing. Moreover, after 1934, the anti-Semitic activities of
Mosley's British Union of Fascists in London's Jewish East End neighbor-
hoods produced an additional incentive to join the CPGB. The CPGB
and its front organizations took the leading role in combating Mosley's
Blackshirts' anti-Semitic attacks, such as the well known October 1936
"Battle of Cable Street." Several Jewish intellectuals, including Harold
Laski and Sir Victor Gollancz, also found a political home within the
CPGB.[85]

We now turn our attention to the role the British press played in
reinforcing the myth of a "Jewish" Bolshevism. The infamous "Jewish
Peril" article published on May 8, 1920, in the prestigious *Times* of
London, in which Jews were linked to worldwide subversive activities,
had followed a series of anti-Semitic reports in that paper dating back to
World War I. The lack of enthusiasm among many in Britain's Russian
Jewish community for Great Britain's military alliance with czarist
Russia during World War I had already prompted suspicions about Jewish
loyalty in the British press. The highly conservative *Morning Post*, with
a readership of roughly 60,000, had begun in August 1917 to draw a connection between the Jews and the Russian Revolution. By early 1918,
the *Morning Post* had warned its readers that the Russian Revolution was
part of the global plan of international Jewry to dominate the world and
alerted them to the dangers of spreading Bolshevism. The newspaper
charged further that Russian Jews, both in Russia and in Great Britain,
were at work to aid Germany in its war against Great Britain. Picking
up on the theme of Jewish capitalist sponsorship of subversive activities,
the *Morning Post* alleged that Russian Jewish capitalists were secretly
funding the Bolshevik cause. The *Morning Post*'s anti-Semitic campaign
received an unexpected boost from leading British Jews in April 1919.
The newspaper had published on April 23, 1919, the famous "Letter of
the Ten" submitted to the paper by several prominent British Jews, including Rothschild, Montefiore, Samuel, and Swaythling. In the letter,
"the Ten" criticized elements of the Jewish press in Britain for allegedly
encouraging foreign Jews residing in Great Britain to embrace the theoretical principles of the Russian Bolsheviks. The chief inspiration behind
the "Letter of the Ten" came from two articles published in March and

---

[85] Kadish, *Bolsheviks*, 242, 246; Rubinstein, *History*, 244, 266–67; Pelling, *Communist*, 82–83; Benewick, *Political*, 223–24.

April 1919 in the *Jewish Chronicle* by Leopold J. Greenberg, the news-paper's editor. The articles highlighted some consonance between the ideals of Bolshevism and Judaism and an explanation for the attachment of many Jews to Bolshevism. The upshot of this published letter from "the Ten" was the suggestion by the Jews themselves that many of their co-religionists identified with revolutionary Bolshevism.

The *Morning Post* was certainly not alone in drawing a connection between Jews and Bolshevism during World War I. As early as November 23, 1917, the influential *Times* referred to the Bolsheviks in an editorial as "adventurers of German-Jewish blood in German pay." The *Times* did not stop here; it went on to describe Leon Trotsky as "a Jew of the Jews" and claimed that the Jews form the executive element of the Bolshevik movement. That Lenin and several high-ranking Bolshevik leaders (many of Jewish background) were smuggled back to Pretrograd through Germany in a sealed train fueled the allegation, published in the *Times* and other newspapers, of a connection between Bolshevism, Jews, and Germany.[86]

The initial English language version of the "Protocols" appears in January 1920 under the title of *The Jewish Peril*. This first English ver-sion of the "Protocols" carried the imprint of a reputable printing house, His Majesty's Printers Eyre & Spottiswoode. Silence within the British press followed the publication of the "Protocols." Four months later, however, the *Times* published its widely read and lengthy article "A Disturbing Pamphlet: A Call for Enquiry" that propelled the myths of "Jewish" Bolshevism and a Jewish worldwide conspiracy to new heights in the English-speaking world. The *Times* article asserted: "Have we been struggling these tragic years to blow up and extirpate the secret or-ganization of German world domination only to find beneath it another,

---

[86] Kadish, *Bolsheviks*, 22–23, 36, 122–24; Shmuel Almog, "Antisemitism as a Dy-namic Phenomenon: The 'Jewish Question' in England at the End of the First World War," *Patterns of Prejudice*, vol. 2, no. 4, 1987, 9–12; Zosa Szajkowski, *Jews, Wars, and Communism: The Impact of the 1919–20 Red Scare on American Jewish Life*, vol. 2 (New York, 1974), 167; Rubinstein, *History*, 201; Lipman, *Social*, 152–53; Finestein, *Short*, 178. Kadish (*Bolsheviks*, 24) observes that the anti-Semitic tone of the *Times* reporting on the Russian Revolution may have been partly due to the reporting of two of its foreign correspondents for Russian affairs who harbored well-known anti-Semitic sentiments. According to Kadish, one of these correspondents, Robert Wilton, published a book in 1918 entitled *Russia's Agony* suggesting that hate-filled Jews of the Pale of Settlement con-tributed hugely to Lenin's success.

more dangerous because more secret? Have we by straining every fibre of our national body, escaped a '*Pax Germanica*' only to fall into a '*Pax Judaeica*'?"[87] The anonymous author of the *Times* article suggested that the Bolshevik Revolution provided proof of a worldwide Jewish plot against Western civilization and cautioned the British prime minister, Lloyd George, against negotiating with the Bolshevik government because he would actually be negotiating with representatives of the Jewish worldwide conspiracy.[88] The infamous *Times* article was followed by an anti-Semitic barrage of eighteen articles published during the summer of 1920 in the *Morning Post* that focused on the link between Jews and Bolshevism. A collection of the eighteen articles subsequently appeared in book form under the title of *The Causes of World Unrest*. The *Morning Post* also published a list of the fifty key Bolshevik leaders, claiming that forty-two of the fifty were Jews. Wilson observes that the sales of the *Morning Post* climbed from roughly 65,000 to nearly 76,000 during the summer of 1920, and Kadish notes that the paper's circulation ultimately reached 119,000 during 1920.[89]

Before the *Times* publicly exposed the "Protocols" as a grand forgery, several British newspapers and periodicals, including the *Times*, the *Morning Post*, the *Spectator*, *Blackwood's Magazine*, and the *Plain English*, had published articles that gave credence to the allegation of a worldwide Jewish conspiracy and Jewish responsibility for the Bolshevik Revolution. Between August 16 and 18, 1921, nearly fifteen months after the publication of its initial article on the "Protocols," the *Times* published three consecutive articles by Philip Graves citing evidence that the authors of the "Protocols" had plagiarized Maurice Joly's 1864 political satire.[90]

Support for the notion of "Jewish" Bolshevism need not rest only on explicit connections made by the British press. Occasionally, the British press succeeded in making the association of Jews with Bolshevism implicit, yet obvious. Here are three examples from my own examination of the *Daily Mail*, one of Great Britain's widest-circulating newspapers. In a July 15, 1919, story on Bela Kun, the head of the Soviet government in Hungary, the *Daily Mail* employed the leader's seldom-used Jewish

[87] Kadish, *Bolsheviks*, 32.
[88] Ibid.; V. D. Lipman, *A History of the Jews in Great Britain since 1858* (Leicester, 1990), 152.
[89] K. M. Wilson, "The Protocols of Zion and the *Morning Post*, 1919–1920," *Patterns of Prejudice*, vol. 19, no. 3, July 1985, 12; Kadish, *Bolsheviks*, 43.
[90] Kushner, *Persistence*, 12; Lebzelter, "Political," 393.

surname and entitled its article "Advance on Bela Cohen." In an article entitled "Austria and Russian Jews" published in the *Daily Mail* on February 15, 1924, the paper's correspondent reporting from Vienna wrote: "In view of this fact, and of the fact that the Russian Government is dominated by Jews . . ." And, finally, in a June 16, 1924, *Daily Mail* article on the official visit to London of Maxim Litvinoff, at the time the Bolshevik assistant commissar of foreign affairs, the newspaper described him as "the agile M. Finkelstein-Litvinoff."

Certainly the British press contributed to the popularization of political anti-Semitism during and after World War I. But it was not alone. The British Foreign Office and several prominent British politicians helped to fan the flames of political anti-Semitism as well. In a series of reports, the Foreign Office commented on the disproportionate number of Jews within the Bolshevik hierarchy, the Jewish role in the assassination of the Romanov imperial family, and the advantages garnered by the Jews from the Bolshevik Revolution. Though many politicians lent credence to the myths of a worldwide Jewish conspiracy and "Jewish" Bolshevism, few had the stature of Winston Churchill.[91] Churchill had already made a name for himself throughout the United Kingdom as an adventurous correspondent during the Boer War, a member of the House of Commons, and a minister in a couple of British governments before and during World War I. As early as February 8, 1920, in an article entitled "Zionism versus Bolshevism: A Struggle for the Soul of the Jewish People" appearing in the *Illustrated Sunday Herald*, Churchill had linked well-known revolutionary Jews to the overthrow of and reconstitution of society. Churchill's list of revolutionary Jews stretched back to antiquity and included the names of Weishaupt, Marx, Trotsky, Kun, Luxemburg, and Goldman. Churchill, fiercely opposed to the Russian Revolution, insinuated in this long article that although non-Jews appear to hold positions of authority within the Bolshevik leadership, their power is actually eclipsed by that of Jews, serving sometimes as their co-equals and at other times as their subordinates. For Churchill, the major inspiration and driving force of the Bolshevik regime emanated from its Jewish leadership. But Churchill saw within "this mystic and mysterious race" a battle between two opposing Jewish prototypes and two contrasting Jewish philosophies. In Churchill's interpretation, pitted against the diabolical, international, and anti-Christian

---

[91] Indeed, Churchill's reputation as one of the greatest statesmen of the twentieth century bore more on his stewardship of Great Britain during World War II.

revolutionary Jew was the national-minded and "Zionist Jew," who sought to establish a Jewish national homeland in Palestine. Churchill envisioned the "Zionist Jew" as a constructive alternative to the "revolutionary Jew" and hoped that a Jewish homeland might direct Jewish energies away from radical politics.[92]

Not withstanding the import of the debunking of the "Protocols" by the *Times,* the myths of a Jewish worldwide conspiracy to sow disorder and Jewish sponsorship of Bolshevism had embedded themselves within the popular British consciousness and would burst forth anew at several intervals during the interwar period. Although after 1924 outright charges of "Jewish" Bolshevism or of an alleged international Jewish conspiracy became rare in the mainstream press and in speeches by British politicians, rightwing anti-Semitic groups continued to carry out a campaign in which Jews and communism were inextricably linked. In the 1920s, Henry Beamish, Admiral Domvile, Lord Sydenham, and Joseph Bannister, along with the extreme right-wing Britons movement, preached the dangers of the alleged international Jewish conspiracy and its sponsorship of revolutionary socialism. During the mid-1920s and early 1930s, the British Fascists published several articles in their principal newspaper, the *Fascist Bulletin,* accusing the Jews of spreading communism and German Jews of running the Soviet Union. The threat of "Jewish" communism became a central theme of Mosley's British Union of Fascists during the 1930s. Mosley declared fascism to be the mortal enemy of communism. In its publications, such as the *Action,* the BUF claimed that "International Jewish Finance," in its efforts to foment a world conspiracy, subsidized the Conservative, Labour, and Socialist Parties in Great Britain and ruled Soviet Russia.[93] The survival of the Bolshevik regime in Russia and the overrepresentation of Jews in the British Communist Party would continue to give life to political anti-Semitism throughout the 1920s and 1930s.

### ROMANIA

As we have seen in the cases of France, Germany, and Great Britain, political anti-Semitism before the Holocaust found inspiration in the

---

[92] Lebzelter, "Political," 386–88; Lebzelter, *Political,* 100; Kadish, *Bolsheviks,* 135–41.

[93] Benewick, *Political,* 42–43, 136–37; Lunn, "Ideology," 150–51; Lebzelter, *Political,* 101–02; Skidelsky, *Oswald,* 342–43, 370, 388; Eatwell, *Fascism,* 235–36.

myths of Jewish disloyalty to the nation and Jewish involvement in revolutionary socialist movements. These two myths shaped Romanian political anti-Semitism as well. Throughout the nineteenth and early twentieth centuries, Romanian nationalists accused Romanian Jews of harboring non-Romanian allegiances. The obstacles erected by various Romanian governments to block Romanian Jewish efforts to obtain legal rights can certainly explain a large part of Jewish resistance to Romanian acculturation before the Holocaust. The charge of Jewish disloyalty has its origins at least as early as 1879, when, in front of the Romanian parliament, the eminent philosopher and parliamentary deputy Vasile Conta spoke of the universal threat of Judaism. Conta claimed that the Jews sought to dominate the world through economic conspiracies, the control of the world press, and through organizations such as the French-based Alliance Israélite Universelle, which he referred to as a government of the "yids." Conta warned his parliamentary colleagues that international Jewry had selected Romania as the national home-land for the Jews.[94] The theme of Jewish disloyalty would reemerge constantly during and after World War I. In the last weeks of World War I, Romanian Jews were accused of being traitors and of being in the pay of the German military. The fact that so many Romanian Jews spoke Yiddish made them suspect in the eyes of many Romanians, who confused Yiddish with German. At the moment of the German troop withdrawal from Bucharest and Brăila on November 11, 1918, a pogrom erupted in these two cities lasting several days.[95] The annexation of Bessarabia, Bukovina, and parts of Transylvania, with their large Jewish populations, after World War I further reinforced Romanian suspicions about Jewish loyalty. Not surprisingly, Cuza's anti-Semitic LANC and Codreanu's Iron Guard political movements obtained a large proportion of their electoral support from the non-Jewish populace of the recently annexed provinces of Bukovina and Bessarabia. Both Cuza and Codreanu opportunistically linked Jewish disloyalty to "Jewish" Bolshevism.[96]

The fear of revolutionary socialism and the belief that Jews participated in and orchestrated revolutionary socialist movements had firmly

---

[94] Volovici, Nationalist, 14–15.

[95] Iancu, L'Emancipation, 95–99.

[96] Zeev Barbu, "Psycho-Historical and Sociological Perspectives on the Iron Guard, the Fascist Movement of Romania." In S. U. Larsen, B. Hagtvet, and J. P. Myklebust, eds., Who Were the Fascists (Bergen, 1980), 383; Volovici, Nationalist, 64; Weber, "Romania," 519–21; Livezeanu, Cultural, 291–92.

implanted itself in the Romanian popular consciousness during the interwar period. In the case of Romania, the lack of industrial development retarded the growth of a socialist labor movement before World War I. Although a small socialist movement sprang forth in the 1890s, within which Jews, Hungarians, Bulgarians, and Ukrainians played leading roles, political anti-Semitism as an expression of the threat of Jewish socialism would be seen as a potent challenge only after 1917. Political anti-Semitism in post-1917 Romania did not emanate chiefly from the size of the socialist constituency or the fear of a seizure of power by the indigenous revolutionary socialist movement, as was often the case in Western Europe. (During the interwar period, the Romanian socialist left, comprised of the Romanian Socialist, the Social Democratic, and the Worker and Peasant Bloc parties' share of the electoral vote, ranged between a high of 5.8 percent of the vote in 1931 to a low of 0.9 percent in 1937). Rather, political anti-Semitism in Romania resulted from Romania's nervousness about Soviet Russian irredentism and the overrepresentation of Russian, Hungarian, and Ukrainian Jews within the leadership of the Romanian left.

Even before socialism entered the Romanian lexicon, Romanians saw resident Jews as a different kind of foreigner than the Greeks, Hungarians, Poles, Russians, and Turks. Alleged Jewish international networks were thought to have played a role in the continual attempts by the Great Powers to intervene in Romanian internal affairs on behalf of Romania's Jews, and these networks supposedly financed Jewish ownership of Romanian economic resources. These alleged links between foreign Jews and Romanian Jews facilitated the image of a Jewish worldwide conspiracy within which revolutionary socialism found a logical home.

The first socialist movement within Romania emerged in the 1870s, led by Romanians who had studied in czarist Russia. Among the Russian emigres were Zubcu Codreanu, Nicolae K. Sudzilovski, and Constantin Dobrogeanu-Gherea. The founding of the Romanian Social Democratic Party occurred in 1893 in Bucharest. Until World War I, Christian Rakovsky (ethnic Bulgarian) and Constantin Dobrogeanu-Gherea (Russian-Jewish) dominated the party's leadership. Both men had strong ties to the Russian revolutionary movement. Dobrogeanu-Gherea became the party's principal theoretician, advocating a program of "neo-serfdom" by which Romania would undergo a bourgeois-democratic revolution, setting in place the rapid industrialization of the country and establishing a basis for a socialist victory.[97] Prior to World War I, the Romanian Social Democratic Party failed to attract any sizeable following. Between 1899 and 1914, no Social Democratic Party candidate won a seat in the Chamber of Deputies. Overall, the party had few members (perhaps 6,000 members in 1897) and minimal electoral support (roughly 2 percent of the parliamentary vote in the 1911 national elections).[98] The party was hurt in these early years by the lack of Romanian industrial development and the defection of important leaders, including Mortun, Diamandi, and Nădejde, to the Liberal Party. The Social Democratic Party revived in 1910, and at the General Congress of Social Democrats in 1910, the party adopted a program that included a call for action against exploitation and oppression based on class, party, gender, and race.[99]

The specter of "Red Revolution" after 1917 brought political anti-Semitism to the forefront. Whereas the emergence of mass-based revolutionary Marxist parties fuelled the "red scare" in Western Europe, the causes of the red scare and the popularity of political anti-Semitism in Romania derived largely from other sources. The fear of revolutionary socialism after 1917 had much to do with the seizure of power by revolutionary Marxists in neighboring Russia and Hungary and the incorporation into Romania of former Hungarian and Russian territories. Romanian political anti-Semitism benefited additionally from the inordinate worldwide press coverage given to the disclosure that Jews had played a leading role in the Russian and Hungarian communist revolutions and from the publication of a Romanian version of the "Protocols of the Elders of Zion."[100] Reports issued by Romanian authorities in the aftermath of World War I claimed that Soviet, Hungarian, and Ukrainian communist agents were infiltrating the local Romanian communist organizations – organizations populated largely by Jews in the newly acquired Bessarabia, Bukovina, and Transylvania.[101] Because Jews in Bessarabia were of Russian origin and because Soviet Russia refused to recognize Romanian claims to Bessarabia, anti-Semitism was further linked to

---

[97] Robert R. King, *A History of the Romanian Communist Party* (Stanford, 1980), 18; Ghita Ionescu, *Communism in Rumania 1944–1962* (London, 1964), 3–4.

[98] Hitchins, *Rumania*, 134.

[99] International Reference Library, *Politics and Political Parties in Romania* (London, 1936), 241–46.

[100] In 1923, Ion Mota had translated from the French what is believed to be the first Romanian-language version of the"Protocols." It appears that excerpts from the "Protocols" were read into the minutes of the Romanian parliament in 1933.

[101] Livezeanu, *Cultural*, 250–54; Lendvai, *L'antisémitisme*, 70–71.

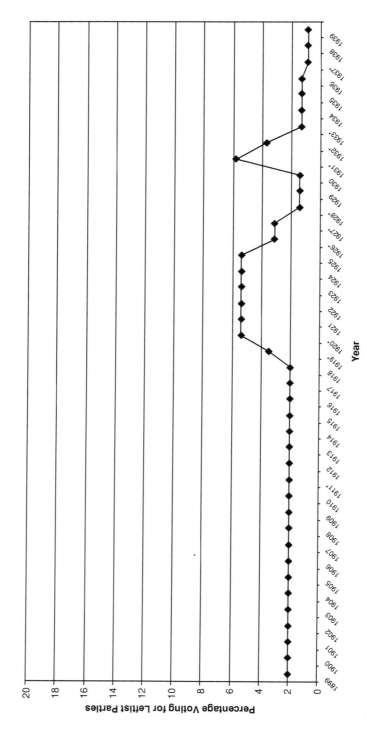

Figure 5.2d. Percentage of votes cast for leftist parties in Romania, 1899–1939. *Note:* Years with an asterisk are national election years. Figures are carried over in off-election years. The earliest data point available was the 1911 election. Due to the lack of reliable data prior to 1911, this level of leftist support is assumed for the period 1899–1910. As stated in the text, there is little evidence to suggest that leftist voting varied considerably prior to 1911. *Sources:* Flora (1983), Mackie and Rose (1982), Dogan (1946), Hitchens (1994).

anticommunism.[102] The linking of Jews with communism in Romania had, in fact, some legitimacy. Volovici suggests that many Jews in the new territories were indeed sympathetic to the Russian and Hungarian revolutions.[103] For other Jews in Transylvania who held no sympathy for the short-lived Hungarian revolution, their allegiance to Hungary and appreciation of Hungarian culture made them appear disloyal in the eyes of ethnic Romanians.[104] Perhaps most importantly, as members of an often "rejected people" or ostracized ethnic minority, large numbers of Romanian Jews found much to their liking in a universalistic socialist ideology, which discounted the criteria of birth and ethnicity for membership in the political community. Furthermore, in its propaganda, the Romanian Communist Party played up its role as the defender of the interests of both the working class and Jews during the interwar period.[105]

In May 1921, the Romanian socialist movement split into social democratic and communist factions. Those socialists who did not back ties with the Comintern reorganized themselves initially into the Federation of Socialist Parties and subsequently, in 1927, into the Social Democratic Party. The Social Democratic Party advocated an end to economic exploitation, the socialization of the means of production, and the creation of a democratic socialist society. Rather than revolution, the Social Democrats called for change through constitutional parliamentary means. The Social Democrats would remain as a minor political force during the interwar years, deriving their support chiefly from the trade unions.[106] The more radical Maximalists, who eventually formed the Romanian Communist Party (RCP), were led by Boris Stefanov and Constantin Dobrogeanu-Gherea's son, Alexandru Dobrogeanu-Gherea. They were joined by a large number of leftist intellectuals, many of

---

[102] King, *History*, 11; Kurt W. Treptow, "Populism and Twentieth Century Romanian Politics." In Joseph Held, ed., *Populism in Eastern Europe: Racism, Nationalism, and Society* (New York, 1996), 203; Mendelsohn, *Jews*, 187–88; Vago, *Shadow*, 21.

[103] Volovici, *Nationalist*, 21.

[104] Marrus, *Unwanted*, 144; Lendvai, *L'antisémitisme*, 70–71.

[105] King, *History*, 33–35; Stephen Fischer-Galati, "The Radical Left and Assimilation: The Case of Romania." In Bela Vago, ed., *Jewish Assimilation in Modern Times* (Boulder, 1981), 93; Janos, "Modernization," 109.

[106] Two other minor leftist parties would emerge during the interwar years. The Unitary Socialist Party sprang forth in July 1928. The party opposed the opportunism of the Social Democrats and the sectarianism of the Romanian Communist Party. The Romanian Socialist Party emerged in 1933. The new party lasted for two years (International Reference Library, *Politics*, 262, 266).

them of Jewish origin, such as Marcel Pauker and his future wife, Ana Rabinovici.[107] By strictly adhering to the policies dictated by the Soviet Union's Communist Party, the RCP solidified the already strong popular conviction that it represented foreign, rather than Romanian, interests. From the beginning, the Soviet Russian Communist Party succeeded in exerting firm authority over the Romanian Communist Party. The RCP depended financially and organizationally on the Russian party, and within the RCP, the Bessarabian group – strongly tied to the Russians – held the commanding positions.[108] Through its control over the Comintern, the Soviet Communist Party oversaw the selection of the RCP leadership and the adoption of party policy. Central to RCP demands was the call for "self-determination up to succession." This came to stand for supporting the Soviet demand for the separation of the province of Bessarabia from Romania, the creation of the autonomous Soviet Socialist Republic of Moldavia, including Bessarabia, and separation of Transylvania, Bukovina, and Dobrodgea from Romania. Further exacerbating the situation for the RCP within Romania, the Soviet-led Comintern instructed the RCP to launch a vigorous public campaign in favor of the Soviet Union's positions. This campaign included assertions that the workers and peasants of Bessarabia had suffered under Romanian rule and that they would prosper only as part of the USSR.

The 1924 Soviet announcement of the new Socialist Republic of Bessarabia and the failed communist-led revolt in 1924 in the Bessarabian town of Tatar Bunar gave the Romanian government the excuse it needed to outlaw the RCP on April 11, 1924.[109] Interestingly, the Soviet Union went ahead and established the autonomous Moldavian Soviet Socialist Republic on the Soviet bank of the Dniester River. Although Romania and the USSR officially recognized each other in June 1934, the two countries were never able to resolve the Bessarabian question during the interwar period.[110] The Tatar Bunar uprising and the Soviet creation of an autonomous Moldavian republic fanned anti-Semitic feelings in Romania, as Romanian politicians assigned blame to a Judeo-Communist conspiracy directed by Moscow. In the subsequent

---

[107] Ionescu, *Communism*, 13; Treptow, "Populism," 420–21; King, *History*, 18; Hitchins, "Rumania," 401–02.

[108] Ionescu, *Communism*, 18.

[109] Ibid., 18, 23; King, *History*, 31; Hitchins, *Rumania*, 400; Treptow, "Populism," 422–23; Fischer-Galati, "Radical," 91.

[110] King, *History*, 28–29.

months, anti-Semitic riots occurred in Bessarabia and neighboring Moldavia.[111]

After the institution of the ban on RCP activities in 1924, the party continued to carry out its objectives through its various front organizations, such as the Worker-Peasant Bloc. The Worker-Peasant Bloc ran candidates in Romanian national elections in 1926, 1927, 1928, 1931, and 1932. In the 1931 elections, the Bloc ran candidates in 47 different electoral districts and gained nearly 74,000 votes (twice the average number it had won in the earlier elections) along with five seats in the Romanian parliament. Unfortunately for the Bloc candidates, their electoral victory was immediately invalidated, and they were blocked from taking their parliamentary seats. By 1932, the Worker-Peasant Bloc's vote had fallen to 9,941.[112]

During the interwar period, membership in the Romanian Communist Party remained low compared to Western European levels. King places total membership at 2,000 in 1922, whereas Hitchins observes that party membership reached its high point in 1936 with roughly 5,000 adherents.[113] As was the case with the Romanian revolutionary left movement before World War I, ethnic minorities continued to be disproportionately represented as members of the Romanian revolutionary Marxist movements and especially as leaders of these movements during the interwar period. Membership appealed to Jews because they belonged to an ethnic group without a territorial base, and to other groups, such as the Hungarians, Bulgarians, and Russians, who were dissatisfied with their inclusion in the new Romania.[114]

Ethnic minority participation in revolutionary events in Romania during the interwar period was certainly significant. In the aftermath of the German military withdrawal from Bucharest in November 1918, the Maximalist wing of the left organized a series of demonstrations in November and December 1918. The demonstrations were violently suppressed by Romanian troops, and a number of arrests of Marxist revolutionaries ensued. One of the chief organizers was the young Ana (Rabinovici) Pauker, the daughter of a Moldavian rabbi.[115] The link between Jews and revolutionary Marxism gained further public attention

---

[111] Fischer-Galati, "Radical," 91–92.

[112] King, *History*, 19; Hitchins, *Rumania*, 400–01; Ionescu, *Communism*, 40.

[113] King, *History*, 18; Hitchins, *Rumania*, 400–01.

[114] King, *History*, xiii, 33–34; Lendvai, *L'antisémitisme*, 70–71.

[115] Ionescu, *Communism*, 11–12; Robert Levy, *Ana Pauker: The Rise and Fall of a Jewish Communist* (Berkeley, 2001).

after the violent repression of the strike at the Grivita railroad works. In the ensuing well-publicized trial of strike organizers, Jews were shown to have been overrepresented among the communist leaders.[116] Among the most famous Jews sentenced at these trials was Ana Pauker. Treptow notes that the Comintern did not trust ethnic Romanian communists and consistently assigned leadership positions in the RCP to ethnic minorities.[117] At the Fifth Congress of the Romanian Communist Party in 1931, only nine of twenty-four delegates with voting rights were ethnic Romanians; the remaining fifteen delegates were made up of six Jews, four Hungarians, three Ukrainians, and two Bulgarians. Although Jews constituted one of several ethnic groups within the RCP, they did dominate the intellectual wing of the party. Three prominent Jews played leading roles in the interwar Romanian communist movement – Ana Pauker, Marcel Pauker, and Alexander Dobrogeanu-Gherea. Fischer-Galati observes that many of the Jewish party intellectuals identified little with Romanian interests.[118] The perception of Jewish overrepresentation within the Romanian revolutionary left created a context for Codreanu and his associates, who proclaimed at the launching of the Legion of the Archangel Michael in the spring of 1930 that one of the principal aims of the new organization was "combatting *kike* communism."[119]

Overall, the electoral popularity of and active membership in the Romanian revolutionary left never reached the levels seen in Western Europe during the interwar period. At its peak, the left obtained roughly 6 percent of the national vote in the 1931 general elections. The fear of the left may have had more to do with Romania's proximity to the USSR and the overrepresentation of Jews and other minorities within the rank and file and leadership of the leftist parties. In short, the attenuated appeal that communism had among native Romanians may be attributed to a number of factors. We should include among those factors that the Romanian Communist Party attracted to its ranks members

[116] Ionescu, *Communism*, 50–51; Butnaru, *Silent*, 51.
[117] Treptow, "Populism," 422.
[118] Fischer-Galati, "Radical," 91. In terms of the overall membership of the Romanian Communist Party, the party's statistics show 18.12 percent Jewish membership in 1933. However, according to Levy (*Ana Pauker*, 5), many Jewish party members claimed that the proportion of Jewish membership was significantly higher, given that many of those claiming Hungarian nationality were Magyarized Jews from Transylvania.
[119] Livezeanu, *Cultural*, 291.

of ethnic minorities, that the Jews and other minorities dominated the party leadership, and that the RCP appeared to back the interests of the Comintern. These factors, moreover, led many Romanians to believe that the country's ethnic minority population was disloyal and that the minorities constituted a threat to Romania's nationalist aspirations and to its social order.

## ITALY

Italian political anti-Semitism before 1938 presents a number of striking contrasts to political anti-Semitism found in our other cases. We have seen elsewhere that political anti-Semitism incorporated charges of Jewish disloyalty to the nation, the existence of an international Jewish conspiracy seeking to seize world power, and Jewish sponsorship of and involvement in revolutionary socialist movements. Certainly, in the years before 1938, Italian anti-Semites sought to mobilize support by focusing upon these themes, but their efforts generally failed to arouse much popular support. The failure of political anti-Semitism to attract a popular following in Italy cannot be attributed to a dearth of economic and political crises or to the absence of a threatening revolutionary socialist left. The Italian state confronted a series of financial and political challenges, as well as a threat from a rapidly growing Italian socialist left, before the fascist seizure of power in October 1922. The strong degree of Jewish assimilation, the widely held belief that Italian Jews were highly patriotic, and the surprisingly hearty participation of Italian Jews in the Italian fascist movement attenuated the potency of Italian political anti-Semitism before the Holocaust.

Italian Jews strongly identified with and participated enthusiastically in the Italian movement for unity and independence during the nineteenth century. Jewish support for Italian unity and independence can be attributed largely to the fact that the principal leaders of the Risorgimento embraced full civil and political equality for the country's Jews. Italian Jews participated energetically in the Carboneria from its beginnings in 1815; in the liberation struggles of the early 1830s in Modena, Reggio Emilia, and Vercelli; as volunteers in Garibaldi's Mille (the Thousand) in 1860; and in the 1866 campaign to liberate Venice from the Austrians. The fact that Jews contributed significantly to the movement for unity and independence did not go unnoticed by many in the new Italian kingdom. Between 1860 and 1866, the Italian king bestowed titles of nobility upon a number of Italian Jews for their contributions.

More than fifty years later, in the aftermath of World War I, the Jews of Trieste figured centrally in the Italian effort to make this highly contested city Italian.[120]

Jewish emancipation and recognition of Jewish patriotism also contributed significantly to the rise of Italian Jews into positions of prominence during the last half of the nineteenth century and the first third of the twentieth. As early as 1848, Daniele Manin, an Italian Jew who had fought bravely against the Austrian forces in Venice, became president of the short-lived Venetian Republic. Isacco Artom became the private secretary of the Kingdom of Sardinia's prime minister, Camillo di Cavour, in the 1850s. In 1861, three Jews won election to the first Italian parliament, and nine Jews held seats in the Italian parliament in 1870. The number of Jewish parliamentarians climbed to eleven in 1874, with the inclusion of Venice and Rome in the newly unified Italian nation. The Italian Senate, consisting of roughly 350 notables appointed by the king, contained 6 Jews in 1902. In 1920, the number of Jews in the Senate climbed to nineteen. Giacomo Malvano, like Artom a Piedmont Jew, served as secretary general at the Italian Foreign Office from 1876 to 1907. In 1891, Luigi Luzzatti became minister of finance. In 1910, he became the first Jewish prime minister of Italy and thereby the first Jew to serve as prime minister in Europe.[121] In 1907, Ernesto Nathan became the first Jewish mayor of the city of Rome. Baron Sidney Sonnino, a Christian convert, held the esteemed positions of finance minister and foreign minister before becoming Italy's prime minister on two separate occasions between 1906 and 1910. Italy also had Europe's first Jewish minister of war: General Giuseppe Ottolenghi held the position between 1902 and 1903. In Italy, Jews distinguished themselves in military careers. Italian Jewish soldiers took part in Italian colonial wars from Eritrea in 1889 to Tripoli in 1911. In World War I, two Italian Jews received the gold medal for heroism, Italy's highest military honor, and Jews won more than a thousand medals for bravery – an extraordinary number given the small proportion of Jews within the Italian population. A Jewish general, Roberto Segre, commander of the artillery in the Battle of Piave in June 1918, is generally credited as the mastermind behind the strategy that saved Italy. In all, fifty Jewish generals

---

[120] Gunzberg, *Strangers*, 84–85; Milano, *Storia*, 356–57; Stille, *Benevolence*, 24; Cohen, "Jews," 4; Canepa, "Christian," 29–30; Rossi, "Emancipation," 118; Momigliano, *Ottavo*, 371.

[121] Disraeli, who had served as prime minister of Great Britain, was a convert to Christianity.

served in World War I, and one of those generals, Emanuele Pugliese, became Italy's most highly decorated World War I general. Nowhere else in Europe had so many Jews risen to the rank of general, and in no other European nation was the participation and sacrifice of the Jewish population in World War I as recognized as it was in Italy. The Jewish presence in the Italian military continued into the interwar period. In 1932, the Italian king reported that eleven Jews served as generals; and two Jewish admirals, Ascoli and Capon, were at the helm of the Italian navy in the late 1930s.[122]

Insinuations of Jewish disloyalty or split allegiance were rare before the 1930s in Italy. However, the issue of Zionism was a source of some anxiety to the Italian Jewish population at the turn of the century and continued to fuel concerns about Jewish sympathies among some segments of the Italian Christian population until the Holocaust. De Felice has observed that anti-Zionism served to unite several anti-Semitic strands in Italy.[123] The Roman Catholic Church saw the effort to establish a Jewish homeland in Palestine as detrimental to its interests to reestablish authority over the Holy Land. For many Italian liberals and democrats, Zionism posed an issue of potential Italian Jewish dual loyalty. Among Italian nationalists, Zionism held the possibility that Italian Jews might support opponents of Italian colonial designs. In particular, before 1914, some Italian nationalists feared that Italian Jews would exhibit pro-Turkish sympathies in the Italo-Turkish dispute in North Africa, given the willingness of Ottoman authorities to permit a Jewish homeland in Palestine. After 1919, many Italian nationalists feared that Italian Jews might side with the British and thwart Italian colonial plans in North Africa and the Middle East, in light of Britain's Balfour Declaration and Britain's new mandate over Palestine. But again, the lion's share of acrimony in regard to Zionism focused on foreign, rather than domestic, Jews. Anti-Semitic nationalists, such as Coppola in his 1911 anti-Zionist articles in L'Idea Nazionale, stressed their opposition to foreign Jews' standing in the way of Italian interests in the Middle East and North Africa, while expressing their conviction that Italian Jews were good Italians and supported Italian interests.[124]

---

[122] Zuccotti, Italians, 15–18; Gunzburg, Strangers, 224; Cohen, "Jews," 4–5; Canepa, "Christian," 14; Bookbinder, "Italy," 98–99; Stille, Benevolence, 30; Momigliano, Ottavo, 369–70.

[123] De Felice, Storia, 55–64.

[124] Toscano, "L'uguaglianza," 231–32.

Mussolini's position on Zionism has appeared to many as ambivalent. In the 1920s, he had tried to woo Chaim Weizmann and Nahum
Sokolov, two Zionist leaders, in an effort to extricate the British from
their base in the eastern Mediterranean. To that end, as well as to advance the notion of a Jewish homeland in Palestine, the Italian fascist
state erected in 1928 the Comitato Italia-Palestina. However, after his
1935 invasion of Ethiopia, Mussolini referred to the Zionist movement
as "English Zionism," or pro-British, and criticized powerful foreign Jews
for belonging to a coherent organization coordinated by the British that
sought to thwart Italian interests. The Italian fascist leader had hoped
that the Zionist leadership would assist Italian efforts to have the sanctions against Italy imposed by the League of Nations removed. When
that did not occur, he blamed world Zionism for failing to come to
Italy's aid. Consequently, Mussolini unshackled Roberto Farinacci and
Giovanni Preziosi, two fascist and anti-Semitic ideologues; the two published a series of anti-Semitic articles in 1936. Yet again, the anti-Semitic
tirade distinguished between international and Italian Jews.[125]

Why did Italian Jews remain largely untouched by the anti-Zionist
rhetoric issuing forth from Italy's nationalist right wing? Perhaps the answer lies in the response of the Italian Jewish community to the Zionist
movement. Unlike the multitude of Jews in Eastern and Central Europe
for whom a Jewish homeland in Palestine, possessed enormous appeal,
Italian Jews approached Zionism tepidly. The high degree of Italian
Jewish assimilation and social mobility dampened the appeal of a Jewish
homeland for the typical Italian Jew. Not one Italian Jewish representative attended the first Zionist Congress in 1897. Rabbi Sonino of Naples
attended the second Zionist Congress in 1898 and told those assembled
that the majority of the Italian Jewish clergy and Jewish leadership opposed the notion of a Jewish homeland in Palestine, since Italian Jews
confronted no discrimination within Italy. Among prominent Italian
Jews expressing sympathy for Zionism was Dante Lattes. However, Lattes
spoke in favor of a Jewish homeland not for Italian Jews, but for Eastern
and Central European Jews fleeing persecution.[126]

More than any other factor, the difficulty in linking Italian Jews to
revolutionary socialism, particularly after the Bolshevik Revolution, ex-
plains the failure of political anti-Semitism to take root in the Italian

---

[125] Ledeen, "Evolution," 7–8, 13–14; Molinari, *Ebrei*, 104, 113; Michaelis, *Mussolini*,
14; Bernadini, "Origins," 440–41; Zuccotti, *Italians*, 31–35.
[126] De Felice, *Storia*, 16–25.

popular consciousness. We have seen that in France, Germany, Great Britain, and Romania, the myth of "Jewish Bolshevism" had gain widespread appeal. In Italy, there were certainly voices accusing Jews of sponsorship of revolutionary socialism, but the targeted Jews were rarely Italian Jews. Italian political anti-Semites were, for the most part, careful to distinguish between Italian Jews and foreign Jews. The failure of political anti-Semitism to flourish in Italy cannot be attributed to the absence of a "red menace," for the Italian revolutionary left before 1922 came close to taking power in Italy. The share of votes for the Italian socialist left had risen dramatically between 1897 and 1919. In the 1897 national elections, the Socialist Party garnered 8.9 percent of the total vote, while in the 1919 elections, the socialist left (Socialist Party, Independent Socialists, and Reformist Socialists) won 34.3 percent of the popular vote. In the last free elections of 1921 before the fascist takeover, the combined left vote (Socialist Party, Independent Socialists, and Communist Party) declined to 29.9 percent of the total vote. If revolutionary socialism did indeed constitute a threat to the Italian social and political order before 1922, why were Jews not linked to this threat? Had the "Protocols" failed to reach the Italian public? Did Italian Jews stand aloof from Italy's revolutionary socialist movements?

The first two Italian-language translations of the "Protocols" appeared in 1921. Giovanni Preziosi, the ardent anti-Semitic nationalist, translated and circulated an Italian version under the title of I Protocolli dei Savi Anziani di Sion. In the same year, Monsignor Jouin, a right-wing Catholic author, also brought out an Italian version of the "Protocols." In a context of worldwide revolutionary upheaval in the aftermath of World War I, the myth of "Jewish Bolshevism" and a worldwide Jewish conspiracy to sow disorder had attracted a following in Italy, as elsewhere. Nationalists, fascists, and conservative clerics of the Roman Catholic Church pointed to the large number of Jews within the worldwide revolutionary socialist movement. The anti-Semitic nationalist Giovanni Preziosi published in 1921 his Giudaismo-bolscevismo-plutocrazia-massoneria, in which he attempted to document a Jewish revolutionary socialist lineage that included the names of Marx, Lassalle, Trotsky, Radek, Joffe, Litvinoff, and Bela Kun. In a series of articles published in his fascist newspaper, Il Popolo d'Italia, between 1917 and 1921, Mussolini highlighted the alleged Jewish role in revolutionary socialism. He labeled Lenin's Bolshevik regime as Jewish-German and eventually as "Jewish pure and simple." In two separate articles on June 4, 1919, and October 19, 1920, in Il Popolo d'Italia, Mussolini claimed that 80 percent

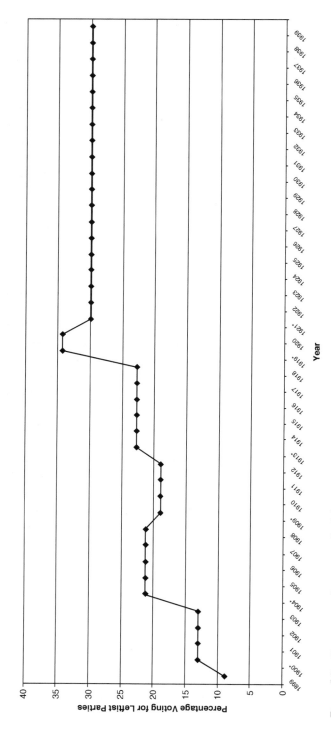

Figure 5.2e. Percentage of votes cast for leftist parties in Italy, 1899–1939. *Note:* Years with an asterisk are national election years. Figures are carried over in off-election years. *Sources:* Flora (1983), Mackie and Rose (1982).

of the Soviet leadership was Jewish and that Jews made up seventeen of the twenty-two people's commissars in Bela Kun's Soviet government in Hungary. Moreover, in the summer of 1919, he described Bolshevism as a worldwide Jewish conspiracy against the Aryans and claimed that rich Jewish bankers from London and New York, including the Rothschilds, Warnberg, the Schiffs, and Guggenheim, had funded the Bolsheviks. Also, the Catholic Church journal *La Civiltà Cattolica* published an article, "La rivoluzione mondiale e gli Ebrei," in 1922 claiming that 447 of the 545 Russian Bolshevik government's state functionaries and 17 of the 21 Soviet people's commissars were Jewish.[127] But again, in these discussions concerning a purported link between Jews and revolutionary socialism, there was seldom any mention of a propensity among Italian Jews for the revolutionary socialist left.[128] Instead, these anti-Semitic polemics concentrated on Central and Eastern European Jews.

With the return of relative calm after the establishment of the Italian fascist regime, interest in the "Protocols" and the myth of "Jewish Bolshevism" subsided until 1938. The one notable exception was the so-called Ponte Teresa incident of March 1934 that supposedly linked Italian Jews to an antifascist conspiracy. The Ponte Teresa incident involved the arrest of seventeen alleged antifascist conspirators. Among the seventeen detainees, eleven were Jewish. The Italian daily press gave considerable coverage to the sizeable Jewish contingent arrested. The influential and widely circulated Italian newspaper *Corriere della Sera*, in its March 31, 1934, edition, accused the detained Jews of being in the pay of expatriate antifascist Italians. In the end, an Italian court acquitted all but two of the accused.[129] The year 1938 marked a dramatic turn in official Italian anti-Semitism. In 1938, three new editions of the "Protocols" appeared, with a new preface and introduction fashioned by two noted Italian fascist anti-Semites, Giovanni Preziosi and Julius Evola.[130] The release of these new editions of the "Protocols" coincided with the beginnings of the fascist anti-Jewish campaign. The fascist anti-Jewish campaign may have been ignited by Mussolini's rapprochement with

---

[127] Ibid., 42–43, 48–50; 69–70; Goldstaub, "Rassegna," 409–33; Zuccotti, *Italians*, 31; Michaelis, *Mussolini*, 6–9, 12–13; Molinari, *Ebrei*, 91–92.

[128] According to Sodi ("Italian," 46), Preziosi may be a notable exception to the rule. Preziosi, in addition to linking Jews worldwide to revolutionary socialism, made the observation that two of the three founding leaders of the Italian Socialist Party were Jewish. The two were Treves and Modigliani.

[129] Zuccotti, *Italians*, 28–29, 291; Michaelis, *Mussolini*, 58–60.

[130] Goldstaub, "Rassegna," 409–33.

Hitler, Mussolini's mounting frustration with the policies of Léon Blum in France, the continuation of the Spanish Civil War, and the imposition of the League of Nations sanctions against Italy. Also, at this juncture, a plethora of fascist anti-Semitic publications surfaced attacking "Jewish Bolshevism" and cautioning Italian Jews to stay clear of abetting their antifascist co-religionists outside of Italy.[131]

Like Jews in other European countries, Italian Jews had become members and, in a number of instances, notable leaders of Italian socialist groups. Italian Jews contributed to the leadership of the Italian Socialist Party from its inception in 1892. Among the best-known Italian Jews in Italy's socialist movement were Achille Loria, Giuseppe Emanuele Modigliani, Claudio Treves, Rodolfo Mondolfo, Umberto Terracini, Emilio Sereni, Enzo Sereni, and Alberto Cavaglion. Loria, a respected economist and critic of Marxian socialism from the University of Turin, had gained some notoriety before the turn of the century through his heated philosophical battles with Engels. Both Modigliani and Treves were moderate socialists who were instrumental in the leadership of the Italian Socialist Party; Terracini, along with Antonio Gramsci, Palmiro Togliatti, and Angelo Tasca, founded the Italian Communist Party, and Terracini and Sereni became two of the most important leaders of the party.[132] However, as Roth and Hughes have adroitly observed, a marked difference was evident between the political attachments of Italian Jews and those of Jews in so many other European nations: Jews in Italy were not overwhelmingly identified with leftist political parties, as Jews were in most other European nations. In Italy, Jews were identified with *both* left-wing and right-wing parties.[133] The high degree of assimilation and social equality experienced by Italian Jews attenuated the appeal of

---

[131]　Ibid., 412; Michaelis, "Fascist," 46, 118–19; Stille, *Benevolence*, 65; Zuccotti, *Italians*, 33. Coincidentally, in the mid-1930s, a few novels appear that depict Jewish characters as part of revolutionary movements in general and as adherents of Bolshevism in particular. Papini's *Gog* and Gotta's 1934 *Lilith* and its 1935 sequel, *Il Paradiso Terrestre*, are prime examples (Gunzberg, *Strangers*, 249–56).

[132]　Momigliano, *Ottavo*, 371–74; Molinari, *Ebrei*, 84–85; Zuccotti, *Italians*, 247–48; Stille, *Benevolence*, 102; Steinberg, *All or Nothing*, 224. Michaelis (*Mussolini*, 5–6) claims that, overall, very few of the Italian Bolshevik leaders were Jews. Also, a number of Jews – including Carlo Rosselli, Leone Ginzburg, Carlo Levi, and Vittorio Foa – played a central role in the left-leaning antifascist Giustizia e Libertà during the 1930s. These non-Marxist antifascists advocated a *"socialismo liberale"* in place of a *"dittatura russa"* (Stille, *Benevolence*, 102; Molinari, *Ebrei*, 81–85).

[133]　Roth, *History*, 476; Hughes, *Prisoners*, 22.

political parties advocating societal leveling. In what may appear to be one of the great political ironies of the twentieth century, Italian Jews were from the beginning overrepresented in Mussolini's Italian fascist movement.

When we think of twentieth-century fascism, whether it be the plethora of interwar fascist movements and parties in France, the Iron Guard of Romania, the Arrow Cross of Hungary, Mosley's British Union of Fascists, or Hitler's German NSDAP, we typically associate the phenomenon with pronounced anti-Semitism. Anti-Semitism figured prominently in all of these fascist movements. In the case of Italy, this association does not hold before 1938. With few exceptions, the Italian fascist movement, from its inception in 1919 until 1938, showed no inclination to embrace anti-Semitism. Moreover, from the beginning of the Italian fascist movement, many Italian Jews enthusiastically embraced the new movement and rose to positions of prominence within the movement and party.

Of the 117 "fascists of the first hour" or "founding fathers" of the Italian fascist movement who joined together on March 23, 1919, in Milan's Piazza San Sepolcro, 5 were Jews. One of them, Cesare Goldmann, secured the meeting room for the first meeting of the Fasci Italiani di Combattimento in Milan. Enrico Rocca, a Jew, is frequently cited as the founder of Roman fascism. Counted among the early fascist martyrs (*martirologio ufficiale*) who lost their lives in the so-called fascist revolution before 1922 were three Jews: Gino Bolaffi, Bruno Mondolfo, and Duilio Sinigaglia. Among Mussolini's earliest financial backers were three Jews: Giuseppe Toeplitz of the Banca Commerciale Italiana, Elio Jona, and the industrialist Gino Olivetti. Participating in the famous fascist "March on Rome" in October 1922 were 230 Italian Jews. (It has been reported that the commander of the military garrison in Rome at the time of the march, who allowed the fascists to enter the city, was Massimo de Castiglioni, a Jew). Jewish membership in the Italian Fascist Party rose dramatically between 1922 and 1938. There were 746 Jewish members in October 1922 in the two political parties that merged to form the new Italian Fascist Party. By October 1928, Jewish membership in the party had climbed to 1,793, and by 1933, 4,800 additional Jews had joined the Italian Fascist Party. In 1933, roughly 10 percent of the Italian Jewish population belonged to the Italian Fascist Party. Before the declaration of the "Manifesto of the Racist Scientists" in 1938, more than 10,000 Italian Jews held membership in the Italian Fascist Party, out of a total Jewish population of approximately 50,000.

After the "March on Rome," Mussolini appointed notable Jews to government posts. Here is a partial list of Jews holding important positions in fascist Italy: Dr. Aldo Finzi (undersecretary of the interior and member of the Fascist Grand Council), Dante Almansi (vice-chief of the fascist police), Guido Jung (minister of finance and ex officio member of the Fascist Grand Council), Alberto Liuzzi[134] (consul-general in the fascist militia), Lodovico Mortara (lord chief justice and first president of the Court of Appeals), Margherita Sarfatti (Mussolini's first official biographer, his mistress, and coeditor of *Gerarchia*, the influential fascist monthly review), Professor Carlo Foa (editor of the *Gerarchia*), Gino Arias (chief fascist theorist of the *Stato corporativo*, the Italian brand of corporatism, and regular contributor to *Il Popolo d'Italia* and *Gerarchia*), Edoardo Polacco (general secretary of the Fascist Party in the province of Brindisi), Gino Olivetti (head of Confindustria), and Giorgio del Vecchio (first fascist rector of the University of Rome). Of the fifteen learned jurists asked by Mussolini to draft the fascist constitution, three were Jews. They were Professors Arias, Barone, and Levi. During the fascist regime, the Jewish proportion of university professors and high-ranking officers in the Italian military remained high. In fact, 8 percent of all Italian university professors in 1930 were Jewish.[135]

Italian Jews, like their non-Jewish Italian counterparts, joined the Italian fascist movement for diverse reasons. For many Jews and Christians, Italian fascism's appeal lay in the movement's support of middle-class material interests, anticommunism, fervent nationalism, and restoration of law and order. Attempts to label Jews as disloyal or Marxists were made all the more difficult because Italy's Jews were well represented in the Italian Fascist Party from its beginnings. In such a context, political anti-Semitism had great difficulty in establishing itself before 1938. Mussolini's apparent *volte-face* in 1938 came as a major shock to both Italian Jews and Christians and ushered in the darkest chapter in the history of modern Italian Jewry.

No factor did more to galvanize political anti-Semitism after World War I than the fear of revolutionary socialism. By advocating social and economic leveling, dismissing religion, and opting for internationalism

---

[134] Michaelis (*Mussolini*, 52) notes that Liuzzi was a baptized Jew.
[135] Michaelis, *Mussolini*, 11, 52; Gunzberg, *Strangers*, 224; De Felice, *Storia*, 70–83; Zuccotti, *Italians*, 18, 25–27; Molinari, *Ebrei*, 101–02; Roth, *History*, 510–11; Steinberg, *All or Nothing*, 224; Leeden, "Evolution," 4; Ernst Nolte, *Three Faces of Fascism* (New York, 1969), 230; Momigliano, *Ottavo*, 373; Cohen, "Jews," 5; Marrus, *Unwanted*, 280; Eatwell, *Fascism*, 85–86.

over nationalism, revolutionary socialists spawned substantial resentment among many groups in society who failed to share their vision. As we have seen, linking Jews to the socialist threat was not difficult for anti-Semites for a number of reasons. First, two of the most eminent early European socialists, Karl Marx and Ferdinand Lassalle, had Jewish roots. Second, Jews were overrepresented in the leadership of most European socialist/communist parties. Third, Jews joined European socialist movements in large numbers. Fourth, the alleged conspiratorial and internationalist characters of socialism struck some non-Jews as consistent with the diasporic nature of the Jewish people and the messianic message of Judaism. Indeed, for many people prone to accept conspiracy theories, Jewish socialism replaced Freemasonry as the principal worldwide conspiracy seeking to bring down the Western status quo. However, political anti-Semitism varied across space and time in our five cases. In places and at times where an imminent socialist takeover appeared possible (e.g., Germany between 1919 and 1922 or France between 1936 and 1938), and/or where Jews were closely identified with the leadership of the revolutionary socialist movement (e.g., Germany between 1919 and 1922 or Romania from 1919 to 1939), heightened political anti-Semitism issued forth. Without question, increasing levels of Eastern and Central European Jewish immigration and growing economic problems further exacerbated political anti-Semitism. Overall, we should expect to find the highest levels of political anti-Semitism in Germany, France, and Romania and lower levels in Great Britain and Italy. In both Germany and France, the revolutionary socialist left remained a viable threat to take power throughout much of the interwar period (in Germany until 1934). Furthermore, in both countries, Jews were closely identified with the socialist leadership. The left in Romania failed to present a viable threat, although it, more than the left in any of the other cases, stood out for its foreign and Jewish composition and could always be identified as a possible conduit for Romania's interwar archenemy, the Soviet Union. The fear of the movements of Hungarian and Russian irredentism in alliance with the Romanian Communist Party was no chimera for many Romanians during the interwar years. In Great Britain, political anti-Semitism emerged less from the perception of a political takeover by the ILP or the Communist Party of Great Britain – for both failed abysmally to gain adherents – than but more from the threat of revolutionary socialism to British colonial and imperial interests. Nonetheless, few Englishmen feared an imminent socialist takeover at home. Italy stands out as an intriguing case, since the revolutionary left came quite close to achieving state power in 1919 and 1920, and Italy's economic situation deteriorated dramatically in the immediate aftermath of World War I – factors that nourished political anti-Semitism elsewhere. Yet in Italy, linking the revolutionary left to Italian Jews encountered insurmountable hurdles. The high degree of Jewish assimilation into Italian social, political, and economic life, the absence of major waves of Eastern and Central European Jewish immigration, and the fact that Italian Jews were as likely to join the right-wing Italian fascist movement as any leftist movement attenuated the alleged "Jewish Bolshevik" myth, at least until Mussolini's abrupt change in 1938.

What does the evidence from the examination of anti-Semitic acts and attitudes suggest about societal variation in European political anti-Semitism? The data presented in Figure 5.3 show that Germany (with sixty-six recorded laws and acts) and Romania (with thirty-one recorded laws and acts) were most active in the promulgation of laws and acts relating to political anti-Semitism between 1899 and 1939. For Germany, forty-three of the sixty-six laws and acts were issued during the pre–World War II Nazi period (1933–39). Moreover, nine of the remaining twenty-three laws and acts in Germany were issued in the year 1920 – the aftermath of the political left's stunning surge in the national elections. In Romania, by contrast, only nine of the thirty-one laws and acts transpired between 1933 and 1939, indicating once again a temporal consistency in Romanian anti-Semitism. The issuance of laws and acts relating to political anti-Semitism remained rather low in Great Britain, France, and Italy throughout the period of this study. In Italy, three of the six laws and acts transpired between 1938 and 1939. Newspaper reportage on political anti-Semitism contrasts sharply with the quantity of laws and acts, as can be seen in Figure 5.3. Italy and Great Britain led the group in the number of articles discussing political anti-Semitism. The importance of Palestine/Zionism to the interests of both countries contributed greatly to the volume of articles. For Italy, the lion's share of articles appeared during two periods: sixteen between 1899 and 1900 and eighteen between 1937 and 1939, and all but eight of the articles dealt with non-Italian Jews. In the case of Germany, we see once again a significant divergence between the pre-Nazi and Nazi periods, with twenty of the twenty-three articles dealing with political anti-Semitism emerging in the 1933–39 period.

Although Great Britain and Italy had the largest quantity of articles discussing political anti-Semitism, few of those articles exhibited an

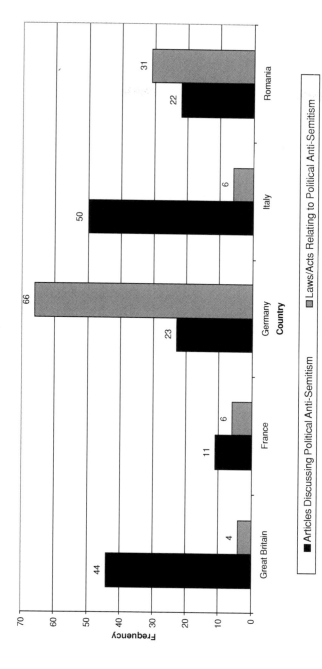

Figure 5.3. Newspaper articles discussing political anti-Semitism and laws/acts relating to political anti-Semitism by country, 1899–1939. *Note:* Articles are taken from the fifteenth day of the month for every month between 1899 and 1939. Articles were taken from the *Daily Mail* in Great Britain (N = 299), *Le Petit Parisien* in France (N = 199), *Berliner Morgenpost* in Germany (N = 269), *Corriere della Sera* in Italy (N = 101), and *Universul* in Romania (N = 136). Laws and acts against Jewish organizations are taken from the volumes of the *American Jewish Year Book* and include two categories from the typology (see Table 1.1). The first includes raids, confiscations, shutdowns, and dissolutions of organizations or media. The second category is false accusations, arrests, or imprisonments. Additionally, I have included deportations or acts that disenfranchise Jews, which were selected from the sixth category in Table 1.1.

unfavorable orientation, as evidenced by the findings in Figure 5.4. Germany and Romania had the highest percentage of unfavorable articles. The French newspaper carried the fewest unfavorable articles among the five national presses.[136]

Figure 5.5 focuses on political anti-Semitism in terms of three specific questions from the anti-Semitic coding instrument. Coders were asked to ascertain if the articles associated Jews with political problems, blamed Jews for political problems, and/or associated Jews with the Marxist left. The findings are quite revealing. The principal newspapers of Great Britain and Italy carried the largest number of articles associating Jews with political problems. Again, much of this reportage may have emanated from the keen interest in both countries in events transpiring in Palestine. However, when it comes to assigning blame to the Jews for the political problems, the data in Figure 5.5 indicate that the British press was relatively less likely to assign blame to the Jews than the French, German, Italian, and Romanian presses. In the cases of Germany, nine of the ten articles blaming Jews for the political problems appeared between 1933 and 1939, while in Italy, twelve of the thirty-six articles were published between 1937 and 1939, and sixteen of the thirty-six articles came out between 1899 and 1900 (coverage of the Dreyfus Affair). Importantly, of the thirty-six articles blaming Jews for political problems carried in the Italian newspaper, only four dealt with Italian Jews. All the others discussed Jews or Jewish issues outside of Italy. One of the more interesting findings of Figure 5.5 relates to the question concerning the association of Jews with the Marxist left. I have argued in this chapter that the charge that Jews were linked to the revolutionary left encountered a major obstacle in Italy, given the large number of Italian Jews associated with the nationalist and Italian fascist movements. Consistent with my contention, we find that among all five countries, the association of Jews with the Marxist left is weakest in Italy, with only two articles. These two articles, moreover, were not about Italian Jews, and both appeared between 1936 and 1937. Equally revealing in terms of political anti-Semitic reportage is the strong proportion of articles in France, Germany, and Romania associating Jews

---

[136] The within-country comparison of newspaper reportage regarding unfavorable articles discussing political anti-Semitism reveals a high degree of consistency. The only exception is in the German reportage, where, once again, for the selected years, the *Muenchner Neueste Nachrichten* diverged significantly from the *Berliner Morgenpost*. The Munich paper contained nine unfavorable articles to the Berlin paper's two articles.

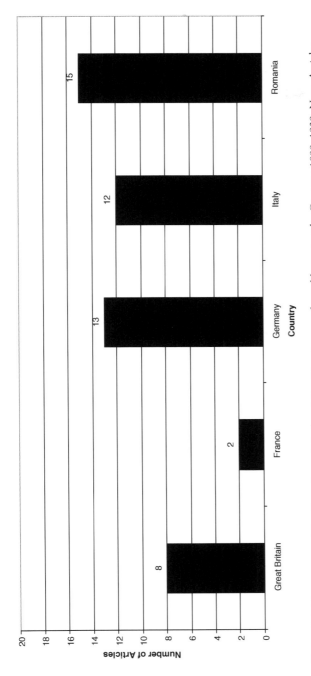

Figure 5.4. Newspaper articles discussing political anti-Semitism in an unfavorable context by Country, 1899–1939. *Note:* Articles are taken from the fifteenth day of the month for every month between 1899 and 1939. Articles were taken from the *Daily Mail* in Great Britain (N = 299), *Le Petit Parisien* in France (N = 199), *Berliner Morgenpost* in Germany (N = 269), *Corriere della Sera* in Italy (N = 101), and *Universul* in Romania (N = 136). Articles were coded "unfavorable" if the article reflected negatively on Jews, if the author's tone expressed disdain for Jews, or if the article supported actions that adversely affected Jews.

with the Marxist left. The case of Romania is of particular interest, given the relative electoral weakness of its political left. In Romania, fourteen of the twenty-two articles discussing political anti-Semitism associated Jews with the Marxist left. Regardless of the relative political weakness of the left in Romania, the generally recognized overrepresentation of Jews in the Romanian Communist Party should have contributed to the popular perception of a Jewish and Marxist connection. Furthermore, not surprisingly, the preponderance of articles linking Jews to the Marxist left appeared during the 1933–39 period. More specifically, eleven of the twelve German articles and ten of the fourteen Romanian articles were published between 1933 and 1939.[137]

Throughout my examination of the four roots of anti-Semitism, I have for heuristic or analytical reasons assigned equal weight to each root and have treated each root independently. Notwithstanding what the empirical evidence from my research suggests about the weight of each root, my study does not allow for an accurate assessment of the variation of the extent to which each root engrained itself within the psyches of individuals and groups. Some might opine that the religious root of anti-Semitism, by virtue of its longevity and embeddedness within Christian theology, has a greater staying power than the other roots. This study is unable to ascertain the validity of this proposition. Moreover, one can present much viable evidence for how these four roots combine with one another. Here are a few examples. Jews, for instance, were charged with conspiring to undermine the existing political and social order. To that end, it was alleged, Jews sponsored and joined revolutionary socialist movements. The reasons presented by people holding this view frequently touched on religious leitmotifs. The Jewish religion fostered a messianic tendency; Jews sought to avenge centuries of Christian discrimination; Jews were atheistic. Economic anti-Semitism often highlighted a supposed "Jewish" acquisitiveness and avarice. Many

---

[137] Examining the results of the intranational newspaper reportage on political anti-Semitism for the selected years, we find little divergence in reportage for the French and Italian newspapers. On the other hand, the *Daily Herald* gave slightly greater coverage to political anti-Semitism than the *Daily Mail*, while *Lumea* provided less coverage than *Universul*. The largest divergence in the intranational reportage emerged from the German press. For the selected years, the *Muenchner Neueste Nachrichten* carried on average six times the number of articles associating Jews with political problems, blaming Jews for political problems, or associating Jews with the Marxist left than the number appearing in the *Berliner Morgenpost*.

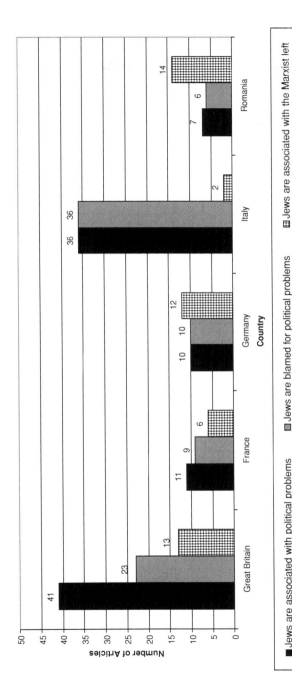

Figure 5.5. Newspaper articles discussing political anti-Semitism by country, 1899–1939. *Note:* Articles are taken from the fifteenth day of the month for every month between 1899 and 1939. Articles were taken from the *Daily Mail* in Great Britain (N = 299), *Le Petit Parisien* in France (N = 199), *Berliner Morgenpost* in Germany (N = 269), *Corriere della Sera* in Italy (N = 101), and *Universul* in Romania (N = 136).

anti-Semites attributed these economic practices to inherent or Jewish "racial" traits or to Talmudic scriptures (religious origins). And racial anti-Semites frequently distinguished between Christian Aryans and other races. For what made the Aryan race so creative and successful, according to many racial anti-Semites, such as Drumont and Chamberlain, was in large part its Christian religious heritage. There are clearly many other examples of how these four roots – religious, racial, economic, and political – interact with and bolster one another. To that end, in the concluding chapter, we turn to a more comprehensive examination of the data on anti-Semitic acts and attitudes. We are particularly interested in the relationship between changes in the volume and character of these acts and attitudes resulting from changes in the rate of Jewish immigration, economic conditions, and popular support for the political left.

# CHAPTER SIX

# CONCLUSION

This book has focused on a number of issues regarding anti-Semitism in Europe before the Holocaust. I have examined the rise of European anti-Semitism through the lens of the religious, economic, racial, and political roots of anti-Semitism. These four roots of anti-Semitism appear to have been instrumental in the formation of anti-Jewish narratives emerging between 1879 and 1939. The four anti-Jewish narratives gained credence from the effects of declining economic well-being, increased Jewish immigration, growth of leftist support, and identification of Jews with the leadership of the political left. However, popular support for anti-Semitism varied temporally and spatially. Anti-Semitism, as measured by acts and attitudes, reached its highest points between the two world wars, particularly in Germany and Romania. Anti-Semitic levels in both Great Britain and France were significantly lower than those in Germany and Romania. The case of France may come as a surprise to many, in light of France's Dreyfus Affair experience and the oft-cited writings of many of France's rightist intellectuals. The conventional wisdom would have it that France, notably during the mid-1930s, with the circulation of the popular slogan *vaut mieux Hitler que Blum* (better Hitler than Blum), was a hotbed of anti-Semitism. The empirical data do not support this contention, however, at least as it may apply to the French middle and lower classes. Italy remained relatively untouched by anti-Semitism, at least until 1936. We have seen that in the case of Italy, the immigration of Eastern European Jews and the identification of Jews with the Italian revolutionary left never materialized as significant issues.

Though I have limited my study to five European nations, I would propose that these findings may be generalized to other European societies.

The case of Bulgaria is illustrative. The Jewish community of Bulgaria largely escaped the destruction of the Holocaust. During World War II, Bulgaria was an ally of Nazi Germany. In March 1943, when Nazi officials ordered the deportation of Bulgaria's 50,000 Jews, King Boris and the Bulgarian government refused to implement the Nazi order. Why? Bulgaria, much like Italy, possessed low levels of anti-Semitism. Like Italy's, Bulgarian Jews were not overrepresented in the Bulgarian communist movement; like Italy's, Bulgarian Jews were largely Sephardic Jews, who had come to Bulgaria from Spain after 1492; and like Italy's, Bulgarian Jews were highly assimilated into Bulgarian society.[1] In brief, pre-Holocaust Gentile attitudes toward Jews in Europe may have been largely shaped by the degree to which declining economic well-being, increased Jewish immigration, growth of leftist support, and identification of Jews with the leadership of the political left were capable of igniting the religious, racial, economic, and political roots of anti-Semitism.

In the following paragraphs, I will attempt to demonstrate empirically the relationship between spatial and temporal variations in anti-Semitism and Jewish immigration, declining economic conditions, and popular support for the left. I have proposed that, within the context of the four roots of anti-Semitism, temporal and spatial variations across the five nations resulted chiefly from the effects of four critical factors. I propose, in short, that increased levels of Jewish immigration (typically from Eastern and Central Europe) should affect levels of popular anti-Semitism in several ways. Since many of the new Jewish immigrants from Eastern Europe possessed few resources and little formal education, they typically competed with many in the host population for low-paying jobs. Competition often bred animosity, resulting in heightened levels of anti-Semitism. Furthermore, the Yiddish-speaking new arrivals from

---

[1] I suggest that the Sephardic–Ashkenazic distinction is far from perfect in terms of differences in Gentile antipathy toward Jews or rates of Jewish victimization during the Holocaust. We cannot forget the bravery of the Danes in resisting Nazi persecution of Danish Jews. The saved Jews of Denmark were largely Ashkenazic, rather than Sephardic. What is essential here is the degree to which Jews were assimilated. Avaham Ben-Ya'akov, "The Bulgarian Jewish Community, 1879–1950: A Model of Zionist Fullfillment," *SHVUT*, vol. 6, no. 22, 1997, 184–205; Tzvetan Todorov, *The Fragility of Goodness: Why Bulgaria's Jews Survived the Holocaust*, trans. A. Denner (Princeton, 1999), 31, 122. In forthcoming research, I am applying my model of the rise of and variations in anti-Semitism to a study of Bulgaria before the Holocaust.

Eastern Europe's Jewish ghettos (Ashkenazic Jews), with their strange customs and religious practices, frequently struck Western European Gentiles as very different from the more assimilated Sephardic Jews, who had lived in the West for centuries. The influx of Eastern European Jews should have fueled the negative racial stereotypes existing within Western European culture and thereby have contributed to growing anti-Semitism. Particularly in the aftermath of the 1917 Bolshevik Revolution, many European Gentiles associated recent Eastern European Jewish immigrants with Bolshevism. Given that many of these Jewish immigrants appeared impoverished, had fled persecution, and came from the former Russian empire, they were perceived to favor parties of the political left. Thus, increased Jewish immigration should have heightened religious, racial, economic, and political antipathies toward Jews, and we should expect that increasing Jewish immigration fueled increasing anti-Semitism. A decline in a nation's economic well-being, particularly in an environment in which Jews are seen as controlling or owning major economic resources, should produce higher levels of anti-Jewish feelings. On the other hand, we should not expect to find high levels of anti-Semitic sentiment in times of economic stability or growth or in situations where Jews are not perceived to be in positions of dominance within a nation's economy. The dramatic rise of the revolutionary left at the end of the nineteenth century led to the fear of a violent overturn of the existing social, economic, political, and religious order in Europe. In the popular consciousness, Jews were often linked to the revolutionary left. Many anti-Semites cited Jews as the founders of revolutionary socialism and anarchism and saw the hand of Jews in periodic labor unrest. Thus, we should expect to see increased anti-Semitism in societies where the political left exhibited growing strength and where prominent leftist leaders were identified as Jews. However, where support for the political left was weak or declining, or where Jews were not seen as playing important roles in the left, we should expect lower levels of anti-Semitism. Unfortunately, there exists no comparable empirical yardstick to measure the magnitude of the public's perception of Jewish identification with the revolutionary left within the five countries. Throughout this study, I have relied principally upon the secondary literature's accounts of the alleged association between Jews and the revolutionary left in each of the five countries.

Table 6.1 presents the results of a regression analysis of anti-Semitic acts for the 1899–1939 period on GDP per capita, Jewish immigration,

TABLE 6.1. *Regression of anti-Semitic acts in Great Britain, France, Germany, Italy and Romania on predictor variables, 1899–1939*

| Variable | Unstandardized Coefficient (Standardized Coefficient) |
|---|---|
| Year | .010** |
|  | (.255) |
| Great Britain | .308 |
|  | (.250) |
| France | .128 |
|  | (.103) |
| Germany (1899–1932) | .296** |
|  | (.107) |
| Germany (1933–39) | .954** |
|  | (.189) |
| Romania | .590** |
|  | (.478) |
| GDP | −.013* |
|  | −(.341) |
| Jewish immigration | .188* |
|  | (.089) |
| Leftist vote | −.003 |
|  | −(.091) |
| Constant | −18.086** |
| R-square | .502 |

\* $p < .05$, one-tailed; \*\* $p < .05$, two-tailed

*Note:* Italy is the reference category for country variables. Numbers in parentheses represent the standardized coefficients.

and leftist vote. To test my proposition, I employ least squares regression with dummy variables (LSDV).[2]

---

[2] To test my hypothesis I utilize pooled time series methods, which allow me to capture variation in all variables both over time and across space. LSDV is a pooled time series estimator applicable when the dependent variable is heterogeneous across groups, as is the case in the present analysis (Lois Sayrs, *Pooled Time Series Analysis*, Newbury Park, CA, Sage 1989). The LSDV model includes dummy variables representing the respective countries of interest, thus making it a fixed-effects model. Since Italy recorded the fewest anti-Semitic acts, it was used as the reference category in the dummy set. Further, I included a dummy variable representing Hitler's rule in Germany (1933–39). I propose that this is necessary

The results of the regression analysis show clearly that GDP per capita and Jewish immigration are good predictors of variations in anti-Semitic acts for the five countries. More specifically, while controlling for the effects of year, country, and Jewish population, the relationship between GDP per capita and anti-Semitic acts and between Jewish immigration and anti-Semitic acts are significant and in the predicted direction. However, the relationship between leftist voting and anti-Semitic acts does not conform to my model's expectations. The variables together (both control and independent) explained more than one-half the variance in anti-Semitic acts.[3]

The multiple regression analysis found no significant relationship between leftist voting and anti-Semitic acts. However, the scholarly literature on European anti-Semitism, especially for the interwar period, points explicitly to a link between leftist voting strength and anti-Semitism. It should be added that this link frequently included the charge of Jewish identification with the revolutionary left. Why doesn't the empirical analysis pick up this relationship? I believe there are a couple of reasons for this. In large part, we can attribute the weak relationship to Romania's high number of anti-Semitic acts and low level of

---

because the political and social climate in Germany was vastly different during this period. Moreover, I control for year in the analysis, again in order to control for sociopolitical changes not encompassed by the set of independent variables. Finally, although I justify the use of Italy as the reference category in the LSDV analysis, the choice is still rather arbitrary. Thus, I employ Stimson's (James A. Stimson, "Regression in Space and Time: A Statistical Essay," *American Journal of Political Science*, vol 29, no. 4, 1985, 914–47) approach and do not interpret the dummy variable coefficients, even though they do make substantive sense in the present analysis. Also, because I have no exact measure of annual immigration by country, I choose to measure immigration by change in the percentage of Jews residing in a country from the previous year. Since it is generally recognized that between 1881 and 1940 Jewish immigrants come almost exclusively from Central and Eastern Europe, the figures for increased Jewish population should largely represent Jewish immigration.

[3] I ran a random effects model to help correct for correlated errors, and the substantive findings held. Thus, it appears that the model employed for the analysis of anti-Semitic acts is robust across model specifications. Additionally, the three variables of theoretical interest—immigration, GDP per capita, and leftist voting – by themselves explain 28 percent of the variance in anti-Semitic acts for the 1899–1932 period and 20 percent of the variance for the 1899–1939 period. Moreover, I ran additional models controlling for Jewish population, and all results in all analyses replicated, but I did not include Jewish population because it is highly collinear with the variable representing Romania.

leftist voting. As mentioned earlier, Romania's relatively lower level of industrialization throughout the period of this study failed to nurture the growth of a large industrial proletariat – a class from which the Marxist left traditionally drew adherents. The left was never a major political contender in Romania's politics. Nevertheless, fear of the left and iden-tification of Jews with the left were obsessions among many segments of the Romanian population. This fear derived largely from the proxim-ity of Bolshevik Russia, the perception that Bolshevik Russia sought the reannexation of parts of Bessarabia and Bukovina, and the oft-publicized claim that Jews were significantly overrepresented within the leadership of the small and highly antinationalist Romanian Communist Party. The lack of an empirical relationship between leftist voting and anti-Semitic acts in the regression analysis may also be due to the particular case of the Italian left. Italy before 1936 witnessed few anti-Semitic acts, but the political left before Mussolini's seizure of power in 1922 drew substantial popular support. Yet, as I have argued earlier, the allegation of Jewish identification with the Italian left never materialized before 1936 in Italy, due largely to the high proportion of Jews in the Italian Fascist Party.

Table 6.2 shows the results of a regression analysis of anti-Semitic attitudes for the 1899–1939 period on GDP per capita, Jewish immi-gration, and leftist vote.[4] Again, I include the same control variables as used in Table 6.1. Unlike the previous analysis of anti-Semitic acts, the regression analysis of anti-Semitic attitudes does not conform to my expectations. From Model 1 in Table 6.2, we see that the three in-dependent variables do not emerge as good predictors of variations in anti-Semitic attitudes for the five countries over the 1899–1939 period. In fact, the explanatory power of the combined control and independent variables accounts for a little more than one-quarter of the explained variance in anti-Semitic attitudes.[5] That the zero-order correlation be-tween the measures of the two dependent variables (anti-Semitic acts

---

[4] I employ the annual proportion of articles unfavorable toward Jews as the measure of anti-Semitic attitudes. Also, as in Table 6.1, I ran additional models controlling for Jewish population, and all results in all analyses replicated, but I did not include Jewish population because it is highly collinear with the variable representing Romania.

[5] The three variables of theoretical interest–immigration, GDP, and leftist voting – by themselves explain only 5 percent of the variance in anti-Semitic attitudes for the 1899–1932 period and 2 percent of the variance in the dependent variable for the 1899–1939 period.

TABLE 6.2. *Regression of anti-Semitic attitudes in Great Britain, France, Germany, Italy, and Romania on predictor variables, 1899–1939*

| Variable | Model 1 | Model 2 | Model 3 |
|---|---|---|---|
| Year | .009** | .010** | .009** |
| | (.492) | (.514) | (.493) |
| Great Britain | .154 | .153 | .163 |
| | (.285) | (.283) | (.303) |
| France | −.023 | .013 | .022 |
| | −(.042) | (.025) | (.041) |
| Germany (1899–1932) | .048 | .069 | .057 |
| | (.082) | (.118) | (.097) |
| Germany (1933–39) | .358** | .342** | .344** |
| | (.305) | (.291) | (.292) |
| Romania | −.103 | −.130* | −.101 |
| | −(.191) | −(.242) | −(.188) |
| GDP | −.006 | −.006 | −.006* |
| | −(.340) | −(.347) | −(.389) |
| Jewish immigration | .009 | −.226** | −.590** |
| | (.010) | −(.246) | −(.644) |
| Leftist vote | −.005** | −.006** | −.005** |
| | −(.356) | −(.402) | −(.321) |
| Jewish immigration * Leftist voting | – | .056** | – |
| | | (.317) | – |
| GDP * Jewish immigration | – | – | .041** |
| | | | (.669) |
| Constant | −17.306** | −18.065** | −17.305** |
| R-square | .265 | .298 | .281 |

$* p < .05$, one-tailed; $** p < .05$, two-tailed

*Note:* Unstandardized coefficients reported with standardized coefficients in parentheses.

Italy is the reference category for country variables.

The dependent variable in the analysis is the proportion of articles in a given year unfavorable toward Jews.

and attitudes) is a less-than-robust .285 indicates that the relationship between these two measures is far weaker than we might have expected.[6]

[6] The bivariate correlations show that the relationship between anti-Semitic acts and attitudes is positive and significant for Italy, Germany, and Romania, but negative and nonsignificant for Great Britain and France.

However, before concluding that the explanatory model for anti-Semitic attitudes is unsatisfactory, I decided to examine interaction effects among the independent variables of interest. The theory outlined in this study suggests that anti-Semitic acts and attitudes should vary with changes in GDP per capita, Jewish immigration, and leftist voting. While I posit that these factors will affect anti-Semitism independent of one another, it is also likely that the variables will operate interactively. For example, the expected effect of Jewish immigration may be exacerbated when leftist voting is high, but may be muted when leftist voting is low. Similar conditional relationships may hold for other combinations of variables as well. Thus, I added interaction terms to the models in order to test for conditional relationships between the variables.

The interaction term in Model 2 of Table 6.2 represents the interaction of Jewish immigration and leftist voting. The coefficient, in conjunction with the main effects portion of the model, suggests that Jewish immigration has a weak and positive effect on anti-Semitic attitudes when leftist voting is low. However, the effect is strong and positive when leftist voting is high.[7] Conversely, leftist voting has a negative effect on anti-Semitic attitudes when Jewish immigration is decreasing, but has a positive effect when immigration is increasing. This finding is consistent with my theory.

As presented in Model 3 of Table 6.2, I also found a significant interaction effect between GDP per capita and Jewish immigration. In this case, the effect of Jewish immigration on anti-Semitic attitudes is positive and strong when GDP per capita levels are higher. Conversely, the negative effect of GDP per capita is exacerbated when Jewish immigration is declining. This finding did not support my theory.[8]

---

[7] To test for interaction at high and low levels of leftist voting, I use the values at plus and minus one standard deviation from the mean to represent high and low levels. This strategy was repeated when testing interaction effects with other variables as well.

[8] These were the only interactions that proved robust across both fixed effects and random coefficient models. There was evidence of a significant three-way interaction between GDP per capita, leftist voting, and Jewish immigration, which increased the explained variance in the model (R-square) to .364, but the coefficients were sensitive to changes in the model, and thus I would report them only tentatively. Also, aggregate graphs of GDP per capita, Jewish immigration, and leftist voting suggested that there are very few times and places where the three variables converge in a manner that would lead the theory to predict high levels of anti-Semitism (i.e., low GDP, high immigration, and leftist voting). This may partially explain the absence of more significant interaction effects. Interestingly,

Notwithstanding the value of adding interaction terms to the model of anti-Semitic attitudes, the relationship between the theoretically important variables and anti-Semitic attitudes is weaker than expected. How might one explain this finding? The relatively low number of unfavorable articles contained in the various newspapers certainly contributes. For the entire 41-year period, the sampling produced a total of 141 unfavorable articles for the five countries (compared to 1,295 anti-Semitic acts for the same period). With so few articles for a study of five countries over a forty-one-year period, it is often difficult to locate statistically significant relationships. However, the sample size does permit us to detect broad spatial and temporal patterns. To that end, we have seen in Figures 1.8a through 1.8d that the number of unfavorable articles about Jews was nineteen between 1899 and 1913, twelve between 1914 and 1923, eighteen between 1924 and 1932, and ninety-two between 1933 and 1939. Clearly, the 1930s marked a dramatic shift in newspaper reportage on Jews, most notably in Germany, Italy, and Romania. It should be pointed out that only thirty-seven of the ninety-two unfavorable articles published between 1933 and 1939 were published in the principal German newspaper.

Though this book has primarily sought to examine temporal and societal variations in European anti-Semitism before the Holocaust, it has touched upon a set of issues quite relevant to the phenomenon of anti-Semitism. Among those issues are the uniqueness of German anti-Semitism; the place of anti-Semitism within the pantheon of ethnic, religious, and racial prejudice; and the likelihood of another Holocaust. I now address each of these points.

In one of the most provocative assertions characterizing German anti-Semitism, Daniel J. Goldhagen recently opined: ". . . much *positive* evidence exists that anti-Semitism, albeit an anti-Semitism evolving in content with the changing times, continued to be an axiom of German culture throughout the nineteenth and twentieth centuries, and that its regnant version in Germany during its Nazi period was but a more accentuated, intensified, and elaborated form of an already broadly accepted basic model."[9] If Goldhagen is correct, we might expect to find

these aggregate graphs (not shown) indicate that immediately after World War I, there was a drop in GDP and a simultaneous increase in Jewish immigration and leftist voting. Incidentally, this time point also represents the highest levels of anti-Semitic acts prior to Hitler's election in Germany.

[9] Goldhagen, *Hitler's*, 32.

consistently higher levels of anti-Semitism, as expressed by acts and attitudes, in Germany than in our other four countries, as well as relatively high levels of anti-Semitism in Germany prior to the Nazi period. The empirical data do not support Goldhagen's claim. As presented in Chapter 1, 401 of the 703 anti-Semitic acts reported for Germany for the 1899–1939 period occurred between 1933 and 1939. In other words, between 1933 and 1939, Germany experienced roughly fifty-seven anti-Semitic acts per year, contrasted to approximately nine anti-Semitic acts per year between 1899 and 1932. What about the newspaper reportage on German anti-Semitism? In Figures 1.8a through 1.8d, we also witnessed a dramatic turnabout in German newspaper reportage beginning in 1933. Prior to 1933, the reportage on Jews by Germany's largest circulating newspaper, the *Berliner Morgenpost*, indicated a generally benign treatment. A skeptic might allege that the *Berliner Morgenpost's* reportage on Jews prior to 1933 was unrepresentative of the German newsprint medium. Indeed, we glean clearly from Figure 1.9 that for the years 1921, 1933, 1935, and 1939, the reportage on Jews by the *Muenchner Neueste Nachrichten* was substantially more extensive than the *Berliner Morgenpost's* reportage. But it would be premature to conclude from this that the two German newspapers differed significantly in regard to *orientation* toward Jews or that an unfavorable tone existed in German newspaper reportage both before and after 1933. The results shown in Figure 1.9 derive from a selection of years that includes only one time point prior to 1933: Hitler's ascension to power.

In order to examine more precisely variation in German newspaper reportage before and after 1933, as well as to look more closely at the thesis of a German *Sonderweg* of anti-Semitism, I directed my German research assistants to compare the reportage on Jews in the *Berliner Morgenpost* and the *Muenchner Neueste Nachrichten* for selected years between 1919 and 1939.[10] The years, chosen at random, were 1919, 1921, 1925, 1930, 1933, 1935, and 1939. Figure 6.1 presents the results. Without question, the reportage on Jews in *both* German newspapers is hardly unfavorable. All thirteen articles in the pre-1933 sample of the *Berliner Morgenpost* are neutral in tone, while ten of the fourteen articles from the *Muenchner Neueste Nachrichten* are neutral. Of the remaining four articles in the *Muenchner Neueste Nachrichten*, three are favorable

---

[10] In Figure 1.9, which focused on intranational newspaper reportage for the five countries, there is only one year, 1921, that is prior to 1933 included in the analysis.

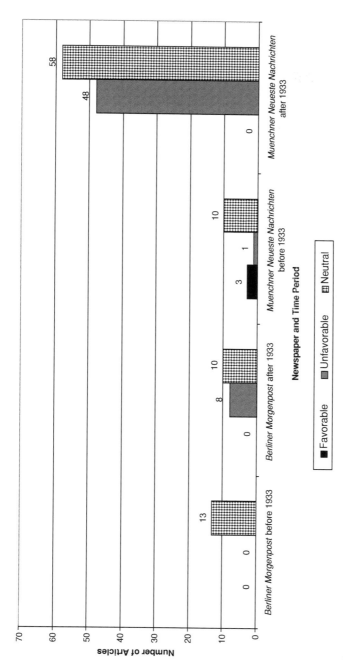

Figure 6.1. German newspapers' orientation toward Jews by newspaper for the years 1919, 1921, 1925, 1930, 1933, 1935, and 1939. *Note:* Articles were coded "unfavorable" if the article reflected negatively on Jews, if the author's tone expressed disdain for Jews, or if the article supported actions that adversely affected Jews. Articles were taken from the fifteenth of the month for every month in the respective years and newspapers.

and one is unfavorable. The comparison of these two newspapers prior to 1933 shows consistency in both tone and volume of articles. The results demonstrate that the 1933–39 period marked a clear divergence in both the volume of articles and the tone of both German newspapers. For the 1933–39 time frame, the Munich paper's coverage of Jews far surpassed the coverage of the Berlin newspaper. Both newspapers exhibited a pronounced increase in unfavorable articles about Jews after Hitler's ascension to power. All told, the results of Figure 6.1 manifestly point to 1933 as a defining fork in German newspaper reportage on Jews, and dash water on the contention that anti-Semitism is an axiom of German culture.

How does anti-Semitism compare to other forms of religious, ethnic, and racial prejudice? Earlier, I suggested that what made anti-Semitism different from other forms of xenophobia or dislike of minorities is that Jew-hatred is more multidimensional than other kinds of prejudice. In the preceding chapters, I have argued that anti-Semitism incorporated religious, racial, economic, and political forms of hatred. Jews were disliked and *feared* for their religious beliefs and attitudes, their alleged racial characteristics, their perceived economic behavior and power, and their assumed leadership or support of subversive political and social movements. The multifaceted nature of anti-Semitism should help to explain why Jews, rather than other minorities, were frequently sought out as scapegoats or useful targets during periods of both worldwide and national difficulties, and why antipathy toward Jews appealed to so many complex groups. The complex character of anti-Semitism may also imply that Jew-hatred is a more intense form of antipathy than other forms of prejudice. Helen Fein's poignant observation about the Holocaust appears to suggest such a claim. Fein wrote: "Now we know how many of Hitler's orders were averted, subverted, or countermanded – extermination of tubercular Poles, mass deportation of the Dutch, catching the Jews of Denmark, burning of Paris, destruction of Germany. The order to exterminate the Jews was not checked because it was already taken for granted that getting rid of the Jews was a legitimate objective."[11] But quantitative assessments of the magnitude of religious, racial, and ethnic hatred are intrinsically difficult to make. For who could state without hesitation that the hatred of Jews by European anti-Semites attained greater force than the loathing of Kurds in Iraq, Armenians in Turkey, Chinese in Indonesia, Muslims in the former

---

[11] Fein, *Accounting*, 91–92.

Yugoslavia, or Gypsies in Central Europe by large segments of the host populations?

In search of a clearer understanding of the heterogeneous nature of anti-Semitism and how anti-Semitic prejudice might compare to other forms of prejudice against minorities, I decided to compare popular antipathies toward Jews and Gypsies (Roma) before the Holocaust. There are many compelling reasons to compare anti-Jewish and anti-Gypsy sentiments. As is the case with the Jews, the Gypsies are a minority that has often suffered from widespread discrimination in Europe. Both Jews and Gypsies encountered hostility for their alleged racial and economic traits.[12] And like the Jews, the Gypsies were targeted for elimination by the Nazis.

Based on linguistic evidence, it is commonly believed that the Gypsies originated in India. They supposedly migrated westward from India beginning nearly one thousand years ago. By the fifteenth century, small groups of Gypsies had reached Western Europe, after sojourning in Asia Minor and Eastern Europe. The word "Gypsy" is an English adulteration of Egyptian and most likely gained currency in early sixteenth century England.[13] Like the Jews of medieval Europe, the Gypsies made their living from a small number of trades. They worked primarily as smiths, metalworkers, producers of baskets, combs, and jewelry, and as fortune-tellers.[14] Within a century after their arrival in Central and Western Europe, the Gypsies were subjected to persecution. Again, as in the case of the Jews of medieval Europe, several European states between the sixteenth and nineteenth centuries expelled the Gypsies, accusing

---

[12] Unflattering myths about the Gypsies certainly would include references to their alleged racial and economic behavior. Interestingly, Kenrick and Puxon have suggested the presence of religious leitmotifs within the constellation of anti-Gypsy sentiment. According to these authors, among some groups in Christian Europe, it was thought that Gypsies denied shelter to Joseph and Mary on their escape from Egypt, and that they shared blame with the Jews for Christ's crucifixion. By one such account, a Gypsy artisan made the nails used to crucify Christ (Donald Kenrick and Grattan Puxon, *The Destiny of Europe's Gypsies*, London, 1972, 26–27).

[13] The Gypsies have been referred to by various appellations, including Sinti and Roma. In the British Isles, they were frequently called Travellers and Tinkers (Judith Okey, *The Traveller-Gypsies*, Cambridge, 1983, 18–19). And as is the case for the word "Jew," official English-language dictionaries include a derogatory definition for a derivative of the word "Gypsy." To "gyp" is defined as to cheat or swindle.

[14] Okey, *Traveller-Gypsies*, 1–11; Kenrick and Puxon, *Destiny*, 13–17, 23–24.

them of trickery, dishonesty, and petty crimes. By the nineteenth century, in many areas of Europe where Gypsies continued to practice a nomadic lifestyle, the authorities treated them as rogues, vagabonds, and vagrants and instituted laws making their daily existence quite precarious.[15] In fact, Mayall cites the enactment of fourteen separate statutes against the Gypsies in Great Britain between 1871 and 1908.[16]

My empirical examination comparing anti-Gypsy and anti-Semitic sentiments is by no means definitive. It should be interpreted as simply suggestive. The examination sought to compare popular attitudes toward Jews and Gypsies as expressed in the newsprint medium. The comparison of attitudes was based on the reading of the widely circulated British daily the *Daily Mail* for the fifteenth day of the month for each year between 1899 and 1939. All articles mentioning Jews or Gypsies were examined. All told, the sample of newspapers contained 299 articles about Jews and 21 articles about Gypsies. The results are presented in Table 6.3. Of the 299 articles pertaining to Jews, my research team coded 44 favorable, 225 neutral, and 29 unfavorable. Of the twenty-one articles dealing with the Gypsies, one was coded favorable, sixteen neutral, and four unfavorable. Among the themes emerging from the articles about Gypsies, three dominate. They are the association of Gypsies with criminal activities (twelve of the twenty-one), the Gypsy nomadic life style, and the association of Gypsies with magic and mystery. While 76 of the 299 articles about Jews included allegations of Jewish criminal activities, we also find a large proportion of articles about Jews referencing purported Jewish political, racial, and economic traits. No article in our sample from the *Daily Mail* suggested that Gypsies constitute a threat to society or to the national interest, while six articles about Jews accused them implicitly or explicitly of posing a danger to British national or societal interests. Certainly, the fact that Jews represented a larger minority in Great Britain than did Gypsies should account for a large part of the divergence in the number of articles. However, what cannot be discounted in any explanation of the results is the significance of the unique multidimensional nature of anti-Semitism vis-à-vis other forms

---

[15] Kenrick and Puxon, *Destiny*, 23–24; Jim Mac Laughlin, "Nation-Building, Social Closure and Anti-Traveller Racism in Ireland," *Sociology*, vol. 33, no. 1, 1999, 129; David Mayall, *Gypsy-Travellers in Nineteenth-Century Society* (Cambridge, 1988), 147–49; Okey, *Traveller*, 1–4.

[16] Mayall, *Gypsy-Travellers*, 189–92. By a rough estimate, the Gypsy population of England and Wales reached 30,000 in 1911 (Mayall, *Gypsy-Travellers*, 24).

TABLE 6.3. Daily Mail *coverage of Jews and Gypsies, 1899–1939*

| | Jewish Articles | Gypsy Articles |
|---|---|---|
| Article Orientation | | |
| Favorable | 44 (15%) | 1 (5%) |
| Unfavorable | 29 (10%) | 4 (19%) |
| Neutral | 225 (74%) | 16 (76%) |
| Discrimination | | |
| Religious | 13 (4%) | 0 |
| Economic | 35 (12%) | 0 |
| Racial | 31 (10%) | 7 (33%) |
| Political | 44 (15%) | 0 |
| Discriminatory Themes | | |
| Associates with criminal activities | 76 (25%) | 12 (57%) |
| Mentions as wandering or in caravans | NA | 11 (52%) |
| Associates with magic, mystery, hypnosis | NA | 6 (29%) |
| Violence against | | |
| Supports | 0 | 0 |
| Opposes | 12 (4%) | 0 |
| Neutral | 31 (10%) | 3 (14%) |
| Organized bans, boycotts, prohibitions | | |
| Supports | 1 (1%) | 0 |
| Opposes | 3 (1%) | 0 |
| Neutral | 13 (4%) | 1 (5%) |
| Threat to society/national interest | | |
| Accept | 6 (2%) | 0 |
| Reject | 3 (1%) | 0 |
| Neutral | 8 (3%) | 0 |
| Use of quotas for group | | |
| Accept | 0 | 0 |
| Reject | 0 | 0 |
| Neutral | 3 (1%) | 0 |
| Total number of articles | 299 | 21 |

*Note:* All articles are from the fifteenth of the month for every month between 1899 and 1939.

of racial, religious, and ethnic prejudice. That Jews could be disliked for religious, racial, economic, or political reasons made them, as I have argued, a more visible target for popular antipathy.

The Western world's anti-Semitism contributed to the Holocaust. As we embark upon a new millenium, we may wonder if anti-Semitic prejudice could once again raise its ugly head to the extent that world Jewry would again be threatened with mass annihilation. As I write this chapter, reports abound of the reawakening of the ancient anti-Semitic demon in Europe. By way of illustration, one of the lead articles in the May 4, 2002, edition of *The Economist* stated: "In the months since September 11th, Europe has seen an increase in attacks on synagogues and other Jewish centres, a rise in threats and intimidation directed at individual Jews, and an increase in anti-Jewish propaganda of one sort or another. On April 21st, Jean-Marie Le Pen, the blithely anti-Semitic leader of the far-right National Front, gained second place in the first round of the French presidential election – a remarkable victory, however bad a drubbing he gets in Sunday's second round. In Germany armed police guard Jewish schools, and Jews are advised not to wear visible signs of their faith. In Britain, often praised for its tolerance, a synagogue was attacked and desecrated this very week."[17] Do these recent events conjure up a revival of European anti-Semitism on the scale of the 1930s? My examination of European anti-Semitism suggests that the likelihood of history repeating itself vis-à-vis the Jews in the West is highly unlikely. Indeed, the recent upsurge in anti-Semitic acts in Europe has more to do with the Israeli-Palestinian dispute than with what some commentators are referring to as the unleashing of Europe's anti-Semitic demon.[18] These attacks on Jews and Jewish property emanate almost exclusively from particular segments of Europe's Muslim population.

My more optimistic assessment of the future of Jewish-Gentile relations in Europe is not based solely upon my belief in the value of learning, but largely on the attenuation of the underlying foundations of the four roots of anti-Semitism in the West. Much has occurred in the Christian-Jewish relationship since 1945 to dampen Christian religious anti-Semitism. In particular, the *Nostra Aetate* declaration embraced by the Second Vatican Council in October 1965, withdrawing the blanket accusation of Jewish guilt for the murder of Christ, and the public pronouncements of Pope John Paul II documenting the historical mistreatment of Jews by Christians have eliminated official Christian

---

[17] "Europe and the Jews," *The Economist*, May 4, 2002, 12.

[18] My interpretation of the recent outbreak of anti-Semitic acts in Europe contrasts with that proposed by Charles Krauthammer: "As French attitudes prove, the anti-Semitic demon is loose again in Europe." *Pittsburgh Post-Gazette* (reprinted from *The Washington Post*), April 27, 2002, A-10.

support for anti-Semitism.[19] The science of race, which had successfully
dug deep roots into Western society before World War II, has been convincingly debunked. Few serious scholars would today pay heed to such
notions as a hierarchy of races and inferior and superior races. Clearly, the
racial basis of anti-Semitism has largely disappeared. With the collapse
of the Soviet Union and the state socialist system in Eastern and Central
Europe, the foundation for political anti-Semitism has been dealt a mortal blow. Revolutionary socialism provided anti-Semites a key weapon in
their assault on Jews, given the magnitude of the perceived threat from
revolutionary socialism and the alleged association of Jews and the political left. Perhaps no other fact has done more to alleviate anti-Semitism
than the collapse of communism. The fate of economic anti-Semitism
diverges from the other forms. Economic anti-Semitism, while somewhat abated, still appears to draw adherents. Economic anti-Semitism
in the West today is more implied and subtle than before World War II.
Murmurings about inordinate Jewish influence in banking, the media,
and the arts are less common now, but still present. Recent events in
Russia and the Ukraine point to the resiliency of resentment among
large segments of the population of the alleged economic power of
Jews. Equally disturbing has been the tendency by some in the anti-
globalization camp to blame Jews for the purported evils of globalization. However, these anti-Semitic voices have failed to resonate widely –
a big difference from the pre–World War II period, when anti-Semitic
attitudes were widely held by respected elites as well as by the lower and
middle classes.

If, on the one hand, popular anti-Semitism in Europe has lost considerable steam by virtue of the attenuation of the religious, racial, and
political roots, it has, on the other hand, gained strength recently from
popular resentment toward Israeli policies in the Middle East. Increasingly, the distinction between a dislike of Israeli policies and a dislike
of Jews has become blurred in the minds of many people. This is truly
unfortunate. Even more alarming is the explosive rise of anti-Semitism
within the Islamic world. While Christian-Jewish relations have vastly
improved since the Holocaust, Muslim-Jewish relations have tragically

[19] Albeit a cartoon appearing in an April 2002 edition of the Italian newspaper *La
Stampa*, commenting on the Israeli siege of Bethlehem's Church of the Nativity,
depicted a baby Jesus wondering if the Jews plan to kill him anew. Such distasteful
editorial decisions remind us that within certain quarters, religious anti-Semitic
residues have not fully disappeared.

fallen upon hard times. Fueled largely by the Israeli-Palestinian dispute, anti-Jewish antipathies wrapped in religious, racial, economic, and political narratives have entered the public discourse throughout the Muslim world.[20] Sadly, the curtain of history has yet to drop on society's longest hatred.

[20] See Goetz Nordbruch, "The Socio-Historical Background of Holocaust Denial in Arab Countries: Reactions to Roger Garaudy's *The Founding Myths of Israeli Politics*," ACTA, no. 17, 2001.

# Coding Instrument —

# Anti-Semitic Questionnaire

# for European Press

# (1899 — 1939)

NEWSPAPER TITLE:
NEWSPAPER DATE:
PAGE (S):
ARTICLE TITLE:

1. For the newspaper edition published on the 15th day of the month, is there an article mentioning Jews or Jewish issues?
   (Yes, No, Cannot Identify, or Not Applicable)
   IF YES OR IF THE ARTICLE COVERS A CRITICAL DISCOURSE MOMENT INVOLVING JEWS OR JEWISH ISSUES ANSWER THE FOLLOWING QUESTIONS:

*Prominence of Article*
2. Does the subject of Jews or Jewish issues appear in either the title or lead paragraph of the article?
   (Yes, No, or Cannot Identify)

3. Are Jews or Jewish issues the central theme of the article?
   (Yes, No, or Cannot Identify)

4. Does the article focus primarily on either domestic Jews or domestic Jewish issues?
   (Yes, No, or Cannot Identify)

5. Does the article employ the words "Jew," "Jewish," "Hebrew," "Israelite," or "Zionist"?
   (Yes, No, or Cannot Identify)

*General Anti-Semitic Attitudes*
6. Is the article favorable, unfavorable, or indifferent toward Jews?
   Favorable (Yes, No, or Cannot Identify)

Unfavorable (Yes, No, or Cannot Identify)
Neutral (Yes, No, or Cannot Identify)

7. If the article mentions violence against Jews, does it support or oppose violence against Jews or Jewish property?
Support (Yes, No, Cannot Identify, or Not Applicable)
Oppose (Yes, No, Cannot Identify, or Not Applicable)

8. If the article mentions the institution of organized bans, boycotts, or prohibitions on Jews or Jewish activities, does it support or oppose them?
Support (Yes, No, Cannot Identify, or Not Applicable)
Oppose (Yes, No, Cannot Identify, or Not Applicable)

9. Does the article mention the existence of a "Jewish Question"?
(Yes, No, or Cannot Identify)

10. If the article mentions the existence of a "Jewish Question," does it accept or reject its existence?
Accept (Yes, No, Cannot Identify, or Not Applicable)
Reject (Yes, No, Cannot Identify, or Not Applicable)

11. Does the article speak of Jews as having too much power or influence?
(Yes, No, or Cannot Identify)

12. If the article speaks of the power or influence of Jews, does it accept or reject the claim?
Accept (Yes, No, Cannot Identify, or Not Applicable)
Reject (Yes, No, Cannot Identify, or Not Applicable)

13. Does the article mention Jews as a threat to society or to the national interest?
(Yes, No, or Cannot Identify)

14. If the article mentions Jews as a threat to society or to the national interest, does it accept or reject the claim?
Accept (Yes, No, Cannot Identify, or Not Applicable)
Reject (Yes, No, Cannot Identify, or Not Appliicable)

15. Does the article mention the use of quotas for Jews?
(Yes, No, or Cannot Identify)

16. If the article mentions the use of quotas for Jews, does it accept or reject their use?
Accept (Yes, No, Cannot Identify, or Not Applicable)
Reject (Yes, No, Cannot Identify, or Not Applicable)

17. Does the article employ derogatory names for Jews (e.g., kikes, yids, youpin)?
(Yes, No, or Cannot Identify)

18. Does the article associate Jews with criminal activities?
(Yes, No, or Cannot Identify)

19. Does the article discuss religious, economic, racial and/or political forms of anti-Semitism?
RELIGIOUS (Yes, No, or Cannot Identify)
Articles or editorials are coded as *religious* anti-Semitism if contents implicitly or explicitly emphasize alleged negative Jewish religious accusations (e.g., anti-Christ, desecrators of host wafer, Christ killers, blood rituals, antiprogressive, ritualistic).
ECONOMIC (Yes, No, or Cannot Identify)
Articles or editorials are coded as *economic* anti-Semitism if contents implicitly or explicitly emphasize alleged negative Jewish economic practices (e.g., cheating, avarice, cheap, moneylending, profit making, hoarding, controlling markets, and manipulating prices).
RACIAL (Yes, No, or Cannot Identify)
Articles or editorials are coded as *racial* anti-Semitism if contents implicitly or explicitly emphasize alleged negative immutable, inherent, or evolutionary traits of Jews – physical (e.g., facial characteristics, stature, skin and hair color and texture), social (e.g., aloofness, clannishness, arrogance, materialist, unrootedness, deceitfulness, cosmopolitan, corruptness, parasitic), mental (e.g., intellectual and plotting), or spiritual (e.g., devoid of social morality) – in order to explain differences between Jews and non-Jews.
POLITICAL (Yes, No, or Cannot Identify)
Articles or editorials are coded as *political* anti-Semitism if contents implicitly or explicitly emphasize alleged negative Jewish political activities and attachments (e.g., Marxism, Bolshevism, communism, socialism, Zionism, controlling governments, divided loyalties, internationalism, unpatriotic, worldwide conspiracy, world domination).

20. If the article is unfavorable toward Jews, does it emphasize religious, economic, racial and/or political anti-Semitism?
RELIGIOUS (Yes, No, Cannot Identify, or Not Applicable)
ECONOMIC (Yes, No, Cannot Identify, or Not Applicable)
RACIAL (Yes, No, Cannot Identify, or Not Applicable)
POLITICAL (Yes, No Cannot Identify, or Not Applicable)

*Religious Anti-Semitic Attitudes*
21. If the article involves religious anti-Semitism, is it critical of Jewish religious practices and/or beliefs?
(Yes, No, Cannot Identify, or Not Applicable)

22. If the article involves religious anti-Semitism, does it associate Judaism with antiprogressive beliefs?
    (Yes, No, Cannot Identify, or Not Applicable)

23. If the article involves religious anti-Semitism, does it claim that Judaism seeks to undermine or destroy Christianity?
    (Yes, No, Cannot Identify, or Not Applicable)

*Economic Anti-Semitic Attitudes*

24. If the article involves economic anti-Semitism, does it associate Jews with economic problems?
    (Yes, No, Cannot Identify, or Not Applicable)

25. If the article involves economic anti-Semitism, does it blame Jews for economic problems (e.g., recessions, depressions, bank failures, rising or falling prices)?
    (Yes, No, Cannot Identify, or Not Applicable)

26. If the article involves economic anti-Semitism, does it associate Jews with control of major banks and financial institutions?
    (Yes, No, Cannot Identify, or Not Applicable)

*Political Anti-Semitic Attitudes*

27. If the article involves political anti-Semitism, does it associate Jews with political problems?
    (Yes, No, Cannot Identify, or Not Applicable)

28. If the article involves political anti-Semitism, does it blame Jews for political problems (e.g., revolutionary unrest, labor strife, government collapse, class conflict)?
    (Yes, No, Cannot Identify, or Not Applicable)

29. If the article involves political anti-Semitism, does it associate Jews with the leadership of the Marxist left?
    (Yes, No, Cannot Identify, or Not Applicable)

*Racial Anti-Semitic Attitudes*

30. Does the article discuss ethnic distinctions among Jews (e.g., Sephardic, Ashkenazic, Polish, Eastern European, assimilated, Western, Oriental)?
    (Yes, No, Cannot Identify, or Not Applicable)

31. If the article mentions ethnic distinctions among Jews, which ethnic type is referenced?
    Western/Assimilated (Yes, No, Cannot Identify, or Not Applicable)
    Eastern/Nonassimilated (Yes, No, Cannot Identify, or Not Applicable)

32. If the article mentions ethnic distinctions among Jews, does it speak more favorably of Western/assimilated or Eastern/nonassimilated Jews? More Favorably Western (Yes, No, Cannot Identify, or Not Applicable) More Favorably Eastern (Yes, No, Cannot Identify, or Not Applicable)

33. Does the article discuss Jewish immigration? (Yes, No, or Cannot Identify)

34. If the article mentions Jewish immigration or immigrants, does it call for increasing Jewish immigration, limiting Jewish immigration, or expelling recent Jewish immigrants? Increasing immigration (Yes, No, Cannot Identify, or Not Applicable) Limiting immigration (Yes, No, Cannot Identify, or Not Applicable) Expelling recent immigrants (Yes, No, Cannot Identify, or Not Applicable)

# Bibliography

Abraham, David. *The Collapse of the Weimar Republic*, 2nd ed. New York, 1986.

Alderman, Geoffrey. "The Anti-Jewish Riots of August 1911 in South Wales." In H. A. Strauss, ed., *Hostages of Modernization: Studies on Modern Antisemitism 1870–1933/39 Germany–Great Britain–France*, vol. 3/1. Berlin and New York, 1993.

Almog, Shmuel. "Antisemitism as a Dynamic Phenomenon: The "Jewish Question" in England at the End of the First World War." *Patterns of Prejudice*, vol. 2, no. 4, 1987.

Almog, Shmuel. "The Racial Motif in Renan's Attitude to Jews and Judaism." In Shmuel Almog, ed., *Antisemitism through the Ages*, trans. Nathan H. Reisner. Oxford. 1988.

Almog, Shmuel. *Nationalism and Antisemitism in Modern Europe 1815–1945*. Oxford, 1990.

Ancel, Jean. "The Image of the Jew in the View of Romanian Anti-Semitic Movements: Continuity and Change." *SHVUT*, vol. 16, 1993.

Angress, W. T. "The Political Role of the Peasantry in the Weimar Republic." *Review of Politics*, vol. 21, 1959.

Arendt, Hannah. *The Origins of Totalitarianism*. San Diego, 1975.

Armon, Theodore. "The Economic Background of Antisemitism in Romania between the Two World Wars: C. Z. Codreanu and the Jewish Trade, 1918–1940." *SHVUT*, vols. 1–2, nos. 17–18, 1995.

Ascheim, Steven E. *Strange Encounters: The East European Jew in German and German Jewish Consciousness 1800–1923*. Madison 1981.

Ascheim, Steven E. "The Double Exile: Weimar Culture and the East European Jews, 1918–1923." In M. N. Dobkowski and I. Wallimann, eds., *Towards the Holocaust: The Social and Economic Collapse of the Weimar Republic*. Westport, CT, 1983.

Ballinger, Pamela. "Submerged Politics, Exhumed Pasts: Exodus, Collective Memory, and Ethno-National Identity at the Borders of the Balkans." Ph.D. dissertation, Johns Hopkins University, 1998.

Bankier, David. *The Germans and the Final Solution: Public Opinion under Nazism*. Oxford, 1992.

Barbu, Zeev. "Psycho-Historical and Sociological Perspectives on the Iron Guard, the Fascist Movement of Romania." In S. U. Larsen, B. Hagtvet, and J. P. Myklebust, eds., *Who Were the Fascists*. Bergen, 1980.

Bauer, Yehuda, *A History of the Holocaust*. New York, 1982.

Ben-Ya'akov, Avaham. "The Bulgarian Jewish Community, 1879–1950: A Model of Zionist Fullfillment." *SHVUT*, vol. 6, no. 22, 1997.

Benewick, Robert. *Political Violence and Public Order*. London, 1969.

Berding, Helmut. *Moderner Antisemitismus in Deutschland*. Frankfurt, 1988.

Bergmann, Werner. "Psychological and Sociological Theories of Anti-semitism." *Patterns of Prejudice*, vol. 26, nos. 1–2, 1992.

Bernardini, Gene. "The Origins and Development of Racial Anti-Semitism in Fascist Italy." *Journal of Modern History*, vol. 4, September 1977.

Bernstein, Richard J. *Hannah Arendt and the Jewish Question*. Cambridge MA, 1996.

Birnbaum, Pierre. *Anti-Semitism in France: A Political History from Léon Blum to the Present*, trans. Miriam Kochan. Oxford, 1992.

Birnbaum, Pierre. "Affaire Dreyfus, culture catholique et antisémitisme." In Michel Winock, ed., *Histoire de l'extrême droite en France*. Paris, 1993.

Birnbaum, Pierre. *La France aux Français: Histoire des haines nationalistes*. Paris, 1993.

Blackbourn, David. *Class, Religion and Local Politics in Wilhelmine Germany: The Centre Party in Wuerttemberg before 1914*. New Haven and London, 1980.

Blackbourn, David. "Roman Catholics, the Centre Party and Anti-Semitism in Imperial Germany." In Paul Kennedy and Anthony Nicholls, eds., *Nationalist and Racialist Movements in Britain and Germany before 1914*. London and Basingstoke, 1981.

Blalock, Hubert, Jr. *Toward a Theory of Minority Group Relations*. New York, 1967.

Bookbinder, Paul. "Italy in the Overall Context of the Holocaust." In I. Herzer, ed., *The Italian Refuge: Rescue of Jews During the Holocaust*. Washington, DC, 1989.

Bracher, K. D. *The German Dictatorship: The Origins, Structure, and Effects of National Socialism*, trans. J. Steinberg. New York, 1970.

Brustein, William I. *The Social Origins of Political Regionalism: France, 1849–1981*. Berkeley, 1988.

Brustein, William I. *The Logic of Evil: The Social Origins of the Nazi Party, 1925–1933*. New Haven and London, 1996.

Brustein, William I. "Who Joined the Nazis and Why?" *American Journal of Sociology*, vol. 103, no. 1, July 1997.

Brym, R. J. *The Jewish Intelligentsia and Russian Marxism*. New York, 1978.

Burks, R. V. *Dynamics of Communism in Eastern Europe*. Princeton, 1961.

Burns, Michael. "Boulangism and the Dreyfus Affair 1886–1900." In H. A. Strauss, ed., *Hostages of Modernization: Studies on Modern Antisemitism 1870–1933/39 Germany–Great Britain–France*, vol. 3/1. Berlin and New York, 1993.

Butnaru, I. C. *The Silent Holocaust: Romania and Its Jews*. New York, 1992.

Byrnes, Robert F. *Antisemitism in Modern France*, vol. 1. New Brunswick, 1950.

Cafagna, Luciano. "Italy 1830–1914." In Carlo M. Cipolla, ed., *The Fontana Economic History of Europe: The Emergence of Industrial Societies – 1*, trans. Muriel Grindrod. London and Glasgow, 1973.

Cameron, Rondo. *A Concise Economic History of the World: From Paleolithic Times to the Present*. New York and Oxford, 1989.

Canepa, Andrew M. "The Image of the Jew in the Folklore and Literature of the *Postrisorgimento.*" *Journal of European Studies*, vol. 9, 1979.

Canepa, Andrew M. "Christian-Jewish Relations in Italy from Unification to Fascism." In I. Herzer, ed., *The Italian Refuge: Rescue of Jews during the Holocaust*. Washington, DC, 1989.

Caron, Vicki. "The Antisemitic Revival in France in the 1930s: The Socioeconomic Dimension Reconsidered." *The Journal of Modern History*, vol. 70, March 1998.

Caron, Vicki. *Uneasy Asylum: France and the Jewish Refugee Crisis, 1933–1942*. Stanford, 1999.

Carroll, James. *Constantine's Sword: The Church and the Jews*. Boston and New York, 2001.

Carsten, F. L. *The Rise of Fascism*, 2nd ed. Berkeley, 1980.

Cesarani, David. "Joynson-Hicks and the Radical Right in England after the First World War." In Tony Kushner and Kenneth Lunn, eds., *Traditions of Intolerance: Historical Perspectives on Fascism and Race Discourse in Britain*. Manchester and New York, 1989.

Cheyette, Bryan. "Jewish Stereotyping and English Literature 1875–1920: Towards a Political Analysis." In Tony Kushner and Kenneth Lunn, eds., *Traditions of Intolerance: Historical Perspectives on Fascism and Race Discourse in Britain*. Manchester and New York, 1989.

Childers, Thomas. *The Nazi Voter: The Social Foundations of Fascism in Germany, 1919–1933*. Chapel Hill, 1983.

Childers, Thomas. "The Social Language of Politics in Germany: The Sociology of Political Discourse in the Weimar Republic." *American Historical Review*, vol. 95, 1990.

Cohen, Israel. "The Jews in Italy." *The Political Quarterly*, vol. 10, July–September 1939.

Cohen, Richard I. "The Dreyfus Affair and the Jews." In Shmuel Almog, ed., *Antisemitism through the Ages*, trans. Nathan H. Reisner. Oxford, 1988.

Cohn, Norman. *Warrant for Genocide: The Myth of the Jewish World-Conspiracy and the Protocols of the Elders of Zion*. London, 1967.

Connell, R.W. "Why Is Classical Theory Classical?" *American Journal of Sociology*, vol. 102, no. 6, 1997.

Conway, J. S. "National Socialism and the Christian Churches during the Weimar Republic." In P. D. Stachura, ed., *The Nazi Machtergreifung*. London, 1983.

Cuker, Simon, et al. *Juifs Révolutionnaires: Une page d'histoire du Yidichland en France*. Paris, 1987.

Dawidowicz, Lucy S. *The War against the Jews, 1933–1945*. New York, 1975.

De Felice, Renzo. *Storia degli ebrei italiani sotto il fascismo*. Turin, 1993.

Della Pergola, Sergio. "Precursori, convergenti, emarginati: trasformazioni demografiche degli ebrei in Italia, 1870–1945." In Ministero per I Beni Culturali E Ambientali Ufficio Centrale per I Beni Archivistici, ed., *Italia Judaica: Gli ebrei nell'Italia unita 1870–1945*. Rome, 1993.

Dimont, Max I. *Jews, God, and History*. New York, 1962.

Dinnerstein, Leonard. *Antisemitism in America*. New York and Oxford, 1994.

Dogan, Matei. *Analiza Statistică A Democratiei Parlamentare din România*. Bucuresti, 1946.

Dreyfus, Jean-Marc. "Banquiers et financiers juifs de 1929 à 1962: transitions et ruptures." *Archives Juives*, vol. 29, no. 2, 1996.

Eatwell, Roger. *Fascism: A History*. New York, 1996.

*Editor and Publisher*, vols. 61–63, nos. 36–37.

Efron, John M. *Defenders of the Race: Jewish Doctors and Race Science in Fin-De-Siecle Europe*. New Haven and London, 1994.

Eidelberg, Philip G. *The Great Rumanian Peasant Revolt of 1907: Origins of a Modern Jacquerie*. Leiden, 1974.

Ettinger, Shmuel. "Jew-Hatred in Its Historical Context." In Shmuel Almog, ed., *Antisemitism through the Ages*, trans. Nathan H. Reisner. Oxford, 1988.

Falter, Juergen W. "Economic Debts and Political Gains: Electoral Support for the Nazi Party in Agrarian Commercial Sectors, 1928–1933." Unpublished paper presented at the eighty-fifth annual meeting of the American Political Science Association. Atlanta, Georgia, 1989.

Fein, Helen. *Accounting for Genocide: National Responses and Jewish Victimization during the Holocaust*. New York, 1979.

Fein, Helen. "Explanations for the Origin and Evolution of Antisemitism." In Helen Fein, ed., *The Persisting Question: Sociological Perspectives and Social Contexts of Modern Antisemitism*, vol. 1. Berlin and New York, 1987.

Feldman, David. *Englishmen and Jews: Social Relations and Political Culture 1840–1914*. New Haven and London, 1994.

Feldman, G. D. *The Great Disorder: Politics, Economics, and Society in the German Inflation, 1914–1924*. New York, 1993.

Ferguson, Niall. *The World's Banker: The History of the House of Rothschild*. London, 1998.

Field, Geoffrey. "Anti-Semitism with the Boots Off." In H. A. Strauss, ed., *Hostages of Modernization: Studies on Modern Antisemitism 1870–1933 / 39 Germany–Great Britain–France*, vol. 3/1. Berlin and New York, 1993.

Finestein, Israel. *A Short History of Anglo-Jewry*. New Haven, 1957.

Finzi, Roberto. *Anti-Semitism: From Its European Roots to the Holocaust*. New York, 1999.

Fischer, Conan. *The German Communists and the Rise of Nazism*. London, 1991.

Fischer-Galati, Stephen. "Fascism, Communism, and the Jewish Question in Romania." In Bela Vago and George L. Mosse, eds., *Jews and Non-Jews in Eastern Europe 1918–1945*. New York, 1974.

Fischer-Galati, Stephen. "The Radical Left and Assimilation: The Case of Romania." In Bela Vago, ed., *Jewish Assimilation in Modern Times*. Boulder, 1981.

Fitch, Nancy. "Mass Culture, Mass Parliamentary Politics, and Modern Anti-Semitism: The Dreyfus Affair in Rural France." *American Historical Review*, vol. 97, no. 1, 1992.

Flora, P. *State, Economy, and Society in Western Europe, 1815–1975*, vol. 1. Frankfurt, 1983.

Foreman-Peck, James. *A History of the World Economy: International Economic Relations since 1850*. Totowa, NJ, 1983.

Franzosi, Roberto. "The Press as a Source of Socio-Historical Data: Issues in the Methodology of Data Collection from Newspapers." *Historical Methods*, vol. 20, no. 1, 1987.

Friedlaender, Saul. "Political Transformations during the War and Their Effect on the Jewish Question." In H. A. Strauss, ed., *Hostages of Modernization: Studies on Modern Antisemitism 1870–1933/39 Germany–Great Britain–France*, vol. 3/1. Berlin and New York, 1993.

Friedlaender, Saul. *Nazi Germany and the Jews*, vol. 1: *The Years of Persecution, 1933–1939*. New York, 1997.

Gamson, William. *Talking Politics*. Cambridge, 1992.

Gannon, Franklin Reid. *The British Press and Germany 1936–1939*. Oxford, 1971.

Garrad, John. *The English and Immigration: A Comparative Study of the Jewish Influx 1880–1910*. London, 1971.

Gentile, Emilio. "The Struggle for Modernity: Echoes of the Dreyfus Affair in Italian Political Culture, 1898–1912." *Journal of Contemporary History*, vol. 33, no. 4, 1998.

Gessner, D. "The Dilemma of German Agriculture during the Weimar Republic." In R. Bessel and E. J. Feuchtwanger, eds., *Social Change and Political Development in Weimar Germany*. London, 1981.

Gies, H. "The NSDAP Agrarian Organization in the Final Phase of the Weimar Republic." In H. A. Turner, ed., *Nazism and the Third Reich*. New York, 1972.

Gilman, Sander L. *Smart Jews: The Construction of the Image of Jewish Superior Intelligence*. Lincoln and London, 1996.

Glock, Charles Y., and Stark, Rodney. *Christian Beliefs and Anti-Semitism*. New York and London, 1966.

Golding, Louis. *The Jewish Problem*. London and Aylesbury, 1938.

Goldstaub, Adriana. "Rassegna Bibliografica Dell'Editoria Antisemita nel 1938." *Rassegna Mensile di Israel*, vol. 54, 1988.

Gonen, Jay Y. *The Roots of Nazi Psychology: Hitler's Utopian Barbarism*. Lexington, 2000.

Good, D. F., and Ma, T. "New Estimates of Income Levels in Central and Eastern Europe, 1870–1910." In F. Baltzarek, F. Butschek, and G. Tichy, eds., *Von der Theorie zur Wirtschaftspolitik-ein Oesterreichischer Weg. Festschrift zum 65. Geburstag von Erich Streissler*. Stuttgart, 1998.

Gordon, Sarah. *Hitler, Germans and the "Jewish Question."* Princeton, 1984.

Gould, Stephen Jay. *The Mismeasure of Man*. New York, 1981.

Green, J. *Social History of the Jewish East End in London 1914–1939*. New York, 1991.

Grill, J. H. "The Nazi Party"s Rural Propaganda before 1928." *Central European History*, vol. 15, 1982.

Grosser, Paul E., and Halperin, Edwin G. *Anti-Semitism, Causes and Effects: An Analysis and Chronology of 1900 Years of Anti-Semitic Attitudes and Practices*. New York, 1978.

Gunzberg, Lynn M. *Strangers at Home: Jews in the Italian Literary Imagination*. Berkeley, 1992.

Hagen, William W. "Before the 'Final Solution': Toward a Comparative Analysis of Political Anti-Semitism in Interwar Germany and Poland." *The Journal of Modern History*, vol. 68, no. 2, 1996.

Hatheway, Jay. "The Pre-1920 Origins of the National Socialist German Workers' Party." *Journal of Contemporary History*, vol. 29, no. 3, July 1994.

Hechter, Michael. "Group Formation and the Cultural Division of Labor." *American Journal of Sociology*, vol. 84, 1978.

Hertzberg, Arthur. *The French Enlightenment and the Jews*. New York, 1968.

Herzer, Ivo. "Introduction." In I. Herzer, ed., *The Italian Refuge: Rescue of Jews during the Holocaust*. Washington, DC, 1989.

Higham, John. *Strangers in the Land: Patterns of American Nativism 1860–1925*. New Brunswick and London, 1988.

Himmler, H. "Bauer, wach auf!" *Der Nationale Sozialist fuer Sachsen*, August 1, 1926.

Hiro, Dilip. *Black British White British: A History of Race Relations in Britain*. London, 1991.

Hirshfield, Claire. "The British Left and the 'Jewish Conspiracy': A Case Study of Modern Antisemitism." *Jewish Social Studies*, vol. 28, no. 2, Spring 1981.

Hitchins, Keith. *Rumania 1866–1947*. Oxford, 1994.

Holborn, Hajo. *A History of Modern Germany 1840–1945*. Princeton, 1982.

Holmes, Colin. *Anti-Semitism in British Society 1876–1939*. New York, 1979.

Holmes, Colin. "Anti-Semitism in British Society, 1876–1939." In H. A. Strauss, ed., *Hostages of Modernization: Studies on Modern Antisemitism 1870–1933/39 Germany–Great Britain–France*, vol. 3/1. Berlin and New York, 1993.

Hughes, H. Stuart. *Prisoners of Hope: The Silver Age of the Italian Jews 1924–1974*. Cambridge, MA, 1983.

Iancu, Carol. *Les Juifs en Roumanie (1866–1919): De L'Exclusion à L'Emancipation*. Aix-en-Provence, 1978.

Iancu, Carol, *L'émancipation des Juifs de Roumanie (1913–1919)*. Montpellier, 1992.

International Reference Library. *Politics and Political Parties in Romania*. London, 1936.

Ioanid, Radu. *The Holocaust in Romania: The Destruction of Jews and Gypsies under the Antonescu Regime, 1940–1944*. Chicago, 2000.

Ionescu, Ghita. *Communism in Rumania 1944–1962*. London, 1964.

James, H. *The German Slump: Politics and Economics 1924–1936*. Oxford, 1986.

Janos, Andrew C. "Modernization and Decay in Historical Perspective: The Case of Romania." In Kenneth Jowitt, ed., *Social Change in Romania, 1860–1940*. Berkeley, 1978.

Johnson, Eric. *Nazi Terror: The Gestapo, Jews, and Ordinary Germans*. New York, 1999.

Jones, G. L. *Hard Sayings: Difficult New Testament Texts for Jewish-Christian Dialogue*. London, 1993.

Jupp, James. *The Radical Left in Britain 1931–1941*. London, 1982.

Kadish, Sharman. *Bolsheviks and British Jews: The Anglo-Jewish Community, Britain and the Russian Revolution*. London, 1992.

Kaplan, Alice. *The Collaborator: The Trial and Execution of Robert Brasillach.* Chicago and London, 2000.

Kater, Michael. *The Nazi Party.* Cambridge, MA, 1983.

Katz, Jacob. *From Prejudice to Destruction: Anti-Semitism, 1700–1933.* Cambridge, MA, 1980.

Kauders, Anthony. *German Politics and the Jews: Duesseldorf and Nuremberg 1910–1933.* Oxford, 1996.

Kele, M. *Nazis and Workers: National Socialist Appeals to German Labor, 1919–1933.* Chapel Hill, 1972.

Kendall, Walter. *The Revolutionary Movement in Britain, 1900–1921.* London, 1969.

Kenrick, Donald, and Puxon, Grattan. *The Destiny of Europe's Gypsies.* London, 1972.

Kershaw, Ian. *Popular Opinion and Political Dissent in the Third Reich: Bavaria 1933–1945.* Oxford, 1983.

Kertzer, David I. *The Kidnapping of Edgardo Mortara.* New York, 1998.

Kertzer, David I. *The Popes against the Jews: The Vatican's Role in the Rise of Modern Anti-Semitism.* New York, 2001.

Kindleberger, Charles P. *A Financial History of Western Europe.* London, 1984.

King, Robert R. *A History of the Romanian Communist Party.* Stanford, 1980.

Kingston, Paul J. *Anti-Semitism in France during the 1930s: Organizations, Personalities and Propaganda.* Hull, 1983.

Krauthammer, Charles. "As French Attitudes Prove, the Anti-Semitic Demon Is Loose Again in Europe." *Pittsburgh Post-Gazette* (reprinted from the *Washington Post*), April 27, 2002, A-10.

Kuehl, Stefan. *The Nazi Connection: Eugenics, American Racism, and German National Socialism.* New York and Oxford, 1994.

Kushner, Tony. "The Paradox of Prejudice: The Impact of Organized Antisemitism in Britain during an Anti-Nazi War." In Tony Kushner and Kenneth Lunn, eds., *Traditions of Intolerance: Historical Perspectives on Fascism and Race Discourse in Britain.* Manchester and New York, 1989.

Kushner, Tony. *The Persistence of Prejudice: Antisemitism in British Society during the Second World War.* Manchester and New York, 1989.

Lane, B. Miller, and Rupp, L. J. *Nazi Ideology before 1933: A Documentation.* Austin, 1978.

Langmuir, Gavin I. "Toward a Definition of Antisemitism." In Helen Fein, ed., *The Persisting Question: Sociological Perspectives and Social Contexts of Modern Antisemitism,* vol. 1. Berlin and New York, 1987.

Langmuir, Gavin I. *History, Religion, and Antisemitism.* Berkeley, 1990.

Laqueur, Walter. *Russia and Germany: A Century of Conflict.* Boston and Toronto, 1965.

Lebovics, H. L. *Social Conservatism and the Middle Classes in Germany, 1914–1933*. Princeton, 1969.

Lebzelter, Gisela. *Political Anti-Semitism in England 1918–1939*. New York, 1978.

Lebzelter, Gisela. "Anti-Semitism – A Focal Point for the British Radical Right." In Paul Kennedy and Anthony Nicholls, eds., *Nationalist and Racialist Movements in Britain and Germany before 1914*. London and Basingstoke, 1981.

Ledeen, Michael A. "The Evolution of Italian Fascist Antisemitism." *Jewish Social Studies*, vol. 37, no. 1, January 1975.

Lendvai, Paul. *L'antisémitisme sans juifs*. Paris, 1971.

Lerner, Richard M. *Final Solutions: Biology, Prejudice, and Genocide*. University Park, PA, 1992.

Levine, Hillel. *Economic Origins of Antisemitism: Poland and Its Jews in the Early Modern Period*. New Haven and London, 1991.

Levy, Richard S. *The Downfall of the Anti-Semitic Political Parties in Imperial Germany*. New Haven, 1975.

Levy, Richard S. "Introduction: The Political Career of the Protocols of the Elders of Zion." In Richard S. Levy, trans. and ed., *A Lie and a Libel: The History of the Protocols of the Elders of Zion*. Lincoln and London, 1995.

Levy, Robert. *Ana Pauker: The Rise and Fall of a Jewish Communist*. Berkeley, 2001.

Lindemann, Albert S. *The Jew Accused: Three Anti-Semitic Affairs (Dreyfus, Beilis, Frank) 1894–1915*. Cambridge, 1991.

Lindemann, Albert S. *Esau's Tears: Modern Anti-Semitism and the Rise of the Jews*. Cambridge and New York, 1997.

Lipman, V. D. *Social History of the Jews in England 1850–1950*. London, 1954.

Lipman, V. D. *A History of the Jews in Great Britain since 1858*. Leicester, 1990.

Livezeanau, Irina. *Cultural Politics in Greater Romania: Regionalism, Nation Building and Ethnic Struggle, 1918–1930*. Ithaca and London, 1995.

Lohalm, Uwe. "Voelkisch Origins of Early Nazism: Anti-Semitism in Culture and Politics." In H. A. Strauss, ed., *Hostages of Modernization: Studies on Modern Antisemitism 1870–1933/39 Germany–Great Britain–France*, vol. 3/1. Berlin and New York, 1993.

Lunn, Kenneth. "The Ideology and Impact of the British Fascists in the 1920s." In Tony Kushner and Kenneth Lunn, eds., *Traditions of Intolerance: Historical Perspectives on Fascism and Race Discourse in Britain*. Manchester and New York, 1989.

Luzzatto, Gadi. "Aspetti dell'antisemitismo nella 'Civilta cattolicà' dal 1881 al 1903." *Bailamme*, vol. 1, no. 2, December 1987.

Mackie, T. T. and Rose, R. *The International Almanac of Electoral History*, 2nd ed. New York, 1982.

MacLaughlin, Jim. "Nation-Building, Social Closure and Anti-Traveller Racism in Ireland." *Sociology*, vol. 33, no. 1, 1999.

Maddison, Angus. "Economic Policy and Performance in Europe 1913–1970." In Carlo M. Cipolla, ed., *The Fontana Economic History of Europe: The Twentieth Century, Part II*. Glasgow, 1976.

Maddison, Angus. *Dynamic Forces in Capitalist Development: A Long-Run Comparative View*. Oxford and New York, 1991.

Maddison, Angus. *Monitoring the World Economy 1820–1992*. Paris, 1995.

Magocsi, Paul Robert. *Historical Atlas of East Central Europe*. Seattle and London, 1993.

Maiocchi, Roberto. *Scienza italiana e razzismo fascista*. Florence, 1999.

Mandle, W. F. *Anti-Semitism and the British Union of Fascists*. London, 1968.

Marrus, Michael R. *The Politics of Assimilation: A Study of the French Jewish Community at the Time of the Dreyfus Affair*. Oxford, 1971.

Marrus, Michael R., and Paxton, Robert O. *Vichy France and the Jews*. Stanford, 1981.

Marrus, Michael R. "The Theory and Practice of Anti-Semitism." *Commentary*, vol. 74, no. 2, August 1982.

Marrus, Michael R. *The Unwanted: European Refugees in the Twentieth Century*. New York and Oxford, 1985.

Marrus, Michael R., and Paxton, Robert O. "The Roots of Vichy Anti-Semitism." In H. A. Strauss, ed., *Hostages of Modernization: Studies on Modern Antisemitism 1870–1933/39 Germany–Great Britain–France*, vol. 3/1. Berlin and New York, 1993.

Massing, Paul W. *Rehearsal for Destruction: A Study of Political Anti-Semitism in Imperial Germany*. New York, 1949.

Massoutié, Louis. *Judaisme et Marxisme*. Paris, 1939.

Mayall, David. *Gypsy-Travellers in Nineteenth-Century Society*. Cambridge, 1988.

McCarthy, John D., McPhail, C. and Smith, J. "Images of Protest: Estimating Selection Bias in Media Coverage of Washington Demonstrations, 1982 and 1991." *American Sociological Review*, vol. 61, 1996.

Mendelsohn, Ezra. *The Jews of East Central Europe between the World Wars*. Bloomington, 1983.

Michaelis, Meir. *Mussolini and the Jews: German-Italian Relations and the Jewish Question in Italy 1922–1945*. Oxford, 1978.

Michaelis, Meir. "Fascist Policy toward Italian Jews: Tolerance and Persecution." In I. Herzer, ed., *The Italian Refuge: Rescue of Jews during the Holocaust*. Washington, DC, 1989.

Milano, Attilio. *Storia degli ebrei in Italia*. Turin, 1963.

Molinari, Maurizio. *Ebrei in Italia: un problema di identità (1870–1938).* Florence, 1991.

Mollier, Jean-Yves. "Financiers juifs dans la tourmente des scandales fin de siècle (1880–1900)." *Archives Juives,* vol. 29, no. 2, 1996.

Momigliano, Arnaldo. *Ottavo contributo alla storia degli studi classici e del mondo antico.* Rome, 1987.

Montias, M. "Notes on the Romanian Debate on Sheltered Industrialization: 1860–1906." In Kenneth Jowitt, ed., *Social Change in Romania, 1860–1940.* Berkeley, 1978.

Morse, Arthur D. *While Six Million Died: A Chronicle of American Apathy.* New York, 1968.

Mosse, George L. *Germans and Jews: The Right, The Left, and the Search for a "Third Force" in Pre-Nazi Germany.* New York, 1970.

Mosse, George L. *Toward the Final Solution: A History of European Racism.* Madison, 1985.

Nagy-Talavera, Nicholas M. *The Green Shirts and the Others: A History of Fascism in Hungary and Rumania.* Stanford, 1970.

Niewyk, Donald L. *The Jews in Weimar Germany.* Baton Rouge, 1980.

Niewyk, Donald L. "Solving the 'Jewish Problem' – Continuity and Change in German Antisemitism 1871–1945." *Leo Baeck Institute Year Book,* vol. 35, 1990.

Niewyk, Donald L. "The Jews in Weimar Germany: The Impact of Anti-Semitism on Universities, Political Parties and Government Services." In H. A. Strauss, ed., *Hostages of Modernization: Studies on Modern Antisemitism 1870–1933/39 Germany–Great Britain–France,* vol. 3/1. Berlin and New York, 1993.

Nolte, Ernst. *Three Faces of Fascism.* New York, 1969.

Nordbruch, Goetz. "The Socio-Historical Background of Holocaust Denial in Arab Countries: Reactions to Roger Garaudy's *The Founding Myths of Israeli Politics.*" *ACTA,* no. 17, 2001.

Novick, Peter. *The Holocaust in American Life.* Boston and New York, 1999.

Okey, Judith. *The Traveller-Gypsies.* Cambridge, 1983.

Oldson, William. *A Providential Anti-Semitism: Nationalism and Polity in Nineteenth Century Romania.* Philadelphia, 1991.

Olzak, Susan. *The Dynamics of Ethnic Competition and Conflict.* Stanford, 1992.

O'Rourke, Kevin, and Williamson, Jeffrey. *Globalisation and History: The Evolution of a Nineteenth-Century Atlantic Economy.* Cambridge, MA, 1999.

Panayi, Panikos. *Immigration, Ethnicity, and Racism in Britain: 1815–1945.* Manchester, 1994.

Pauley, Bruce F. *From Prejudice to Persecution: A History of Austrian Anti-Semitism.* Chapel Hill, 1992.

Pelling, Henry. *The British Communist Party*. London, 1958.

Petzina, D. "Germany and the Great Depression." *Journal of Contemporary History*, vol. 4, 1969.

Peukert, D. J. K. *The Weimar Republic: The Crisis of Classical Modernity*, trans. R. Deveson. New York, 1989.

Pierrard, Pierre. *Juifs et catholiques français: D'Edouard Drumont à Jacob Kaplan 1886–1994*. Paris, 1997.

Pippidi, Andrei. "The Mirror and Behind It: The Image of the Jew in the Romanian Society." *SHVUT*, vol. 16, 1993.

Piva, Francesco. *Lotte contadine e origini del fascismo*. Venice, 1977.

Poliakov, Leon. *The Aryan Myth: A History of Racist and Nationalist Ideas in Europe*, trans. Edmund Howard. New York, 1971.

Pollins, Harold. *Economic History of the Jews in England*. East Brunswick, 1982.

Pulzer, Peter. *The Rise of Political Anti-Semitism in Germany and Austria*. Cambridge, MA, 1988.

Pulzer, Peter. *Jews and the German State: The Political History of a Minority, 1848–1933*. Oxford, 1992.

Quinley, Harold E., and Glock, Charles Y. "Christian Sources of Anti-Semitism." In Helen Fein, ed., *The Persisting Question: Sociological Perspectives and Social Contexts of Modern Antisemitism*, vol. 1. Berlin and New York, 1987.

Rosenberg, Hans. "Anti-Semitism and the 'Great Depression', 1873–1896." In H. A. Strauss, ed., *Hostages of Modernization: Studies on Modern Antisemitism 1870–1933 /39 Germany–Great Britain–France*, vol. 3/1. Berlin and New York, 1993.

Rossi, Mario. "Emancipation of the Jews in Italy." *Jewish Social Studies*, vol. 15, April 1953.

Rossi-Doria, Anna. "La diffidenza anti ebraica liberale e democratica." In Dataneus, ed., *L'Italia E L'Antisemitismo*. Rome, 1993.

Roth, Cecil. *The History of the Jews of Italy*. Philadelphia, 1946.

Rubenstein, Richard L. *After Auschwitz: History, Theology, and Contemporary Judaism*, 2nd ed. Baltimore and London, 1992.

Rubinstein, W. D. *A History of the Jews in the English-Speaking World: Great Britain*. New York, 1996.

Ruether, Rosemary R. "The Theological Roots of Anti-Semitism." In Helen Fein, ed., *The Persisting Question: Sociological Perspectives and Social Contexts of Modern Antisemitism*, vol. 1. Berlin and New York, 1987.

Ruppin, Arthur. *The Jews in the Modern World*. London, 1934.

Sabatello, Eitan F. "Trasformazione economiche e sociali degli ebrei in Italia nel periodo dell'emancipazione." In Ministero per I Beni Culturali E Ambientali Ufficio Centrale per I Beni Archivistici, ed., *Italia Judaica: Gli ebrei nell'Italia unita 1870–1945*. Rome, 1993.

Sayrs, Lois. *Pooled Time Series Analysis.* Newbury Park, CA: 1989.

Scammon, Richard M. "The Communist Voting Pattern in British Parliamentary Elections." In James K. Pollock et al., eds., *British Election Studies, 1950.* Ann Arbor, 1951.

Schatz, Jaff. *The Generation: The Rise and Fall of the Jewish Communists of Poland.* Berkeley, 1991.

Scheil, Stefan. *Die Entwicklung des politischen Antisemitismus in Deutschland zwischen 1881 und 1912: Eine wahlgeschichtliche Untersuchung.* Berlin, 1999.

Schor, Ralph. *L'opinion française et les Etrangers 1919–1939.* Paris, 1985.

Schor, Ralph. *L'Antisémitisme en France Pendant les Années Trente.* Paris, 1992.

Schuker, Stephen A. "Origins of the 'Jewish Problem' in the Later Third Republic." In Frances Malino and Bernard Wasserstein, eds., *The Jews in Modern France.* Hanover and London, 1985.

Segel, Benjamin. *A Lie and a Libel: The History of the Protocols of the Elders of Zion,* trans. and ed. Richard S. Levy. Lincoln and London, 1995.

Sering, M. *Deutsche Agrarpolitik: Auf geschichtlicher und landeskundlicher Grundlage.* Leipzig, 1934.

Serpieri, Arrigo. *La guerra e le classi rurali italiane.* Bari, 1930.

Shapiro, Paul A. "Prelude to Dictatorship in Romania: The National Christian Party in Power, December 1937– February 1938." *Canadian-American Slavic Studies,* vol. 8, no. 1, Spring 1974.

Sherman, A. J. *Island Refuge: Britain and Refugees from the Third Reich 1933–1939.* London, 1973.

Skidelsky, Robert. *Oswald Mosley.* New York, 1975.

Smith, David N. "Judeophobia, Myth, and Critique." In S. D. Breslauer, ed., *The Seductiveness of Jewish Myth: Challenge or Response.* Albany, 1997.

Smith, Elaine R. "Jewish Responses to Political Antisemitism and Fascism in the East End of London, 1920–1939." In Tony Kushner and Kenneth Lunn, eds., *Traditions of Intolerance: Historical Perspectives on Fascism and Race Discourse in Britain.* Manchester and New York, 1989.

Snyder, David, and Kelly, W. R. "Conflict Intensity, Media Sensitivity and the Validity of Newspaper Data." *American Sociological Review,* vol. 42, 1977.

Sodi, Risa. "The Italian Roots of Racialism." *UCLA Historical Journal,* vol. 8, 1987.

Soucy, Robert. *French Fascism: The First Wave, 1924–1933.* New Haven and London, 1986.

Sperber, Jonathan. *The Kaiser's Voters: Electors and Elections in Imperial Germany.* Cambridge, 1997.

Stammer, Larry B. "Scholars Revisit 'Betrayal' of Judas: Studies of Old Texts Cloud Traditional Tale of Villain," *Minneapolis Star Tribune*, April 29, 2000, p. B10. (reprinted from the *Los Angeles Times*).

Steiman, Lionel B. *Paths to Genocide: Antisemitism in Western History*. New York, 1998.

Steinberg, Jonathan. *All or Nothing: The Axis and the Holocaust 1941–1943*. London and New York, 1990.

Sternhell, Zeev. "The Roots of Popular Anti-Semitism in the Third Republic." In Frances Malino and Bernard Wasserstein, eds., *The Jews in Modern France*. Hanover and London, 1985.

Stille, Alexander. *Benevolence and Betrayal: Five Italian Jewish Families under Fascism*. New York, 1991.

Stimson, James A. "Regression in Space and Time: A Statistical Essay." *American Journal of Political Science*, vol. 29, no. 4, 1985.

Strauss, Herbert A. "Hostages of 'World Jewry': On the Origin of the Idea of Genocide in German History." In H. A. Strauss, ed., *Hostages of Modernization: Studies on Modern Antisemitism 1870–1933/39 Germany–Great Britain–France*, vol. 3/1. Berlin and New York, 1993.

Strauss, Herbert A. "Introduction: Possibilities and Limits of Comparison." In H. A. Strauss, ed., *Hostages of Modernization: Studies on Modern Antisemitism 1870–1933 /39 Germany–Great Britain–France*, vol. 3/1. Berlin and New York, 1993.

Summers, Anne. "The Character of Edwardian Nationalism: Three Popular Leagues." In Paul Kennedy and Anthony Nicholls, eds., *Nationalist and Racialist Movements in Britain and Germany before 1914*. London and Basingstoke, 1981.

Szajkowski, Zosa. *Jews, Wars, and Communism: The Impact of the 1919–20 Red Scare on American Jewish Life*, vol. 2. New York, 1974.

Teller, Judd L. *Scapegoat of Revolution*. New York, 1954.

Temin, Peter. *Lessons from the Great Depression: The Lionel Robbins Lectures for 1989*. Cambridge, MA, 1989.

Thayer, John A. *Italy and the Great War: Politics and Culture, 1870–1915*. Madison and Milwaukee, 1964.

Todorov, Tzvetan. *The Fragility of Goodness: Why Bulgaria's Jews Survived the Holocaust*, trans. A. Denner. Princeton, 1999.

Toscano, Mario. "L'uguaglianza senza diversità: Stato, società e questione ebraica nell'Italia liberale." In Mario Toscano, ed., *Integrazione e Identità: L'esperienza ebraica in Germania e Italia dall'Illuminismo al fascismo*. Milan, 1998.

Treptow, Kurt W. "Populism and Twentieth Century Romanian Politics." In Joseph Held, ed., *Populism in Eastern Europe Racism, Nationalism, and Society*. New York, 1996.

Vago, Bela. *The Shadow of the Swastika*. Farnborough, 1975.

Vago, Raphael. "The Traditions of Antisemitism in Romania." *Patterns of Prejudice*, vol. 27, 1993.

Voight, Klaus. "Jewish Refugees and Immigrants in Italy, 1933–1945." In I. Herzer, ed., *The Italian Refuge: Rescue of Jews during the Holocaust*. Washington, DC, 1989.

Volovici, Leon. *Nationalist Ideology and Antisemitism: The Case of Romanian Intellectuals in the 1930s*. Oxford, 1991.

Weber, Eugen. *Action Française: Royalism and Reaction in Twentieth-Century France*. Stanford, 1962.

Weber, Eugen. "Romania." In Hans Rogger and Eugen Weber, eds., *The European Right: A Historical Profile*. Berkeley and Los Angeles, 1965.

Weber, Eugen. *The Hollow Years: France in the 1930s*. New York and London, 1994.

Wehler, Hans-Ulrich. "Anti-Semitism and Minority Policy." In H. A. Strauss, ed., *Hostages of Modernization: Studies on Modern Antisemitism 1870–1933/39 Germany–Great Britain–France*, vol. 3/1. Berlin and New York, 1993.

Weinberg, Meyer. *Because They Were Jews*. New York and London, 1986.

Weiss, John. *Ideology of Death: Why the Holocaust Happened in Germany*. Chicago, 1996.

Wertheimer, Jack. *Unwelcome Strangers: East European Jews in Imperial Germany*. New York and Oxford, 1987.

Wilson, K. M. "The Protocols of Zion and the *Morning Post*, 1919–1920." *Patterns of Prejudice*, vol. 19, no. 3, July 1985.

Wilson, Stephen. *Ideology and Experience: Anti-Semitism in France at the Time of the Dreyfus Affair*. Rutherford, NJ, 1982.

Winock, Michel. "L'héritage contre-révolutionnaire." In Michel Winock, ed., *Histoire de l'extrême droite en France*. Paris, 1993.

Winock, Michel. *Nationalism, Anti-Semitism, and Fascism in France*, trans. Jane Marie Todd. Stanford, 1998.

Winkler, H. A. *Mittelstand, Demokratie und Nationalsozialismus*. Cologne, 1972.

Wistrich, Robert S. *Socialism and the Jews: The Dilemmas of Assimilation in Germany and Austria-Hungary*. Rutherford, NJ, 1982.

Wistrich, Robert S. *Antisemitism: The Longest Hatred*. New York, 1991.

Woodroffe, Martin. "Racial Theories of History and Politics: The Example of Houston Stewart Chamberlain." In Paul Kennedy and Anthony Nicholls, eds., *Nationalist and Racialist Movements in Britain and Germany before 1914*. London, 1981.

Zenner, Walter P. "Middleman Minority Theories: A Critical Review." In Helen Fein, ed., *The Persisting Question: Sociological Perspectives and*

*Social Contexts of Modern Antisemitism*, vol. 1. Berlin and New York, 1987.

Zofka, Z. *Die Ausbreitung des Nationalsozialismus auf dem Lande*. Munich, 1979.

Zuccotti, Susan. *The Italians and the Holocaust: Persecution, Rescue, and Survival*. New York, 1987.

# INDEX

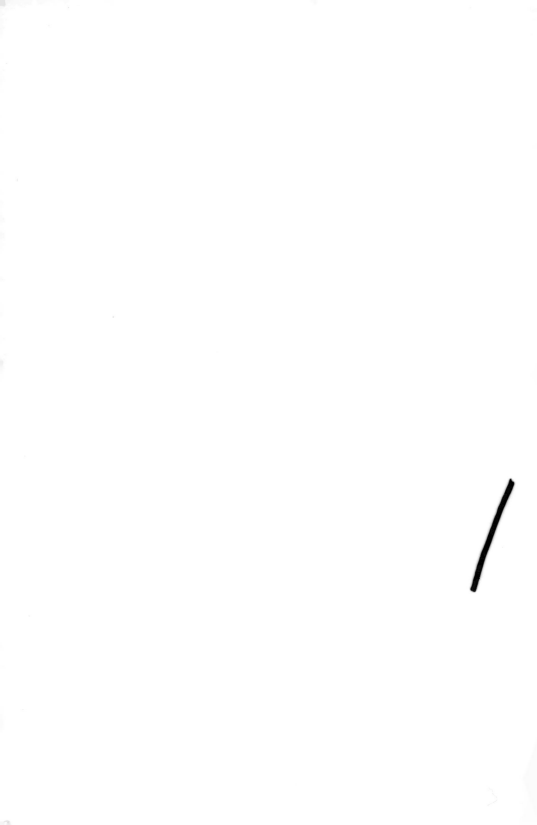

Printed in Great Britain
by Amazon